CW01189525

Gogarth North

Editor Simon Panton

Contributors Simon Marsh, Graham Desroy, Al Leary, Adam Wainwright, Martin Crook, George Smith, Pete Robins and James McHaffie

Design Al Williams, Manual Design

Printing Fratelli Spada, Rome, Italy

Distribution Cordee www.cordee.co.uk

Publisher Ground Up Productions Ltd.

December 2008

ISBN 978-0-9554417-1-4

© Ground Up Productions Ltd

All rights reserved. No part of this publication may be reproduced, stored in a retrieval system, or transmitted in any form or by any means, electronic, mechanical, photocopying or otherwise without written permission of the copyright owner.

A CIP catalogue record is available from the British Library

Guidebook Disclaimer
The writers and publisher of this book accept no responsibility for the way in which readers use the information contained herein. The descriptions and recommendations are for guidance only and must be subject to discriminating judgement by the reader. Advice and training should be sought before utilising any equipment or techniques mentioned within the text or shown in any of the photographic images. Climbing and bouldering are activities with a danger of personal injury or death. Participants in these activities should be aware of, and accept, these risks and be responsible for their own actions and involvement.

This one's for Mick Tolley "Get yourself to Gogarth kid!"

www.groundupclimbing.com

V12 OUTDOOR
rock climbing specialists

With the largest selection of technical hardware, more than 50 different rock shoe styles, plus men's and women's crag gear, the only other place to visit is the crag!

Live the dream

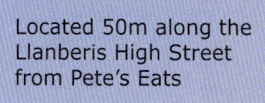

Located 50m along the Llanberis High Street from Pete's Eats

Old Baptist Chapel, High Street, Llanberis, Gwynedd, LL55 4EN

tel: **01286 871534**

Keep checking our website for the best deals on the net:

www.V12outdoor.com

Tim Neill cruising Gogarth classic
The Strand E2 5b, Upper Tier
photo: Jethro Kiernan

Contents

Introduction	6
Getting there	9
Access and Conservation	12
Local accommodation and facilities	14
Safety on the crags	15
A Question of Style	21
Grades	23
Graded list	24
A Pre-Cambrian Trip	28
Holyhead Mountain	30
Upper Tier	58
Main Cliff	90
Easter Island Gully	162
A Dream of White Horses, Gogarth	176
Wen Zawn	178
Flytrap area	208
North Stack	220
Tsunami Zawn	235
Breakwater Quarry	242
Craig Badrig	248
Porthllechog	253
Miscellaneous Crags	261
Benllech	264
Fedw Fawr	280
Sea level traversing	290
History	296
Route Index	322
Acknowledgements	326
Bibliography	327
Advertisor's directory	327

high sports

alpine
trad
sport
boulder
splashing out !

the shop for
all climbers

www.highsports.co.uk
51-52 Wyle Cop, Shrewsbury   01743 231649

Andy Newton MIC

- **Instruction**
- **Guiding**
- **CWA, SPA, ML Courses**

Andy also offers days tailored to clients wishes: sea-cliff climbing, lead coaching, ropework, scrambling, mountain navigation and other group leadership skills.

Please contact Andy to discuss the possibilities:

www.andynewtonmic.org
andy@andynewtonmic.org
tel: **01286 872 317**

Gogarth North Introduction

The magnificent sea cliffs of Gogarth, situated on the western tip of Anglesey (or Ynys Môn as it is known in Welsh), provide an unparalleled range of exciting traditional routes in a beautiful and atmospheric coastal location.

Gogarth has a well deserved reputation for wildness; it certainly tends towards the untamed and adventurous side of the modern climbing experience. Moreover, it seems to hold its many devotees in a wild-eyed state of neo-religious zeal, each fresh day at the crag fuelling an ever-deepening passion for this most special of crags. The character and quality of the climbing alone justifies such devotion, but there is also a strong sense of treading on hallowed ground; Gogarth after all, bears the irremovable stains of a rich climbing mythology left by several generations of committed climbers operating at the forefront of Welsh climbing. Indeed, the development of these crags presents a fascinating pageant stretching back to the heady days of the mid 1960s when the first tentative steps were taken on to the towering walls of Main Cliff.

As modern visitors, armed to the teeth with lightweight racks, colour topos and detailed descriptions we will never truly understand the disturbing levels of risk and fear that the original pioneers faced as they edged nervously upwards into loose and unknown territory, often with little more than a rope, a few slings and a peg hammer for security. Yet, regardless of how the cliff has cleaned up, and how much better modern equipment is, there is still great adventure to be found here. Gogarth definitely suits the competent climber; many of the routes are tidal and some loose rock will still be encountered. On the main crags there is little in the lower grades, and a degree of experience and composure is required to deal with the infamous Gogarth 'grip' factor.

As a counter to all that seriousness, Holyhead Mountain and a number of the crags spread along the north and north east coast of Anglesey provide a less committing option. The intensive outcrop style predominates here, but there are also gentler routes in the lower grades which will suit those looking for a more relaxed day out.

Finally, one of the most attractive things about the Anglesey crags is the relatively clement weather patterns which visit the island. Often when the nearby mountain crags are besieged by rain, the weather out on the coast can be surprisingly benign. Many of the cliffs (particularly at Gogarth) are west or south facing suntraps, permitting climbing throughout the year.

Looking across Gogarh Bay to Main Cliff and beyond photo: Jethro Kiernan ʌ

Introduction 7

The guidebooks: Gogarth North and Gogarth South

It became obvious from an early stage of guidebook production that placing all the routes and information in one guide (as had previously occurred) was just not practical. It is nearly twenty years since the previous Climbers' Club guide was produced and since then there has been over 300 new routes done on the various Anglesey sea cliffs. An obvious north-south split presented itself as a solution; leaving two separate volumes of similar size.

Gogarth North

Gogarth North covers the series of crags found on the western side of Holyhead Mountain on the outskirts of Holyhead town, itself the key ferry port for traffic travelling to and from Ireland. Here there is a range of dramatic sea cliffs running across Gogarth Bay and round the North Stack promontory. It also includes a number of little known crags situated along the north coast of Anglesey, including several limestone sport crags in the Benllech and Fedw Fawr area which have undergone a re-equipping program in the last year. In total there are over 500 action packed routes to go at – plenty to keep even the keenest cragger going for a year or ten.

In the period since the last guide there has been a wave of impressive new climbs, equally as groundbreaking as anything that previous generations came up with. But it's not all about desperate E7s, there have been developments throughout the grade range and a number of forgotten classics dug out of the encroaching fluff by intrepid crag researchers Al Leary and Simon Marsh.

Gogarth South

The sister volume, Gogarth South is due for publication in 2009; it will cover the equally dramatic range of crags running south from the South Stack lighthouse and around the Range to Rhoscolyn.

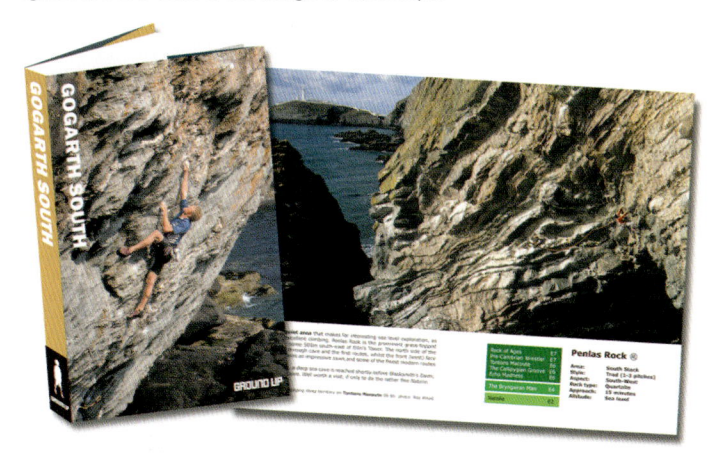

North Stack

Tsunami Zawn

North Stack
Flytrap Area
Wen Zawn
Easter Island Gully
Main Cliff
Upper Tier

Holyhead

Breakwater Quarry

Breakwater Country Park

Holyhead Mountain

Pont Hwfa

Holyhead

South Stack

cafe

250m

Introduction

Getting There

Anglesey is dissected by the A55 dual carriageway, which allows quick access across the island to Holyhead. Holyhead is also well served by the public transport network and it is entirely possible to get within reasonable walking distance of the crags by using trains or buses. The following descriptions assume that visitors will be arriving by car, but will be equally useful for those walking out of Holyhead.

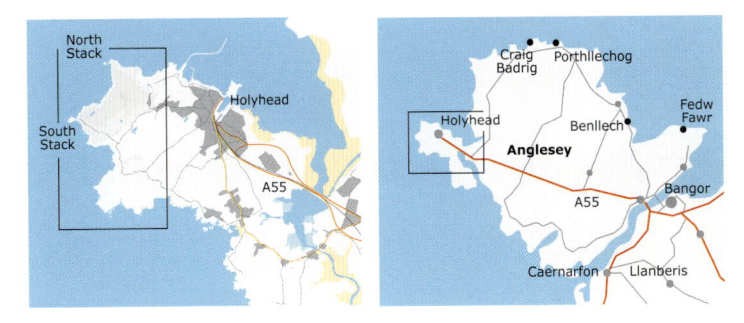

South Stack

Take the A55 dual carriageway directly into Holyhead. Once in the town, follow the road straight through passing the large clock tower on its right side. Continue until you reach a left hand turn signposted for South Stack (Prince of Wales Road). Follow this road to a mini roundabout; turn left here up Walthew Avenue, as instructed by the South Stack signpost. Turn right at the next T-junction (again signposted) and follow the road out of Holyhead. Continue through open countryside for 2km until a signposted right turn presents itself. This leads in 1km to a café on the left. There is parking available here, but only for customers of the café. If you don't fancy a pre-cragging brew or are short on time continue along the road for a further few hundred metres where a couple of small car parks will be found. If the car parks are full, various other parking spots are available along the wider parts of the road close to the cafe.

North Stack

Go straight across the previously mentioned mini roundabout, and straight across the next mini roundabout. Then take the left turn immediately on the left (signposted: Breakwater Country Park). Follow the narrow road along over numerous speed bumps to the car park on the right at the end.

Individual crag approach descriptions from the South and North Stack car parks are given in each chapter.

North Coast

The north coast crags of Craig Badrig, Porthllechog, Benllech and Fedw Fawr have independent descriptions given in the crag introductions.

climbing walls

cave systems

rock sculpture

skateparks

- indoor
- outdoor
- mobile
- design
- manufacture
- installation
- maintenance
- matting

BENDCRETE

0800 146778   mail@bendcrete.com   www.bendcrete.com

fiona roy on the 'evolution' climbing centre   photo : john hartley

GOGARTH NORTH

GROUND UP

Cover: George Smith and Adam Wainwright fully engaged with the first ascent of **The Mad Brown** E7 6b, Wen Zawn photo: Ray Wood

This page: Streaky Desroy bringing the 70s Californian vibe to **Bruvers** HVS 5a, Holyhead Mountain photo: Jethro Kiernan

Don't waste your time on home improvement.

If you want to improve your climbing rapidly, there's no better way than to get some professional coaching.

At Plas y Brenin our instructors are not only highly skilled, accomplished and experienced climbers, they're expert coaches too. They know exactly how to help you achieve your maximum potential as a climber.

Whether you're an absolute beginner, you've reached a plateau in your development, or you're simply ready to move up a grade and improve your technique, our coaches will help you improve - fast.

For a free 72-page colour brochure call us on 01690 720214, e-mail brochure@pyb.co.uk or take a look at our website at www.pyb.co.uk

MOUNTAIN EQUIPMENT GORE-TEX PLAS Y BRENIN

Plas y Brenin, Capel Curig, Conwy LL24 0ET Tel: 01690 720214

www.pyb.co.uk

Access

With regard to the locations described few access difficulties exist, at least with the main climbing zones. The cliffs at Gogarth, Holyhead Mountain and along the north coast are mostly located within areas designated as access land under the Countryside and Rights of Way Act 2000, and can be accessed along the Isle of Anglesey Coastal Path. In other locations where no legal right of way exists, please show respect for the landowner's wishes, as in a number of these locations on-going discussions are being undertaken with a view to improving access. It is possible that significant trespass and damage to fences/walls will only cause these discussions to stall.

Access situations can change, so it is recommended that prior to your crag visit a quick reference is made to the British Mountaineering Council regional Access database which provides dynamic updates for all crags in the UK: **www.thebmc.co.uk/outdoor/rad/rad.asp** For example, a temporary seasonal restriction may be applied if a rare bird is found nesting close to climbing routes. Of course, this restriction will be removed if or when nesting at the location ceases.

Inconsiderate parking can cause friction with land owners and local residents. Where parking is unavailable within a designated car park, please park sensibly and do not block access tracks or gates. Alternatively, why not consider leaving the car behind; regular bus services are available to the main climbing areas, and Holyhead has a main line railway station.

Conservation

Anglesey's geology is incredibly diverse, containing some of the oldest rocks found south of the Scottish Highlands in the form of the Pre-Cambrian quartzite upon which we climb at Gogarth. This underlying geology has resulted in an equally diverse range of habitats forming on the surface, many of which are incredibly rare not only in Wales, but Europe as a whole. As such the coastal heath sites seen at Holyhead Mountain and various sites along the north coast have been designated as Sites of Special Scientific Interest, and in the case of the Gogarth area higher designations indicating their importance on a European level. It is vital that as users of these important sites we are aware of both the importance of these designated sites but also their fragility. The heathlands are in the main a matrix of heathers, gorse and grasses, but rarer plants such as the heath spotted orchid, bee orchid and spotted rockrose are also present. Please keep to existing paths as straying off these can lead to the erosion of the very thin soils, and damage to rarer plants through trampling. The spotted rockrose for example is so small that it's hardly noticeable, and interestingly has dropped its distinctive petals by the time the lazy climber has finished their egg and chips at the café!

Sea cliffs are also important sites for lichens and bryophytes, which colonise both the exposed and sheltered sections of the cliffs. Please be aware that many of these species are not only rare, but form a major component of the coastal ecosystem. Gardening of existing routes should be sympathetic, and exploration of new routes and areas should be consulted upon with the Countryside Council for Wales before vegetation is removed: **www.ccw.gov.uk** (tel: 01248 672500)

Please follow the countryside code at all times and above all else please appreciate and enjoy the wildlife you see, before scaring yourself silly on your next project!

Access and Conservation • Introduction

Countryside Code: Respect - Protect - Enjoy
As a general guide to good behaviour, the Countryside Code provides some sensible advice:

- Be safe - plan ahead and follow any signs
- Leave gates and property as you find them
- Protect plants and animals, and take your litter home
- Keep your dog under close control
- Consider other people

The approach path to Holyhead Mountain, Upper Tier and Main Cliff
photo: Jethro Kiernan

Local accommodation and facilities

Anglesey is a popular holiday destination, and as such it is well served with accommodation choices. There are a numerous campsites on the island, but a popular option with climbers has always been Outdoor Alternative (see their advert on page 26) at Rhoscolyn, which also has bunkhouse accommodation, as does Anglesey Outdoors in Holyhead. There is also the usual array of youth hostels, bed and breakfasts and hotels, plus numerous cafes, pubs, ice cream parlours, restaurants, and takeaway food establishments in the local towns and villages. Food shopping is well catered for too with various wholefood shops, bakeries, butcher shops and supermarkets throughout the area.

The main climbing wall on the island is the Indy Wall, based at the Joint Services Mountain Training Centre at Llanfair PG (see their advert on page 27). On the mainland the Beacon Climbing Centre in Waunfawr (see their advert on page 26) and the Plas y Brenin wall (see their advert on page 11) in Capel Curig are also popular options. The nearest dedicated climbing equipment shops to the crags are in Bangor (Great Arete) and Llanberis (V12 Outdoor - see their advert on page 3, Joe Brown).

Rest day recommendations include sea level traversing (see page 291), hiring a sit on top kayak from Outdoor Alternative, walking sections of the Anglesey Coastal Footpath (see details at **www.islandofchoice.com/doc.asp?cat=693&Language=1**), sea fishing, and boat trips out to the Skerries or around Gogarth Bay, cycling the Cefni Cycleway, bird watching, various watersports at Rhosneigr beach, or perhaps a game of golf.

snowdonia-active.com is the No.1 resource for news, what's on and information about outdoor things for active locals and visitors alike. If you are looking for somewhere to stay, the nearest cafe, or anything to do with the outdoors then check out the map search. For things to do on days-off download our free activity guides.

Snowdonia-Active is a social enterprise working to support and develop the outdoor sector in North West Wales.

Safety on the crags • Introduction

All of the crags described in this guide are potentially dangerous places to climb. The following notes will help you to reduce the level of risk encountered in a typical day out climbing.

Tides

On the sea cliffs the biggest threat to your safety is arguably the sea. Make sure you have a copy of the tide tables, which are available from most local climbing shops or water sport shop, or that you have consulted one of the many online tide prediction websites prior to your crag visit.

It also pays to understand the changing tidal conditions. Spring Tides, which coincide with a full moon, cover the biggest range (i.e. lowest and highest tide levels) and thus have the fastest speed of water movement. Neap Tides rise and fall over a smaller range. The two tidal types switch over on a fortnightly basis, with the time of low and high tide moving on by just over half an hour each cycle. The highest tide mark is denoted by the band of black lichen at the cliff base; however a big swell and/or high winds can send waves breaking right up the crag to alarming heights.

High Speed Ferry Wake

There is an additional safety issue which relates specifically to the main Gogarth sea cliffs; that being the wake generated by the high speed ferry service which runs a few times a day from Holyhead to Ireland. Outgoing ferries don't seem to cause a significant wake, but as a rule of thumb you can expect a sizeable wake from an incoming ferry to hit the crag approximately 5-10 minutes after it has passed the headland of North Stack. The impact of the wake varies a good deal depending on the tide level, sea conditions and the nature of the cliff topography. Tight zawns such as Wen Zawn are particularly vulnerable, whilst the open stretch of Main Cliff is less affected. Another factor to consider is that the wake appears to cause a more violent disturbance to the water at low tide.

Copies of the ferry timetables can be found at **www.irishferries.com** and **www.stenaline.co.uk** Currently you can expect an incoming high speed ferry to pass the North Stack headland at approximately 10.30, 13.15 and 19.30; however these times may be subject to change. Either way, a degree of vigilance should allow evasive action to be taken should a wake be spotted heading towards the crag.

Abseiling/Ropework

If the approach involves an abseil, it is much safer to use an extra static abseil rope, which can be left in situ as a potential means of escape should it be required. The use of a prussic back up on the abseil rope may take a few more seconds to set up, but it could save your life in an accident situation.

Most of the routes on the main Gogarth cliffs are multi pitch. Consequently it makes sense to use double ropes; these will reduce drag on big pitches and allow quick abseil retreats. You should also keep a pair of prussic loops and/or lightweight rope ascending devices clipped to your harness at all times. These will be of great use in rescue situations and will get you out of all sorts of tricky scenarios should the need arise. Indeed, it is wise to have a good working knowledge of basic rope rescue techniques, such as escaping the belay system and creating a pulley system.

Introduction • Safety on the crags

Climbing Equipment

On the majority of non-bolted routes it makes sense to use double ropes (normally 8 or 8.5mm x 50m, and dry treated); these will help to reduce drag and allow quick abseil retreats. On a big sea cliff route it is not unusual to take in excess of 15 quick draws (most of which should be extra long), half a dozen or more 120cm or 60cm slings, a double set of cams up to size 4, a full double set of wired nuts and some lightweight hexes. You will also need extra gear to set up any abseils.

There are of course many crags in the area (such as Holyhead Mountain) where a more basic rack will suffice. On the north coast sport routes a single 50m rope and 10 quickdraws will normally be enough, although it is common practice to carry some wires.

You will encounter numerous ageing pegs, stuck nuts or even the odd old bolt on the Gogarth sea cliffs. These rusty relics should all be treated with suspicion, and backed up with wires, cams or slings wherever possible. The marine environment is a particularly harsh one and rapid corrosion of metals should be expected. The bolts used in the newly re-equipped limestone crags on the north coast are nearly all marine grade stainless steel (and thus resistant to degradation caused by salt water), however they should also be subject to scrutiny. Use your judgement; if a bolt looks suspect, treat it with caution.

Be aware that traversing at sea level to access your chosen route is a potentially risky business. If you slip, or are washed into the sea by a rogue wave (or the ferry wake) then it will be difficult to swim with a full rack and rope tied to you. It is much safer to carry your rack on a bandolier or sling which can be jettisoned in an emergency. Similarly, you should consider carrying your climbing rope in the traditional 'looped over the shoulder' method, allowing quick removal in the water.

The more time you spend climbing in the salty sea cliff environment, the more maintenance your climbing rack will need. Rinsing your kit with fresh water (before drying it out) and lubricating all moving parts on cams and karabiners should keep everything in working order.

Loose Rock

Loose rock is often encountered on sea cliffs; this being particularly so on the upper sections and hill side exits. Great care should be taken on loose ground; a steady, considered climbing style, where weight is carefully distributed between all limbs, is the best tactic. Try to press down rather than pull out. Finally, take care not to knock loose material off with trailing ropes, neither your second nor others climbing/traversing in the fall line will thank you for it.

Helmets

Head injuries are common in climbing and abseiling accidents, so it seems sensible that all climbers, whatever grade they climb, should consider wearing a helmet. Luckily there is a wide range of lightweight helmet designs currently available. If you haven't got one, go and try a few on at your local climbing shop, you'll be surprised how comfortable (and stylish) they are these days.

The advantage is *clear*

From Gogarth to grit or Central Icefall to Smiths route this revolutionary helmet is an awesome new tool and the first true modular helmet built just for climbers. Worn 'naked' it's superlight for hard rock action yet, at the turn of a screw, the exclusive *Alpine Shield* cover gives the added stone & icefall protection needed for winter wearability. Tested to extremes, simple to switch around and a joy to wear, the Alpine Shield is the first helmet with this convertible capability. So from Gogarth games to winter workouts it goes from best in class to a class of its own.

alpine shield

www.wildcountry.co.uk

WANT TO FIND OUT THE DEFINITIVE ACCESS SITUATION TO CLIMBING VENUES IN NORTH WALES?

THEN YOU NEED TO CHECK THE BMC REGIONAL ACCESS DATABASE (RAD)

The RAD contains details of over 700 crags in England and Wales where access issues have been reported and where special arrangements apply.

RAD features include:
- The latest, most accurate information – our network of Area Access Representatives can log in and update site details whenever situations change
- Intuitive "traffic light" access status categories, incorporating seasonal nesting restrictions
- Quick print summary of search results – ideal for sticking in the back of your guidebook
- General information, parking and group use advice
- All the new CRoW Act Information
- Crag photos, access routes, and information about important flora and fauna
- Additional notes and resources for all major climbing areas

Visit the RAD now on **www.thebmc.co.uk/bmccrag**

FEEDBACK AND FURTHER INFORMATION

The ongoing development and success of the BMC's access work and RAD depend on your feedback. For any questions, comments, or suggestions about RAD please contact Guy Keating, BMC Access & Conservation Officer –
e: **guy@thebmc.co.uk** or t: **0161 438 3309**

BMC Cymru/Wales represents climbers and walkers in North Wales. It's run by locals and is directly involved with crag restorations and access negotiations. It supports the North Wales Bolt Fund and also resolves problems with fixed gear, erosion and footpaths. It's an active and positive bunch of people who would love to meet you. Get in touch with them via **bmccymruwales@live.co.uk**, or through Martin Kocsis at the BMC Office –
e: **martin@thebmc.co.uk** or t: **0161 438 3336**

BMC WORKING FOR CLIMBERS, HILL WALKERS & MOUNTAINEERS

Safety on the crags • Introduction

Clothing

The temperature on a sea cliff has an annoying tendency to fluctuate wildly from boiling hot to freezing cold, sometimes in the time it takes you to get yourself half way up your chosen route. Even on sky-blue summer days it pays to carry a spare lightweight top. Applying sun block cream to any exposed skin is also a sensible precaution during the summer months.

Conditions

Sea cliffs can often be blighted by damp, slippy rock, rendering otherwise straightforward ground treacherous and strenuous. To the lay person the occurrence of the 'dreaded dampness' can seem almost mystical, however seasoned campaigners soon learn to spot the tell tale signs, such as the darker colouring of the rock. It's actually quite simple: in the morning the lower sections of most tidal routes will normally be damp. If you wait until mid day the sun and the wind will have had time to dry out the rock to a climbable state. On certain still and humid days this process can be slowed to a virtual halt and your chosen route may not come into condition at all.

Accident Procedure • First Aid

If spinal or head injuries are suspected, do not move the patient without skilled help, except to maintain breathing or if this is essential for further protection.

If breathing has stopped, clear the airways and start artificial respiration. Do not stop until expert opinion has diagnosed death.

Summon help as quickly as is compatible with safety.

Rescue

In the event of an accident on a sea cliff where further assistance is required dial 999 and ask for the Coastguard. Give as many details as possible including a grid reference of the crag which is given in each of the crag introduction sections in this book. Do bear in mind that mobile phones cannot always be relied upon to work; signal quality will be found to vary considerably.
In the event of a helicopter evacuation secure all loose equipment, clothing, rucksacks etc. All climbers in the vicinity should try to make themselves safe. Do not approach the aircraft unless told to by the crew.

RNLI and Mountain Rescue teams

The local Royal National lifeboat Institution (RNLI) and Mountain Rescue teams are manned by volunteers and funded almost entirely by donations. Please help to support their valuable work by making a donation. Details of how to donate can be found on the following websites:

www.rnli.org.uk
www.llanberismountainrescue.co.uk
www.ogwen-rescue.org.uk
www.aberglaslyn-mrt.org

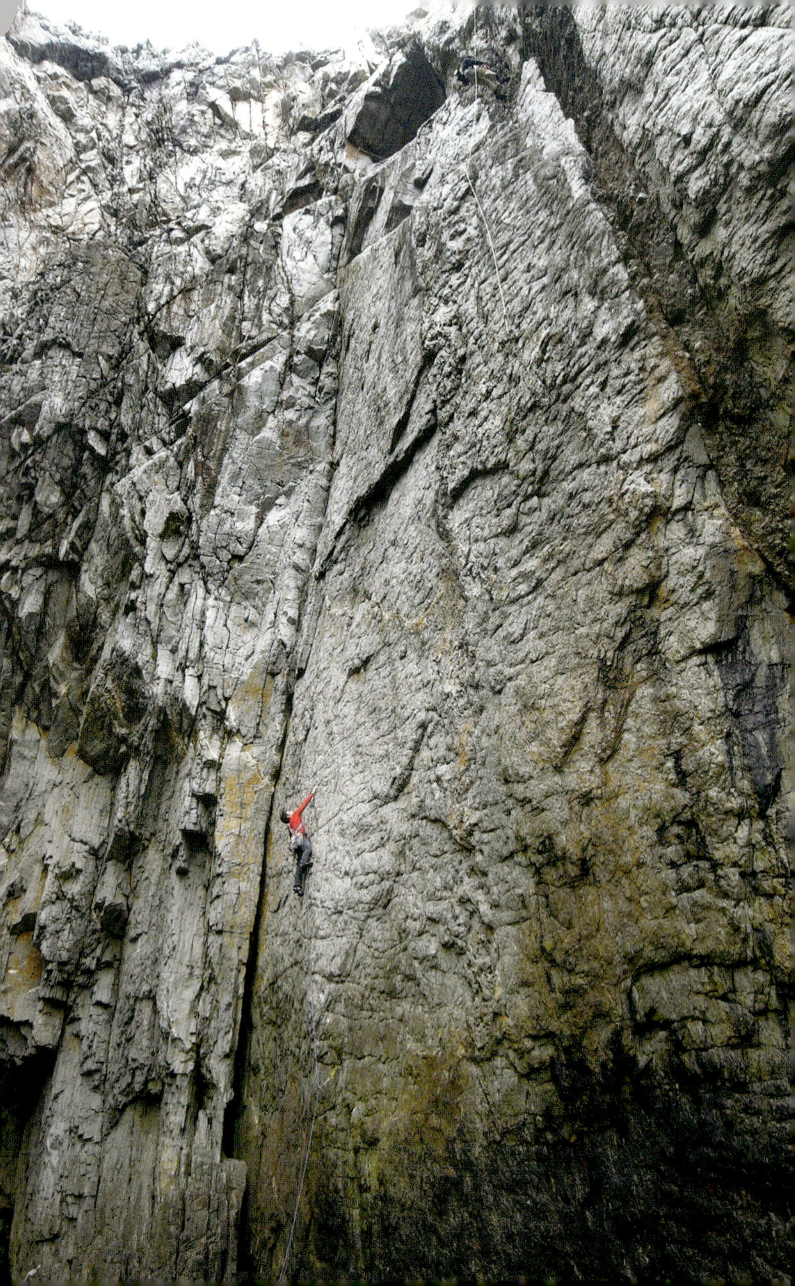

A Question of Style • Introduction

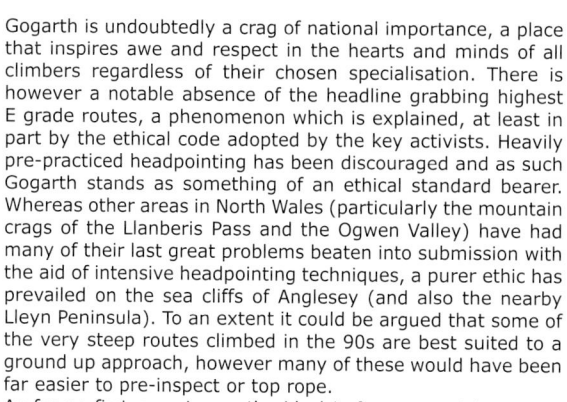

Gogarth is undoubtedly a crag of national importance, a place that inspires awe and respect in the hearts and minds of all climbers regardless of their chosen specialisation. There is however a notable absence of the headline grabbing highest E grade routes, a phenomenon which is explained, at least in part by the ethical code adopted by the key activists. Heavily pre-practiced headpointing has been discouraged and as such Gogarth stands as something of an ethical standard bearer. Whereas other areas in North Wales (particularly the mountain crags of the Llanberis Pass and the Ogwen Valley) have had many of their last great problems beaten into submission with the aid of intensive headpointing techniques, a purer ethic has prevailed on the sea cliffs of Anglesey (and also the nearby Lleyn Peninsula). To an extent it could be argued that some of the very steep routes climbed in the 90s are best suited to a ground up approach, however many of these would have been far easier to pre-inspect or top rope.

As far as first ascents go, the ideal is for an on-sight ascent, stepping into the unknown, route finding and cleaning as you go. Once a fall has brought an on-sight attempt to an end then ground up is considered the next best thing; a style that can cover everything from a one fall ascent to a multi day aid climbing extravaganza, but one that is tailored to suit by the climb and not the climber with an abseil or top rope. Therefore, whilst Gogarth may not contain some of the biggest numbers in the country, it arguably has the highest concentration of routes that have been climbed in a fair manner from the 1960s to the present day, an ethic that will hopefully continue well into the future.

All that being said, it must be acknowledged that numerous routes in the last 30 years (particularly on North Stack Wall and on the Upper Tier) were cleaned and inspected on abseil prior to a successful lead. There is of course a world of difference between an abseil inspected ascent and a clinical headpoint, the latter it has recently been argued might be better represented by a combination of a French grade with an additional risk/danger assessment similar to the one used in the United States. Once a successful ground up ascent has been made then a true E grade can be applied.

There is one notable exception to the Gogarth headpointing embargo: in 2003, Tim Emmett climbed the steep and clearly desperate *Chicama* at Trearddur Bay (an area covered in the forthcoming Gogarth South book). Tim practiced the route on a top rope prior to his ascent, offering a grade of E9 6c upon completion. Under the new system this route could be given F8a+ R, with R indicating relatively poor protection and the likelihood of injury in a fall.

James McHaffie attempting an onsight ascent of Johnny Dawes' ground up masterpiece, **Hardback Thesaurus** E7 6b, Wen Zawn photo: Nick Bullock

Pegs

Steel protection pegs have played a big part in the development of Gogarth. This is particularly true of the early days of exploration, but they have also helped to tame some of the harder modern routes. Clearly they allowed the first ascentionists to overcome some very loose and challenging territory, although it should be recognised that when the routes were done ground up many of the pegs were placed in extremis on lead.

Obviously pegs rust quickly in the salty sea cliff environment and as such are not sustainable. However, over the years most pegged routes have cleaned up considerably and become much more reasonable propositions. Where the pegs have rusted away modern protection equipment (i.e. lightweight wires and cams) have often kept the overall grades at a similar level, or in some cases made the route safer.

In some cases, such as the crux of *Big Groove*, as the peg (which is difficult to back up) deteriorates the route will inevitably become more serious.

So, whilst pegs are not the most sustainable protection solution, they are part of the fabric of the Gogarth experience. Occasionally it might be possible, and desirable to maintain the character of a specific route by replacing broken pegs, however in many cases it may be better to simply accept that routes will change and evolve over time.

Bolts

Bolt protected sport climbing has never been accepted as a suitable style for the main Gogarth cliffs. The odd bolt or two has been placed over the years, most famously by Ron Fawcett on *The Cad* on North Stack Wall, however the hangers were soon removed (although it is still possible to hook a wire over one of the remaining studs). More recently a bolt protected aid route was established in Parliament House Cave – this was quickly de-geared by local climbers keen to enforce the no bolt ethic.

Nevertheless, sport routes have been accepted elsewhere on Anglesey. The nearby Breakwater Quarry has a few bolt protected routes and the limestone crags in the Benllech and Fedw Fawr area have numerous fully equipped sport routes. These peripheral crags suit the application of pre-drilled protection and in no way represent a threat to the traditional ethic. In fact several traditional routes have been established adjacent to the clip ups – it is simply a case of deciding what will yield the best route. On a small limestone crag, sometimes that is a line of bolts, sometimes (and normally if there is meaningful natural protection) that is a bolt free or partially bolted line.

Grades

This guide uses the standard British grading system for traditional runner protected climbs. This runs in ascendance through the full range of difficulty, from straightforward climbs suitable for beginners, right up to state-of-the-art test pieces: Difficult, Very Difficult, Severe, Hard Severe, Very Severe, Hard Very Severe, and Extremely Severe, an upper range which is subdivided into numbered E grades (the hardest climb described in this book is E8). This adjectival grade gives an overall impression of the difficulty of the climb, taking into account factors such as how serious it is, how physically sustained it is and how technically difficult the climbing is. There is also an additional technical grade (4a, 4b, 4c, 5a, 5b, 5c, 6a, 6b, 6c, 7a), which gives an indication of the hardest single move on a given pitch. The grades are based on the assumption that the route will be attempted onsight.

The sport routes are described with the simple linear French system: F5, F5+, F6a, F6a+, F6b, F6b+, F6c, F6c+, F7a etc. There is an approximate parity between a given sport grade and a well protected traditional route, however there are so many other factors governing the difficulty of a Welsh traditional route - beyond the physical and technical difficulty, which are covered by a sport grade - that any comparisons should be treated as no more than very rough guides. For example, F6a would be similar to a well-protected E1, but only to someone familiar with placing natural protection and dealing with the myriad challenges of a typical traditional route (e.g. loose rock, navigation of line etc.).

Boulder problems, where mentioned, are described with a split grade of the American 'V' system, which runs from V0- to V16, and the Fontainebleau system, which runs from Font 3 to Font 8c+.

The introductions to each of the crags gives a quick-reference, colour-coded list of the starred routes. The grade ranges are as follows:

	UK (adjectival/technical)	**French** (sport)	**American**
E6 and above	E8 6c/7a	F8b,8b+	5.13d/5.14a
E3 – E5	E7 6b,c/7a	F8a,8a+	5.13b,c
HVS – E2	E6 6a,b,c	F7b+,7c,7c+	5.12c,d/5.13a
S – VS	E5 5c/6a,b,c	F7a,7a+,7b	5.11d/5.12a,b
D – VD	E4 5b,c/6a,b	F6c,6c+	5.11b,c
	E3 5b,c/6a	F6b+	5.11a
F7c and above	E2 5a,b,c/6a	F6a+,6b	5.10c,d
F7a – F7b+	E1 5a,b,c	F6a	5.10b
F6a+ - F6c+	HVS 4c/5a,b	F5,5+	5.9/5.10a
F5 – F6a	VS 4b,c/5a	F4+	5.8
	HS 4a,b,c	F4	5.6/5.7
	S 4a,b	F3+	5.5/5.6
	VD	F2+,3	5.3/5.4
	D	F2	5.2

< A rusty relic of times past; one of the old bolt studs on **The Cad**, North Stack Wall
photo: Ray Wood

24   Introduction • Graded List

E8
Extinction

E7
The Hollow Man
Hardback Thesaurus
Heinous Flytrap
The Wild Underdog
Roof Rack
The Ultraviolet Exterminator
The Mad Brown
The 4th Dimension
Sex and Religion
The Bells! The Bells!
The Collection Plate
The Undertaker
The Angle Man
The Unridable Donkey
The Clown
The Demons of Bosch
Rubble

E6
Hang Ten (in the Green Room)
Bar Fly
Psychocandy
(It's a) Broad Church
Barbarossa
A Wreath of Deadly Nightshade
Stroke of the Fiend
Billy Bud
Skinhead Moonstomp
Conan the Librarian
Dead and Bloated
The Porcelain Arena
Food and Drink
Mister Softy
Cruise on through
Games Climbers Play, Original Start
Coming on Strong
ET
Flower of Evil
The Big Sleep
Alien
For Madmen Only
Art Groupie
The Long Run Direct
The Cad

E5
The Boston Struggler
Mammoth Direct
Trhern Arête

Spiders Web
Flytrap Roof
Instant Van Goch
Energy Crisis
Bury My Knee
The Shadowy World of the Nemotodes
The Three Amigos
Blackleg
Mammoth
Afreet Street
The Horrorshow
Manor Park
Forgery
The Cruise
A Limpet Trip
Eraserhead
Evidently Chickentown
Captain Mark Phillips
Hunger
Ramadan
The Long Run
Ordinary Route
Return to Garth Gog
The Tet Offensive
Holyhead Revisited
The Red Sofa
Dinosaur
Annihilator
The Ancient Mariner
Not Fade Away
Sebastopol
Positron
Run Fast, Run Free
Citadel
I Wonder Why
Fifteen Men on a Dead Man's Chest
Puzzle Me Quick

E4
A Seagull Ate My Crisps
Ormuzd
The Camel
Metal Guru/The Golden Bough Finish
The Crossing
Three Day Event
Mirrored in the Cleft
Snakebite Wall
Skinned Up
The Mustapha Twins
Graduation Ceremony
The Wastelands
Sarah Green
Penny
Blue Peter

Bubbly Situation Blues
The Big Groove Direct
20,000 Leagues Under the Sea
Syringe

E3
Big Jim
Trunk Line
Strike
The Needle
T. Rex
Croissant
The Assassin
Wonderwall
Idris Mad Dog
Sai Dancing
North by North West
Hyena
Sex Lobster
Vicious Fish
Pequod
Tumbling Dice
Winking Crack
Who was EB?
Dislocation Dance
Gobbler's Arête
The Rat Race
The Big Groove
The Tail
Skerries Wall
Darkness
Stimulator
Final Solution
Achilles
The Echoes
This Year's Model
South Sea Bubble
The Electric Spanking of War Babies
Supercrack

E2
Aardvark
Fail Safe
Devotee
Hypodermic
Bran Flake
Genuflex
Toiler on the Sea
The Eternal Optimist
Zeus
Vend-T
Archway
The Bluebottle
Ibby Dibby
Faller at the First
Talking Heads

Graded List • Introduction

Jaborandi
U.F.O.
Echo Beach
Tequila Sunrise
Flytrap
Resolution Direct
The Quartz Icicle
Morphine
The Strand
Resolution
Point Taken
Merchant Man
Sisters Crack
Tidal Wave
Belvedere
The Seventh Wave
Park Lane/Doomsville Connection
Ramble On
Trampled Underfoot

E1

Sunstroke
Nightride
Green Gilbert
Emulator
Swastika
Hombre
Grendel
Drag
Uhuru Direct Start
Breaking The Barrier
Dream Seller
The Night Prowler
The Third Man
Sneaky Seal
Gringo
Gogarth
Fifth Avenue
Mestizo
Nice 'n' Sleazy
Peepshow
Spider Wall
The Whispers
Shag Rock

HVS

The Concrete Chimney
The Gauntlet
Belial
Force 8
The Girdle Traverse
The Trap
The Ramp
Central Park
Diogenes
King Bee Crack

Hud
Scavenger
A Dream of White Horses
The Paranoid Duck
Puffin Direct Start/Force 8
Heulwen
Scavenger Direct
Bloody Chimney
Phagocyte
Sprung
The Hustler
Caught by the Skerries
Wen
Bruvers
Shagger's Start
Exit Groove
Pentathol
Flooze
Dde
Registration Blues
Cordon Bleu
Ahriman
Tape Worm
Gazebo
Britomartis

VS

The Groove
The Rift
Bezel
Maverick
Imitator
Black and Tan
Birthday Passage
Tension
Pantin
Cursing
Patience
Puffin
Carlsberg Crack
Teaser
Dirtigo

HS

Pleasant Surprise
Candlestick

S

The Elephant's Arse
Tempest
Stairs
Pebbledash
The Wandering Primrose

VD

Hardcore Prawn
Away With the Fairies

F7c+–F8a+

The Terrible Thing F7c+

F7a–F7b+

Dream of the Crane Fly F7b+/7c
The Wasp Factory F7b
Gone Fishing F7b
The Crimson Crimp F7b
Hip to be Square F7a

F6a+–F6c+

Trigonometry F6c+
Boys From the Black Stuff F6c
Puppy Power F6c
Statement of Roof F6c
Sir Lobalot F6c
Waking the Witch F6c
Six Blade Knife F6c
Costa Del Benllech F6c
Sportingly Pocketed F6b+
Down to the Waterline F6b+
Vi Et Armis F6b+
Crackpot Crack F6b+
River of Steel F6b+
Sexy Garcon F6b+
Wind of Change F6b
Mike's Glory F6b
Christmas Cracker F6b
Contraflow F6b
42 Moves F6b
Hit me like a Hammer F6b
A Pocketful of Pockets F6a+
Cracking Sport F6a+
Sporting Crack F6a+
Bunty F6a+
The Song Remains the Same F6a+
Fossil Zone F6a+
Hard Shoulder F6a+
Tricky Fruitbat F6a+

F5–F6a

Mr Hulo F6a
Carousel Ambra F5+
Escape Route F5+

Anglesey Adventures

Adventure courses for schools, colleges, youth groups, plus skill based Climbing and Mountaineering courses.

- **Coasteering, Sea Level Traversing**
- **Climbing, Abseiling**
- **Mountain Walking, Scrambling**
- **Kayaking, Canoeing, Raft Building**
- **Gorge Scrambling, Orienteering**

tel: **01407 761777**

36 Porth y Felin
Holyhead
Anglesey

AALA
AMI

www.angleseyadventures.co.uk

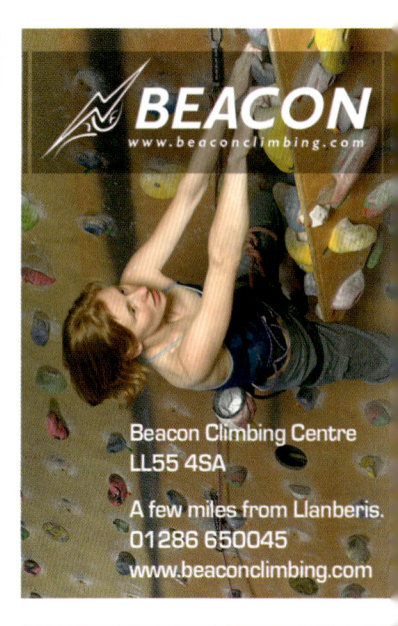

BEACON
www.beaconclimbing.com

Beacon Climbing Centre
LL55 4SA

A few miles from Llanberis.
01286 650045
www.beaconclimbing.com

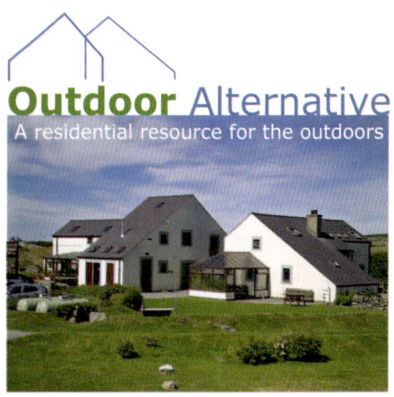

Outdoor Alternative
A residential resource for the outdoors

Rhoscolyn, Anglesey
01407 860469
centre@outdooralternative.org

Group accommodation & camping close to Rhoscolyn crags and a short drive from world famous climbing on Gogarth.

NITA'S B&B

IF I'M NOT HERE - 07769 851681

Home from Home...
...in the heart of Llanberis

- www.surfsister.co.uk -
- 01286 870087 -

THE INDY CLIMBING WALL

[Anglesey's best kept secret]

- **Extensive top rope and lead walls**
- **Featured resin bouldering wall**
- **Free standing competition spec boulder**
- **Top quality route setting; frequent resets**
- **Café and shop for climbing essentials**
- **Open 7 days a week until 10 pm**
- **Something for everyone, from beginners to honed beasts!**

01248 716058 - call for more info or email: indyclimbingwall@hotmail.com

Indefatigable, Llanfair PG, Anglesey, LL61 6NT

A Pre-Cambrian Trip

The lads said a 'visit' to Gogarth was just part of the Welsh circuit - along with Trem and Cloggy. No big deal, but it was a sea cliff.

To me the café seemed to be positioned at an un-nerving elevation. Swirling mist added to the atmosphere (slightly dampening it). A sense of foreboding made me secretly want to will-on a bit of light rain, so that we could brew up for longer, and the tatty guide was so full of mystery it merited a bit of a looking over. Strange route names without obvious meaning or explanation, each the work of a different crowd. The Holliwells, Joe Brown, Jim Moran, The Wintringhams - they'd all frequented the unseen world below us, so it couldn't be too bad.

As we approached the cliff edge the sun was breaking through to make the rocks look unfeasibly bright. "Look at the bloody drop!" Descending the tightly gripped and fluffy abseil rope I watched the sea coming up at me, restless and irregular, foam rippling down from the sun flecked crests. Too much to take in, I watched my feet bump past contorted rocks, the flat surfaces covered in sponge like plant life sporting pink flowers on tiny stalks, gawping at you as you went past them. The abseil rope was too long, it trailed off into the depths as if inviting any souls who dared, to continue down through the gesturing fronds of kelp weed. The lads debated our whereabouts, interpreting and deciphering various cracks, chimneys and gaping grooves. Drips launched from a distant highpoint, depositing themselves on holds just above us in an unhelpful way. Even if it was the wrong part of the zawn I was having a belay, festooning the alien shaped spikes with slings as another boot splashing swell rolled through. After further decoration of the ledges with ropes and the like we soon had a leader out of sight among the flanges and flakes, seeming to shuffle rather than to climb. Was this the method?

Later as the second set off upwards I was left to my senses. I watched waves being consumed by a dark cave at the back of the zawn, emitting the occasional 'UMFF'. Beyond the green entrance its innards were throat red and pitted with limpets. "A SEAL!" I exclaimed to myself in surprise. His great mottled body had loomed past before the quizzical face emerged, sniffing in what seemed like disdain. The big eyes. The whiskers. I moved to call the lads, but this was enough to prompt a bullet-speed bob from view.

With an unmanageable rush the ropes went from slack to bar tight and tugging. Calls were futile in the face of competition from the birds; their shrill calls an orchestra of anti-music. As I left the stance I glanced down one more time to witness a jet black auk swimming deep below the surface. Did they do that or was it dehydration?

The rock was really hard. And really soft. The hard bits stuck out like stegosaurus fins frozen from movement in some past moment of chaos. The soft bits were cavernous bands of bad cement. Climbing it appeared to be straight forward if a bit distracting. Our leader had stopped at the discovery of an ancient piton forced into apparently solid strata above a foot ledge. We must, from a distance have looked like a small and tragically misplaced queue of lost souls stood immobile, awaiting some unknown fate. This was more or less the case. The book was out again, and pitch two read out like a poetry recital. A new leader was selected and despatched. We watched attentively before being drawn again to the spectacle below us. The reappearance of mist and a lower sun resulted in a complicated light show. The foot ledge was too small. So were our boots.

Pitch two was, we all agreed, pretty steady, because nobody had fallen off. Mind you nobody had any skin left on their hands. After jamming there was a pleasant warm sensation about the scraped and reddened grazes. Karabiners seemed harder to undo. Sweat and salt were creeping into our eyes. Apparently the final ungraded pitch was mine. The rack was handed over amid more chanting from the sacred texts. Grooves and chimneys would 'lead to easier ground'. What was it – an escalator? Weighed down by the battle dress and still too big for my boots, I set off in an angst infused search for runners. Mild interest in rock forms gave way to an obsessive clamour for thread holes, spikes and cracks, deep enough to bury some metalwork. A piece of rock (a handy sort of pinch grip) detached itself completely in mid usage. I stood holding the thing for a second as if the moment could somehow be reversed. It could not. Neither for that matter could the pitch. I was visiting myself now - a fall was unthinkable as the unprotected upper reaches of the cliff sprouted green lichenous fluff, which crinkled and jumped into your eyes.

In placing this last piece of the jigsaw colour began to drain from the scene, all at once the returning sea mist had wiped out height and perspective. My mouth was a pocket of dust. The ropes dragged behind me like loathsome tails. Above were the lolling pink flowers again, their bulbous rootstocks making a strange anchorage as fingers were pushed deeper and deeper. Out of the nothingness came a solemn boom. It was the lighthouse. Time's up. My torso grovelling back over the top, I still held on tightly to the flat world as if it might try to get away.

I shouted "Safe" into the mobile greyness - "it's pretty steady that pitch".

Ed Bellthorpe

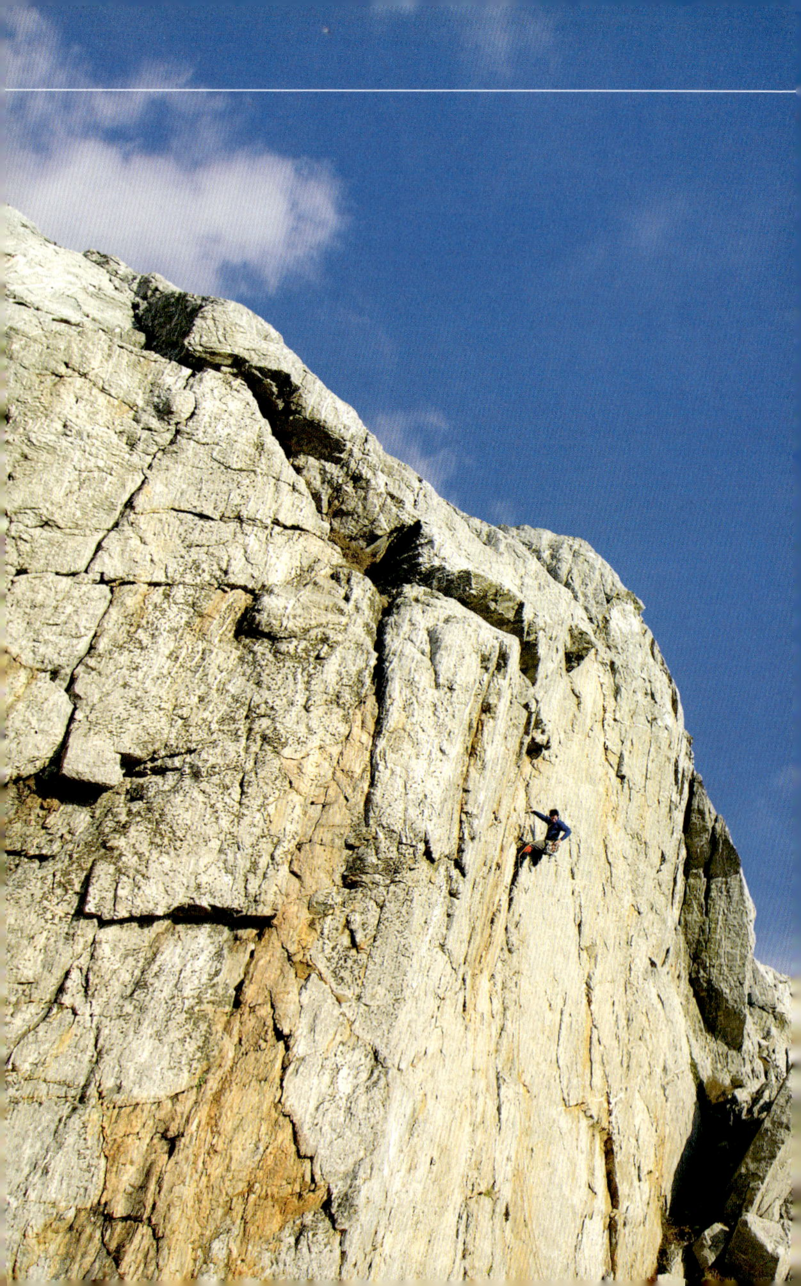

Holyhead Mountain

Area:	Holyhead Mountain
Style:	Trad (1 - 2 pitches)
Aspect:	South-West
Rock type:	Quartzite
Approach:	15 minutes
Altitude:	150m
OS Grid ref:	218 827

A delightful, sunny outcrop, with much excellent climbing; a good deal of which can be found in the lower grades. This is a much underrated area of the Gogarth range, unfairly written off in the past as a mere sideshow to the bigger cliffs. Given the quality of the routes and the sunny aspect, it really deserves to attract more attention.

The relaxed ambience provides the perfect counter to the seriousness and intimidation of the nearby sea-level cliffs. However, don't be fooled into thinking this is the 'easy' option; invariably the climbing is a good deal more action packed than first appearances might suggest.

The Quartz Wall and Yellow Wall are the star attractions, but exploration of the Ramps should not be discounted, as there are many fine routes hidden away in this area. The slabs at the right side of the crag offer something of a rarity for the area; a number of pleasant routes in the lower grades.

Andy Scott on crag classic
King Bee Crack HVS 5a
photo: Jethro Kiernan

Trhern Arête	E5/6
The Three Amigos	E5
A Seagull Ate My Crisps	E4/5
Mirrored in the Cleft	E4
Snakebite Wall	E4
Skinned Up	E4
Penny	E4
Big Jim	E3/4
Croissant	E3
Sai Dancing	E3
Final Solution	E3
The Electric Spanking of War Babies	E3
The Echoes	E3
Bran Flake	E2
Point Taken	E2
Sisters Crack	E2
Grendel	E1
Uhuru Direct Start	E1
Breaking The Barrier	E1
King Bee Crack	HVS
Bruvers	HVS
Black and Tan	VS
Tension	VS
Cursing	VS
Birthday Passage	VS
Patience	VS
Teaser	VS
Sump Direct	HS
Pleasant Surprise	HS
Candlestick	HS
The Elephant's Arse	S
Tempest	S
Stairs	S
D'Elephant	VD

There is a limited amount of bouldering to be had in amongst the jumble of large blocks that lie below the crag. Dan Warren has recently climbed 2 particularly taxing roof problems in the V8-9/Font 7b–7c range, but at a more approachable standard, the large split block in the centre of the boulder field has a number of easier highball problems. Also of note, on the right side of the boulder field, is a fine bulging wall split by a diagonal crack. The chaotic nature of the landings means that pads and spotters are essential - lone boulderers beware!

The specific first ascent details for many of the routes at Holyhead Mountain are unknown. Over the years members of the RAF Valley Mountain Rescue team and various local climbers have climbed on the crag extensively, and it seems likely that the majority of routes below the grade of E1 can be attributed to these 2 groups.

Conditions: The sunny aspect and exposed position ensure that the crag dries very quickly, even in winter! The rock quality varies from smooth and solid on the faces of the 2 Walls, to sections of flaky and friable on the Ramps.

Approach: The crag is clearly seen from the A55 while driving towards South Stack, as it forms the steep left hand side of Holyhead Mountain itself. It is reached from either of the small car parks at the end of the South Stack road, where a path or a track leads off right (the path and track soon join). Continue towards the microwave relay stations, and bear rightwards past them. The crag now presents itself a few hundred metres directly ahead. Numerous heathery tracks cut up to the rocks from the network of paths below.
The crags are situated on the Southwest side of the summit and comprise (from left to right) a series of 6 ramps (A to F), 2 compact walls, (the Yellow and Quartz Walls), some slabs, and finally a short steep crag well over to the right.

Descent: Straightforward descent gullies and paths can be found by all the sections of the crag. For Yellow Wall, come down gullies on either side of the crag. For Quartz Wall, go leftwards to just before you reach Yellow Wall; take the path down towards *Tension*.

Approach • **Holyhead Mountain** 33

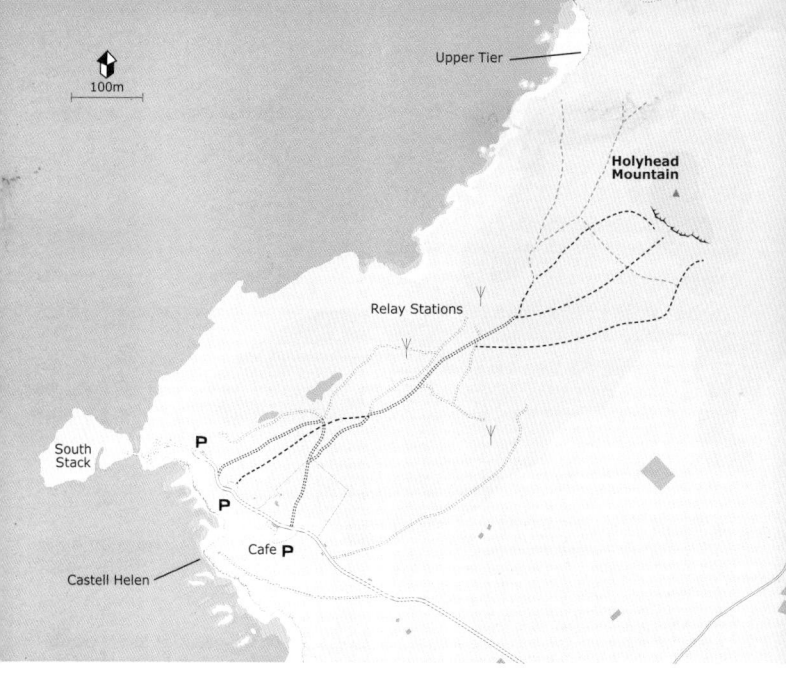

Labels on upper photo: Quartz Wall, Central Slab, Sub Slab, Red Rocks, The Pillar

Labels on map: Upper Tier, Holyhead Mountain, Relay Stations, South Stack, Castell Helen, Cafe, 100m

∧ The crag as seen from the approach path from South Stack

34 **Holyhead Mountain** • Ramp A

The crag is described left to right, starting with:

Ramp A

The smallest of the ramps is just off the South to North Stack path, and has a reddish base-wall and a central V-groove.

▶ **1. Corkscrew VS 5a** 6m
The central V-groove provides a good tussle.

▶ **2. Thumbscrew VS 5a** 6m
The cracks in the vague arête right of *Corkscrew*.

Ramp B

Higher up and to the right of the first scree slope is a larger buttress. The left wall of this has a prominent M-shaped overlap.

▶ **3. Vegetable Garden VD** 22m
Better than the name suggests. Start by *Candlestick* and follow the ramp on the left-hand side of the buttress. Near the top it is better to finish up the Y crack on the right.

▶ **4. M Wall HVS 5b** 18m
Climb the thin crack up the left side of the 'M', past an old peg.

▶ **5. M...M...Mother E4 6a** 18m
Poor rock and poor protection. Climb the right leg of the 'M', and then move left to its apex. Continue direct.
[K Neal, D Hazelaar 05.11.94]

▶ **6. Candlestick HS 4b** * 22m
A fine groove up the left edge of the buttress. Start at a pair of short cracks, below the groove. Climb the cracks to gain the groove, and follow it to exit right from the top.

Ramp B • **Holyhead Mountain** 35

▶ **6a. Puffin Shuffle HVS 5c** 25m
A difficult start, interesting mid section, and a wild-chop finish. From top of square pedestal (just left of *Romulus*), make a very difficult move into the left-hand groove, follow this easy to a thin crack up the steep right-hand wall, to a jug on the right edge – hands on edge, feet on wall and lay-away to the top!
[D Durkan, solo-back rope from below, 2007]

▶ **7. Romulus VS 5a** 25m
In the front of the buttress are 2 wide cracks and this takes the left hand crack. Start below a square pedestal. Climb up onto the wide crack, and follow it to finish up a shallow groove in the arête above.

▶ **8. Remus HS 4c** 25m
The right hand crack, starting just right of *Romulus*. Climb the crack, then gain a shallow corner on the left, and finish up an open groove in the slab above.

36 **Holyhead Mountain** • Ramp C

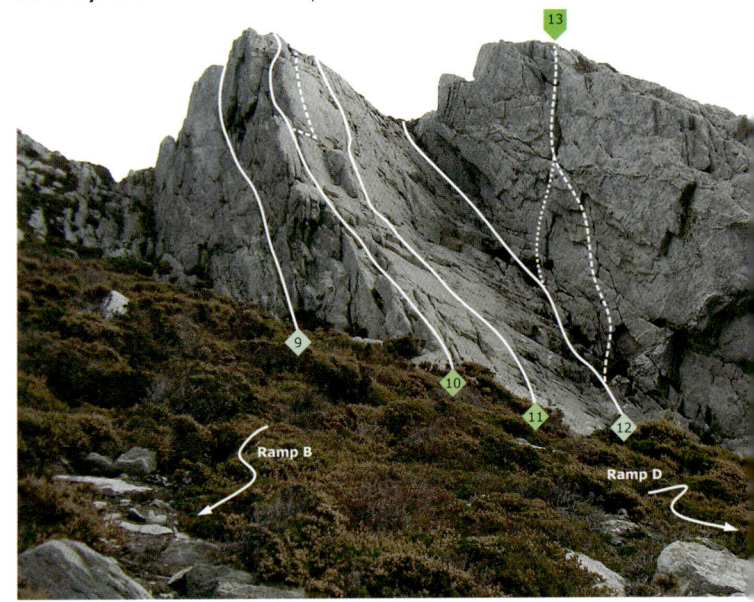

Ramp C

This ramp consists of a white slab, a dirty corner, and an extensive but inconsistent area of rock on the right.

▶ **9. Wally's Folly VD** 30m
Climbs the wall around left of the corner. Start just higher than the bottom right end of the wall and climb a ramp to a square niche. Pull out left to gain a slab then move left again before finishing up a crack on the right.

▶ **10. Pigeon Hole Crack S 4a** 28m
This varied climb takes the left slabby arête of the slab. Follow the arête to gain a wide crack, and then go up this to a ledge. Continue up the steepening groove above with interest before exiting right to finish more easily up the slab.

▶ **10a. Primrose Hill VD** 28m
From the ledge step right onto the main slab and follow the slight line to the top.

▶ **11. The Wandering Primrose S 4a** 30m
A combination of two earlier insignificant lines. Start in the centre of the slab and climb straight up until it is possible to move left over an overlap to a spike and a small ledge (level with the ledge of *Pigeon Hole Crack* on the left). From the righthand side of the ledge follow a faint groove to the top on good holds.

There are 2 or 3 parallel lines right of *The Wandering Primrose*, offering worthwhile and sustained climbing at a VS standard.

12. Primrose Hill Gutter M 25m
The right-hand corner, almost all unpleasantly dirty.

13. P.C.H. E1 5b 15m
Climbs the diagonal crack in the wall over looking *Primrose Hill Gutter*. Loose in parts, and quite strenuous. Climb up the slab, step right and follow a crack, jamming over an overlap at 10m. An easier start is possible further up left.
[J.Dalton, M.Petty 28.05.93]

14. Breakaway E2 5c 37m.
Climbs the steep crack on the overhung buttress. Layback round the overhang at 5m to a bridging position. A tricky move up gains an arm-swallowing pocket. Go up over a bulge at a shallow groove and finish easily up slabs.
[J.Dalton, M.Petty 28.05.93]

To the right is a broad area of rock, which has been climbed at various points, but only by poor and inconsistent routes. Perhaps try somewhere else instead.

Ramp D

15. Stairs S * 37m
A pleasant route, although a little vegetated.
P1 25m Climb diagonally right to a short corner, and go up this then back left above the overhang to the edge. Ascend this to the next roof then traverse right to a stance on the arête.
P2 12m Go left to the edge and up to a square block. Finish up an exposed groove on the left side of this.
Variation: **Stairs Direct VS 5a** 34m
Climb the short corner as for P1 of *Stairs* but step left and climb through the 1st roof with a crack in its middle, mantel, then continue up rightwards to the next roof, move right to a short wall and finish up this.

16. Teenage Kicks S 4a 30m
The arête right of *Stairs*. Start in the gully right of that route, and climb up leftwards to the arête. Follow it to join *Stairs* at its stance, then move left and finish directly up a cracked slab. [S Jones, D Hazelaar 1981]

17. The Grip VS 4c 36m
To the right is a very steep reddish wall, left of the big horizontal projection.
P1 4c 18m Climb the short corner, trending left to a dirty gully. Ascend a shallow groove on the right, then go across the slab to a corner and belay here.
P2 4b 18m Climb the corner above, or the slab on the right.

18. Spreadeagle Crack HVS 5a 36m
The broken crack just left of the big projection. Often damp, but worth doing.
P1 5a 18m Climb the crack to a poor, sloping ledge on the left, then step right and continue up the crack, exiting right to a small stance.
P2 4c 18m Go left beneath an overlap then up a crack in the left arête.

18a. The Three Amigos E5 6b * 26m
A recent, but apparently classic addition tackling the hanging fin right of *Spreadeagle Crack*. Go up easy ground to the roof; continue with bizarre moves past some hanging fangs. After an initial hard pull the leftward trending groove feature on the headwall leads into a bold finish. [J McHaffie 2008]

Jon Ratcliffe feeling the pump on the pushy test piece, **Branflake** E2 5b photo: Jethro Kiernan

Holyhead Mountain • Ramp E

Ramp E

A boulder-choked chimney splits the left-hand ramp while the right-hand side of this is a huge pinnacle.

▶ **19. Curtains VS 4c** 30m
A good but somewhat serious climb up the narrow rib just left of *Plimsole*. Start at the foot of the rib, behind a large block.
P1 4c 18m Climb the left edge, over a small bulge (spike), and cross rightwards to a slight groove that leads to a crack. Follow the crack up to reach a short steep corner above; climb directly to the belay.
P2 12m Go up the groove behind the stance, step left into a deeper groove, then finish directly on the left arête.

▶ **20. Plimsole HD** 27m
The obvious boulder-choked chimney. Start at the foot of the chimney.
P1 18m Climb the right-hand side of the chimney to a cave. Go left to a groove, and then back up right to a block platform.
P2 9m Finish up the wide crack in the back wall.

▶ **21. Nuts HVS 5a** 30m
P1 5a 20m Start up *Plimsole* until a difficult and poorly protected move leads into the hanging groove on the right wall. Go up the groove to a ledge, and then follow the thin steep crack, stepping right around onto the slab. Belay at top of pinnacle.
P2 4c 10m From the platform on *Plimsole*, step down and left to gain the thin crack, follow this to the top.

▶ **22. Grendel E1 5c** * 22m
A monster! This follows the overhanging crack in the centre of the pinnacle, starting just right of *Plimsole*. Step up right onto a large flake, and go up the groove in the centre of the buttress to the overhang. Rest on the right. Step left into the brutal crackline, and follow it with no little effort to the top of the pinnacle.
[K Robertson, M Gresham 1980]

▶ **23. Cursing VS 4c** * 22m
A well-situated route with good climbing, starting as for *Grendel*. Follow *Grendel* for a few metres, then layback up a flake on the right wall and continue to the overhang. Move around right and follow the crack (exposed position) to reach the slab above. Climb to the top of the pinnacle and belay behind. P2 of *Little Women* provides a good finish.

▶ Variation: **Direct Start HVS 5a** 12m
Climb the crack in the arête, just right of the parent route, to join it at the overhang.

Around to the right is a steep wall, bounded on the right by an obvious tall cave mouth. A conspicuous project line sports an old peg; to its right lies the striking line of:

▷ **24. Skinned Up E4 6b** * 20m
A fine strenuous pitch with good protection, taking the thin crack in the wall. Start at the cave and pull into a crack on the left. Go up to the first bulge, pass this with difficulty, pegs, and pull over the crux second bulge. This gains a dubious spike, and easier ground leads to the top of the pinnacle.
[First ascended as an aid route called *The Peeler* in the 70s: A1+ D Durkan 1968
FFA: M Gresham 04.07.86]

▷ **25. Little Women HVS 5a** 24m
Interesting, with 2 contrasting pitches, starting in the tall cave.
P1 5a 15m Bridge up the cave and pull into the steep shallow corner above. Ascend this, and another shorter corner, to a block platform.
P2 4c 9m Climb the centre of the blank-looking wall behind the stance, just right of *Plimsole* P2. Serious.
[M Gresham, D Birch 11.09.82 - P2 T Carter 1968/9]

Ramps E and F are joined together by a slabby back wall. With this, the two ramps form a square amphitheatre.

▷ **26. Teaser VS 4c** * 22m
A good pitch up the obvious white corner in the back left-hand side of the amphitheatre. Start at the contorted short wall below the corner and climb up boldly but easily to the foot of the corner. Climb the corner to the top.

▷ Variation: **26a. Step on the Wild Side HVS 4c** 24m
As for *Teaser* until halfway up the corner, when a gigantic stride left is made to a ledge on the back wall (right of *Little Women* P2). Climb up the blank wall with no protection! [T Carter, D Durkan 1968/9]

27. Birthday Passage VS 4c * 22m
A good climb with one difficult move. Start right of *Teaser*; climb up until the back wall is reached. Follow the sustained crack (3m right of *Teaser*) directly to under the small overlap near the top. From here go direct, or as for the original line, make an interesting move left and then continue directly to the top.

28. Pleasant Surprise HS 4c * 23m
Nice varied climbing up the crackline right of *Birthday Passage*. Start up the short contorted wall, as for *Birthday Passage*, to gain the broken slab. Go up to the back wall, and follow a shallow corner to a small ledge on the right, passing the odd dubious hold. Step left and finish on good holds.

28a. A Seagull called My Name HS 4b 22m
Start 4m right of *Birthday Passage*. Climb up the steepish wall on small holds, and then head slightly right to reach a groove. Go up this and then move left to follow a thin crack leading to the top.

29. New Boots and Panties S 4a 22m
A scrappy start amongst huge blocks leads to a fine finish up the diagonal crack 10m right of *Teaser*. Start 6m right of *Birthday Passage*, below a short wide crack, and climb up just left of the crack. Go right to the top of a large pinnacle and step off the top of this onto the crack, which is followed with interest to the top.

Variation: **29a. Rhiannon HS 4b** 23m
From the top of the pinnacle, traverse confidently left to twin cracks, and go up these to the top.

30. Old Boots and Cut-Offs HS 4b 20m
Start as for *New Boots* and climb the wide crack above. Continue to a point just right of the pinnacle, then step right and climb thin cracks in the white wall to the top.

31. Mrs Murdock S 4a 18m
The broken corner line on the right-hand side of the back wall of the amphitheatre. Climb the short, steep corner crack to reach an earthy ledge. Continue up the obvious corner above to the top. It is possible to finish more airily by stepping right onto the front face of the right-hand bounding wall of the corner from a few moves up the upper corner.

Right of *Mrs Murdock* is a broken area, before the rock improves again to the right of the rift.

Ramp F

32. Mental Block VS 5a 12m
Climb the short steep corner, just right of the rift, finishing up the slab on the right.

33. Oh Man, I Gotta Have a Wildebeast E1 4c 10m
This slab right of *Mental Block* follows a quartz streak. 1 very low runner.

Ramp F • **Holyhead Mountain** 43

▸ **34. Duffel HS 4b** 30m
This climbs the blank-looking wall and arête bounding the right side of the amphitheatre. Start just right of the short, steep corner of *Mental Block*.
P1 4b 12m Follow a vague line of flakes diagonally right to the arête, and follow this up left to a big broken ledge.
P2 4b 18m Traverse left, above a broken gully, to climb the left-hand crack of the trio on offer.

▸ **35. C'est la Vie HVS 5b** 18m
Climbs the arête right of *Duffel*. Not particularly worthwhile.
[M Gresham, D Hazelaar 19.01.83]

▸ **36. The Abbey VS 4c** 36m
The line between *C'est la Vie* and *The Sump*, starting 2m right of the arête.
P1 4c 18m Climb a thin crack, and a chimney to a big broken ledge.
P2 4b 18m Walk left to finish up *Duffel* P2.

▸ Variation: **Direct Finish HVS 5b** 8m
From the big broken ledge climb the central groove in the short back wall.

▸ **37. The Sump D** 27m
Take the 'V' feature in the centre of the ramp starting just right of *The Abbey*.
P1 15m Step right steeply and go up into the slabby 'V' groove. Ascend this to the back wall, and then go up the slab on the right to a cosy nook above a cave (The Sump).
P2 12m Stride across The Sump to the right, and cross the slab to finish up a shallow groove near the right-hand edge. (Either descend carefully down the back of the ramp, or go up to the top of the ramp to gain the descent gully).

▶ **38. Sump Direct HS 4b** ∗ 25m
5m to the right is an obvious corner. Start at broken rocks a little to the right of the corner.
P1 4a 15m Move into the corner and follow the left wall on good, sometimes friable, holds. Climb into the continuation groove on the right and go up to belay on *The Sump*.
P2 4b 10m Climb the steep corner above the stance.

▶ **39. The Elephant's Arse S 4b** ∗ 24m
An amusing, though escapable, struggle up a system of rocky through-caves. Start 3m up and right of *Sump Direct*, 3m below a hole.
P1 4a 8m Climb directly up to the hole then squirm up the slot directly above this to land in an 'alley'.
P2 4b 16m Go up directly into the roof of the cave before escaping through a side exit onto a big, block-covered ledge. Either go left to finish up *Duffel*, or go right to descend a short tricky chimney.

▶ **40. Kit Kat VS (HVS?) 4c** 8m
Gain and climb the short steep corner. Awkward, strenuous, and sustained.
[1986]

Further right and at a higher level is a short steep white wall.

▶ **41. Pisa E1 5b** 10m
The slanting crack in the centre of the wall.

▶ **42. Minime E2 5b** 10m
The right hand arête of the wall of *Pisa*, climbed on its left hand side. Fiddly cams and a thin sling protect.
[I.O.Roberts, D.Noden 1999]

▶ **42a. Crack VD** 8m
Climb the crack direct. This feels bigger than it is.

Yellow Wall • **Holyhead Mountain** 45

To the right, across a wide heather gully, is an area of rock that boasts the highest concentration of quality routes on this crag.

Yellow Wall

A gleaming sheet of solid, clean rock, this is the most impressive part of the crag. A central crack cleaves the cliff from top to bottom, providing *King Bee Crack*, a useful landmark. Descents may be made down gullies on either side of the cliff.

▶ **43. The Raver S 4a** 10m
This takes the slabby left groove, high up, reached by a start up the adjacent overgrown slab.

▶ **44. Bloody Fingers HS 4b** 11 m
Start up the overgrown slab and ascend the steep green corner.

▶ **45. A Seagull Ate My Crisps E4/5 6b** ∗ 20m
A fine, pumpy route tackling the slanting crack in the steep wall right of *Bloody Fingers*. Climb up to a huge flake and traverse left along the slanting crack until a hideous jam enables a rest to be appreciated in a niche. Move up left and climb the arête on the edge of the *Bloody Fingers* groove to the top.
[M.Turner, M Griffiths 06.98]

On the left-hand side of Yellow Wall itself is a slabby grey buttress, in the centre of which is a broken chimney containing a huge jammed flake.

▶ **46. Thread S 4a** 34m
Start a couple of metres up and left of the broken chimney.
P1 4a 12m Climb up to an overlap slanting up rightwards and follow this almost to the chimney. Make a hard move over the bulge on the left, and go up to belay near the back wall.
P2 22m Go left to a huge flake, and from halfway up this, step right around the arête to gain a ledge. Follow heathery steps rightwards to a corner. Ascend this and the cracks above to finish.

46 Holyhead Mountain • Yellow Wall

▸ **47. Wind E1 5b** 37m
Right of the broken chimney is a steep arête.
P1 5b 15m Climb the right-hand side of the arête with difficulty, and then trace a quartz band around to the left. Follow the arête to exit a shallow groove and gain block belays at the back wall.
P2 4c 22m Climb a short steep crack, just right of the huge flake on *Thread*, to gain that route. Step up and left to follow the slabby left edge; thin and poorly protected.
[M Gresham, K Neal 05.02.84]

Right again is a deep chimney in a corner:

▸ **48. Uhuru VS 4c** 40m
A good route when combined with the *Direct Start*, less so without it. Start in the corner chimney of *Jones' Crack*.
P1 4c 18m Climb the chimney for about 8m, then swing left on good holds to reach a narrow ledge leading out left. Traverse left until it is possible to step up right to the centre of the wall, and boldly climb this (no protection) to gain the big ledge.
P2 4b 22m Step up to a horizontal break, and follow this rightwards to an open groove (junction with *Bran Flake*). Climb up this for 3m before stepping right onto a slab. Finish directly up this.
[D Durkan 1969/70]

▸ Variation: **Direct Start E1 5c** * 17m
Climbs the centre of the bulging wall left of the chimney, to eventually gain the narrow ledge on the parent route. Finish up this.
[M Gresham, K Neal 11.10.86]

▸ **49. Jones' Crack VD** 18m
Named after a Holyhead school teacher who got stuck in the crack!
Climb the chimney corner direct, starting at the foot of the chimney. Climb up the outside for 3m then enter the chimney. Climb up the inside, quite a struggle, to finish on the big ledge. Finish up *Thread* P2.

▸ **50. Bran Flake E2 5b** ** 30m
A brilliant, action packed route.
Ascend the outside of the chimney of *Jones' Crack/Uhuru* for 3m before stepping right to a scoop, which leads to a bulge. Pull through this leftwards to gain the steep crack; race up this to reach easy ground on the upper slab. It is possible, and perhaps desirable to belay at the top of the steep section.
[K Robertson, S Robertson 31.01.81]

▸ **51. Shreddies E2 5c** 40m
Start at a thin crack between *Bran Flake* and *Croissant*.
P1 5c 17m Climb to the overlap and go leftwards to base of large flake. Go round this on the right to belay up in a cave.
P2 23m Climb easily up slabs to finish.
[N Sharp, J Dalton 12.05.94]

▶ **52. Croissant E3 6b** ∗ 30m
A very difficult and steep route taking the crack just left of the arête, 6m right of *Jones' Crack*, starting just left of the arête. A hard start leads to the foot of the main crack, which is followed, steep and sustained, to a cave. Finish easily up the slab above.
[K Robertson, A Lewandowski 11.07.81]

▶ **53. Mirrored in the Cleft E4 6b** ∗ 30m
Obviously desperate, this follows the shallow groove high in the arête, right of Croissant. Start at the foot of the arête. Climb the arête for 3m, and then trend rightwards to a vague crack. Follow this up and left, to a long horizontal pocket, left of the groove. Climb the groove, move left to the cave, and finish up *Croissant*.
[J Redhead, J Perrin 1982]

▶ **54. Big Jim E3/4 6b** ∗ 30m
A technical and strenuous number attacking the system of deceptively steep cracks between *Mirrored in the Cleft* and *King Bee Crack*. Start 2m left of *King Bee Crack* and climb up to a left-sloping ramp. Follow this to its top, gain a steep flake crack, and climb this with much difficulty to a horizontal break. Phew! Exit leftwards up the easy slab above.
[K Robertson, A Lewandowski 12.07.81]

▶ **55. King Bee Crack HVS 5a** ∗∗∗ 37m
Well protected and well strenuous: a classic of the crag. Start just right of the main crack, and climb a subsidiary crack to a small ledge at about 5 metres. Step left to the main crack and climb it, past a bulge near the top, crux, to gain the slab. Finish more easily up the crack in the slab.

48 Holyhead Mountain • Yellow Wall

▶ **56. Snakebite Wall E4 6a** * 37m
Although essentially an eliminate, this is a very worthwhile route with excellent, if a little bold climbing. Starting at the base of a short diagonal crack a couple of metres right of *King Bee Crack*. Go up the crack for 3m, and then make a reachy manoeuvre rightwards past a flat handhold to gain a line of pockets and edges leading up to a peg. Trend slightly rightwards to join *Penny* at some quartz. Follow *Penny* to the top.
[K Neal, M Gresham.10.10.86]

▶ Variation: **56a. Trouser Snake E4/5 6a** 37m
From hollow flakes down and left of *Penny*, crimp up the wall leftwards to join *Snakebite Wall* after its rightwards traverse. Follow this to just before it joins *King Bee Crack*. Arrange gear then traverse up and right to a poor tied off peg, then up to a good jug/spike just left of *Final Solution*. Ignore thoughts of escape into *Final Solution*, instead head up and left to finish via a left facing groove and the easy upper slab.
[T Neill, T Keep 22.06.03]

▶ **57. Penny E4 6a** ** 37m
The striking diagonal crack yields a suitably rewarding climb. (NB. This route was mistakenly identified as *Katana* in the previous guide.) Climb the wall just left of the crack past an overlap to gain the crack (crux). Follow the pumpy crack up leftwards into the top of *King Bee Crack*.
[J Redhead, K Robertson 1982]

▶ **58. Sai Dancing E3 6a** ** 37m
An absorbing and rather difficult route navigating a line up through the highest point of Yellow Wall. Start just right of *Penny*, and climb straight up the wall, following a faint groove, to the halfway ledge on *Final Solution*. Follow this to its 2nd peg then go diagonally right past a small square overhang to reach a thin crack. From good holds at the top of this, hidden peg, go diagonally left to an overhanging groove and improvise your way up it, to finish on an easy slab.
[M Gresham 18.06.88]

▶ **59. Final Solution E3 5c** ** 37m
Another good climb, (mistakenly identified as *Penny* in the previous guide) taking the upper of the 2 diagonal cracks, right of *King Bee Crack*. Start 3m right of the crack, behind a huge leaning flake. Climb the steep wall, and swing left to a groove formed by the crack. Ascend this to a small ledge on the left and continue up the crack, past 2 old pegs, to make a hard exit into the finishing slabby corner above.
[K Neal, M Gresham 23.04.84]

▶ **60. Trhern Arête E5/6 6a** * 37m
The obvious hanging arête feature right of *Final Solution* and the upper section of *Sai Dancing* provides an exciting and serious prospect with big fall potential. Start up *Final Solution*, but climb straight up to a small heather ledge. Attack the steep arête; if you make it past the snatchy crux section in one piece, easier, but still bold climbing leads up the slab above to the top.
[M Griffiths, M Turner 06.98]

Yellow Wall • **Holyhead Mountain**

▶ **61. Twilight Zone E4 6b** (1 pt) 35m
A sustained pitch up the ramp and overhanging groove directly above the start of *Final Solution*. Start as for *Final Solution* and climb straight up to a small heather ledge. Climb the steep ramp, poor peg, to the foot of the overhanging groove, and ascend this with great difficulty, to a fine flake crack at its top. Finish up this, and the wall above, trending left. (A rest point was used in the difficult groove.)
[K Neal, M Gresham (1 pt) 30.08.86]

▶ **62. The Electric Spanking of War Babies E3 5c** * 25m
Good steep climbing, with dubious rock and protection, up the flaky scoop right of *Twilight Zone*. Start just right of a thin crack, some 3m left of Patience. Climb a thin crack to gain a big tottering spike, wedged in a horizontal break. From the top of the spike step leftwards onto the wall then go up trending rightwards to a thin crack formed by the left-hand side of a flake. Climb the crack, move right past a pencil of fragile rock, and gain the leftward slanting groove. Ascend this exiting slightly right on flaky holds.
[M Gresham, K Neal 10.10.86]

▶ **63. The Electric Lady Charlotte E3 5c** 27m
The diagonal line running leftwards out of *Patience*, crossing *The Electric Spanking...* near the top. A bit loose in places.
[R Parry, M Gresham 08.96]

▶ **64. Patience VS 4c** * 25m
The shattered overhanging corner at the right hand end of the crag has a spectacular move at its climax. It is however quite loose in places and should be treated with caution. Start at the foot of the corner, and climb it to a sloping ledge. Move right to a jagged crack and go up to the overhang. Go left to the chimney, climb up a couple of metres, and then swing right across the overhanging wall to the arête. Finish up the slab above.

▶ **65. A Slow Brew E3 6a** 25m
Climbs the sharp arête between *Patience* and *Drying Out*.
Starting just right of the arête, climb up to a flake and then step leftwards off this onto the arête itself. There is a poor cam and fragile thread around to the left. Climb a thin discontinuous crack to eventually gain good holds just below where the angle eases. Follow the arête more easily to the top.
[K Neal 04.10.86]

▶ **66. Drying Out E3 6a** 22m
The eye-catching and very steep curving crack in the wall to the right of *Patience*. Start 2m right of the sharp arête, by a large boulder. Climb easily up rightwards to the start of the main crack. Follow this round a bulge, crux, old peg, to the upper part of the slab, and finish up the continuation crack in this.
[J Donelly 06.85]

Holyhead Mountain • Quartz Wall

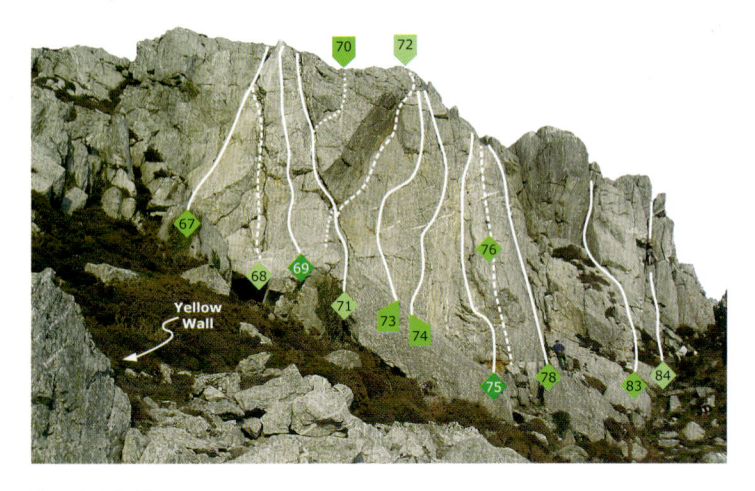

Quartz Wall

30m to the right of Yellow Wall is an appealing wall of grey quartz-streaked rock where another run of superb routes can be found. Descent is by walking back from the crag top rightwards to descend a short wall, and double back down a gully, past *Tempest*, to the foot of the crag.

▶ **67. The Unblue Crack E1 5b** 25m
The slanting pink crack in the left side of the wall, doesn't quite live up to expectation. Start in the broken corner, 10m left of the corner of *Tension*. Go easily up the corner to a heathery ledge, step right and climb the slanting crack diagonally rightwards, crux. Finish up an easier wider crack

▶ **68. Andover VS 5a** 25m
Climbs the straight crack line 6m left of *Tension*. Climb the crack, passing a bulge at half-height, crux, before moving left to finish up *The Unblue Crack*. Some loose rock.
[J Donnelly 1980]

▶ **69. The Arrow E3 5c** 25m.
Climb the narrow slab of rock between *Andover* and *Tension*, passing an overhanging section at half height.
[G Mitchell, J Loveridge 1999]

▶ **70. See Emily Play HVS 5a** ∗ 28m
Although essentially a variation on *Tension*, this provides good exciting climbing. Start just left of *Tension*, at the foot of an arête. Climb the serious left side of the arête to join *Tension* at the roof. Go left and follow *Tension* for 5m, before moving right using an undercut flake to finish up a vague groove.
[M Gresham, J Dalton 03.04.83]

71. Tension VS 4b ** 25m
An approachable and satisfying excursion. Climb up the central corner to the large roof. Move left past a block and ascend a groove to a bulge. Large holds allow a swing left to gain the finishing crack.

72. Black and Tan VS 4c * 28m
The striking diagonal line is quite a tough proposition, and certainly hard for the grade. Follow *Tension* to the roof, and then trace the diagonal crack up rightwards beneath the roof, to a steep and daunting finale.

73. Point Taken E2 5c * 25m
Start as for *Breaking the Barrier*, but instead of stepping right to the triangular niche go straight up to gain a short, shallow corner a few feet below the big roof. From here go diagonally right to twin cracks, above a small overhang, and finish up these. The twin cracks originally formed a variation finish (known as *Pointless*) to either *Breaking..* or *Black and Tan*.
[J Hope, K Neal, A Hulbert 07.91]

74. Breaking the Barrier E1 5b *** 26m
Immaculate, technical face climbing up the centre of the attractive quartzy wall. From a few metres right of *Tension*, move up and right to a large triangular foothold. Continue up the thin crack above, stepping right to follow another thin crack line to a good hold. Finish up a steep, shallow corner.
[J Donnelly 1980]

75. The Echoes E3 6a ** 28m
The shallow groove right of the previous route is guarded by an obstinate start. Start below and just right of the groove, beneath some triangular pockets. Climb steeply up the overhanging wall and swing left into the bottomless shallow groove. Ascend this to its top, and continue up the wall above, to finish up a short shallow corner.
[M Gresham, K Neal 09.04.83]

76. Sisters Crack E2 5b/c * 25m
Another worthwhile line on this fine wall. Very well protected, after the initial bouldery start. Climb straight up through the bulge via the crack and continue directly up the headwall above finishing on the arête.
[G Smith 11.03.07]

77. Relief E2 5c 26m
An enjoyable eliminate which follows the arete just right of *The Echoes*. Climb the crack of *Bruvers* for 3m then balance left on reasonable footholds to gain the arete. Follow its slabby left hand side until tricky moves rightwards gain a flake and the top.
[M Gresham, K Neal 15.02.86]

78. Bruvers HVS 5a ** 25m
This classic strenuous crack has plenty of gear, and you'll be glad of it.
[K C Jones, C C Jones 1969]

79. Apostrophe HVS 5a 28m
A wandering line up the wall right of *Bruvers*, starting just right of that route. Climb a disjointed layaway crack to gain the left end of a rightwards-sloping gangway, and follow this to near its right end. Take a short steep crack back up left to finish. [D Hazelaar, S Jones 1981]

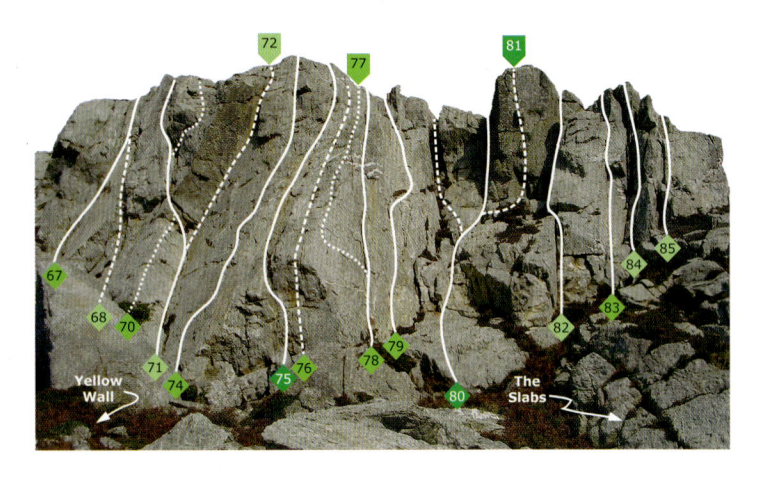

▶ Variation: **Direct Finish E2 6a** 26m
From the left-hand end of the gangway, step up left and climb the hairline crack, with difficulty, to the top. A poor blade peg protects the crux.
[M Gresham, K Neal 15.02.86]

▶ **80. Contestant VD** 30m
Start 3m right of *Bruvers*, at the foot of the slab, and climb it to a steep open groove. Go up this to the slab above. There are two finishes from here: the chimney on the left, or better, the steep green corner on the right.

▶ **81. Dreaming of Home E3 5c** 28m
A variation with no clear parentage and an extremely dangerous hanging flake; one to be avoided by all but the seriously deranged. The route takes the front of the steep tower at the back of the recess, and right of the top corner of *Contestant*, starting as for that route. Follow *Contestant* to the back wall, then move right to a steep crack splitting the centre of the overhanging wall. Climb this, past a dangerously detached flake, to the top. [1986]

▶ **82. Blackfoot HS 4b** 22m
Scrappy and contrived, starting a few metres right of *Contestant*. Climb a smooth slab up a short heathery corner. Ascend this to the slabby corner above, and follow it to climb a wide chimney on the right.
[M Gresham 1982]

▶ **83. Time to Reflect HVS 5c** 15m
This follows the short capped groove, just left of Tempest. Climb up to the groove and gain a standing position on the good ledge. Place a good nut above you, make one very hard move over the roof, then finish much more easily, pull leftwards over the roof, and continue up a vague crack and pockets to a pinnacle stance. Well named.
[D Hazelaar, M Gresham 21.02.83]

▶ **84. Tempest S 4a** * 15m
The obvious cracked groove in the right-hand edge of the buttress. Start at the foot of the groove, and climb it to finish up an awkward wide crack.

Streaky Desroy enjoying
Black and Tan VS 4c
photo: Jethro Kiernan

54 Holyhead Mountain • Quartz Wall

▶ **85. Momser S 4a** 12m
A poor route up a groove and crack just right of *Tempest*.

▶ **86. Scissorhands E1 5b** 8m
Up the gully from *Tempest* is an undercut arête, with a crack that stops at 6m.
[N.Ashton 29.08.91]

▶ **87. Tinseltown Rebellion E2 5c** 50m
This interesting girdle of the Quartz Wall is fairly serious with good technical climbing. Start at the foot of *The Unblue Crack*, by an undercut horizontal break running rightwards.
P1 4b 20m Step up and right to gain the break, and follow it rightwards to a belay on Tension, at the top of the corner.
P2 5c 30m Step down onto the wall and follow the quartz bands rightwards to a good hold, on Breaking the Barrier. Move right and around the arête to gain the crack of Bruvers, and finish up this.
[D Hazelaar, M Gresham 20.03.82]

Central Slab

The slab right of Quartz Wall has 2 vegetated Moderate routes, but they are not worth describing. Right of this is a steep gully marking the left edge of the Central Slab, a broad expanse with the dirty corner line of *Route 66* up the centre.

▶ **88. Black Owen VD** 38m
A wandering line with pleasant climbing, starting at the foot of *Slab Direct* and trend left to climb the arête to the back wall, then traverse right to the foot of a shallow chimney, and climb it to finish up the wall above.

▶ **89. Slab Direct VD** 30m
Good climbing, but not very direct! Start 5m right of *Black Owen*, on a small blunt pinnacle. Step off the pinnacle and trend leftwards to the top edge of the slab, spike. Move up to gain a steep slabby groove in the left edge of the back wall, and ascend this to the top.

▶ **90. Lost Hope HS 4b** 28m
Pleasant, but contrived. Start on a large block leaning against the slab, up and right of *Slab Direct*. Climb straight up the centre of the clean slab to the large overlap. Traverse left under this, and then pull up rightwards to gain the base of a crack, just right of the *Black Owen* chimney. Climb the crack and finish up the wall above.
[M Gresham, I Williams 09.02.84]

▶ **91. Route 66 D** 28m
A poor climb up the vegetated corner right of *Lost Hope*, in the middle of Central Slab. Finish rightwards up a shallow groove in the back wall.

▶ **92. Slippers VD** 34m
A worthwhile route up the arête right of *Route 66*, starting in a grassy bay down and right of that route. Climb the slab directly to a horizontal break, pull left over the bulge and continue up the left edge to a ledge (possible belay). Move up and climb the front face of the white pillar, then step left and finish

Central Slab • **Holyhead Mountain** 55

up a pleasant slabby wall. Belays well back on left. The original finish stepped right across to a heathery ramp and twin-crack finish.

▶ **93. D'Elephant VD** ∗ 34m
This follows the obvious vegetated break just right of *Slippers*, to finish up a fine hand crack in the headwall. This crack could also be used as a finish to *Slippers* by traversing right from the ledge below the pillar.

▶ **94. Snowfall VD** 34m
The right hand edge of the main slab, starting at the foot of the slabby edge 6m right of *Slippers*. Climb the edge of the slab to a broken stepped ledge, and go up the short corner above. Make a steep pull right into a broken groove and climb this, passing a ledge on the right, to finish up the wall above. Peg belay.

▶ **95. Rock and Ice HS 4a** 22m
Pleasant, with 1 hard move, starting at the foot of the slab. Climb the centre of the slab to the headwall, and pull up leftwards with difficulty to gain a deep crack. Finish up this, or the left arête.
[Members of Rock and Ice club on a warm up for a Gogarth meet circa 1967]

▶ **96. Comfortably Numb VS 4c** 22m
A pleasant eliminate up the slab and wall, starting just right of *Rock and Ice*. Take a direct line up the slab to reach the back wall, where difficult moves passing an overhang on its right gain a faint crack and a precarious exit. (NB. **The Mad Scientist HS** 28m, climbs directly up the slab from the start of *Slippers*.) [M Gresham, D Birch 12.02.83]

▶ Variation: **Albany Lodge E1 5b** 22m
Follow the parent route to the headwall, then traverse 2m left and finish on small edges. [2002]

Sub Slab

Right of the descent gully is another broken wall, and down and right again is another large sweep of slab, the Sub Slab. The broken wall has a few dirty routes which are short and not distinct enough for description. The slab itself, which steepens up for the last few metres, has a number of lines, but the following pair are the most worthwhile:

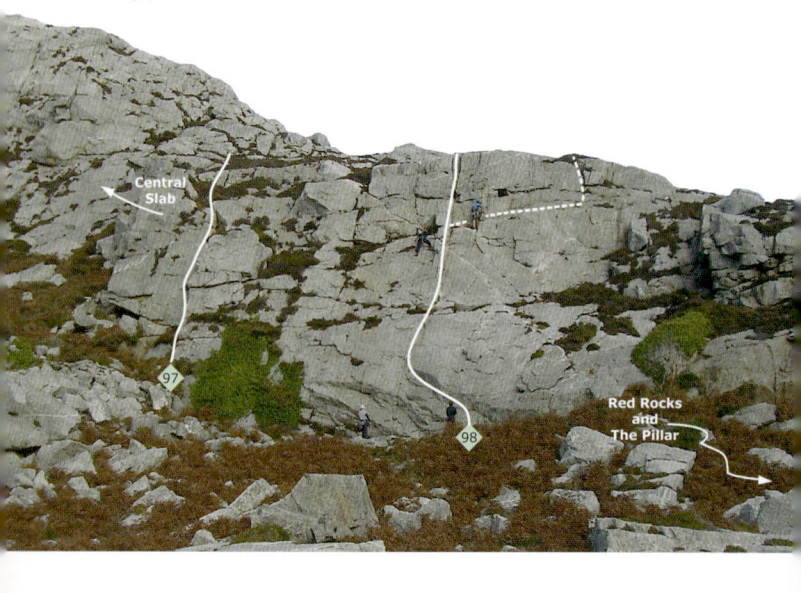

Sub Slab • Red Rocks • The Pillar • **Holyhead Mountain**

▶ **97. Delicate D** 22m
Ascend a series of broken corners on the left side of the slab through some vegetation.

▶ **98. Hat VD** 25m
This takes the weakness up the centre of the slab, starting under an overlap at its foot. Pull up and left to the crack, and follow this to the headwall. Finish up steep twin cracks to gain a niche just below the top. Belays above. **The Right Hand Finish**: this original finish traversed right along small ledges to exit up a small crack.

Red Rocks

The band of rock on the right is the Red Rocks. Fairly diminutive in height, but very steep, it has some potential for short hard routes. All the obvious lines have been climbed, albeit with varying amounts of aid.

The Pillar

The small grey buttress across the path and to the right of Red Rocks. The routes are short and unprotected.

▶ **99. Hammer S 4a** 10m
The obvious central crack.

▶ **100. Gelli VS 4b** 10m
The wall and layaway crack 1m right.

▶ **101. Surprise E1 5b** 10m
The fingery wall and rounded flake 2m right.

Upper Tier

Area: North Stack
Style: Trad (1-10 pitches)
Aspect: South-West
Rock type: Quartzite
Approach: 20 + 10 minutes
Altitude: 70m
OS ref: 216 834

Sex and Religion	E7
Hang Ten (in the Green Room)	E6/7
Psychocandy	E6/7
Barbarossa	E6/7
Dead and Bloated	E6
Cruise on Through	E6

Energy Crisis	E5
Blackleg	E5
Afreet Street	E5
The Horrorshow	E5
Manor Park	E5
The Cruise	E5
Run Fast, Run Free	E5
Fifteen Men on a Dead Man's Chest	E5
Strike	E3
Winking Crack	E3
Who Was EB?	E3

Tequila Sunrise	E2
Fail Safe	E2
The Strand	E2
The Eternal Optimist	E2
U.F.O.	E2
Park Lane/Doomsville Connection	E2
Fifth Avenue	E1
Shag Rock	E1
The Gauntlet	HVS
The Ramp	HVS
Central Park	HVS
Puffin Direct Start/Force 8	HVS
Bloody Chimney	HVS

The Rift	VS
Bezel	VS
Pantin	VS
Puffin	VS
Dirtgo	VS

Andy Scott getting stuck into the infamous **Winking Crack** E3 5c
photo: Jethro Kiernan

An ever-popular section of the crag sporting a rake of quality routes throughout the grades, all of which can be accessed without abseiling. Despite being situated well above the sea the Upper Tier retains an air of seriousness with an unnerving approach path, especially to the first time visitor. Moreover should you venture beyond the starred routes, some alarmingly loose rock and vegetated ground will be encountered; even the popular routes have the odd creaky hold. Rock falls do occur here from time to time, and great care should be taken if you encounter any fresh rock scars.

All that being said, the main lines are visually appealing and generally clean; in the case of the most popular ones (such as *The Strand*) the line is normally defined by a cleaned strip running up through the ubiquitous green fur, which clings to all but the sheerest sections of rock. Protection is normally good (large cams are often useful) and the relative ease of retreat, compared to the tidal crags, combines to give a fairly relaxed cragging atmosphere. The routes on the left side of the crag are often done as extensions to the *Emulator* section of Main Cliff.

60 Upper Tier • Approach

Conditions: As a southwest facing suntrap, the crag dries quickly, although it may be damp in the morning shade.

Approach: From either of the small car parks at the end of the South Stack road a path or a track leads off right (the path and track soon join). Continue towards the microwave relay stations, and bear rightwards past them. The Holyhead Mountain crag can be seen a few hundred metres directly ahead. As you get closer follow a path over a col allowing a first view of the Main Cliff, before bearing left and descending to reach a gearing up area at the top of a steep gully. Once you've racked up and hidden your rucsac from view, drop down the eroding path in the steep and exposed seaward edge of the gully. Traverse back right into the gully bed (try not to pay too much attention to the huge hanging boulder perched above your head) and clamber down over a couple of big blocks until the gully opens out. Thereafter a broken and occasionally collapsed path leads, with some scrambling, across the steep hillside beneath the crag.

Return to the Approach Gully/Gearing Up Area: From the finish of all routes scramble up to join a path, contouring back across the upper slope above the crag. Follow it southwards to a 2.5m heather and rock step. Just beyond the path divides; the right fork leads down to a short rocky gully dropping in to the gearing up area at the top of the approach gully. It is also possible to follow a gentler, but more circuitous route around to the left, then cutting back right to the gearing up area. For more detailed notes, see the Main Cliff section on page 96.

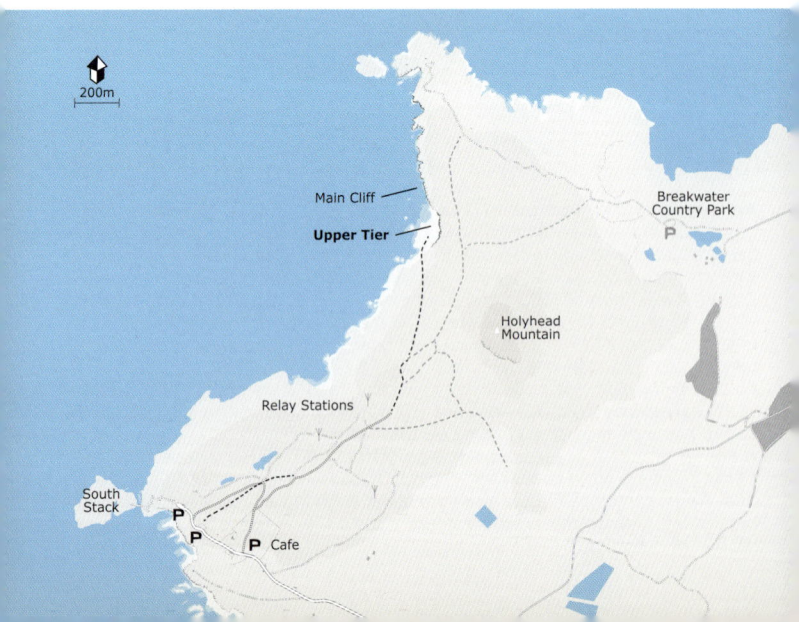

Approach • Upper Tier Right Hand • **Upper Tier** 61

▸ **1. Nomad VS** 52m
A vegetated and rather obscure route, starting beneath a 6m slab at the foot of the descent gully.
P1 30m Take the slab then the groove on the right to a wall. Traverse right and go up a short arête moving left onto a ramp, which is followed to a crack leading to a block belay on the left.
P2 22m. Move across to the crack behind the belay, go up this, and go over blocks to a wide crack on the right, which gains the top.
[D Durkan, D Edwards 05.06.68]

Approach for routes 2-6: Following the now fairly level path around the corner soon brings the obvious twin slanting cracks of *Strike* into view. (NB. The alternative approach path to the Main Cliff breaks off down leftwards from here.) The most feasible access for routes 2 - 6 is a scramble up right from the base of *Strike*.

▸ **2. Trogg's Way HVS 5a** 40m
A chossy route and not recommended. It was originally started by scrambling up to a belay at the foot of the obvious slabby corner (*Dirtgo*) left of the descent gully. The tricky crack on the right leads to a grassy ledge. Climb a slab on the left wall followed by a slight groove. From the top of this gain the flake on the left then take the crack above to finish.
[D Durkan, P Sandall 08.07.70]

Upper Tier • Upper Tier Right Hand

3. Psychocandy E6/7 6c * 18m
A hard and bold proposition tackling the thin rightwards-trending crack. The in situ protection has deteriorated and the grade may now be pushing into E7 territory. Start by scrambling up to the foot of the obvious slabby corner left of the descent gully (as for *Trogg's Way*). Go up the corner for a few metres then move right to the crack, which leads past 2 poor pegs to finish on the arête.
[C Smith 07.86]

4. Dirtigo VS 4c * 49m
With the P2a option this route is much better than the name suggests. Start as for *Trogg's Way*.
P1 4c 34m Climb the corner, past a ledge at half height, until delicate finishing moves gain the base of a grassy alcove/gully. Flake crack belay up on the left.
P2 4a 15m From the belay traverse right and follow the loose, vegetated chimney to the top.
Variation: **P2a** 4a 15m Traverse out left to the edge and follow this to the top. This is the cleanest finish and more in keeping with P1.
[M Yates, J Jordan 07.05.66]

5. Acid HVS 52m
A neglected and overgrown route, which takes the crackline in the centre of the slab to the left of *Dirtigo*. Start as for *Trogg's Way*.
P1 34m Go up and left to gain the crack and follow it over the bulge above, where a slight groove leads to a second bulge. Take this on the left before moving right to belay on the grassy ledge, as for *Dirtigo*.
P2 18m Traverse right and climb the chimney, as for *Dirtigo*, for 5m. Follow the ramp leftwards to the top.
[D Durkan, T Armitage 19.05.70]

6. Dropout E2 5b 49m
A serious and poorly protected pitch, which takes the arête left of *Acid*, starting at the foot of the corner, as for *Trogg's Way*.
P1 5b 37m Follow *Acid* over the 1st bulge, and then traverse left to the arête and climb this, with difficulty, to a small ledge. Move up right and climb the slab just right of the arête to a belay.
P2 4a 12m Ascend easily in the line of the arête to finish.
[B Wintringham, G Milburn 23.07.78]

Although it is not immediately apparent, the very steep wall to the left of *Dirtgo* is actually a huge flake which is seperated from the main crag by the lines of *The Rift* and *Bloody Chimney*.

7. The Rift VS 4c * 57m
A proper old fashioned tussle ('hen ffash' in Holyhead speak). Start by scrambling up rightwards from the start of *Strike* to a ledge and small chockstone belay, at the base of a wide crack. (To reach the start of *Dirtigo*, *Acid* etc, continue scrambling rightwards.)
P1 4c 37m Climb the left edge of the crack, past a small spike, and then stand up a flake just inside the chimney: time to start wriggling. Throw in the occasional 'shoulder scrunch' or 'reverse chicken wing' (or any other known squeeze chimney technique!), trend up and inwards in equal measure until it

Shag Rock

is possible to pull out leftwards onto a ledge. Continue diagonally up and left to reach a spike belay on top of the flake.
P2 5m Scramble up to another spike belay in a small recess.
P3 4c 15m The innocuous looking crack behind the belay proves to be steeper and harder than it looks.
(NB. George Smith has climbed a variation on P1 via "a terrifying scrabble" up the protectionless left hand arete of the chimney.)
[C E Davies, A Cowburn 12.03.66]

8. Dead and Bloated E6 6c * 35m
A safe but desperate direct finish to *Strike*. Follow *Strike* to the shake out. Step right and climb the wall past 4 pegs to a difficult exit onto the sloping top. Finish easily.
[G Farquhar, C Carolan 07.07.94]

9. Strike E3 6a ** 52m
A steep and pumpy pitch best dealt with quickly. Great stuff, although some might be happier with an E4 grade.
P1 6a 37m Climb up and make a hard move left to establish yourself on the line of the twin diagonal cracks. Keep on trucking, pausing briefly at a poor rest midway to arrive at the final crux sequence leading up into the slabby groove above. It is common to belay and abseil off from here. Alternatively continue up the slabby groove and a wide crack on the right to reach a belay on top of the flake.
P2 4c 15m P3 of *The Rift*.
[R Edwards, E Fry (5 pts) 24.05.66, FFA: P Gomersall, S Foster 1976]

Variation: 9a. Strike Direct E6 6c 30m
A vicious and scary direct start up the faint arête, protected by small wires, and starting down to the left of the original start. Boulder out the arête to join *Strike* just below the slabby groove. Continue as for *Strike*.
[J M Redhead 1982]

10. Blackleg E5 6a ** 48m
A vague right-trending depression provides the line of this serious pitch. A good selection of wires and a large sling can be placed en-route, and while few of the runners are really inspiring it is a most worthwhile route.
P1 6a 22m A strenuous start leads up and rightwards to a spike runner. Pull straight up to a small flake on the left, which accepts further protection. Move up right to a good hold where the wall steepens. A very long reach leads to an excellent hold and easier ground on the ramp of *Strike*. Belay.
P2 6a 11m Gain the flake on the right and move up strenuously to its top. Follow a lichenous ramp leftwards, then go up to belay on top of the flake.
P3 4c 15m Finish as for *The Rift*.
[R Fawcett, C Gibb 18.09.78]

11. Sex and Religion E7 6c ** 35m
The obvious left hand finish to *Blackleg* provides a serious and sustained outing; be warned, the protection is poor. Follow *Blackleg* past the flakes to a good, crucial nut placement. Move up and left to a poor peg. Continue with difficulty to gain the vertical crackline above and follow this to join *Strike*. Finish up this. [G Farquhar, C Carolan 26.07.93]

Upper Tier Right Hand • **Upper Tier** 65

▶ **12. Barbarossa E6/7 6b** ✱✱✱ 52m
A superb and bold wall climb, striking a direct line up the crackline in the front face of the huge flake: strenuous and sustained, and a good deal more serious since the demise of the peg on the lower wall. Start left of *Blackleg* directly below a line of pockets in the middle of the wall.
P1 6b 37m Move up to a large pocket (big nut), and then make technical moves slightly leftwards then rightwards to regain the line of pockets and soon thereafter some gear. Follow the pockets and a vague crack line to a small overlap and continue in the same line to an old peg. Step right. and then go easily up to belay on the flake.
P2 4c 15m Finish as for P3 of *The Rift*.
[J Moran, A Evans 30.05.78, FFA J Redhead 06.07.80]

▶ **13. Bloody Chimney HVS 4c** ✱ 55m
A character building adventure, where the grade of P1 depends largely on one's girth! Start at the foot of the slabby corner of the slab.
P1 4c 22m Gain the large block and follow the steep crack until it widens. At the earliest possible opportunity, throw yourself into the chimney and wriggle upwards to welcome holds and a belay just above a narrow section.
P2 4b 18m Shuffle into the back of the widening chimney. Back and foot up past a flake crack, then trend rightwards under the large chockstone to emerge into the daylight.
P3 4c 15m P3 of *The Rift*.
[D Alcock, D Potts 24.04.66]

66 Upper Tier • Upper Tier Right Hand

▶ **14. U.F.O. E2 5b/c** * 62m
A splendid trip; the climbing is engrossing and the interest sustained. Provided a large rack is carried, the first 2 pitches (which offer alternately strenuous then technical climbing) can be run together. Similarly P2 and P3a can also be combined.
P1 5b 27m Go up the slabby corner for 8m to a small foot ledge. Step right and follow a thin crack (a bit creaky in places) first rightwards, then back left to a sharp layback flake. Follow this to the top of a pinnacle, and then descend to the first stance of *Bloody Chimney*.
P2 5b/c 20m Move back up to the top of the pinnacle and gain the groove above via a long reach (5c for the short). From the top of the groove, step right onto a ledge and battle up the wide crack on the left to a ledge and big flake. Belaying here will help reduce the rope drag and the likelihood of the protection lifting out on the final pitch.
P3 5a 15m Trend up and left to a grass ledge. Follow the left trending cracks almost to the arete, and then step up right onto a small quartz ledge. The short groove above leads to the top. Spike and threaded flake belays (a big sling is useful) can be found approx 8m up and to the right.
Variation: **P3a** 5a 15m From the block, follow the wide crack, then step right to a diagonal crack which leads to the top. A better and cleaner way of finishing the route
[L E Holliwell, F Quigley, L R Holliwell 04.11.67]

▶ **15. Pantin VS 5a** * 64m
Despite appearances to the contrary (i.e it's a bit furry in places), this is a good route up an impressive section of the cliff. It is worth waiting until mid afternoon to let the sun dry off the slab and upper corner. P3 is top end for the grade.
P1 4b 26m Go up the slabby corner for 8m to the foot ledge as for *U.F.O.* Continue up to a small flake crack, and then traverse left for a few metres to a faint groove. Follow this, trending up left, then back right to a ledge below twin cracks.
P2 4a 8m Climb up the cracks to a large block belay on the ledge. A big sling (240 cm) is handy.
P3 5a 30m Step back down and traverse boldly rightwards across the steep wall (the level at which you traverse is open to variation), then make a long stride to better holds which lead up to a large spike. (Take care to protect this section; the wires have a habit of lifting out!) Sprint up the short leaning corner to a ledge on the right, then step back into the enclosed groove. Climb this to a grass ledge, then up the continuation to the top.
[A Williams, B Royal 05.64]

Bryn Williams fully engaged with P2 of **Bloody Chimney** HVS photo: Al Leary

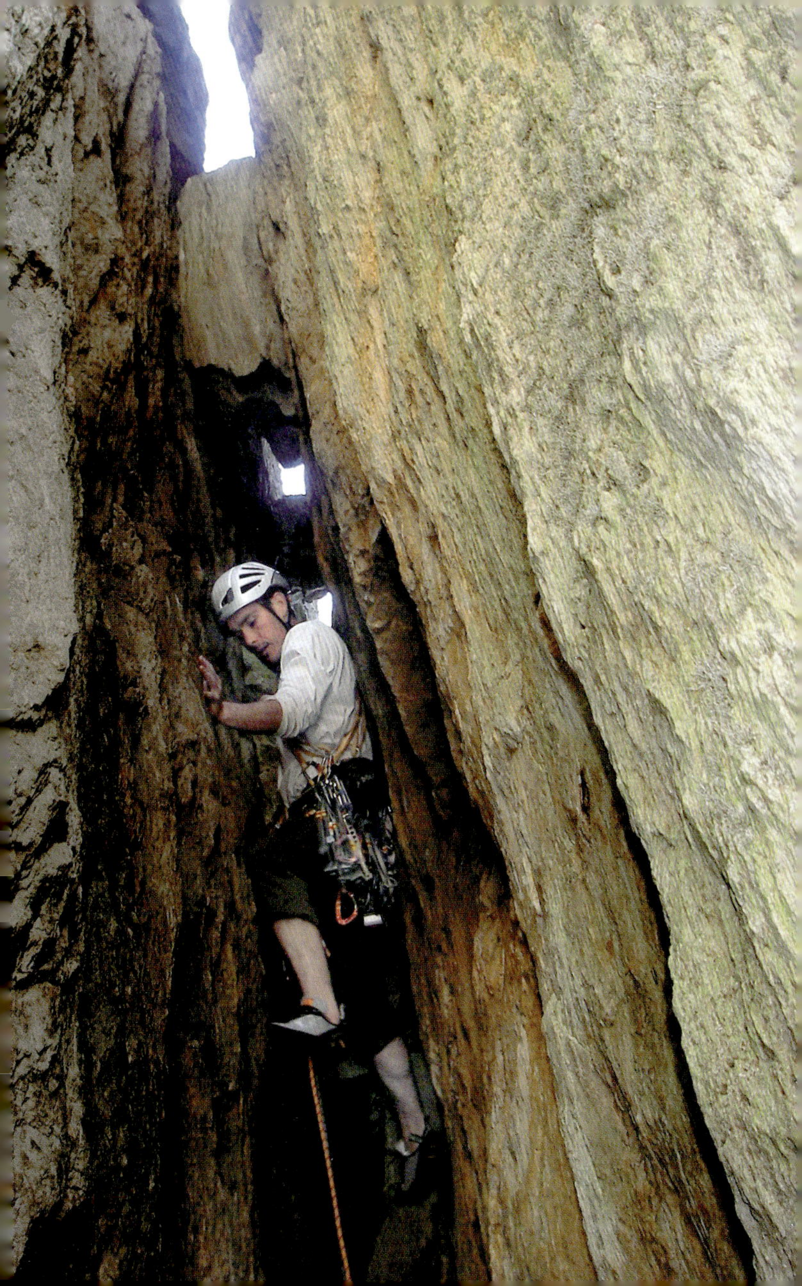

68 Upper Tier • Upper Tier Right Hand

Up and left of *U.F.O* is a steep wall tackled by *Run Fast, Run Free, Get The Stroll* etc. Traditionally these were accessed via *Pantin* P1 with a short rightwards traverse to gain the start of the main pitches; however the *Puffin Direct Start* (followed by a quick traverse accross the slab) offers a vastly superior approach pitch and warm up for the aforementioned strenuous challenges.

▶ **16. Get The Stroll E3 5c** 65m
Bold but not as strenuous as *Run Fast, Run Free*, with the same start.
P1 4c 22m P1 of *Run Fast, Run Free*.
P2 5c 31m Follow *Run Fast, Run Free* until below the obvious pod in the crack. Traverse delicately right on quartz holds to gain 'rattley' flakes and follow these up rightwards to reach a crack, which leads to a good stance.
P3 5c 12m From the left-hand end of the ledge, follow the obvious leftward slanting crack to the top. (NB. This pitch was originally given 4c in the 1978 and 1981 Supplements; it was not checked for this guide.)
[D Knighton, J Girdley 28.10.78]

▶ **17. Run Fast, Run Free E5 6a ∗∗** 65m
The superb, steep crack on P2 offers a well protected, arm-melting stamina trial.
P1 4c 22m Follow *Pantin* to just below the twin cracks, and then traverse rightwards to nut belays in the corner of the slab.
P2 6a 43m Move up into the soaring crackline in the steep wall and follow it leftwards past a pod and a poor peg. Step right to a continuation crack, which will lead to the top.
[D Knighton, J Girdley (2 pts) 27.10.78, FFA: W Todd or P O'Donovan 1980]

▶ **18. Canned Laughter E2 5c (1 pt)** 67m
The original aid route of this wall has been superseded although it can be followed to give a disjointed route. Start from a belay below the short cracks on *Pantin*.
P1 4c 22m P1 of *Run Fast, Run Free*.
P2 5c 33m Gain and follow the crack, as for *Run Fast, Run Free*. From the top climb leftwards to a 2nd thin crack. Go up a couple of metres, then go left to a corner and peg. Climb this, moving left into the corner of *Pantin* and ascend this to a stance. (One rest sling was used on this pitch.)
P3 12m Move right into a broken chimney and climb this to finish.
[P Seramur, D Durkan as an A2 aid route 22.11.70/Aid reduced to 1 pt by D Knighton, D Cronshaw 02.10.78]

▶ **19. Dangerous Rhythm E3 5c** 56m
The meat of this route is provided by the golden corner left of *Run Fast, Run Free*. Start at the foot of the slab a couple of metres left of *Pantin*.
P1 4c 22m P1 of *Run Fast, Run Free*.
P2 5c 34m Climb up the shallow the depression just left of the initial crack of *Run Fast, Run Free* and continue up the wall above to reach a large hollow spike (peg on the wall out left). Ascend the shallow corner above to the overlap, which is passed on the right, and continue for 5m before moving left into a chimney. Finish up this.
[D Knighton, D Cronshaw 05.11.78]

20. Force 8 HVS 5a * 68m

A good route, although the overgrown nature of P1 undermines the overall quality. Start at the left arete of the *Pantin* slab. A better alternative is to swap P1 for *Puffin Direct Start,* then continue up the twin cracks of *Pantin*.

P1 4c 43m Climb up and right for 5m, then head back left to gain the arête at a small bulge. Follow the crack up the edge of the slab then take a slight groove leading to the back wall. Go up the break in the wall to gain a ledge on the skyline. Step right and go up the crack to belay at the top block.

P2 5a 25m Step onto the wall and trend up and leftwards to the top of a big flake. Continue steeply up for a few moves, then swing right into an alcove. Follow the finely positioned left hand ramp/groove until it is possible to step right onto a good ledge. A short diagonal flake crack leads back leftwards into the easy finishing chimney. Belay at some embedded blocks.
[D Durkan, P Sandall, P Brown 20.08.70]

21. Puffin VS 4b * 65m

The easiest route hereabouts and despite a smattering of vegetation and loose rock, it is a pleasant introduction to the cliff. Start below the left hand groove.

P1 4a/b 15m Up the groove (some loose rock) to belay on top of the flake. (Large/240cm sling is useful.)

P2 4b 17m Traverse right along the ledge for 3m and climb up to gain a steep crackline. Follow this until it is possible to swing right onto the arete. Move up for a few moves, then traverse right and climb a short crack in the slab (past a couple of threads), before trending diagonally rightwards to a ledge at the base of the twin cracks.

P3 4a 8m Up the cracks to a block belay on the ledge. The big sling is again handy.

P4 4a 25m Move left and climb the deep groove/corner to the top. A good finish.
[R Edwards, J Fletcher, 22.05.66]

21a. Puffin Direct Start HVS 5b * 36m

This underrated climb, which follows the right hand stepped flake, is well worth doing in it's own right. When combined with the twin cracks of *Pantin*, followed by P2 of *Force 8,* a very fine route at a consistent standard is produced.

Start 2m right of the original route. Layback and bridge up the initial bulges (immediately discovering that it's a touch steeper than it looked!) to a smoother section of rock. Sprint up this to better holds at the top of the leaning crack, then continue more easily to the right hand end of the ledge on *Puffin P2*. Continue up this to the belay ledge below the twin cracks.
[R Edwards, J Hutchinson (1pt) 14.11.67]

The path now descends slightly and undulates across the hillside. Just below some big boulders, it narrows considerably and shuffles around a faint rib (best not to look down at this point!). Shag Rock is the obvious white, detached pinnacle over on the left, and *Winking Crack*, *The Cruise* etc, climb the brown wall overhead.

22. Campion HVS 5a 81m
A varied climb, loose in places, with some frightening grass climbing on P3. After the first 2 pitches, it would be possible to traverse across and gain either *Puffin* or *Force 8*; both of which will provide a better finish. Start below and left of the slab of *Puffin* at some large blocks, below a groove.
P1 4b 25m Climb the groove and crack above the belay to the top of the pinnacle.
P2 4c 9m Go up the crack behind the belay to a small stance on the edge of the upper slab.
P3 5a 22m Move right to a short crack and take this until it is possible to move onto the wall on the left. Climb this, peg, and then step left onto a short brown slab. Move left again then go up over vegetated ledges to reach a large spike belay.
P4 4c 25m The crack in the wall above leads to a flake. From this transfer to another crack on the left and finish up this.
[R Edwards, J Edwards, F Hutchison (1 pt) 07.11.67]

23. Hang Ten (in the Green Room) E6/7 6c * 56m
A hard and scary lead with a committing crux slab. Start by the pinnacle, up and left of *Campion*.
P1 6c 28m Gain the top of the pinnacle, and step onto the arête. Climb this on the right hand side, past a peg to reach a 2nd peg. Swing round left and climb the blunt arête direct to a desperate slap for a good hold in a serious situation. Continue more easily up the rib to a belay.
P2 4c 28m Finish as for P2 of *The Cruise*.
[P Pritchard, C Waddy 03.06.88]

24. The Cruise E5 6b ** 55m
This popular crack pitch provides a pumpy stamina test.
P1 6b 37m Scramble up from the path to belay in a corner. Step left and go up the arête to a small ledge underneath the crack. Move into the crack and follow it past pegs to a brief resting position beneath the short chimney that guards access to the ledge above - medium sized cams serve to protect the inevitable tussle.
P2 4c 28m Easy slabs and vegetated ledges lead to the top.
[Originally done as an aid route (*Nod*) by D Durkan, P Sandell 08.70, FFA: J Moran, P Williams, J Sonczak 1984]

25. Cruise on Through E6 6c * 38m
A hard direct on *The Cruise*. Follow *The Cruise* to the rest below the final pod. Thin moves out left, past 2 rusty pegs, and through the scoop lead to a break and a vertical crack. Follow this up to the ledge.
[M Turner, L Thomas 2002]

26. Noddy E4 6b 66m
A somewhat contrived beginning leads to a well-positioned climax passing the old aid point (a meagre RURP!!) on the wall between *The Cruise* and *Winking Crack*. There is good gear before the traverse, but potential for a sizeable swing. Start as for *Winking Crack*.
P1 5a 30m Follow P1 of *Winking Crack*.
P2 6b 18m Gain the prominent crack out right (*Who Was EB?*) directly behind the belay and follow it to a horizontal break. Cross this passing the old aid peg to reach a flake slanting away up right. This leads to easier ground and belays.
P3 4c 18m Finish up broken rocks to the top.
[D Cronshaw, D Knighton (1 or 2 pts) 21.10.78, FFA: C Parkin , F Ball 1991]

27. Who Was EB? E3 5c * 60m
A fine parallel line to *Winking Crack*, which supersedes the contrivances of *Noddy*. Originally climbed in a big single pitch, although there is the obvious option of splitting the route at the *Winking Crack* belay. Start as for *Winking Crack*, but (from the 1st stance) break off to follow the crack line to the right, until a step left at the 'V' junction. Finish up the right hand crack.
[T Turner, L Thomas 2006]

28. Winking Crack E3 5c *** 67m
A route with a fearsome reputation built upon its final man-eating offwidth crack: be afraid!
P1 5a 30m Scramble up from the path to belay on a large ledge. Move right and start up the first corner on *The Cruise*, traversing left around the arête and climbing up left to follow a groove until block belay can be reached on the left.
P2 5c 37m Follow the crack to a ledge on the left where it divides. Continue up the left branch to a small overhang. Move left, then back right, before heading up the cracks to the final offwidth section. Dive in and swim upwards, improvising as you go. (It is possible, although hardly sporting, to avoid the offwidth by striding out right on to the right arête.)
[J Brown, A Cowburn (6 pts) 05.06.66, FFA: J Street 1966]

72 Upper Tier • Upper Tier Right Hand

▶ Variation: **Blue Oyster Cult E3 5c** 55m
A spiralling line weaving in and out of *Winking Crack*, on which it is based. Start beneath the overhanging corner left of the start of *Winking Crack*.
P1 5c 10m Climb the corner to a nut belay halfway up P1 of *Winking Crack*.
P2 5a 15m Move left around the corner and gain a ramp/groove, which is followed to an awkward exit rightwards to the block belay at the end of P1 of *Winking Crack*.
P3 5c 30m Move up into the corner then boldly gain the arête, rounding it by blind moves before climbing up into the crackline of *Winking Crack*. This is followed to the swing right onto ledges, and so to the top.
[D Knighton, A Hyslop, M Tuerney 22.04.78]

▶ **29. Blind Pew E2 5b** 74m
This rather vegetated but worthwhile route climbs the area of rock between *Winking Crack* and the back of the bay. So named from the amount of debris dislodged onto the first ascentionists face! (NB. P1 is overgrown, however this is easily bypassed by following the scramble approach to *Winking Crack* and walking left along the ledge.) Start by a short scramble up to a short wall, split by a crack, a few metres right of the start of *Crowbar*.
P1 4c 10m Climb the crack to a good ledge. Belay below the lefthand groove.
P2 5b 15m Follow the groove to an easier groove. This leads to a good stance.
P3 5b 15m The overhanging crack leads to the next belay.
P4 5b 12m Continue up the crack to the final stance.
P5 4c 22m Climb the detached flake above on its left side and continue in a similar line to the top.
[J Brown, J Cheesmond (10 pts) 23.06.66, FFA: D Knighton, D Cronshaw 12.09.78]

▶ **30. The Emotionary E5 6a** 25m
This takes the once brushed wall high up between *Blind Pew* and *Winking Crack*, starting from the belay at the end of P3 of *Blind Pew*.
P1 6a 15m Step right to a peg then climb straight up to a second poor peg at the overlap. Continue rightwards with difficulty to a handhold before following a leftward-slanting crackline, peg, to a good stance.
P2 5a 10m Climb the slab on the left to finish up the headwall via a short, thin crack.
[D Knighton, D Cronshaw 22.09.78]

▶ **31. Fifteen Men on a Dead Man's Chest E5 6a** ∗ 62m
Good, technically interesting climbing that in its current condition is a committing and fairly dirty prospect. Start by scrambling up to a ledge just left of the start of P2 of *Blind Pew,* as mentioned in the *Blind Pew* description.
P1 6a 25m Move boldly left around the arête and go up to the first of a line of pockets. Continue in the same line with increasing difficulty until it is possible to move right to a ledge and pinnacle belay.
P2 5c 25m From the top of the pinnacle follow a flaky crack until scary moves up and slightly right lead to a ledge and belay. A friable, serious pitch.
P3 4c 12m Ascend a short groove on the right to a ledge, trend right up a short slab into a corner and finish up the easy crack.
[M Boysen, D Alcock, D Howard Jones (3 pts) 05.71, FFA: A Sharp 1983]

32. The Horrorshow E5 6b * 74m
The main pitch on this neglected route is now somewhat overgrown and the ageing in situ gear is not beyond suspicion. In its hay day it was said to offer excellent sustained climbing with good protection. It would probably clean up well, but there would still be the friable and serious P2 of *Fifteen Men..*, up which the route continues, to deal with. Start by scrambling up leftwards from the main path to the base of the right hand groove.

P1 4a 12m Follow *Crowbar* to the slabby ledge and take a belay below a short crack in the right wall.

P2 6b 25m Climb the short crack in the right wall, then work up right to a peg before trending back leftwards to a second peg, deep in a pocket. Follow the faint crackline to a peg (high on the right) before a tricky move left gains a good hold above. Traverse right along the obvious line then move up and right to a junction with *Fifteen Men..* in a corner on the sloping ledge.

P3 5c 25m As for P2 of *Fifteen Men...*

P4 4c 12m As for P3 of *Fifteen Men...* Ascend a short groove on the right to a ledge, trend right up a short slab into a corner and finish up the easy crack.

[J Moran, A Evans, G Milburn (1 pt) 08.07.78, FFA: R Fawcett 01.80]

33. Crowbar E1 5b * 78m
A big striking line that follows the overhanging corner system up the back of the bay Despite a slightly unnerving approach, and a scrappy finish, the climbing in the main groove is consistently good and well protected; it is however prone to dampness, and as such, is best left until mid afternoon when the sun will hopefully have dried up any residual moisture.

P1 4b 18m Climb the broken left wall of the groove, past a slabby ledge, to reach the main corner. (Alternatively follow P1 of *Black Spot*, then descend the ledge diagonally rightwards to the stance above).

P2 4c 15m The bulging flake crack leads to a ledge. Belay a few metres to the left of the groove.

P3 5b 45m The corner leads to a small sloping ledge and possible belay at 12m (4c to this point). Continue up the steep, finely positioned groove until possible to step left onto a ramp. Follow this via easier but rather vegetated terrain towards the arete, then step back right onto a grass ledge. Belay just above on a quartz ledge. Descent: Scramble up left, then diagonally down leftwards on steep grass to gain a worn area and belays at the top of *Fifth Avenue*, *Central Park* etc.

[D Scott, W Cheverst (7 pts) 21.05.66]

34. The Grim Reaper E3 6a 53m
This eliminate fills the gap between *Crow Bar* and *Black Spot* with difficult climbing in a good position. Start as for *Crowbar*, below the corner.

P1 5a 25m Climb steep slabs to a ledge and peg, as for *Crowbar*. Move left, climb the steep ledged wall to a large ledge then take the groove, rising from the middle of the back wall, moving right to belay as for *Crowbar*.

P2 6a 28m Go left along the ledge then climb steep rock diagonally rightwards and go up rightwards to good footholds. Move steeply up right until forced left to a small pillar. Go up rightwards to a ledge where an easy escape is possible up to the left.

[J Moran, G Milburn 24.07.78]

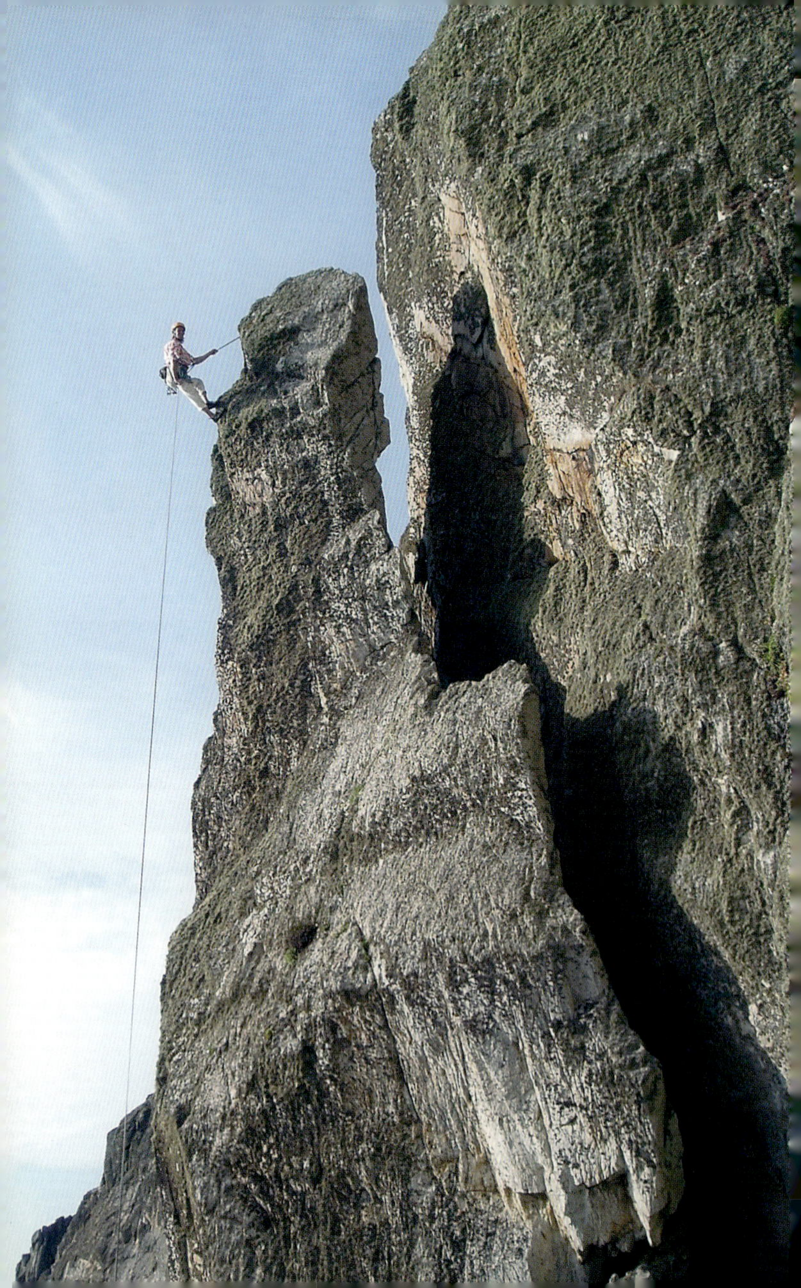

35. Black Spot HVS 5a 55m
The left hand corner/groove yields a reasonable route that covers some interesting terrain. It is a little dusty in places though and some of the rock, especially on P2 demands care.(Take a good range of cams.) Start by scrambling up a rising leftwards traverse from the path to reach a comfy haven at the base of the Shag Rock spire and beneath the left hand corner/groove.
P1 5a 20m Climb a steep crack/groove, then move right to a ledge. Follow the continuation groove until it is possible to step right. Belay on the ledge.
P2 4c/5a 35m Layback briskly up the steep, slanting groove then continue up to a ledge. Traverse right, and climb the left trending groove to another ledge, and then follow the slabby corner above until just below a steep, wide crack in the final wall. Step delicately out left onto the slab, and then climb carefully up the wall just to the left of the crack to gain the hillside. Scramble up for 6m to belay at a crack on the right wall; cams useful. A final 20m scramble leads up leftwards, and then back right to the worn area of *Fifth Avenue*.
[L E Holliwell, L R Holliwell 15.10.67]

36. Bitter Days E1 5b 62m
A well positioned climb up the arete overlooking Shag Rock. Unfortunately at present it is very lichenous. Start as for *Black Spot*.
P1 5a 25m Follow *Black Spot* up the short steep wall, or go up behind *Shag Rock*, to gain the arête. The wall above leads to a sloping ledge which is traversed to a semi-hanging stance, approximately 5m below the first stance on *Black Spot*.
P2 5b 37m Traverse back left to the ledge and climb up leftwards to a crack near the arête (peg). Climb the crack, peg, to easier ground. Traverse left onto the arête and finish up this.
[B Wintringham, M Wintringham 16.03.78]

37. Shag Rock E1 5a * 25m
The unique Gogarth summit vista is ample reward for this esoteric outing. Start as for *Black Spot*. Clamber up over blocks, then follow the chimney until a ledge on the left arete is reached. Climb the steepening arete via a hollow flake crack, traverse rightwards onto the inside face for a few moves, then direct to the summit. Victory salutes and banter are de rigueur; warrior poses or headstands are optional (just be careful not to flick off the belays!). It is worth carrying a large sacrificial sling for the abseil descent.
[M A Boysen, B Ingle (1 pt) 04.04.64]

38. Shagorado E3 5c 37m
An unusual route, which spirals its way up *Shag Rock*, with some friable rock at the start. Start beneath a right-trending crack in the front face of the pinnacle. The crack leads to a ledge, where a step right gains holds leading up and left to reach a small ledge. Climb steeply up the crack above to reach the slab above. Trend left up this, peg, to reach the arête and move around this to the start of a narrow ledge crossing the face. Follow this across to the other arête and climb this to the summit.
[D Knighton, B Conlon 30.09.78]

< Streaky Desroy abseiling off Shag Rock. Photo: Desroy collection

The path now drops down around the base of Shag Rock and follows a slippery traverse above a rather alarming drop to a safer area just before *The Strand*; the path to the Main Cliff descends from here.

▶ 39. Fifth Avenue E1 5c ** 63m
One of the best routes of its grade on the Upper Tier, with varied and sustained climbing.
P1 5b/c 33m Climb the chimney on the left side of Shag Rock until possible to pull into the bulging groove that runs up leftwards. Layback the groove and gain the upper ramp via a precarious high step (crux). Follow the still sustained ramp/groove past an initial spike (the first belay of *Tequila Sunrise*), to an old peg and spike belay below the upper wall.
P2 5b 30m The short wall proves to be steeper and harder than it looks; a further 25m of scrambling up steep grass and boulders leads to a solid flake belay at a worn/level area at the base of a gully.
[M Boysen, M Yates 14.05.66]

▶ 40. Tequila Sunrise E2 5c * 43m
A route of contrasts: an initial bold wall pitch, precedes a sparkling finish up the sort of crackline that cams were invented for. Start just to the left of the chimney of *Fifth Avenue*.
P1 5b 25m Follow the flake/groove on the left to its top, then move boldly up the wall past a small spike to pegs. Trend up and leftwards to gain a thin crack that leads to a spike belay halfway up the ramp of *Fifth Avenue*.
P2 5c 18m Climb the steep crackline with the usual technical dilemmas; thumbs up or thumbs down? From some good spikes on the arete follow thin cracks, just right of the edge, until it is possible to belay at twin cracks immediately below the broken hillside. Approximately 25m of steep scrambling leads up and leftwards to the worn area at the top of *Fifth Avenue*.
[A Evans, J Moran, D Knighton 27.05.78]

▶ 41. Times Square E1 5a 49m
A character building finale along a 'booming' left-trending gangway contrasts with the better protected, balancey nature of the pitch below. Not as clean as Fifth Avenue, the top pitch of which would provide a safer/better exit. Start just above the path at a left trending groove, down and left of the chimney of *Fifth Avenue*.
P1 5a 35m Climb directly up the groove, then follow blocks up leftwards to a ledge below the crack of *Street Survivor* (good wires). Step right (crux) and follow thin cracks past some hollow spikes to gain a right trending groove that leads to the belay of *Fifth Avenue*.
P2 5a 14m Go out left and shuffle along the line of creaky flakes, which in places appear to be held together by the grass! Just before these run out, follow the diagonal line (small cams/micro wires useful), up and left to the hillside (14m to here). Continue up to a variety of belay options as for *Central Park*.
[P1: F Cannings, D Peers 15.04.67/P2: F Cannings, T Lewis 09.03.69]

Shag Rock
30
28
24
17
16
14
44
42
4
2
33
27
25
24
11
8
3
47
32
28
31
29
23
7
15
13
12
10
9a
9
49
46
45
43
41
39

Upper Tier • Upper Tier Right Hand

42. Street Survivor E2 5c 53m
An overgrown route, starting directly below the final crack of *Central Park*. The grass slope at the top of the route is very steep and doesn't offer much in the way of secure belays. A pre-placed abseil rope, tied off from the vicinity of the worn/level area of *Fifth Avenue* is recommended.
P1 5a 25m Climb the wall and crack which leads directly up to the stance on *Central Park*, to belay as for that route.
P2 5c 28m Move up the top crack of *Central Park* for 2m then make awkward moves left to gain flakes out on the wall. Climb up the flakes, continuing up the steep shallow groove above, which leads with difficulty to the top. Continue up the steep loose slope at the crag top until decent belays can be found. 50m ropes needed!
[D Knighton, J Tout 27.03.78]

43. Central Park HVS 5a ** 63m
The classic striking crackline of P2 generously repays perseverance on the mediocre initial pitch. Start in a small niche at the left side of the short rock traverse on the path. Start just left of the arch overhang.
P1 5a 33m Go up the slabby wall on the left to reach a shallow groove leading to a ledge on the left. Move up right to gain and follow a leftward trending line and steep groove and the wall above. Traverse delicately right to belay at the foot of the crack. A serious and sparsely protected pitch, particularly since the flake that provided protection for the traverse parted company with the crag.
P2 5a 30m Cruise up the crack passing a problematic section near the top. Belays can be found by scrambling, with care, just up and left of a perched block. (N.B. Bear in mind that your belayer is directly in the fall line of any dislodged rocks, so it is perhaps better to continue up and right on grass steps for approximately 10m to a stance at a slightly hollow boulder choke.)
[P Crew, D Alcock (10 pts) 14.05.66]

44. Manor Park E5 6a/b 58m
Another neglected route, which has become overgrown. The original pegs on P2 have long since crumbled away, along with a few holds, upping the grade a notch. The grass slope at the top of the route is very steep and doesn't offer much in the way of secure belays. A pre placed abseil rope, tied off from the vicinity of the worn/level area of *Fifth Avenue* is recommended. Start as for *Central Park*.
P1 5c 30m Follow *Central Park* for 15m until it is possible to move right and climb a thin crack directly to the belay of *Central Park*.
P2 6a/b 28m Follow the obvious thin crack out and up leftwards to a step left to a large pocket, good nut, and climb to the top with some difficulty (original holds now missing). Continue up the steep loose slope at the crag top until decent belays can be found. 50m ropes needed!
[J Moran, D Knighton, A Evans 27.05.78]

45. Hyde Park E4 6b 75m
This route had a reputation for shedding holds; it has now lost its original 1st belay, which was located at the left end of the *Central Park* traverse. The most feasible alternative belay is at the top of P1 of *Central Park*. Start midway between *Central Park* and *The Strand*.

P1 5b 26m Follow a series of flakes before traversing right into *Central Park* and following to its 1st belay at the base of the main crack.

P2 6b 49m Move back out left to the end of the traverse, step left and climb rattley flakes to reach the top of the groove, on *Transatlantic Crossing*. (N.B. This section has been affected by rockfall and is unclimbed in its current state). A thin crack above leads with difficulty past some old pegs to easier ground and the top. Belay higher up the slope.
[B Wintringham, M Wintringham (1 pt) 26.08.77/FFA: A Sharp 1977]

46. The Strand E2 5b *** 73m
A fantastic route and the line of the crag, which follows the thin crack up the well-cleaned strip; sustained, well protected and very popular. Some people abseil off after the main pitch, however due to the age of the in situ anchors this can't be recommended.

P1 5b 43m Move up right to gain the crack line, which is followed to a belay below a short slab.

P2 4b 30m Ascend the short broken slab, and then scramble up for 25m to a big flake at a level/worn area.
[E Drummond (1 pt) 01.10.67]

47. Park Lane E2 5b * 70m
P1 is excellent and clean, however the main flake feature has a slightly disconcerting hollow feel to it. The rest of the route has unfortunately fallen into serious neglect. Start as for *The Strand*.

P1 5b 30m Climb up rightwards to the crack, but follow holds leading up left to below the bulge. Move up left, then step back right into the crack, and climb up to a stance and peg belay on top of the large flake.

P2 5b 28m Go up left to a crack and gain the groove above. Follow this to exit left onto a stance with peg belays in a corner.

P3 4b 12m Take the slab above then scramble up the slope to belay high up the slope.
[L E Holliwell, L R Holliwell 22.10.67]

The obvious **Park Lane/Doomsville Connection** (E2 5b, 5b/c **) yields a superb and popular combination.

48. Mayfair E3 5c 48m
Although an eliminate, the climbing is worthwhile. P1 has a distinct crux section, while P2 is more sustained with bold, crimpy wall climbing. Start a couple of metres left and up from *The Strand*.

P1 5c 30m Go up to a peg then break out rightwards and climb the right-hand side of the flake to the stance on *Park Lane*. (N.B. P1 is initially overgrown; recent ascents have started up *Park Lane*).

P2 5c 18m Follow *Park Lane* a little way until it is possible to climb flakes to a peg. Climb the slab to the top and belay well back up the slope. It is possible to traverse right to the stance on *Strand*.
[B Wintringham, J Brown (2 pts) 24.07.78/FFA: A Sharp, S lewis, P Williams 08.78]

49. Doomsville E2 5b/c ∗ 91m
The ramp on P3 is a great feature; unfortunately the approach pitches are dirty, overgrown and loose (sounds great, eh?). Start below a groove up left from *The Strand*.
P1 5a 18m The groove leads to grassy ledges and a peg belay.
P2 5b/c 18m Go rightwards, past a peg, to the belay on top of the flake as for *Park Lane*.
P3 5b/c 25m The attractive diagonal ramp trending up right is not as innocent as it first appears. Climb it with a good deal of interest; at its top a short crack leads up to *The Strand* belay below a short slab.
P4 4b 30m P2 of *The Strand*.
[M Yates, A Cram, J Yates (2 pts) 19.05.67]

50. Broadway HVS 5a 64m
An uninspiring climb taking the cracks up the left hand side of the wall, starting as for *Doomsville*.
P1 5a 18m The groove leads to grassy ledges and a peg belay.
P2 5a 34m Climb the thin crack then the wider crack above to belay on slabs as for *Park Lane*.
P3 4b 12m P3 of *Park Lane*.
[C J Phillips, D Cuthbertson, L Dickinson (1 pt) 16.03.69]

51. Transatlantic Crossing E2 5c 123m
This interesting girdle of the *Central Park* wall, starting as for *Fifth Avenue*, is unlikely to be the quoted grade following a significant rockfall on the initial groove on P2 (common with *Hyde Park*). The route is described as finishing as for *Park Lane* but it would seem better to finish up the cleaner *Doomsville* option.
P1 5a 40m Chimney up and gain the groove, as for *Fifth Avenue*. At the first bulge, move down left and around the corner to gain holds leading leftwards past a large spike on *Times Square*. Continue across to belay below the wide crack, as for *Central Park*.
P2 5c 43m Traverse left to climb a groove (site of the rock fall), move left to *The Strand* then climb down this for 6m until it is possible to climb across to the flake on *Mayfair*. Climb up to the stance on top of the flake.
P3 5b 28m As for P2 of *Park Lane*.
P4 4b 12m Finish as for P3 of *Park Lane*.
[E Drummond, S Brown (4 pts) 11.67, FFA: P Whillance, D Armstrong 1977]

The next few routes start in the steep, grassy-floored amphitheatre up and left of the *Central Park* Wall. It is gained by a rather frightening pitch up a vague gully in the centre of the broken rocky band, which leads onto the steep vegetated slope. It is also possible to abseil into this area from the crag top, an approach that requires a detailed knowledge of the cliff topography, and is probably even more gripping than the normal way.

52. Gladiator 50m HVS 5a 50m
Reasonable climbing, but with worrying sections of loose rock on both pitches taking the obvious break slanting up right. Start at the foot of the break, by a pinnacle in the centre of the bay.
P1 5a 22m Climb the broken groove to a ledge, and carry on up the diagonal break to reach a small stance and peg belay.
P2 5a 28m Go up the groove and ramp on the left, and then traverse left into a light-coloured groove and follow it to the top.
[L E Holliwel, L R Holliwell 07.10.67]

53. Kira His E4 6a 48m
This fairly serious route takes the wall right of *Amphitheatre Wall*, starting at a block belay right of the corner of that route.
P1 6a 18m Climb the crack in the red wall, just right of the corner, to a block belay.
P2 5c 30m Go straight up the groove behind the belay to a loose finish.
[M Crook, D Kendall 08.02.89]

54. Amphitheatre Wall HVS 4c 52m
A serious route, taking the broken corner on the lefthand side of the amphitheatre, finishing on some very poor rock. Start by scrambling up to the foot of the corner.
P1 4b 18m Climb the corner crack, past a sloping ledge, to a small niche on the right. Peg belay.
P2 4c 34m Take the groove behind the stance then go right around the arête and onto a slab. Go right again to a wide crack, which leads, through very loose rock, to the top.
[M Boysen, C Rowlands 10.05.64]

55. Mill Street Junction E1 5b 50m
This follows the obvious dog leg crack system right of *The Cracks*, with pitches of 4c and 5b.
[D Knighton, D Cronshaw 1979]

56. The Cracks HVS 5a 50m
A fine route, which tackles the obvious crackline left of *Amphitheatre Wall*, and almost justifies the terrible approach. It can be done in a single run out. Start by scrambling up to the base of a thin crack in the slab.
P1 4c 25m The crack leads to a large ledge.
P2 5a 25m Move right and climb the wide crack, just right of the arête, moving left where it narrows to finish up the arête. Medium and large cams are useful.
[J M Kosterlitz, R J Isherwood 22.10.67]

Helen John seconding P1 of **Fifth Avenue** E1 5b photo: Streaky Desroy

82 **Upper Tier** • Upper Tier Left Hand

57. Staying Alive E4 6a 53m
A serious and aptly named route, with a poorly protected P1. Start 6m down and left of *The Cracks*.
P1 6a 28m Climb the slab, keeping right of the arête and passing a peg at 18m to land on the belay ledge of *The Cracks*.
P2 5a 25m Finish by taking the obvious crack system 3m right of the top pitch of *Ceilidh*.
[P Whillance, D Armstrong 30.03.78]

Approach for routes 58-75: Continuing leftwards across the hillside (towards an obvious yellow rockfall scar), the path again narrows above an impressive drop. Scramble upwards through some boulders to a levelling (*The Gauntlet* climbs the groove above), descend slightly past a pillar leaning against the cliff (start of *The Ramp*), until a small worn area at the edge of the wall is reached; *Bezel, Eternal Optimist* etc. start here.

58. Ceilidh E2 5c 80m
This takes variable rock in a good, exposed situation right of the yellow scar. Start at the base of a groove at the bottom right hand corner of the wall.
P1 4c 18m Climb the groove, keeping left, to belay on top of a block.
P2 4c 9m Move right and climb a deep crack a little way before moving right again, over a bulge, then up to a small stance on the edge of the wall.
P3 5c 28m Take the steep ramp up left, past a peg, then go left and climb onto a loose flake. Take the shallow groove up to and over a small overhang, peg, and continue leftwards to a large ledge.
P4 5a 25m Climb up left to beneath a large pinnacle, traverse right for 6m and take a crack to a narrow ramp leading up left. This is followed to a good spike before moving left to a small spike and finishing direct.
[A R McHardy, P Crew (1 pt) 11.04.66]

59. Mondo Hard E4 6a 81m
An adventurous direct line up the cliff sharing most of P3 and some of P4 of *Ceilidh*. Start left of *Ceilidh*, below an overhanging wall.
P1 6a 18m Layback up fins to reach a crack and enter a yellow niche, peg. Exit right at its top, peg, to easier climbing and a block stance.
P2 5b 10m Climb a short wall and fine crack direct to a poor belay, on P3 of *Ceilidh*.
P3 5c 28m From the top of the steep ramp, go left and climb onto a loose flake. Take the shallow groove up to and over a small overhang, peg, and continue leftwards to a large ledge (*Ceilidh* P3).
P4 5c 25m Go straight up the corner groove to the top, exiting right to easier ground.
[M Crook, D Kendall, J Toombs 29.09.87]

60. Monsoon E2 5b 60m
A big pitch weaving up the wall right of the yellow rock scar. The first ascensionist does not recall the exact line taken!
[M Turner, S Hale 1990s]

73
66
67
56
54
52
70
50
53
47
57
Main Cliff
71
68
67
65
64
63
61
66
Scramble approach to Ampitheatre
59
58
49
46
Emulator

84 Upper Tier • Upper Tier Left Hand

▶ **61. Yellow Scar E1 5b** 78m
An intricate route up the area of rock right of the huge yellow scar (the scene of a large rockfall in 1969), taking in some poor rock. Not really recommended. Start at a small pinnacle below the scar.
P1 5a 18m Climb to the top of the pinnacle and boldly surmount the overlap on the right. Move up left then step right across an overhang into a broken groove. Climb this exiting right to the stance on *Ceilidh*.
P2 5b 30m Go up the short wall on the left, then follow this obvious line left to a pinnacle on the edge of the yellow scar. Move up onto the scar and traverse left then back up right to gain big holds, leading leftwards to a small pinnacle stance.
P3 5a 30m Take the corner crack on the right to the top of a large pillar, then descend (junction with *Ceilidh* P4) and traverse 6m right to a crack. Climb this to a narrow ramp leading up left. This is followed to a good spike before moving left to a small spike and finishing direct.
[L E Holliwell, L R Holliwell 01.10.67]

▶ **62. Hurricane E2 5c** 30m
Start as for *Yellow Scar*. From the pinnacle, climb straight up cracks in the steep wall to an awkward mantelshelf at the top. Continue up a short groove and swing right to belay on *Ceilidh*. Finish up this route.
[S Webster, P Trower 28.07.80]

▶ **63. Nameless Arete XS** 55m
A line up vague arête right of *The Gauntlet* has been climbed. The first ascensionist does not recall the exact line taken (again!)
[M Turner, L Thomas 1990s]

▶ **64. The Gauntlet HVS 5a** ∗∗ 55m
An Upper Tier favourite. To the left of *Yellow Scar* is a shallow groove, which, as usual, is steeper than it looks.
P1 5a 35m The sustained groove (peg) leads to a small roof. Pull steeply into the continuation groove and follow this until possible to move right onto a ledge (optional belay). Traverse back left and follow the deeper curving groove around rightwards until it closes; step right onto a ledge and spike belay below the prominent groove.
P2 4b 20m The classic corner pitch leads to the top. Scramble up and right for a further 10m to belay in a groove.
[P Crew, B Ingle 02.05.64]

▶ **65. Ziggurat E4 6a** 58m
A very dirty and scrappy route. Start 5m left of *The Gauntlet*.
P1 5b 28m Follow a depression up slightly left for 22m, and then traverse right to the good belay on *The Gauntlet*.
P2 6a 15m Go left onto the arête and climb it via a short and technical sequence, peg, before going leftwards across two shallow grooves to an exposed belay above a very steep wall.
P3 5b 15m From the right-hand end of the ledge go straight up to finish up vegetated slabs.
[L E Holliwell, J Kingston (1 pt) 10.71, FFA: A Pollitt, N Clacher 11.10.81]

▶ **66. The Ramp HVS 5a ∗∗ 58m**
Despite being hard for the grade, this is one of the most popular routes on the crag. The line intrigued first ascensionist Pete Crew for weeks on end; "..was it a slab, or an overhanging wall with jugs?" Only one way to find out!
P1 5a 30m Gain the top of the pinnacle, step right and follow the corner of the sustained ramp until possible to traverse left to spikes. Climb rightwards over the bulge and follow the continuation of the groove to a large spike. (Usually furnished with abseil tat.) Traverse left to a belay at the far end of the ledge, below a corner crack.
P2 5a 28m Climb the crack to a ledge. Make a big stride rightwards and grope expectantly for the good holds that allow a steep pull into the bottomless chimney: a spectacular position. Follow the easier chimney to a small bulge which leads, with care, to the hillside. Trend up and right to a cluster of hollow spikes/blocks just above a quartz ledge.
[P Crew, J Baldock 24.04.66]

▶ **67. Energy Crisis E5 6a ∗∗∗ 58m**
A fantastic and pumpy test piece with a puzzling crux. The gear is good (at least on P1), assuming you've got the stamina to place it. Start beneath the right hand of the two wide cracks a little left of *The Ramp*.
P1 6a 28m Race up the steep wall to gain an undercut flake (useful kneebar). Swerve left across the wide crack with some improvisation, then surge upwards before your arms wilt to reach a belay on *The Ramp*.
P2 5c 30m A few bold and tricky manoeuvres lead rightwards into the base of the hanging groove; once ensconced in its protective fold, continue more easily to the top.
[P Whillance, D Armstrong 01.05.78]

68. Afreet Street E5 6a * 53m
A strenuous and surprisingly stubborn route. Start beneath the left hand of the 2 wide cracks.
P1 6a 28m Climb narrow slabs until it is possible to enter the crack on the right. Take this direct, passing the odd ancient peg to the stance on *The Ramp*.
P2 5b/c 25m Climb the slanting 'quartz-speckled' cracks above, finishing up the chimney on P2 of *The Ramp*.
[E Drummond (4pts) 09.03.69, FFA: R Fawcett 1980]

69. Gael's Wall E3 5c 53m
Juggy 'blob' hauling and pinching up the wall between *Afreet Street* and *Fail Safe*.
P1 5c 23m Start as for *Afreet Street*, stepping left onto the ramp of *Fail Safe*. Follow the curving undercut feature, past a good small wire, and then go straight up the wall to an obvious large chickenhead ledge. An exciting mantle onto this leads to a groove and flared crack, which takes you to the exit move of *Fail Safe* and its belay.
P2 5c 30m P2 of *Energy Crisis* provides a suitably challenging finish.
[T Neill, J Garside, S Savage 31.05.02]

70. Fail Safe E2 5b ** 53m
Although not particularly hard for the grade, this bold and sparsely protected route requires a confident approach to avoid the all-too-common grippers. An imaginative flair will help with the protection, as will a good number of thin slings. Start 7-8m right of *The Eternal Optimist* below a vague groove.
P1 5b 28m Climb up to a spike, step left and follow the narrow slabs diagonally leftwards until possible to move back right on 'blobs', to gain the main ramp. Follow this to the overhang (thread usually in situ), then follow the line of sloping shelves up rightwards to a short finishing groove which leads with relief to the belay ledge of *The Ramp*.
P2 5a 25m P2 of *The Ramp*.
[D Alcock, P Crew (1 pt) 07.05.66]

71. The Eternal Optimist E2 5b ** 47m
A steep and funky route taking the obvious corner/crack running up and past the overhang.
P1 5b 37m A steep start gains the crack; follow it with the help of some large holds on the left, and pull through the overhang with difficulty. Easier climbing and a wide crack leads to a ledge and belay on the left.
P2 4c 10m Finish up the wide crack on the left.
[A Sharp, S Humphries 06.02.75]

72. Cartwheel E2 5b 52m
A reasonable but poorly protected route featuring the right hand of two cracks left of *Bezel*. Start a little to the right of *Bezel*.
P1 4c 15m Climb the slab just right of *Bezel*, via the prominent quartz vein. Cross *Bezel* and follow a right trending crack to the *Bezel* stance.
P2 5b 37m Step left and take the crack until a prominent V-niche on the left can be gained. Continue more easily to a ledge and belay. Stay roped up for the exit scramble up easy rocks on the left.
[A Evans, J Moran 05.07.78]

73. Bezel VS 5a * 47m
This popular introduction to the Upper Tier is hard for the grade (especially when combined with the direct finish, as described). Start just left of *The Eternal Optimist* at the base of the slab.
P1 4b 15m Climb up to the top of the pinnacle on the left then follow a diagonal crack up rightwards. Move left, then up to a small ledge with an old peg and nut belays at the foot of the groove.
P2 5a 23m Pull through the bulge via some stretchy bridging and continue up the groove to a block. Traverse rightwards around the arete to belay below a crack.
P3 5a 9m The cleanest finish is up the leaning crack directly above the stance. Climb this with a sense of urgency to a small alcove at half height (large gear is useful). Easier but still steep climbing gains the top and a belay just above.
P3a 4b 12m From the stance, step back left and pull into the short groove. Follow this until possible to traverse back right to the top. Not as clean or good as the direct, but considerably easier.
[B Ingle, P Crew 25.04.64]

74. Slow Dancer E2 5b 49m
A serious pitch up the left hand flake crack between *Cartwheel* and *Sulcus*. Start from the pinnacle just left of *Bezel*. Follow *Sulcus* to a ledge at 9m then climb the discontinuous flake crack to reach the V-niche on *Cartwheel*. Continue more easily to a ledge, and belay. Stay roped up for the exit scramble up easy rocks on the left.
[J Moran, A Evans 05.07.78]

75. Sulcus VS 5a 43m
This follows the obvious crack in the arête left of *Bezel*, and although a little overgrown is quite worthwhile. Start from the pinnacle, as for *Slow Dancer*. Follow the crack as far as the overhang and move left around it into a niche. Step left then go up to spike belays. Stay roped up for the exit scramble up broken ground.
[R Holliwell, J Fitzgerald 06.07.69]

Girdle Traverses

As one might expect on such an intensively developed cliff, there is a choice of 3 different traverses, each of which will provide an adventurous and challenging day out for an experienced team.

76. Rolla Costa VS 257m
A poor route, which avoids the issue of a true girdle line, taking the right hand area of The Upper Tier. Start at the foot of the approach gully.
P1 30m As for *Nomad* P1.
P2 28m Follow cracks right of *Nomad* P2, and then a chimney leads to a crack on the left. Take this to the stance.
P3 21m Go left to a break on the skyline, and then descend a chimney to belay on *Dirtigo*.
P4 12m Traverse left again, around the arête before descending slightly and crossing a chimney to gain a belay.
P5 18m Descend the chimney to belay as for *Bloody Chimney* at the far end.

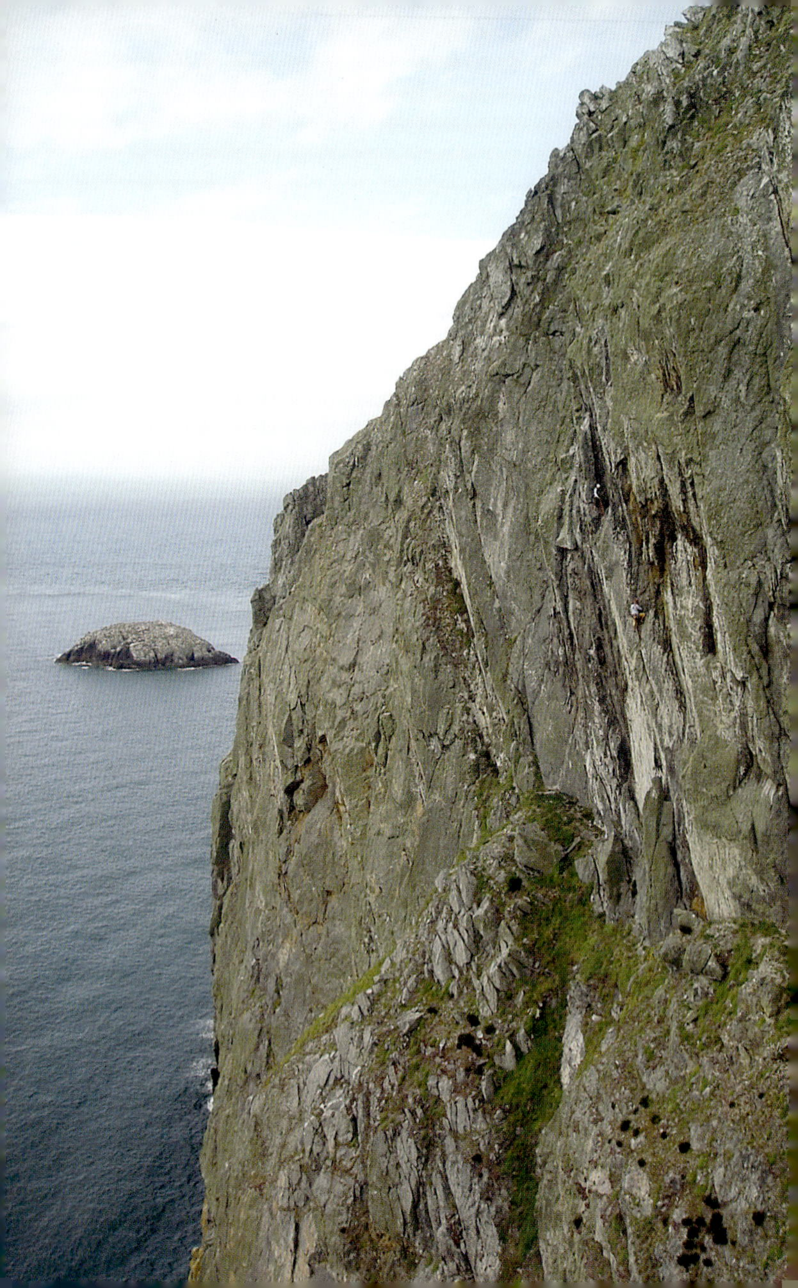

P6 22m Abseil down *Bloody Chimney* P1.
P7 37m As for *Pantin* P1.
P8 28m Go left along the ledge, below the final pitch of *Puffin*, and continue across to near the top of *Winking Crack*.
P9 40m Abseil down *Winking Crack* to the large ledge.
P10 21m Abseil down the groove and wall to the path.
[D Durkin, D Williams 27.07.68]

77. The Underground XS 6a (7 pts) 209m
A potentially entertaining expedition, with some hard and sustained climbing. Some of the pegs mentioned in the description will almost certainly not be still present. Start as for *Strike*.
P1 6a 37m As for *Strike* P1.
P2 5c 37m Pendulum from a pinnacle, on the upper edge of the huge flake, across the wall, on the left, to a peg. Descend the slight groove to another peg before moving left, with difficulty, past a yellow flake into *Bloody Chimney*.
P3 5b 21m As for *U.F.O.* up grooves and cracks to a ledge, block belay.
P4 5b 30m Go to the left-hand end of the ledge. At foot level a peg can be used to gain a small pinnacle, on reddish rock. Tension left from this to a hidden peg at waist level, in the middle of the wall, and using this and a nut, gain the corner on the left. Follow this (*Canned Laughter*) to the corner of *Pantin*. Descend and cross to a spike belay on the left.
P5 4c 15m Go diagonally left to belay at a quartz ledge on the skyline.
P6 5b 18m Use a peg on the left to gain *Winking Crack*. A crack leads left to a steep corner, parallel to the top of *Winking Crack*. Climb this to the top.
P7 4c 30m Descend the broken crack on the left to a ledge, then take the ramp on the left to a corner. Descend the slab to the arête. Go round this to a groove then on to a quartz ledge. Belay on the grass below. A dirty pitch.
P8 5a 21m Climb the centre of the wall behind the stance, trending left to a small bulge near the top. Surmount this and scramble to belay higher up.
[D Durkin, M Bron, J Baker (12 pts) 07.05.70]

78. Suspender E1 5a (2 pts) 129m
A steep and sustained girdle of the left hand area of The Upper Tier, starting below *The Cracks*. Rope manoeuvres are used to pass the steep ground right of *The Ramp*.
P1 4c 21m Drop down a little and move around the corner to a ledge. Carry on left, past a flake, to a shallow groove. Climb this for 3m to a stance.
P2 5a 15m Continue up the groove to a pinnacle on the edge of the yellow scar. Move up onto the scar, peg, and go left then back right to gain big holds leading up left to a stance on a pinnacle, as for *Yellow Scar*.
P3 4b 22m Descend part of *The Gauntlet*.
P4 5a 25m Go left to the arête, peg. Lower 6m on the rope, and swing left to a ledge, peg. Climb up and leftwards across the wall to a peg, and again use the rope to descend and swing across to the slabby corner of The Ramp, peg. Climb down to a ledge and belay.
P5 5a 21m Go back up continuing as for P1 of *The Ramp*.
P6 5a 25m As for *The Ramp* P2.
[A Wilmott, M J Spring (2 pts) 14/15.04.68]

< Al Leary and Bryn Williams on P1 of **The Ramp** HVS 5a   photo: Streaky Desroy

Main Cliff

Area: Gogarth Bay
Style: Trad (2-6 pitches)
Aspect: South-West
Rock type: Quartzite
Approach: 20 + 20 minutes
Altitude: 0 - 30m (mostly tidal)
OS ref: 215 835

Main Cliff is the magnificent centrepiece of Gogarth; a majestic swathe of vertical and overhanging rock that rears proudly straight out of the sea safe in the knowledge that it is the most impressive cliff, not only at Gogarth, but in the whole of North Wales. The routes here are a testament to the exploits of many generations of Britain's best climbers seeking to leave their signature on this quartzite monolith. As can be expected the routes abound in legend with tales of massive run-outs, monster falls and epic retreats being commonplace. This has all given the cliff a forbidding reputation that is only accentuated by the lonely approach and often adverse morning conditions.

Almost invariably first acquaintances are daunting; leaving the Upper Tier and heading steeply downhill on the narrow path heightens the senses to the cliff's reputation and this is further enhanced by the scramble down to sea level and the intimidating traverse around the pinnacle to reach the majority of the routes. It is only at this point that the scale and steepness of the cliff is obvious with the overhanging central section towering above you; be brave because this cliff will provide you with some of the most exhilarating and memorable rock climbs that you will ever know. The climbs are typically sustained and pumpy affairs, requiring much fitness and tenacity. Indeed, an ascent of one of the big lines is enough to send all but the most highly trained stamina machines whimpering to the café in search of a well earned brew break, and with little prospect of a return to the crag that day.

Adam Wainwright going for it on P1 of **Dinosaur** E5 6a photo: Jethro Kiernan

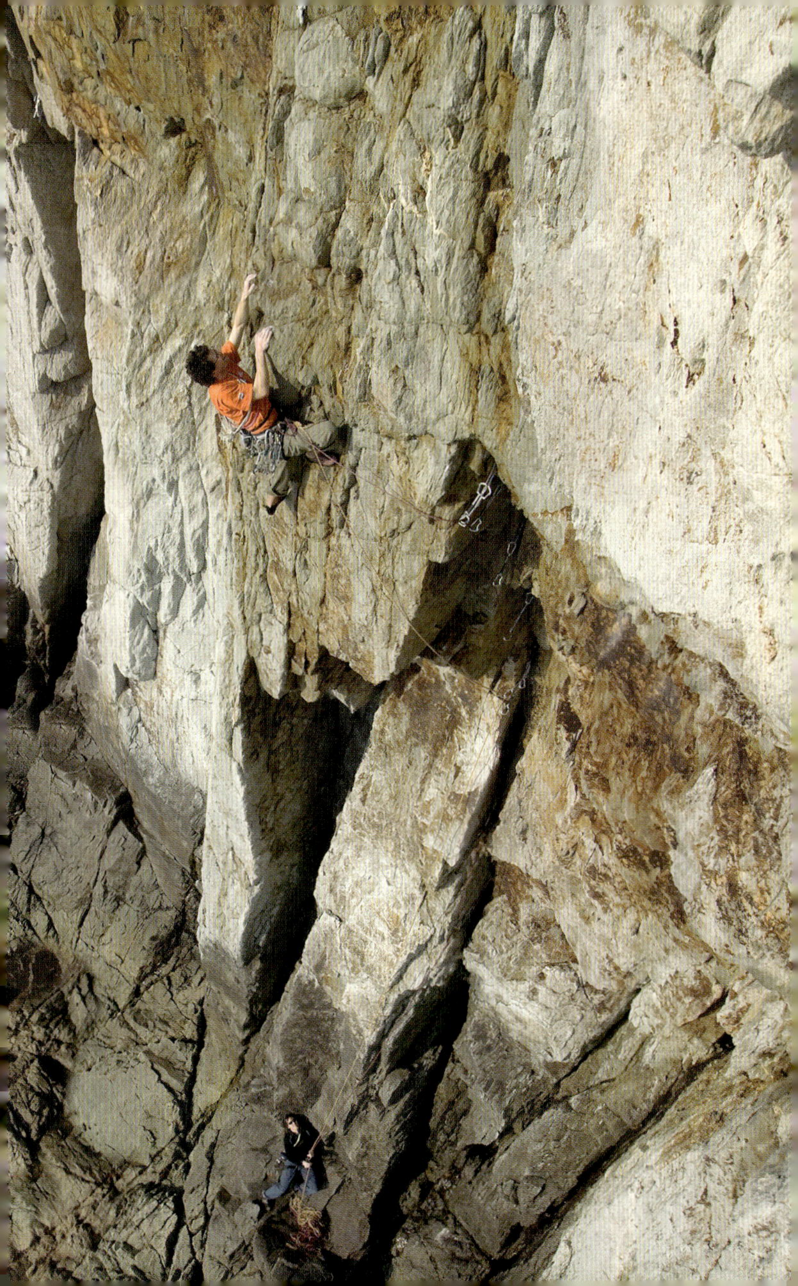

Main Cliff • Introduction

Extinction	E8
Skinhead Moonstomp	E6
Alien	E6
Food and Drink	E6
Coming on Strong	E6
ET	E6
The Big Sleep	E6

Mammoth Direct	E5/6
Ramadan	E5
Mammoth	E5
Eraserhead	E5
The Tet Offensive	E5
Ordinary Route	E5
Return to Garth Gog	E5
Hunger	E5
Sebastopol	E5
Positron	E5
Puzzle Me Quick	E5
Piglet's Left Boot	E5
The Three Musketeers	E5
The Camel	E5
Citadel	E5
Dinosaur	E5
The Horizon	E4
Graduation Ceremony	E4
Mistaken Identity	E4
The Wastelands	E4
Syringe	E4
Bubbly Situation Blues	E4
The Big Groove Direct	E4
The Needle	E3/4
Trunk Line	E3
The Assassin	E3
Hyena	E3
The Rat Race	E3
Darkness	E3
Achilles	E3
The Big Groove	E3
Stimulator	E3

Aardvark	E2
Hypodermic	E2
Devotee	E2
Jaborandi	E2
Resolution Direct	E2
Morphine	E2
Resolution	E2

The Third Man	E2
Sunstroke	E1/2
Nightride	E1
Mestizo	E1
Phaedra	E1
Emulator	E1
Dream Seller	E1
Gogarth	E1
Heroin	E1
The Night Prowler	E1
Gringo	E1
Peepshow	E1
The Girdle Traverse	HVS
Scavenger Direct	HVS
Diogenes	HVS
The Hustler	HVS
Scavenger	HVS
Pentathol	HVS
Hud	HVS
Cordon Bleu	HVS

Imitator	VS

Introduction • **Main Cliff**

The lower 2/3rds of the cliff is blessed with solid fused rock, its heavily featured surface rounded back by the elements to leave a confusing array of open pinches, hidden undercuts and sloping cracks. The quality of the rock deteriorates towards the top of the crag and the upper pitches typically involve some loose rock and lichen, which require a careful approach.

Although the climbing is more conventional than the nearby South Stack cliffs, it is still advisable to carry a large rack with a wide range of cams, long quickdraws and multiple slings often proving very useful. Small cams and very thin slings may normally be considered esoteric, but on the Main Cliff can often provide crucial protection. There are a lot of pegs scattered around the cliff, but virtually none of them are in a safe condition.

The exits of some routes, notably *Dinosaur* and *Alien*, can involve scrambling up steep heather slopes and in dry summer conditions with hefty rope drag, your partner out of sight, the peaty ground crumbling beneath your feet and the heather coming away in your hands this can feel like the psychological crux of the route.

A word should also be made about the tidal wash caused by the high speed ferries which can cause a short lived, but dramatic increase in the height of the water. The wash normally hits the cliff 5 - 10 minutes after the ferry passes by at its closest point on the way into Holyhead. All climbers should be mindful of this potential danger whilst traversing the base of the cliff to access their chosen route

Conditions: Main Cliff is a south west facing suntrap and in the right conditions dries very quickly, however good climbing conditions are a tricky call. It is difficult to predict conditions even when looking down on the cliff from the gearing up area and it can be blowing wildly here and yet be perfectly calm at sea level. In dry conditions the quartzite has excellent friction, but in damp conditions the friction reduces remarkably making many routes very much harder than they should be. The best conditions are usually encountered in the afternoon when there are clear skies and a light wind is blowing onto the cliff. It only takes 30 minutes of sun to dry the surface dampness, but the difference in the rock's friction is remarkable.

All the routes on the crag, particularly those in the central *Dinosaur* area, can be damp in the mornings before the sun has time to burn off the overnight moisture, even in a dry spell with clear skies. As always some routes are affected more than others and this is mentioned in the route text. In general the higher you go the less impact the morning dampness has on climbing conditions. The red coloured rock tends to hold the water on its surface longer than the white rock. A good indicator is the colour of the *Dinosaur* and *Hunger* walls – the darker they are, the damper the crag. It always pays to carry a full chalk bag on the Main Cliff just in case conditions are not perfect.

The weather changes remarkably quickly here and it is not unusual to be baking one minute and then getting cold 15 minutes later as the wind picks up and then cloud covers the sun. A light windproof is often really useful on the higher pitches.

< Photo: Al Leary

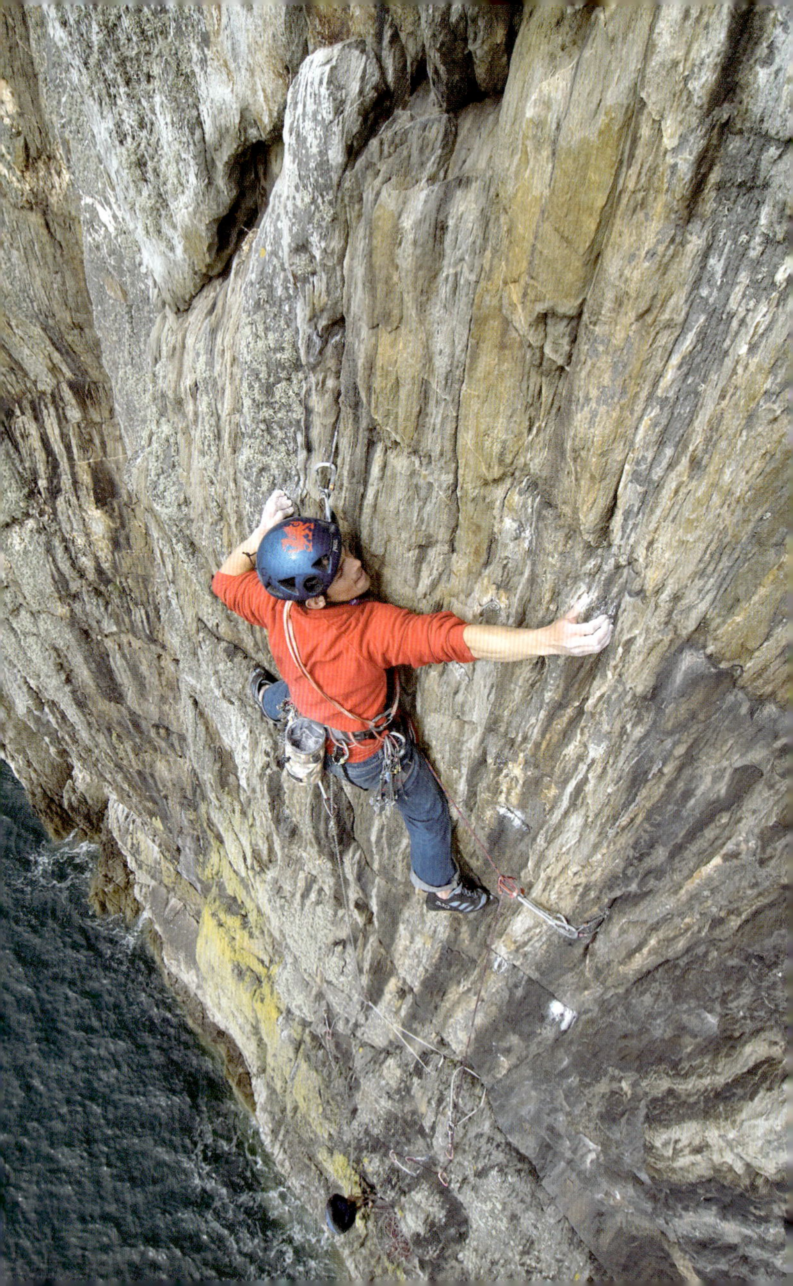

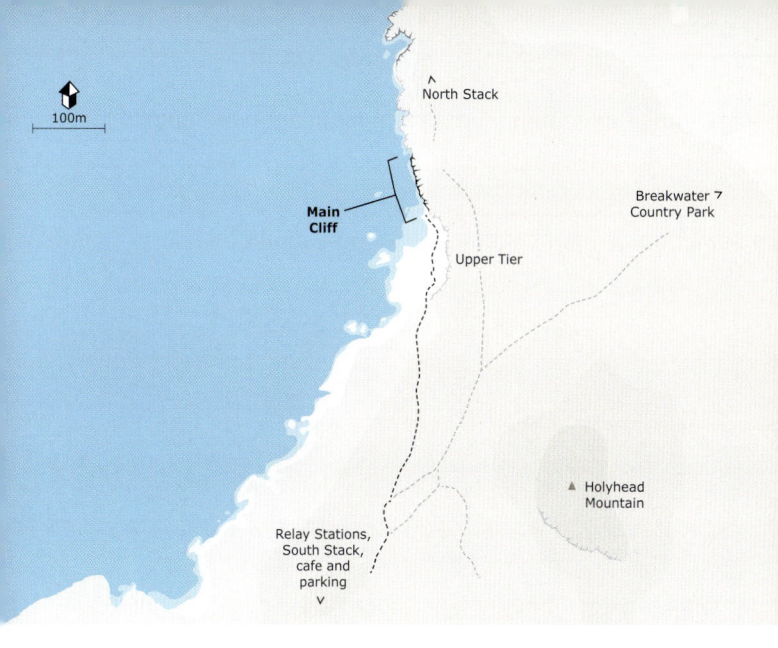

Approach: From either of the small car parks at the end of the South Stack road a path or a track leads off right (the path and track soon join). Continue towards the microwave relay stations, and bear rightwards past them. The Holyhead Mountain crag can be seen a few hundred metres directly ahead. As you get closer follow a path over a col allowing a first view of the Main Cliff, before bearing left and descending to reach a gearing up area at the top of a steep gully. Once you've racked up and hidden your rucsac from view, drop down the eroding path in the steep and exposed seaward edge of the gully. Traverse back right into the gully bed (try not to pay too much attention to the huge hanging boulder perched above your head) and clamber down over a couple of big blocks until the gully opens out. Thereafter a broken and occasionally collapsed path leads, with some scrambling, across the steep hillside beneath the crag. Follow the path until immediately beyond the rock step that is below *Central Park* and 25m before *The Strand*.

All of the sectors, except *Cordon Bleu*, are accessed by the small track that heads steeply downhill from just beyond here. This leads to the slabby *Emulator* buttress. *Cordon Bleu* is accessed by continuing on the Upper Tier path passing 10m under *The Strand* and around the back of the amphitheatre to the start of *Bezel* on the far left hand side of the Upper Tier. A steep grass slope leads down to an embedded flake belay on the edge of the Main Cliff, just before the grass gets really steep. It is probably sensible to rope down this section as the ground is loose and a slip could have dire consequences.

< Lee Roberts on the crux pitch of **The Assassin** E3 5c photo: Jethro Kiernan

96 Main Cliff • Crag Layout

Labels on photo: Big Groove, Cit[adel], Phaedra, The Assassin, Main Cliff Left Hand Routes, Big Groove Area, Phaedra Area, Needle Area, Citadel Area

Returning to the Approach Gully/Gearing Up Area: After you have finished your route and are on top of the crag on the heather slopes you will normally need to get back to the gearing up area at the top of the approach gully.

Most of the routes finish at 90 -110m above sea level and it is necessary to scramble up the slopes to a small path that traverses the area at the 150 – 180m level. The scramble feels longer than this because this is only the vertical distance. There are several small tracks that wind up the slopes from the finishes of the more popular routes and it is worth trying to find these to avoid heather bashing.

Once on the track that traverses the slopes head southwards (rightwards looking in) and follow it as it contours above the Upper Tier until a 2.5m rock and heather step puts you onto a small ridge. The path splits here and you can choose the long, easy way via the uphill split or the shorter, steeper version via the downhill split. It takes 5 to 15 minutes to reach this point from the exit slopes.

The longer easy way follows the uphill track which soon levels and then gradually drops down to the rocky buttress on the right, reaching the walls at their lowest point where they are just 3m high. Scramble down this easy wall and continue following the path to a junction with the cliff's main approach path. Turn right and 100m later you are back at the gearing up area. 10 minutes from the rock step.

The faster route follows the lower path gently downhill for about 40m to a small cairn where the path starts to gain height again. Turn off right here and head steeply downhill on a faint narrow track, generally bearing down and left. This leads with care directly to the gearing up gully. 5 minutes from the rock step.

Crag Layout: As shown above, the crag naturally divides itself into several areas and their specific characteristics are described in more detail in the individual sections. The sections and the routes within them are described from right to left as this is the usual method of approaching them.

98 Main Cliff • Cordon Bleu Area

Cordon Bleu Area • Routes 1-9 *Interrogator* to *Cordon Bleu*.

This is the very right hand of the main cliff where it leans back to meet the grassy slopes running down from the left hand side of the Upper Tier. The buttress is positioned about halfway up the cliff and is identifiable as the shield of clean rock that lies above and slightly left of the *Emulator* buttress.

The *Cordon Bleu* area is approached by following the Upper Tier path to its very end. Thus after passing the 4m rock step below *Central Park* continue on the middle path passing 10m below *The Strand*, then continuing around the back of the amphitheatre past the *Energy Crisis* wall to the slabby corner of *Bezel* on the far left hand side of the Upper Tier. A steep grass slope leads down from here for 25m to a 1.5m high triangular flake that lies embedded next to the edge of the buttress, just before the grass gets really steep. It is probably sensible to rope/abseil down this section as a slip could have dire consequences. All the routes except one start at the embedded flake, and routes 3 to 8 all finish by scrambling up the well worn steps for 8m to a large flake pinnacle with further belays. You can either un-rope here or stay roped to reach another belay in the blocks 45m up on the ridge on the right. Further steps lead up from here to join the descent path.

This section of the crag dries quite fast because of its elevated position, but there is quite a lot of red rock around the steep middle section and this dries more slowly. The most obvious feature for orientation is the wide, squat, red corner in the centre of the cliff. This is the belay corner at the end of P1 of *Sunstroke*. It is common to combine pitches from the *Emulator* buttress that lies below here with a route on the *Cordon Bleu* buttress and so reach the top of the crag.

▶ **1. Interrogator HVS 5b** 60m
A poor route that is largely over-grown and destined to stay that way. Start 10m up from the embedded flake belay below a depression that becomes a vague leftwards trending groove.
P1 5b 25m Climb to the back of the depression and follow the groove to the left for 6m. Traverse left delicately across the slab to gain and climb vertical cracks, which lead to a belay ledge.
P2 4c 35m Step right off a block to climb the short wall and shallow groove above. Trend right and climb over an overlap. Follow the broken rake above for a short distance, until steep broken rock on the right wall can be climbed to the top.
[L E Holliwell, L R Holliwell 30.03.68]

▶ **2. Interpolator HVS 5b** 59m
Reasonable climbing in need of a good clean. Start from the embedded flake belay.
P1 19m Move up from the right from the belay and enter the groove. Climb this until a niche where groove is blocked by an overlap. Move left around this and then move back right to a belay below the slab
P2 40m Climb the very short corner above the belay onto the slab and take the line of weakness leftwards to the crack that runs the remaining height of the buttress. Climb this to the top passing a small overlap
[B. Ingle, P.Crew (1 pt aid) 11.04.66]

Abseil roped scramble to embedded flake

Upper Tier path

embedded flake

Main Cliff traverse line

100 Main Cliff • Cordon Bleu Area

▶ **3. Sunstroke E1/2 5b/c** * 43m
A good route with varied and strenuous climbing. Although one of the first routes to catch the morning sun, the crux red corner can stay damp longer than expected. Start from the embedded flake belay.
P1 5b 19m Move down left a couple of metres from the flake belay and climb the wall leftwards into the corner. Continue up the corner, which gets increasingly strenuous, until it finishes where the right wall of the corner becomes a grey flaky pinnacle. Above there is a short, steep wall with a horizontal crack/faultline running along its base. Jam leftwards along the crack/fault line, passing a small downward pointing nose, before pulling up onto the slab that lies beneath the perfect 6m high, steep red corner. Belay here on medium cams and large nuts.
P2 5b/c 24m The corner above the belay is a bit of a beast, but thankfully short. Escape left at its top to gain a rest on the faint arête before a quick couple of moves up gain the juggy, flake crack of *Diogenes*. Romp diagonally leftwards across the slab on this to a small platform on the left arête and a good sling and nut belay, just to the left.
[D Durkan, M Tolley 24.08.70]

▶ **4. Mistaken Identity E4 6b** * 50m
A big, long pitch that provides a hard variant on *Sunstroke*. Start from the embedded flake belay. Start as for *Sunstroke* by moving down left a couple of metres from the flake belay and climb the wall leftwards into the corner. Continue up the corner, which gets increasingly strenuous, until it finishes where the right wall of the corner becomes a grey flaky pinnacle. *Sunstroke* traverses off left here along the horizontal faultline; ignore this option and instead move up into the short steep crack that lies just above and to the left. Climb powerfully up this to a rest on the slab. Move tenuously left into the slabby groove and follow this with a surprising amount of interest until it ends below a wide V shaped groove 6m from the top. The left wall of the V groove is a massive flake. Trend left past this and climb up on its left to a belay platform on the left of the massive flake.
You can either un-rope slightly back from here or stay roped to reach another belay in the blocks 45m up on the ridge on the right. Further steps lead up from here to join the descent path.
[N Bullock, D McMannus 19.06.2008]

▶ **5. Diogenes HVS 5b** * 54m
A great route that tackles some steep and impressive territory for the grade. Start from the embedded flake belay.
P1 4a 14m Move down the grass ramp for 8m and then scramble diagonally leftwards up a line of weakness across the broken slabs for 6m to gain a belay in the obvious recess that has a block on its right hand side.
P2 5b 18m 7m directly above the belay is a square cut recess in the steep wall. Climb up towards this and then either:
a Climb it directly (hard at first but gets easier) then exit the recess and move 2m left to slabby ground below the steep corners.

b Move 2m left from just below the recess to gain a left trending flake/ramp system in the red rock. Follow this left for 2m and then head back right to bypass the recess (easier at first and then harder) to gain slabby ground below the steep corners.

Climb up into the left side of the first corner and thug rightwards along the break for 3m until it is possible to move upwards into a small corner. A couple more steep pulls gain the comfortable belay ledge with a broken peg. (Medium wires and cams.)

P3 5a 22m Climb the arête above the right wall of the belay for a couple of metres to gain the juggy flake crack that runs diagonally leftwards across the slab to the arête. Follow this to the small stance/ledge on the arête - good sling and nut belays just to the left.
[P Crew, I G MacNaught-Davies 03.04.66]

▶ **5a. Diogenes Direct Start HVS 5b** 41m
There is a direct start recorded that begins at sea level from the same position as *Resolution*. The initial pitch is interesting, but P2 can be overgrown.
P1 5b 13m This climbs the initial crack of *Resolution* but where this bears left along the diagonal crack, continues straight up for another 5m to pull onto a small sloping ledge just left of a very green corner. Belay.
P2 5a 28m Climb the steep crack to the left of the belay and then fight up the often green slab to the belay in the recess at the end of *Diogenes* P1.
[J Kingston, D Mossman, L R Holliwell 12.10.69]

▶ **6. Achilles E3 5c** ** 53m
This takes the well-protected/strenuous vertical crack that lies just to the left of the steep corners on P1 of *Diogenes*. Largely independent and very good climbing; worth seeking out.
P1 4a 17m Start from the embedded flake belay as for *Diogenes* P1, but move 3m further left to a good flake belay directly below a thin crack.
P2 36m 5c Move up from the belay onto a sloping shelf and gain the thin crack; follow it with interest to a position just left of a strange, 1m high upright spike (the 'Finger of Doom') at 12m. Pull into the crack that lies behind the spike with difficulty to gain good finger locks and a resting place. A sustained and burly section then leads into *Diogenes* 2/3 of the way across its final diagonal traverse. Follow *Diogenes* to the small stance/ledge on the arête and a good sling and nut belay, just to the left.
[P Littlejohn, J Mothersele 09.91]

▶ **7. Coming on Strong E6 6b** * 57m
Technical wall climbing on the orange face left of the upper crack of *Achilles*. The gear is good, but a little spaced and can also be fiddly and strenuous to place. It is probably best to leave this route for the afternoon because the red rock tends to retain the damp.
P1 17m Start from the embedded flake belay as for *Diogenes* P1, but move 3m further left to a good flake belay directly below a thin crack.
P2 6b 40m Move left from the belay and climb the wall left of the *Achilles* crack on good edges and layaways to reach easy ground left of the detached vertical spike on *Achilles*. Climb diagonally left up a groove to where it blanks out at a small overlap, break back horizontally right on good incuts to a resting spot below a thin crack. Good peg 3m above. Climb the thin crack with difficulty

to reach the peg and then gain the leftwards leaning rampline by laybacking leftwards off the crack to reach to a blocky incut. Improvise your way along the ramp on blind, but positive holds to a thin crack that splits the bulge. Pull past the bulge with the aid of good holds on the right of the crack. Follow the crack more easily to join *Diogenes* at the end of its leftwards traverse. Belay as for *Diogenes* just past the small stance/ledge on the arête.
[P Littlejohn, M Diggins 10.91]

8. Revelation E1 5b 57m
An eliminate that wanders across the slab looking for new territory. It finds some with a final pitch that is essentially a superdirect finish to *Resolution Direct*.

P1 4a 14m As for *Diogenes* P1: Move down the grass ramp for 7m from the embedded flake belay and then scramble diagonally leftwards up a line of weakness across the broken slabs for 7m to gain a belay in the obvious recess that has a block on its right hand side.

P2 5b 27m 7m directly above the belay is a square cut recess in the steep wall. Climb up almost to the bottom of this and then take the flake system that runs leftwards (as for the left hand variant on *Diogenes*) and continue up this into the small corner. Move leftwards past the strange 1m high spike on *Achilles*, then traverse diagonally left across the slab on the obvious line of weakness, pass the arête and take a belay in the corner groove of *Resolution* (where that route moves steeply left to climb onto the big white flake that lies immediately above).

P3 5b 16m Climb steeply up onto the white flake as for *Resolution* and then step right to the crackline. Climb this, initially difficult, to the good stance and flake belay that is shared with *Diogenes*, *Achilles* and *Coming on Strong*. Finish by scrambling up the well worn steps for 8m to a large flake pinnacle with further belays. You can either un-rope here or stay roped to reach another belay in the blocks 45m up on the ridge on the right. Further steps lead up from here to join the descent path.
[B Wintringham, M Wintringham 23.06.79]

9. Cordon Bleu HVS 5b ** 144m
A thrilling girdle across the upper section of the Main Cliff. Although largely straightforward in technical terms, the crux wall being a notable exception, this is a serious and adventurous route cutting through some wild and exposed territory. Start from the embedded flake belay.

P1 4a 38m Descend to an obvious traverse line leading out left onto the slabby face. Keep going until an arête is reached. Pass the arête and climb down a short chimney to a ledge – belay on the far side beneath P4 of *Gogarth* at the base of a 20m crack formed by a house sized flake leaning against the cliff. Good sling belays.

P2 4b 37m Climb down and move around the base of the massive flake to reach a corner on the other side. Go up this and traverse out left along the top of the flake traverse line to belay just beyond its apex.

P3 5b 20m The steep wall above blocks access to the corner, Pull up the wall on reasonable holds with a few powerful moves. Traverse left from the corner along the slabby ramp (not forgetting to place some decent runners to protect your second) to a small exposed stance.

Emulator Area • **Main Cliff**

P4 4b 25m Climb up the short chimney above and move across a slab to a large groove. Climb up this to a stance on the arête.
P5 4b 24m Move left then up behind a large flake to a short groove which leads to the top. [G Birtles, P Crew 21.05.66]

Emulator Area • Routes 10-16 *Seeyerlater* to *Simulator*.

This is the first buttress reached on the Main Cliff approach path. It lies on a small platform about 15m above the sea, The easiest route to find is *Emulator*, which is the perfectly formed, left facing corner/groove system on the left of the platform that runs the full height of the buttress.

This buttress dries quickly and is not affected by tides or high seas, but seagulls like nesting on the ledges below the routes and can show their dislike for climbers during the nesting season (April/May) with accurate and persistent dive-bombing runs.

All the routes here require you to scramble up the grass slopes above the buttress to reach either the *Cordon Bleu* or Upper Tier buttresses. You can either do a further route on one of these two crags or take the Upper Tier path back to the descent gully. The ground above the buttress has lots of loose debris on it so take care not to dislodge any of it onto parties below.

▶ **10. Seeyerlater HVS 5b** 65m
The route starts in reasonable fashion, but the top pitch is well worth avoiding. It may be best considered as an alternative start to *Imitator*. Start 8m right of the corner of *Emulator* at a small left facing corner that looks like it is formed by a 7m high flake lying against the buttress.
P1 4b 10m Climb the corner to the top and then move right along the ledge for 4m to gain a belay below the crack that runs up the wall above.
P2 5b 18m Climb the crack to an impasse below an overlap. Gain the overlap and then jam and undercut left to gain the crack on the right, move steeply up this to gain a junction with *Imitator* and easier ground. Continue up the crack for 3m to belay in the niche as for *Imitator*.
P3 35m Don body armour, write a quick will and call the air ambulance before heading up above the belay into a wilderness of green looseness. If you are very lucky both you and your belayer will reach the Upper Tier safely. This is not described fully for your own protection. The final pitch of *Imitator* is a much better option.
[S Reid, W Parker 26.07.81]

▶ **11. Aardvark E2 6a** * 62m
A popular test piece; good wall climbing leads to a thin crack crux in the upper section suited to small fingers. Although quite well protected, the slightly run-out crux might prompt some to complain about the E2 grade.
P1 6a 27m Start up the wall 5m right of the *Emulator* corner and climb up and left on good holds that lead to a thin crack. Follow this with difficulty to gain the *Imitator* traverse. Climb up and follow the left hand of 2 thin cracks with increasing difficulty past 2 small overlaps, then move right to good holds in the right hand crack. Climb it to a small ledge and belay.
P2 35m Easy ground leads to the grassy slope. Scramble up to a belay at the foot of *Bezel*.
[A Evans, G Milburn, B Wintringham, J Moran 23.07.78]

12. Imitator VS 4c * 60m
Another popular climb, often linked with *Bezel* on the Upper Tier crags.
P1 4c 30m. Start below the *Emulator* corner. Move rightwards from the ramp at the foot of the corner to climb the steep, blunt groove that blocks access to the long, slim left facing corner above. This has good holds, but is also slightly loose at the top as you pull onto the vegetated ledge. A great little left facing corner heads straight up from here; climb it and pull right at the top with difficulty onto the slabby wall to gain an obvious line of holds trending rightwards. Follow this traverse line almost to the right edge of the buttress where a short crack leads up to a belay.
P2 4b 30m The shallow groove on the left leads to a small bay. Step right and follow the arête to easy ground. Scramble up to a belay at the foot of *Bezel*.
[B Ingle, G Rogan 27.05.64]

13. Lardvark E5 6b 62m
Squeezed in, but offering a hard, technical challenge. This takes the very thin crack in the wall left of Imitator's groove before moving right into Aardvark and climbing this to a variation left hand finish. The gear is adequate, but quite blind and fiddly to place.
P1 6b 27m Start up *Imitator*, pull over the initial bulge and stand on the small ledge below the groove on that route. Move up the groove of *Imitator* for 2m before pulling left into the thin crack. This leads to a crucial, small square undercut in the wall above. Desperate moves on poor side pulls gain small incuts just below the overlap, pull 2m right with haste to gain better holds, gear and a junction with *Imitator* as that route moves right. Pull straight up via the crack to join *Aardvark* just below its crux. Do this and then continue straight up the same crack to the top. Belay as for *Aardvark* on the small ledge.
P2 35m Easier ground leads to the grassy slope. Scramble up to a belay at the foot of *Bezel*.
[M Crook, R Cutler 06.93]

14. Emulator E1 5b *** 62m
This takes the striking corner groove line on the left side of the platform that runs the full height of the buttress and yields an excellent pitch of sustained jamming, laybacking and bridging. Well protected.
P1 5b 32m Pull into the corner and enjoy 32m of great climbing. Belay above the corner on the right. Take care arranging the belay as there are a lot of hollow, loose blocks here.
P2 30m Scramble up the grass slopes to a belay below the corner of Bezel in the far top left corner of the Upper Cliff.
Or head diagonally left to the embedded flake belay below the *Cordon Bleu* buttress and finish up *Sunstroke* or *Diogenes*.
[P Crew, B Ingle 10.05.64]

15. Stimulator E3 5c ** 64m
A good route that deserves to be popular, and a perfect complement to *Achilles* on the *Cordon Bleu* cliff above. P1 and P2 can be run together if you extend the gear as you move right around the arête and this is perhaps the best way of doing the route. The initial groove can stay damp a bit longer than expected because of its aspect – it is a lot easier when fully dry.

5m left of the *Emulator* corner is an arête that runs the full height of the buttress. Start 1m left of this below a steep, shallow groove.

P1 5c 10m The initial groove is much steeper than it looks and there is not a lot of gear until better holds arrive at 7m. Pull up from the ground onto the small ledge and arrange gear (small cam useful) at head height, then make a couple of stiff pulls and high steps to gain jugs. Romp up to the large ledge and belay on the right next to a flake.

P2 5b 24m Move right to the arête, step up onto the small ramp and make a couple of delicate moves around the arête to gain a good, but slightly loose spike. Continue diagonally right to gain a series of finger ledges and climb up these easily to the hand crack that looms above. This hand crack gives good and interesting climbing all the way to the top of the buttress; scuttle rightwards for 2m and pull over as for *Emulator*. Belay with care as for *Emulator*.

P3 30m Scramble up the grass slopes to a belay below the corner of *Bezel* in the far top left corner of the Upper Cliff. Or head diagonally left to the embedded flake belay below the *Cordon Bleu* buttress and finish up *Sunstroke*, *Diogenes* or *Achilles*.

[B Wintrinham, P Jewell 10.07.78]

16. Simulator VS 4c 64m
It all starts so well, and then...

There is a great looking right facing corner 10m left of *Emulator* that sits above the descent corner. Unfortunately the good climbing is limited to the first 18m and there after it rapidly becomes green and a bit loose. It may be best to consider this as an alternative approach to *Diogenes* on the *Cordon Bleu* crag above. It certainly is sensible to make the P1 belay on the embedded flake that sits at the base of the buttress. Scramble up to belay beneath the corner.

P1 4c 32m Climb the corner passing a small overlap to gain the continuation corner, Climb this with increasing care to gain a broken, grassy ledge. Now either follow the small continuation corner or climb the short broken wall to the left before heading diagonally left to the embedded flake at the base of the buttress on the left.

P2 32m Scramble up the grass slopes to a belay below the corner of *Bezel* in the far top left corner of the Upper Cliff.

[P Crew, B Ingle 03.05.64]

Gogarth Area • Routes 17-23 *Resolution* to *Falls Road*.

Continue past the *Emulator* groove for 8m to the top of an open corner/recess at the edge of the platform and scramble down this for 8m with care and then continue traversing leftwards about 25m to the open corner formed by a huge pinnacle resting against the main cliff. This is the start of the route *Gogarth* and the pinnacle is the *Gogarth* pinnacle. Routes 17 to 22 all finish on the upper slope. Either belay immediately on the left after topping out or rope drag allowing continue for another 8m to a position next to a large flaky sidewall which offers both belays and a safe point for unroping. Well-marked steps lead up the slope via the ridge on the right to join the path that leads back to the base at the top of the descent gully.

The routes to the right of *Devotee* are non-tidal and can be climbed in most seas. The routes on the front face of the Pinnacle (*Garth Gog* and *Falls Road*) are more restricted – *Falls Road* needs a low tide and *Garth Gog* needs a medium tide for a direct start. The routes here dry quickly and with the exception of *Devils Marbles*, *Garth Gog* and *Falls Road* do not suffer too much from dampness or seepage.

▶ **17. Resolution E2 5b** * 81m
A good route that, although largely superseded by the direct version, still offers a classic and interesting way up the cliff. Above the traverse that runs from the *Emulator* area descent corner to the Gogarth Pinnacle there is a large bay of steep, brown rock. The route starts via a short vertical crack on the right hand side of the brown rock; this crack leads into a recess before arcing leftwards to form a jagged diagonal traverse line. P2 and P3 can be run together.
Start by scrambling 7m up from the traverse line to the bottom of the crack. The easiest scramble starts 4m right of the Gogarth pinnacle and heads diagonally up and right to the base of the crack.
P1 5b 35m Climb the crack strenuously to a rest in the recess and then move up to gain the leftwards trending diagonal line. Enjoyable climbing along this leads to the arête; move left around this into the groove. Continue up the corner for 16m until forced left onto less clean ground to a large spike belay on the right of a ledge below the clean arête.
P2 5b 26m Climb the steep, cracked wall left of the arête for 5m until it is possible to move rightwards to gain the crack on the arête. Continue up the crack more easily to where it becomes an open groove bounded with a large blocky flake on its left hand side. Belay here in the recess.
P3 5b 20m Haul up the steep blocky flake on good holds to gain a standing position on top of it. A series of fingery moves up the tricky groove on the left leads to an easier finishing crack. If you have run P2 + P3 together you will need to belay very soon after pulling onto the upper slope.
[P Crew, G Rogan 31.12.66]

Abseil roped scramble to embedded flake
Upper Tier path
embedded flake
Main Cliff traverse line
1
2
3
4
5
6
7
8
9
10
11
12
13
14
15
16
17
18
19
20
21
22
23

108 Main Cliff • Gogarth Area

▶ **18. Devil's Marbles E5 6b** 44m
This takes the wall and triangular roof to the right of *Resolution Direct*. It starts about 6m right of the corner formed by the *Gogarth* pinnacle and the Main Cliff. The obvious identifying feature is the triangular roof 20m above the starting ledges.
The route finishes in the middle of the *Cordon Bleu* slab at the first belay of *Diogenes/Achilles/Coming on Strong*; take your pick for a finishing route. Start by scrambling 7m up from the traverse line to the bottom of the crack. The easiest scramble starts 4m right of the Gogarth pinnacle and heads diagonally up and right to a position below the triangular roof.
P1 6b 44m Climb the groove that lies below the right side of the roof to an impasse where a few thin moves bring the roof within reach. Lunge out from the right side of the roof to good holds. Attack the following roof via the crack that leads to a small corner. Hard moves lead to easier ground, which is taken to a ledge right of the *Resolution* belay.
[M Turner, S McAleese, 05.06]

▶ **19. Resolution Direct E2 5b** ★★★ 88+m
A great route that forces an uncompromising line up the right edge of the cliff. It is the most popular E2 on the main cliff with difficulties that are sustained without being excessive. P2 and P3 can be run together.
It is possible to start the route in 2 ways:
P1 a 5b 40m From a point 3m right of the base of the *Gogarth* pinnacle (the start of *Gogarth*) scramble up 5m to a sling belay on a large flake in a recess. This is on the left side of a bay of overhanging, creaky looking rock. From this belay move 3m left to gain the crackline in the arête.
P1 b 5b 45m From a point 2m right of the Gogarth pinnacle climb the slightly rightwards trending cracks in the slight pillar to gain a position just right of the continuation arête. Gain the crack in the arête.
Follow the crack in the arête with sustained climbing until a pull into a corner system (junction with *Gogarth* P2) introduces easier climbing. Continue up the corner for 16m until forced left onto less clean ground to a large spike belay on the right of a ledge below the clean arête. The first 10/15m constitute the crux, but the leader soon disappears from view and rope drag can be a problem if care is not taken,
P2 5b 28m Climb the crack in the arête, initially moving slightly right before a delicate series of moves back left. It pays to spot your footholds here before you launch into the sequence. Continue up the easier continuation crack to where it becomes an open groove bounded with a large blocky flake on it's left. Belay here in the recess.
P3 5b 20m Haul up the steep blocky flake on good holds to gain a standing position on top of it. A series of fingery moves up the tricky groove on the left leads to an easier finishing crack. If you have run P2 and P3 together you will need to belay very soon after pulling onto the upper slope.
[A Pollitt, H Clover 13.03.82]

20. Gogarth E1 5b ** 106m

The first route established on the Main Cliff provides an intricate and classic line, building up to a dramatic finale on the exposed headwall. The top pitch is significantly harder than anything that comes before and the final traverse requires competent rope work from the leader. The route is described in its original and classic format, but P3 and P4 can be run together quite easily. Not tidal. Start by the large crack formed by the right side of the pinnacle and the cliff proper.

P1 4b 18m Ascend the wide crack to a stance on the top of the large pinnacle.

P2 5a 18m Step down 1m and traverse right across the steep wall on good flatties, continuing past the arête to gain a shallow hidden groove. Climb up the groove, keeping left of a small overhang, then traverse back left to take a belay on the right side of the very sloping, 5m x 3m ledge directly above the previous belay. Peg and small wires. (NB. It may be considered better to belay on the left side of the ledge as this gives both an easier and safer belay and a better view with less drag on the next pitch.)

P3 4b 18m Move left to the left side of the ledge and climb the short (4m) groove/crack which leads slightly leftwards to easier ground. When the left trending weakness ends move up and slightly rightwards via the continuation groove for 4m to a belay stance at the base of a wide, slabby crack formed by the right side of a massive, house-sized flake. Good sling and large cam belays.

P4 4c 20m The superb crack leads to a perched stance at the top of the huge flake. Large gear useful on this pitch.

P5 5b 32m Psyche up and traverse out right below the headwall for 7m to reach to reach a ledge beneath a pair of thin cracks. (NB. If you head up too early and climb the 1st flake cracks that rear up 4m along the traverse line you will be doing the harder 5c finish of *Devotee*.) Pull up into the cracks proper with a bit of difficulty and then continue past the sustained 3m crux section to reach easier ground. Continue to the top in the same direct line with one more hardish section 5m from the top.

[B Ingle, M Boysen (1 pt) 04.04.64]

21. Devotee E2 5c * 101m

A direct eliminate on *Gogarth* that looks for trouble and has some good climbing. Not tidal.

P1 5b 20m Start 2m left of the corner formed where the pinnacle meets the Main Cliff (start of *Gogarth*). Climb diagonally left across face of pinnacle via a juggy flake line that ends at a horizontal quartz band. There is a small overhang on your left on the arête at this point. Continue in the same line via some thin face holds, staying on the right side of the arête to a point where your feet are above and just right of the small overhang. A difficult and slightly off-balance move around the arête on sidepulls leads quickly to jugs and easy ground. Continue up easily to the top of the pinnacle and junction with *Gogarth* P1 belay. (A tougher version is also possible by traversing leftwards from the initial flake line under the small overhang onto the left side of the arête. Hard, long moves on sloping holds lead upwards with difficulty from here to gain good jugs after 5m. This is worth E4 6a because the gear is far from brilliant and is strenuous to place.) It is also possible to start 4m lower and climb the groove in the arête to join the original route, at the end of the initial flake line traverse, with no change in grade.

P2 5c 33m The steep wall immediately behind the belay is climbed with difficulty for the first 4m before easier ground leads slightly leftwards to a pull onto the middle of the very sloping 5 x 3m ledge, also used by the *Gogarth P2 belay*. Move leftwards to the crack/groove above the left side of the sloping ledge and climb this slightly leftwards to easier ground. Now trend up and slightly rightwards via the continuation groove for 4m to a belay stance at the base of a wide, slabby crack formed by the right side of a massive, house-sized flake. Good sling and large cam belays. This last section is shared with *Gogarth* P3 and the *Gogarth* P3 belay.

P3 5b 18m Move diagonally left from the belay to gain a faint left trending groove formed by a slightly discontinuous line of blunt flakes, Climb these up and left to their finish and then continue either directly or more easily slightly rightwards to gain the belay on the top of the flake as *Gogarth* P4.

P4 5c 30m A very good exposed pitch that is a fine finale. Traverse out right below the headwall for 4m to a point where you have just pulled past a slight arête into a small corner. A fantastic flake crack line now soars up the crag right above you. This is steep and exposed but has decent gear - small and medium cams prove very useful. Climb it with sustained difficulty to the top and move slightly right to belay as for *Gogarth*.
[B Wintringham, M Wintringham 15.06.79]

▶ **22. Return to Garth Gog E5 6a/b ** 99m**
A modern eliminate based around *Gogarth* that provides fine and difficult climbing and should prove popular. P1 is hard and involves powerful laybacking on rounded holds; it is recommended that you both warm-up before getting on the route, and also let the sun/wind dry it out fully. The start requires a medium tide, although it is possible in higher seas to traverse in from the right.

P1 6a/b 16m A well-protected pitch, but the gear is typically placed blindly from strenuous positions. Start 4m from the right arête below the overhanging, white groove in the front face of the *Gogarth* pinnacle. Pull up into the start of the groove (very thin sling useful) and gain a decent undercut in the wall above (small cam). Layback into the groove proper with a crucial high step to gain a good pocket foothold in the left wall, rock powerfully leftwards to gain a finger pocket in the left wall and then up to better holds just above. A reach back right gains good incuts and then a few more strenuous moves on rounded pinches leads to easy ground. Move left across the pinnacle to belay 5m above the lowest, large flat, black platform on a more pointed, sloping yellow/black platform. This should be below the right hand of two cracks in the red wall above – at the time of writing this crack had a wire stuck at its start.

P2 6a 20m Climb the crack (*Falls Road*) on strange and surprisingly good holds for 8m until just below a 30cm diameter blob of quartzite in the crack; make a hard move diagonally rightwards to gain a good hole and move right past this to gain another crack system. Move up this with sustained interest until the angle eases, but all the holds become flared and sloping; improvise upwards to gain the centre of the *Gogarth* P2 belay ledge, pull over and move leftwards across this to gain a belay below the groove/crack in the corner on its left hand side.

Gogarth Area • **Main Cliff** 111

P3 4c 18m Climb the short (4m) groove/crack, which leads slightly leftwards to easier ground. Now trend up and slightly rightwards via the continuation groove for 4m to a belay stance at the base of a wide, slabby crack formed by the right side of a massive, house-sized flake. Good sling and large cam belays.

P4 5c 45m Climb the corner crack, as for *Gogarth*, for 4m until it is possible to step right into the very slim 5m high corner with a wide (3cm) crack in the back of it. Fight up this for 5m before reaching ledges and easier ground. Continue directly upwards to gain the crux cracks on the last pitch of *Gogarth* directly. Finish as for *Gogarth*.
[M Turner, L Thomas, G MacMahon 11.94]

▶ **23. Falls Road E4 5c** 102m
An interesting route that has some good bits, but lacks overall consistency. The highlights are the great P2 up the technical red wall that lies above the left side of the *Gogarth* pinnacle and the top pitch which was worryingly described by Mountain magazine as 'the mind boggling crack that the *Rat Race* pioneers had prudently avoided'.

Start on the left hand side of the seaward face of the *Gogarth* pinnacle under a wide, dark groove/crack. This is quite smooth and can be quite slimy.

The start of the route requires a low-ish tide and calm seas, if this is not available or if the initial crack is too greasy it is possible to do the first pitch of *Rat Race*.

P1 5a 14m Climb the crack/groove to the ledges at its top. Move up and slightly right across the pinnacle to belay 5m above the lowest, large flat, black platform on a more pointed, sloping yellow/black platform. This should position you below the right hand of two cracks in the red wall above – at the time of writing this crack had a wire stuck at its start.

P2 5c 20m Climb the crack on strange and surprisingly good holds for 8m until just below a 30cm diameter blob of quartzite and make harder moves past this; now move leftwards into the left hand crack and climb this to the left hand end of the sloping *Gogarth* belay ledge. Belay in the left hand corner on good wires.

P3 5a 37m Follow the obvious line trending left to a large block at the base of a corner. Climb the corner for a few moves and then move right into another corner, which leads up onto the slab. Move up to belay on *Cordon Bleu*.

P4 5c 25m The final worrying pitch tackles the wide crack splitting the wall above. Climb up to the overhang from the left, and then move right and up to the wide crack. Follow the crack to the top.
[J Gosling, E Thurrell, B Sullivan, B Cardus 06.09.69]

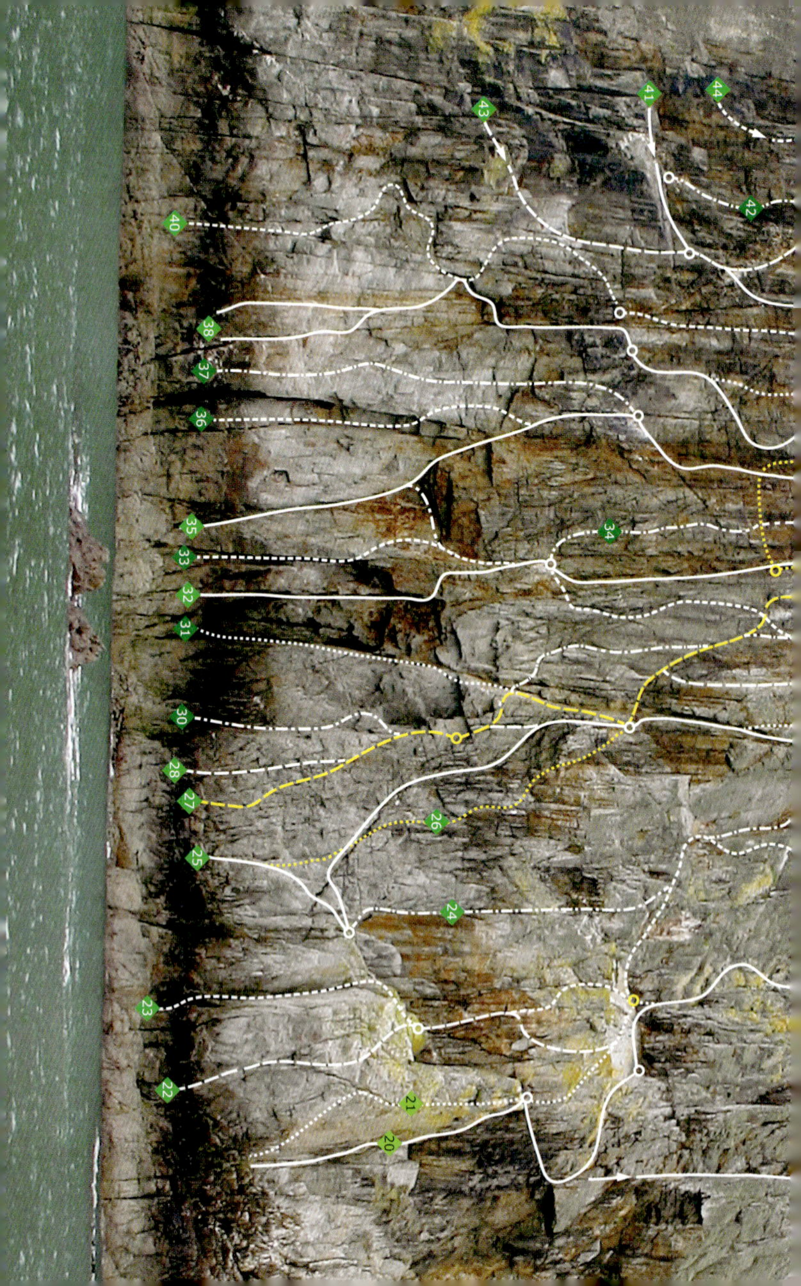

20
21
22
23
24
25
26
27
28
30
31
32
33
34
35
36
37
38
40
41
42
43
44

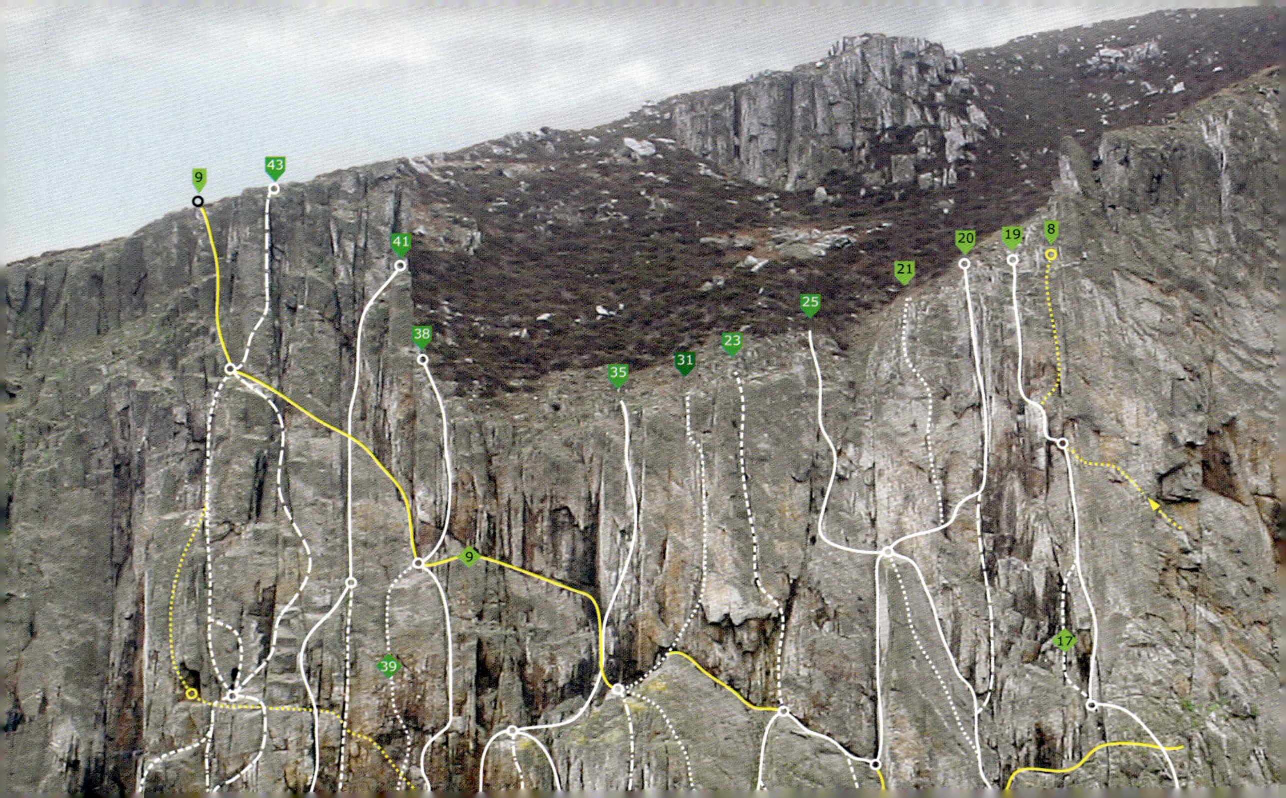
9
43
41
38
9
39
35
31
23
25
21
20
19
8
17

114 Main Cliff • Positron Area

Positron Area • Routes 24-28 *Bubbly Situation Blues* to *Eraserhead*

The routes in the *Positron* area start from a high platform that lies on the far side of the *Gogarth* pinnacle. The platform is non tidal and is not affected by most seas, however access to it is affected by both.

From low to mid tide a fairly simple low level traverse around the pinnacle using large sea washed footholds allows access to the platform. It is possible at higher tides to traverse at two higher levels, the highest of these uses the horizontal hand rail that runs at 3m above the high water line. This has a long/hard, blind reach to pass the *Falls Road* groove that can be exciting, if not dangerous, with the sea crashing at your ankles. Alternatively climb pitch one of *Gogarth* and abseil down the far side to the platform. This area of the crag suffers a little more from dampness on the initial pitches, but nowhere near as much as the neighbouring *Dinosaur* area.

▶ **24. Bubbly Situation Blues E4 6a** 107m
An under-valued gem with testing and contrasting pitches. P2 is very good and despite appearances should not be under estimated. It is steeper than it looks and gives sustained, strenuous climbing. This is in contrast to the technical and bold P3, however this pitch is quite overgrown and most parties join *Cordon Bleu* before finishing up *The Rat Race* or *Devotee*. Start as for *The Rat Race/Ordinary Route* on the upper level of the *Positron* platform 6m left of the corner at a slight weakness.
P1 5a 12m *The Rat Race* P1.
P2 6a 25m Gain the steep left facing groove that lies above the left side of the ledge and follow this with far greater difficulty than expected and strenuous gear placements to an easing in angle and a rest. Move up steeply again into the continuation groove and gain a very sloping ledge. Continue up the easier groove to gain a better ledge with a mediocre belay on the right (#0 cam and wires).
P3 5c 25m The original route moves about 4m left from the belay and climbs the left trending groove that arcs across the slab to join *The Rat Race* at the top of its chimney. The route then continues diagonally leftwards to the *Cordon Bleu* belay under the short, black wall that guards the headwall. Finish up *Dinosaur* or *Alien*. The left trending groove is however fairly over grown and thus most people climb straight up from the belay to gain the large slabby corner that is formed by the left side of the house sized flake that lies against the cliff-junction with *Cordon Bleu*. Climb up to the top of the massive flake and belay at its top as for *The Rat Race*, *Devotee* and *Gogarth*. Finish up the last pitch of any of these routes.
[R Evans, C Rogers 12.06.71]

▶ **25. The Rat Race E3 5c** ** 116m
A challenging and exciting route. Start on the large platform left of the *Gogarth* pinnacle at a point 6m left of the corner below a depression/weakness. If the tide cuts off the approach traverse around the base of the pinnacle, then do P1 of *Gogarth* instead and descend the far side of the pinnacle to reach the belay at the end of P1.
P1 5a 12m Ascend the wall slightly rightwards on good holds; then head steeply diagonally right on even better holds to reach a belay on the lower left hand ledges on the pinnacle.

P2 5c 30m Step left and follow the rising traverse line out leftwards, passing a tricky section to gain a chimney groove. Go up this to reach the curving overlap (usually damp). Ignore the rising pump in your forearms and follow a crack leftwards around the overlap to reach a steep slab. Pull up right to belay below an ominous looking chimney.

P3 5b 25m The overhanging chimney proves to be both a physical and psychological test. Do it quickly, before you get too pumped or scared (or both!). Exit right at its top onto the slab, and move up to belay on the flakey traverse of *Cordon Bleau*.

P4 8m Traverse down to belay at the base of the corner groove.

P5 4c 13m Romp up the corner to reach a perched belay stance on the sloping ledge on top of the huge flake. This is the top of P4 on *Gogarth*.

P6 5a 28m Step down and head left to reach a crack. Climb the crack, taking the right hand branch where it divides, and then move left across a rib to finish up an easier crack. A creaky South Stack style pitch! Belay well back.

[M Howells, B Whybrow (1 pt) 23.07.66]

▶ **26. Ordinary Route E5 6a ∗∗ 158m**
Although a little convoluted in line, this is an amazing route and a great way to see all the really impressive bits of main Cliff in one go. Start on the upper level of the *Positron* platform 6m left of the corner at a slight weakness (the same starting position as *The Rat Race*).

P1 6a 35m Climb steeply up the juggy wall; initially slightly rightwards, then slightly left to join *The Rat Race* traverse. Make a move leftwards along this until below an old peg in the break above and then climb upwards to gain a slim pillar of rock. Up this and move left slightly at its top into the shallow black groove above; exit right from this leftwards with difficulty to gain a rest below a smooth golden wall with a small groove on its left hand side. Curse the person who left the rotting wire that blocks the best gear slot at the start of the groove and boldly make a big move into the groove above. Move leftwards up the groove to *The Rat Race* P2/*Positron* P2 belay.

P2 6a 30m This is an alternative version of the amazing P3 of *Positron*. Once you have pulled over the small roof at the end of the traverse and moved into the *Dinosaur* groove, continue by down climbing the groove for about 6m to belay at an old peg. This is level with the roof at the end of *Positron's* rising traverse. Large cams and wires for the belay.

P3 5c 40m A wild pitch that feels exposed as it works its way upwards along a disconnected series of weaknesses. It moves a long way left so remember to protect your partner. Step down from the belay and teeter left along the obvious ledge into the groove of *Mammoth*. Move up this to a small ledge on the left where a diagonal fault line runs across the steep wall on the left; climb this with difficulty to join the vertical crack of *Citadel*. Climb up the crack to the first small ledges on the left. Cross the ledges leftwards and go up a short corner before stepping left onto a very sloping ledge, around an outside corner to a large sloping ledge and belay.

P4 5c 35m Step left around the corner from the left end of the sloping ledge, where you are presented with a shallow groove line which is heavily fluffed with green fur. Tricky moves lead up the groove to reach a big open bay. Finish up a big sharp flake on the right wall of the bay.

P5 5b 18m *Tet Offensive/Sebastapol* P4. Climb the weakness in the centre of the pillar and then follow the arcing handrail to the right arête; continue to the top on the right side of the pillar. Belay on the short finishing slab above (good sling belays 7m up and right.) There is a reasonably well-marked path leading up the hillside to reach the return path.
[A Sharp, C Dale 11.75]

27. Positron E5 6a *** 87+m

A legendary route that lives up to its reputation as one of the best E5s in the country. It strikes an audacious and sustained line through some breath-taking territory. The climbing is not hard for the grade, but the rising traverse on the headwall is very atmospheric and can feel quite lonely. The platform from which the routes in this area start drops down in level towards its left hand side. *Positron* starts from the left edge of the highest level.

P1 5c 20m Climb up rightwards into a shallow scoop, then move back left to a small (25cm) right facing ear of rock. Continue up and left again via a small ramp to a position on the arete. Move up to the small overlap just above, pull over it and take a belay immediately above. This lies directly below the chimney/groove on P2 of *The Rat Race*.

P2 6a 12m Pull up left through the overlap that lies above the belay and then traverse awkwardly leftwards around the arête into the groove of *Alien*. Follow the groove more easily up to *The Rat Race* belay.

P3 6a 30m A diagonal crack leads up left from the large spike on the arete. The crack is steep and sustained, but the holds are generally positive and there is good gear. The crack fades slightly after 8m and a couple of harder pulls upwards gain a traverse line that leads left to a small overhang. Small cams. Turn the overhang on the left and then continue up more easily, stepping left into the groove of *Dinosaur* and following it to a comfortable belay on insitu tat and blocks.

(NB. It is possible with 60m ropes and a low/mid tide to get back to the ground from this belay if you want to pack another route in without walking all the way round. You do risk getting your ropes wet though...)

P4 5c 25+m P3 of *Dinosaur*.
[A Rouse, P Minks (5 pts) 03.71/FFA: A Sharp]

28. Eraserhead E5 6a ** 84+m

A great route with a fine position. P1 is a good alternative to the first pitches of *Positron*, and P2 is the harder lead, with crimpy climbing that is quite pumpy and a little bold.

P1 5c 28m Climb the weakness just right of the left arête of the wall and continue up this to join *Positron* at the base of the sloping ramp. Follow the ramp up leftwards to the arête and pull over the small overlap as for *Positron*. Continue straight up, past the 1st *Positron* belay and pull over the small overlap into vertical cracks that lead into *The Rat Race* traverse at its crux. Cruise though this and pull left around the roof as for *The Rat Race* to gain the belay at the end of *The Rat Race* P2.

Dinosaur Area • **Main Cliff** 117

P2 6a 34m Step left across the chimney to gain the large spike on the arête at the start of the diagonal crack line of *Positron*, Move up this for 2m and place some good gear in the *Positron* crack. Step up and back right to gain thin incuts in the blunt arête (small wires) and make a series of committing moves in a spectacular position on positive, but well spaced holds. The climbing eases after 8m and a slight move out right gains a small furry corner. Up this and then take the left trending groove line (*Alien*) that leads up to the belay on *Cordon Bleu* beneath the small, black wall. This is just left of the apex of the slab.
P3 5c 22+m P3 of *Dinosaur* or P3 of *Alien*.
[G Farquhar, C Waddy 09.88]

Dinosaur Area • Routes 29-36 ET to *Mammoth Direct*.

The *Dinosaur* area starts in the recess just beyond the *Positron* platform and is easily identified by a series of dark, imposing corners and chimneys that combine to give this area an intimidating aurora. The most obvious identifying feature is the parallel chimney of *Mammoth Direct*, which is the leftmost of the chimneys.

Access to this area and all subsequent areas can be difficult in high seas or beyond mid-tide because the only traverse line is quite low and the corner just beyond the *Positron* platform is one of the worst places on the traverse for rogue swells and big waves.

This area suffers badly from morning dampness and it is not advisable to attempt these routes before the sun hits the wall and dries the surface moisture from the backs of the cracks - normally this doesn't happen until late afternoon. While *Mammoth* and *Mammoth Direct* can be climbed at mid/high tide, if you can get past the corner, all the other routes really need a mid-tide or less, and calm seas.

▶ **29. ET E6 6b** * 74+m
Another difficult excursion finding an independent and rather fine P3 up the slim pillar left of *The Rat Race* chimney. Start by taking the *Skinhead Moonstomp* corner direct.
P1 6b 22m Climb the corner left of *Positron* direct, continuing up beyond the *Skinhead Moonstomp* traverse exit, until level with the *Positron* belay. Traverse right at this level to reach the belay. Quite spicy!
P2 5c 10m As for the upper section of *Eraserhead* P1, continue up above the belay, pulling over the small overlap into vertical cracks that lead into *The Rat Race* traverse at its crux. Cruise though this and pull left around the roof as for *The Rat Race* to gain the belay at the end of *The Rat Race* P2.
P3 6b 30m The crack in the arête is attacked direct via long and hard reaches. A good runner is reached; continue thereafter on spaced holes to the *Cordon Bleu* traverse.
P4 5c 22+m P3 of *Dinosaur* or P3 of *Alien*.
[M. Turner, L.Thomas 1990s]

118   Main Cliff • Dinosaur Area

▶ **30. Skinhead Moonstomp E6 6b *** 88+m**
An outrageous adventure that is one of the best E6s in the country. A modern riposte to *Positron*, it swaggers up the centre of the perfect headwall using that route's crack as a rest before blasting upwards again to *The Big Sleep* bucket seat belay. It is not a soft touch and the penalty for those whose confidence falters or whose stamina fails, is long flight time! As you step around leftwards from the *Positron* platforms there is a huge grey corner straight ahead of you. This is the start of *ET* and *Skinhead Moonstomp*.
P1 6a 22m Ascend the corner mainly using the left hand wall to reach a small bulge; pull past this on the left to gain a sloping shelf. Climb up into the overhanging corner above the shelf and then traverse out right to a jug near the arête. Swing on to the arête to join *Positron* and pull over the small overlap as for that route and take a belay immediately above. This lies directly below the chimney/groove on P2 of *The Rat Race*.
P2 6b 32m Pull up left through the overlap that lies above the belay and then traverse awkwardly leftwards around the arête into the groove of *Alien* as for *Positron* P2. Move up the groove for 1m and then pull diagonally left into a weakness. Continue up diagonally left to gain a shallow niche with a good rest and runners. You are now at the very base of the headwall and above you is an amazing soaring flakeline. Climb up and right to gain the bottom of the flake. Layback this strenuously in a fantastic and increasingly pumpy position to a point where it peters out at a small flake (thin sling runner), continue up via a line of flat jugs to join the diagonal crack of *Positron*. Climb through the crux section of *Positron* to the shake-out on that route before it traverses left to the overhang; instead step right and climb the crack that leads to a small corner and legendary 'bucket seat' belay.
P3 5a 12m Climb up to belay just below the apex of the slab on the *Cordon Bleu* traverse. This is just below a short, steep black wall
P4 5c 22+m Move right and climb *Dinosaur* P3 or *Alien* P3 to finish.
[A Pollitt, S Andrews 12.05.84]

▶ **31. Alien E6 6b *** 84+m**
A Littlejohn masterpiece with a cruel and intimidating P1 that carves a direct line through varied and steep territory. The original route continues in the same vein and nonchalantly throws in *The Rat Race* chimney as dessert, which should give an indication of the fight ahead. This is probably why a lot of people choose to combine the epic P1 with *Positron's* classic P3; this combination creates one of the best routes in the country. 6m left of the *Skinhead Moonstomp* corner there is a huge rectangular recess that contains 3 very wide cracks/chimneys. *Alien* starts up the rightmost chimney and then follows it until it closes and becomes a rightwards-slanting fault line.
P1 6b 34m Bridge up into the chimney, then make a couple of more delicate move across the void onto the slabby, rust coloured right wall. Step up and right onto the arête and make a difficult move past a bulge to a decent rest. Continue strenuously up the fault line (obvious cam #4 in a slot) to the small roof and move right until just under its left hand side (crucial cam #0.5 and a good Rock #1). Pull straight over the roof with difficulty to reach various indistinct, crusty incuts and quickly rock over onto the slab. Relax. Continue up the groove for 8m before moving right to *The Rat Race* belay.

9
43
41
38
35
31
23
25
21
20
19
8
9
17
42
39
44
41
34
43
26
24
21
20
40
38
37
36
35
33
32
31
30
28
27
25
23
22

P2 5c 28m Climb the chimney of *The Rat Race* for 9m until the chimney starts closing up and the angle eases; step left onto a ramp and follow it as it becomes a left trending groove line. Climb the short corner at its top and then cross the slabs leftwards to gain the *Cordon Bleu* belay below the short steep black wall. This is just left of the apex of the slab.

P3 5c 22+m Move right to the base of the crackline that lies above and right of the apex of the slab. Gain and then follow this, very sustained, to a difficult move leftwards out of the top of the crack. Once on top follow the exit notes at the end of the *Dinosaur* description.
[P Littlejohn, S Lewis 16.05.80]

31a. Direct start to Alien E6 6b
If you want to make life really hard then there is this alternative, harder start available that joins the parent route at the top of the red slab on P1. Start halfway between the big grey corner and the rectangular recess where the standard route starts; position yourself under the most defined crack that curves leftwards.

P1 6b 30m Climb the crack and pull up onto the red slab to join the original route. Continue up the original route.
[M Turner, G Farquhar 1989]

32. Dinosaur E5 6a *** 83+ m
Dinosaur is often cited as being the best of the Main Cliff E5s; the quality of the line and the climbing is undoubtedly top class. And whilst it may not be the hardest E5 around it should not be underestimated; even in perfect nick it is a strenuous and fairly bold proposition. As you step around leftwards from the *Positron* platforms there is a huge grey corner that contains the starts of *ET* and *Skinhead Moonstomp*. 6m left of this is a huge recess that contains 3 very wide cracks/chimneys. *Dinosaur* starts up the middle chimney and then pulls left where it closes to climb the buttress on the left.

P1 6a 28m Climb up to the top of the chimney where it closes (cam #3/rock #7) and make wild moves out left past the arête and onto the front face of the bottomless buttress. Continue strenuously up and left with some urgency to gain increasingly better holds. Although small cams are very useful on this section, it is arguably better to run it out. Continue more directly up to a stance on vague ledges just to the left of the continuation chimney. Gear up and left for the belay.

P2 5b 30m Step right into the steep groove that runs all the way up the left side of the *Positron* headwall. Climb this, sustained and spooky, but never desperate, all the way to its top. The normal belay is on the left of the groove on a comfortable ledge with in situ tat and blocks. This is also the *Mammoth* and *Positron* belay,

P3 5c 25+m This pitch is one of the standard ways off the cliff, so learn it well as you could well be doing it a lot in the future. Traverse back rightwards for 5m on good holds and foot ledges until below the short, steep black wall. Climb the steep wall to gain a very sloping ramp with a corner above (as *Cordon Bleu* P3). Pull out right past the arête into a groove system that runs up the right side of the arête. Climb these with constant interest until a move left into a continuation groove signals the arrival of easier climbing. You can either arrange a belay as you pull over the top or you can continue up the heather

slopes for a higher belay on a large boulder. The rope drag can make this latter option feel like hard work.
The best way off is via the long sidewall/ridge on your left. Once you have joined this continue upwards along its side until the ridge becomes less rocky and more rounded; follow indistinct steps leftwards onto the crest of the ridge and less steep ground. Un-rope when you feel safe and follow well-worn steps directly up the heather covered ground to join the return path.
[P Crew, J Brown (10 pts) 19.06.66/FFA: R Fawcett 1980]

33. The Big Sleep E6 6b * 85+m
An eliminate product of the early 80s featuring some good, bold, sustained and insecure climbing on P1, but unfortunately some less well defined climbing on P2. P1 should not to be underestimated; in less than perfect conditions the flat holds and slopers on the upper section can feel insecure and there is not much gear. As you step leftwards around the corner from the *Positron* platforms there is a huge grey corner that contains the starts of *ET* and *Skinhead Moonstomp*. 6m left of this is a huge recess that contains three very wide cracks/chimneys. *The Big Sleep* starts up the left hand crack/chimney.

P1 6a 28m Climb the left hand crack for 15m until it closes at a roof. Pull left around the arête onto good footholds on the slim pillar that bounds the left edge of the crack (poor peg in the crack above) Climb the pillar up and slightly leftwards on insecure holds to the right side of a vague groove that lies on the right edge of the large roof. Sustained moves up the groove on more flat and sloping holds eventually allow you to reach the *Dinosaur* belay with relief. The stance is on vague ledges just to the left of the continuation chimney of *Dinosaur*. Gear up and left for the belay.

P2 6b 30m Traverse rightwards across the chimney of *Dinosaur* and gain undercuts in the hanging flakes on the right. Move rightwards on these to gain a large foothold below the obvious flake crack (large wire). Climb up the rightwards-leaning flake crack to where it starts to move back left and move straight up to gain a large flat hold. Straight up again to a small spike and then hard moves up and right to get a good flat hold under the right side of the small roof. Turn the roof and trend rightwards to the Bucket Seat belay. (NB. This is the direct variation, which is the most logical and frequently climbed line. The original line traversed right from the large foothold for 5m to join *Positron*, before climbing directly to the Bucket Seat.)

P3 5a 12m Climb up to belay at the apex of the slab, on the *Cordon Bleu* traverse.

P4 5c 25+m Move right and climb *Dinosaur* P3 or *Alien* P3 to finish

[R Fawcett, P Williams, J Moran 22.05.80, Direct on P2 by J Redhead]

Main Cliff • Dinosaur Area

▶ **34. Wall of Fossils E6 6b** 85+m
Another eliminate that provides some good climbing. The route starts as for *Mammoth* and climbs to the roof capping the corner before traversing right under the roof to join *The Big Sleep* as it heads up to the *Dinosaur* stance.
P1 6b 30m Climb the corner with increasing difficulty to below the roof and then traverse very strenuously on undercuts with even more difficulty to the groove on the right of the roof. Sustained moves up the groove, on flat and sloping holds, eventually lead to a stance on vague ledges, just to the left of the continuation chimney of *Dinosaur*. Gear up and left for the belay.
P2 6b 30m Step left and move up through overhanging flakes and continue past a good spike to reach the ledge along which *Ordinary Route* traverses. Forceful climbing leads directly up the steep red wall above to a rounded exit onto the slab. Move right to a block belay.
P3 5c 22+m P3 of *Dinosaur*.
[J Moran, R Fawcett, P Williams 27.05.80]

▶ **35. Mammoth E5 6a/6b** ✱✱✱ 88+m
A great route with very traditional character traits, that requires a wide repertoire of climbing skills for a successful ascent. Immediately after the large, forbidding recess that contains the starts of *Alien, Dinosaur* and *The Big Sleep*, and 5m before the parallel chimney of *Mammoth Direct*, is a leftward leaning, left-facing corner. This funnel shaped corner starts modestly at sea level, but widens rapidly to become a massive 'open-book' corner, where it is halted by the overhangs at 18m. The route climbs this corner to start.
P1 6a/b 37m Climb the corner with increasing difficulty to below the roof and make a hard and often slippery traverse out left to a resting position on the arête. Psyche up and continue with commitment to gain a large pocket (old peg) with good holds in it; move up before you get too tired and make the crux moves to reach a small resting niche with good undercuts that provide a welcome respite. Continue up using the grey fins and crack that are slightly left of the red groove. Belay on the right side of the thin ledge 3m above.
P2 5c 26m Psyche up and move rightwards from the belay onto a vague rib that is to the right of the main groove. Climb this until it is possible to pull back left into the groove (peg). Follow the groove with sustained difficulty over a small bulge and up into a thin left-facing corner that leads to a comfortable belay on the sloping platform on the right that is shared with *Dinosaur*, *Positron* etc.
P3 5c 25m + Move right and climb *Dinosaur* P3 to finish
[P Crew, E Drummond (6pts) 06-07.05.67/FFA: A Pollitt, S Andrews 23.05.84]

▶ Variation: **Mammoth Direct Finish**
P3 6a 25+m Follow the standard (*Dinosaur*) finish by traversing rightwards for 5m on good holds and foot ledges until below the short, steep black wall. Climb the steep wall to gain a very sloping ramp with a corner above. However, now climb that corner directly rather than moving right to climb the grooves in the arête.
[E Cooper, P Littlejohn 21.05.95]

Citadel Area • **Main Cliff** 123

36. Mammoth Direct E5/6 6a/6b ★★★ 85+m
An amazing challenge that fires straight up the cliff without compromise. It is, once again, a route with pitches of contrasting character. P1 is obviously intimidating and brutal, but also well protected and fairly straightforward for the fit. P2 is more subtle, albeit still an intricate, bold and strenuous undertaking. The route starts from a flat-topped block that lies below the perfectly parallel left most chimney. This block is safe from most tides and seas.

P1 6a/b 34m Climb up into the chimney with a few bold and difficult initial moves. Continue up with less difficulty to where the chimney closes (large thread normally in situ). Pull across the chimney leftwards using a foothold on the left arête of the chimney to gain good holds on the left wall. A sequential run of moves leads up and then back right (peg) to a junction with the original route. Finish up this (N.B. it is possible to abseil off blocks at the top of *Hunger/Citadel* P2. Two abseils lead back down to sea level. Make the second abseil from a poor thread near the top of *Hunger* P1.

P2 5c 26m As for *Mammoth* P2.

P3 5c 25+m Move right and climb *Dinosaur* P3 to finish
[A Pollitt, M Crook 26.05.84]

Citadel Area • Routes 37-43 *Extinction* to *Sebastapol*.

The routes on the open steep walls to the left of the *Dinosaur* area can be climbed at all but the highest of tides providing you can get past the *Dinosaur* corner, with the exception of *Sebastopol*, *Food* and *Graduation Ceremony* which need a mid tide. The lower pitches of these routes, especially *Hunger*, suffer from the morning dampness, but dry far faster than those in the *Dinosaur* area. The upper walls including the cracks on *Citadel* and *Graduation Ceremony* don't take seepage and dry fast.

The easiest identifying feature is the continuous crack of *Hunger* on the right side of the reddish wall. This runs all the way up the lower wall and is 4m left of the leftmost chimney (*Mammoth Direct*).

37. Extinction E8 6b ★★★ 32m
The stupendous wall right of *Hunger* yields this fierce test piece.
Climb the wall immediately left of the chimney (*Mammoth Direct*) until it is possible to move left and up to a flake with good runners. Move left along the obvious line to a spike and runner. Crux moves lead straight up to another spike and then to a peg where improving holds lead up past the roofs to a wild finish. Continue up to the *Mammoth* belay, and either follow this or abseil off.
[S Mayers 25.04.91]

38. Hunger E5 6a ★★★ 86m
Another great route with 2 big pitches of open climbing that contrast strongly in character. While P1 is pumpy and burly, P2 is a long and lonely lead. P1, despite being open, does retain moisture for longer than expected. Start 4m left of the leftmost (*Mammoth Direct*) chimney on the lower of the 2 highest flat topped blocks that lie beneath a continuous reddish crack. The route can be started in 2 ways:

P1a 6a 32m Climb up the continuous crack for 6m taking care not to go too high (this is about 1m below the small overlap) and then make a tricky move left to gain a hole and then fat, slopey pinches below a situ thread.

P1b 6a 32m Alternatively and easier, start 2m to the left below a series of discontinuous red cracks. Climb up to the fat pinches on decent holds. Now pinch your way tenuously past the thread and then head diagonally left on improving holds to reach the overlaps at the niche on *Citadel* just before its crux. Ignore this easy option and head rightwards along the overlap for 3m to a weakness in the roofs where they are split by 2 cracks. Powerful moves lead up the right hand crack with difficulty to easier angled rock. Continue up for 3m before taking a stance on the right.

P2 5c 36m A strangely unnerving pitch. Climb up the wall on reasonable holds to reach a small white flake at 12m before committing to a slightly rising traverse rightwards, this leads after 6m to a flake that is on the very edge of the *Mammoth* groove. Pull back diagonally leftwards to gain the top of the flake and then the vertical crack line just to the right. Climb the crack to a stance below serrated cracks in the short headwall above.

P3 5b 18m Climb carefully up from the belay to gain the right hand crack that lies immediately above. Ascend this for 3m before moving left into loose grooves that lead to the top. Scramble up the slope for 5m before belaying on the sidewall on the left.

[P Littlejohn, C King 08.06.78]

Variation: **39. Ramadan E5 6b ★★★**
A fierce, direct P2 for *Hunger* that probably pushes the overall grade of the route towards E6. The very good climbing is sustained and pumpy.

P2a 6b 34m An excellent variation climbing more or less directly up the orange wall above the belay on mostly good edges, with a hard crux past an undercut. Sustained, with good gear if you can place it.

[C Waddy and J Dawes 1988]

40. Citadel E5 6b ★★★ 92m
An utterly stunning route that is a contender for best E5 on Main Cliff. P1 is good and infamously 'cruxy' whilst P2 is awesome – a sustained, pumpy crack in a brilliant position. Start 9 m left of the *Mammoth Direct* chimney and 4m down and left of the discontinuous red cracks on the easier direct start to *Hunger*. This should position you just below a shallow (1.5m wide x 1.5m high) rectangular recess that lies immediately above the starting point, which is on or just above the normal traverse line.

P1 6b 30m Move up into the recess and pull out of it without too much trouble before heading diagonally leftwards along a line of weakness to the small corner formed by arching overlaps dropping down the wall. Climb up the rightwards-arcing corner for 1m to where it becomes a roof and traverse diagonally rightwards under it awkwardly on jams, undercuts and sidepulls. Continue doing this for 7m to a resting position in a good niche tucked against a vertical section of the overhangs. There is normally a large piece of tat in the niche. Step out leftwards on undercuts and side pulls that lead leftwards past an inverted peg. The crux follows: hard moves left, then up past a fingery undercut into a slabby groove. Relax. Up the groove to its top and then move 5m right along a thin ledge to the belay. The belay is just below the only grey streak on the wall above you and this is often marked by a piece of tat on a small flake. This point is below and to the left of the continuation crack.

49
46
43
41
38
32
31
46a
48
9
26
47
39
42
27
34
30
51
42
47
38
37
36
33
31
32
35
52
50
49
46
45
44
43
41
40

P2 6a 32m Ascend the steep wall above the belay until a step right gains the crack proper. (NB. The parallel crack to the left is *Graduation Ceremony* P2.) Swarm up the crack, eventually gaining an easing just as the rock becomes more grey than red, at a small corner. Continue up past some ledges on the left, and belay 5m further up the crack at an indistinct sitting belay, in a slight niche on the green slabs.
P3 4c 30m Climb directly up from the belay into the broken continuation groove (it looks worse than it is) then continue straight up to join the large, slabby corner line that comes in from the right, follow this until an impasse where the corner is stopped by a steep wall. Pull steeply onto the right wall of the corner and follow this on hollow jugs for 6m to gain a fine sling and cam belay on the rock saddle above. Finish by dropping down the opposite side of the saddle and scrambling up the sidewall of the ridge. Continue upwards along its side until the ridge becomes less rocky and more rounded; follow indistinct steps leftwards onto the crest of the ridge and less steep ground. Un-rope when you feel safe and follow well-worn steps directly up the heather covered ground to join the return path.
[J Street, G Hibberd (9 pts) 19.11.68/FFA: R Fawcett 1977]

▶ **41. Graduation Ceremony E4 6a ★★★ 92m**
Borderline E5. Excellent climbing and often unfairly overlooked because of its more famous neighbours. The main event is the crack-line on P2, but P1 is no walk in the park and requires careful ropework. Start 7m left of *Citadel* at a black crack that starts at ground level and fades after 5m to become a narrow rightwards-facing corner/groove that leads to small overlaps. There is a small flat 1m x 1.5m square platform just at the bottom of the black crack and the area around the corner groove has splashes of rust colour on the surface of the rock.
P1 6a 35m Climb up the crack, or just to its right, to gain the bottom of the corner. Small to medium cams. A couple of difficult, committing pulls and a high step get you established in the corner on good holds. Continue steeply up this for a couple of metres until a blind reach left gains jugs on a horizontal fault. Yard diagonally leftwards for 3m to gain a large ledge. Move up the steep left facing corner system on the left, which is initially more awkward than it looks. Continue going in this line for about 17m until the large (2/3m x 8m) sloping ledge of *The Big Groove* is on your right. Pull onto this and go to the right hand end to belay on small to medium wires below a quartz corner. (NB. It is possible to make the top of the pitch more interesting by following *Sebastapol* on the upper part of P1 - pull right out of the large left facing corner system 10m earlier at the first weakness on the right; this gains easier ground that follows a slabby line diagonally rightwards for 5m to a position where the rock wall rears steeply upwards again and is split by a crack. A series of delightful, steep pulls on the jugs that are positioned around the crack gains the right hand end of the belay ledge directly.)
P2 6a 27m Up the quartz corner for 4m, then bear rightwards to the crack line. Interesting moves up the crack become increasingly harder as the holds become more rounded; a sustained section past the widest part of the crack almost leads to a junction with *Citadel*, before a pull leftwards gains easier territory. Continue up the crack system for 5m and then move diagonally left for 2m to gain a very awkward bulge. Powerfully over this and then take a

sitting belay slightly up and right in a slight recess directly below the main part of the finishing corner groove that lies above. This belay is shared with *Citadel*.
P3 4c 30m Finish as for *Citadel* P3.
[A Sharp and R Toomer 1976]

Combining *Graduation Ceremony* P1, *The Big Groove* P2 and *The Big Groove Direct Finish* is an excellent and sustained combination at E4.

42. Food and Drink E6 6b *** 102m
An awesome route with strenuous, technical and bold climbing. Initially climbed as 2 separate routes, but best and most logical as a single route.
P1 Food 6b 35m Follow *Graduation Ceremony* until it breaks out left. Continue up the corner to an overlap (small cams) and make difficult moves through this on the right to gain the easier upper corner. This leads you to a position shared with *Sebastopol* below *The Big Groove* belay ledge and at the top of the slabby, post-crux groove on *Citadel*. The route was originally described as going to the *Citadel* P1 belay on the right, but it is now normally finished via the route *Drink* which starts on *The Big Groove* belay ledge. In this case finish straight up via *Sebastopol*, which lands you on the right side of *The Big Groove* belay ledge.
P2 Drink 6b 22m Belay either at *The Big Groove* belay (bomb proof, but 4m left of the route) or 4m to the right below the corner (not so bombproof – small cam/Wallnut #2), but below the leader. Climb up into the bottom of the corner on reasonable flakey holds, and when these run out at 5m, make hard moves up using holds on the left wall to gain 2 good flat holds just left of the corner. Bold crux moves lead up and slightly left – using the mini arête on the left – to reach some poor holds above the arête. Shuffle rightwards with adrenaline flowing to gain good flakes and gear. Much easier climbing remains, before pulling onto the belay ledge. Belay as for *Tet Offensive* and *Sebastopol* on the large sloping ledge (2m x 4m) with 3 natural threads in the back wall. Small wires and brass nuts are useful on this pitch.
P3 5c 27m *Tet Offensive* P3.
P4 5b 18m *Tet Offensive* P4.
[*Food*: P Pritchard, B Pritchard 1992, Drink: A Wainwright, C Waddy 27.05.92, Food and Drink: A Wainwright, T Briggs 24.05.06]

43. Sebastopol E5 6a/b *** 105m
An excellent, strenuous line that is essentially a more direct and harder version of *Graduation Ceremony*. Start 3m left of *Graduation Ceremony* at the base of the crack that is immediately left of the arete.
P1 6a 38m Climb the crack with a fair amount of difficulty, especially in the initial section, to a junction with *Graduation Ceremony* on the first sloping ledge at 15m. Continue as for *Graduation Ceremony* by going slightly left to climb the steep corner system, which is initially more awkward than it looks. Continue going in this line for about 7m until there is an obvious weakness on the right. Traverse right along these slabby thin ledges for 5m to reach a point 10m directly below the right side of the huge sloping belay ledge of *The Big Groove* and where the rock rears steeply upwards again and is split by a crack. A series of delightful steep pulls on the jugs that are positioned around the crack gains the right hand end of the belay ledge directly. Belay beneath

a steep quartz corner on the right of the ledge as for *Graduation Ceremony* on small to medium wires.
P2 6a/b 22m Climb the corner as for *Graduation Ceremony* but then break out left onto the steep, red wall via a slanting crack to reach a small, blunt pillar. Difficult and committing moves leftwards from this gain large layaways in a hidden flake crack that is just right of the arête. A final hard sequence from this gains good holds up on the arête itself and a much easier traverse back diagonally right along a juggy flake line. At the end of this a few upward moves gain a large sloping ledge (2m x 4m) with one of the most convenient belays at Gogarth (*The Tet Offensive* also belays here). Belay on the left hand side using 3 natural threads, taking care not to trust the insitu tat.
P3 5b 27m The original route climbed the groove on the right of the belay to a sloping ledge and then the continuation groove chimney and short wall to reach a slim 3m wide pillar that sits above a very sloping ledge. Belay. (NB. The finish of *The Tet Offensive* is much better – cleaner and harder – and lands you at the same final belay.)
P4 5b 18m Climb the pillar with interest. Belay on the short finishing slab above – good sling belays 7m up and left. There is a reasonably well-marked path leading up the hillside to reach the return path.
[J Moran, P Williams 22.05.79]

The Big Groove Area • Routes 44-54 *Tet Offensive* to *Hypodermic*.

After the *Citadel* area the walls become slightly less intimidating, but also a bit more confusing because there are less obvious and unique features to use as reference points from a sea level vantage point. The best reference point is the large square block that marks the left edge of this sector. This 4m high block lies on the traverse line and has to be climbed over to get any further along the traverse. The top of the block itself is the start of *Syringe* and *Morphine*. This is a haven of safety and sits well above the high tide line. The easiest traverse line drops down slightly at the start of this sector and it can be hard getting past here at low-mid tide or higher. Rough seas and tidal wash will also cause problems in this area.

This area contains a lot of previously over-looked gems. The classics of this sector, *Pentathol* and *The Big Groove*, start 12m right of the block below an indistinct, rightwards trending line of flakes. These routes are not normally badly affected by dampness although the crux pitch of *The Big Groove* can take longer than expected to dry and it also takes seepage. P1 of *Tet Offensive* is also stubbornly resistant to drying out.

▶ **44. The Tet Offensive E5 6b ** 102m**
Another previously overlooked route that should be a classic. It is just a shame that the crux crack on P1 is both so obviously desperate and so often damp. The rest of the route is still really good and well balanced; if the initial crack is off the menu then it may well be worth starting up *The Wastelands* just to the left (this option gives a very good top end E4 6a **). Start beneath the smooth, overhanging black crack 5m from the right arête of the buttress; this is at the lowest section of the approach traverse. (Low tide and calm seas needed.)

43
46
49
41
38
31
32
48
46a
9
26
47
39
42
27
34
30
51
42
47
38
37
36
31
33
32
35
52
53
50
49
46
45
44
43
41
40

P1 6b 35m The initial flared, black and smooth part of the crack looks the worst, but is actually not at all bad in dry conditions. Climb this to where it closes up and the crack becomes thinner and grey. Gain a good hold on the right of the crack and then make a series of hard moves up the flared crack to gain a sloping shelf and 1m above a spikey jug. Pull up into the corner above the right side of the shelf and climb this to gain the larger corner (*Graduation Ceremony*) that leads more easily to *The Big Groove* belay ledge. Belay as for *The Big Groove* on the left side in a small corner (peg). This is below the main continuation corner of *The Big Groove*.

P2 6a 22m Climb up into the base of *The Big Groove* corner either by following *The Big Groove* or by climbing more directly up the leaning wall above the belay; the route was initially described as using the direct variant, but this is very soon forced left into *The Big Groove* version. The direct start is hard, sustained and bold with the possibility of hitting the ledge if you fluff the moves. At a point level with the remains/rust scars of the pegs that mark *The Big Groove* crux make a wild step right onto a square cut hold on the arête. Pull around the arête to gain a good small ledge below a flared flake crack. Climb this with some difficulty to its top and pull onto the left side of a small ledge (1m wide x 3m long - stuck cam just above) and traverse to its right hand side. Climb the short 3m corner above before moving 1m right to gain a large sloping ledge (2m x 4m) with one of the most convenient belays at Gogarth. Belay using 3 natural threads, taking care not to trust the in situ tat.

P3 5c 27m Climb the groove just to the left of the belay - more difficult than you expect - to gain easier ground which leads in the same line to a sloping ledge. An easier version is to climb the weird pockets above the belay for 4m and then traverse leftwards into the groove along a handrail. The sloping ledge is bounded on its back and right by a steep groove. Pull into the groove from the left and climb it strenuously to a rounded exit onto yet another sloping ledge; move up this for 5m to reach a slim 3m wide pillar that runs all the way to the top of the crag. Belay.

P4 5b 18m Climb the weakness in the centre of the pillar and then follow the arcing handrail to the right arête; continue to the top on the right side of the pillar. Belay on the short finishing slab above (good sling belays 7m up and right.) There is a reasonably well-marked path leading up the hillside to reach the return path.
[J Moran, P Williams. 20.05.79]

▶ **45. The Wastelands E4 6a** ∗∗ 109m
Another hard variant based around the corner line of *The Big Groove*. P1 is great and offers perfect Gogarth climbing, firing directly up the wall on cracks and corners to *The Big Groove* belay ledge; P2 is also good, finding a subtle line of weakness up the wall left of *The Big Groove*. The route starts below the crack that is 2m left of the smooth, overhanging black crack of *The Tet Offensive*, 7m from the right arête of the buttress. This is at the lowest section of the traverse. Low tide and calm seas needed.

P1 5c 35m The initial crack is steep, but fortunately there are also holds on either side of the crack to help you out. The angle and the climbing soon ease as you reach a left facing corner system (junction with *The Big Groove* /*Pentathol* as they come in from the left). Up the corner for 7m until the rock becomes steeper (*TBG/P* escape leftwards). Continue up the corner with some interesting bridging. Difficult moves at the top allow an escape rightwards onto a sloping ledge system. Move up and right along this until a short crack allows a large sloping ledge (*Pentathol*) to be gained. Climb the corner on the rear right side to the massive ledge, on *The Big Groove* 3m above. Belay on the left side of the platform in the first corner to the right of the left edge of the platform (1 new peg). This is directly below the main continuation groove.

P2 6a 38m Traverse horizontally leftwards from the left edge of *The Big Groove* belay ledge for 7m on good, but sometimes loose holds to an area with large, well defined flakes. There is a collection of old slings and krabs on a big flake 3m up and left of this point. Move up on more good holds and then step right into a thin crack with difficulty. Climb this with more difficulty and pass a very poor peg – good wires just above – to easier ground. Continue up the crack more easily to the start of a left facing corner groove (junction with *Puzzle Me Quick*). This proves to be quite technical. Keep going until the ground becomes steeper and the groove starts trending leftwards. Move right around the arête onto the slabby right wall. Follow the natural line of holds that tends right and slightly up to a junction with *The Big Groove*. Belay either immediately or 3m higher at a small spike.

P3 5a 18m/25m The original route traversed back to the left arête and followed this to the top (25m). It is better to continue up *The Big Groove* as this offers better and cleaner climbing (18m).

P4 18m Finish as for *The Big Groove*.

[J Moran, G Milburn, A Evans 28.07.78]

▶ **46. The Big Groove E3 5c *** 109m**
This excellent route tackles the huge left facing groove that splits the upper part of the cliff. The route offers very good climbing throughout, but it is slightly unbalanced with the short crux pitch being very much harder than anything that comes before or after. The difficulty of the crux pitch is also affected quite badly by dampness and seepage because lots of the holds on the first half of the pitch are quite rounded.

Start 12m right of the large, high square block below an indistinct, rightwards trending line of flakes. This position is just after the lowest point of the traverse where the traverse gains about 1.5m in height by moving up and over a large sea washed flake with 3 distinctive spiked teeth on its top. Low to low/mid tide needed. (This position can be hit badly by the swell from the high speed ferry as it comes into port.)

There are higher belays available either on the higher block 2m to the left or in more dire situations on a good spike 4m up the initial wall.

P1 5a 39m Climb up steeply from the toothed flake for 4m to reach a line of rightward trending flakes; follow this flake system strenuously rightwards to a ledge beneath a short corner. Go up the corner for 5m until forced left along the easiest line to gain another left facing corner, which leads to a very sloping ledge on the right (*Pentathol* P1 belays here). Ascend the short corner above to a massive sloping ledge. Belay on the left side of the platform in the first corner to the right of the left edge of the platform (1 new peg). This is directly below the main continuation corner groove.

P2 5c 18m Move left from the belay and climb up from the left side of the ledge to surmount a small black wall and gain a corner with a spike at its top (thread). Continue up the black wall right of the thread for 4m until your hands are on a sloping shelf where the rock starts to become brown and then make delicate moves rightwards across the void onto another sloping shelf. Gain the vertical cracks (peg scars) above its right hand side and then make hard moves up and right into the blind flake crack. Climb this and at its top make insecure moves on to the small sloping ledge. The old belay pegs are in poor condition and it is better to belay on the left below the continuation groove on the standard route.

P3 5b 34m From the left side of the ledge step left into the groove and then follow it with sustained interest. Move slightly left 5m from the top of the main corner proper in to a smaller groove with a good flake crack in the back of it. Up this and then choose a spike belay from the many available – there is a big, solid one 5m up the slope above the finishing groove.

P4 18m There are a variety of ways to escape onto the main heather slope, but one of the most convenient is as follows. Head up rightwards towards the rear right corner of the bay and then scramble easily up the short ramp that lies 3m left of the right corner to gain a belay stance on edge of the cliff. Sling and cam belay. Move 6m right (looking in) to gain a path that runs up the ridge to regain the return path.
[P Crew, D Alcock (1 pt) 18.06.66]

Those looking for a harder, more balanced challenge should not overlook the following combinations: *Graduation Ceremony* P1 or *Wastelands* P1, combined with *The Big Groove* P2 and *The Big Groove Direct* to finish. These are excellent and sustained combinations at solid E4.

▶ **46a. The Big Groove Direct E4 5c ✶✶✶ 113m**
A harder, more consistent and perhaps better way of doing the route. The difficulties are in the first half of the pitch and the top is clean and solid. Lots of small wires needed. Highly recommended.
P1 5a 39m *The Big Groove* P1.
P2 5c 18m *The Big Groove* P2.
P3a 5c 35m. This takes the clean continuation corner directly above the right side of the P2 belay ledge rather than moving left to climb the groove in the left wall. It is still best to belay on the left of the ledge. Climb the steep wall/corner past the peg at 2m to gain a creaky flake in the corner and use this with care to gain the shelf. Difficult bridging gains the crux where the crack in the right hand wall doglegs back into the corner. The continuation white crack is still difficult, but gradually eases until you gain a small ledge on the arête. Climb in the same line up the continuation corner via the stepped ramp that leads much more easily past one last bulge to the belay terrace. Belay at your convenience.
P4 18m *The Big Groove* P4.
[E Drummond, B Campbell-Kelly 27.09.69]

44
46
49
46a
47
42
58a
59
48
57
51
60
58
56
55
54
53
52
50
49
48
46
45
44

134 Main Cliff • The Big Groove Area

▶ **47. Puzzle Me Quick E5 6a** ∗ 109m
P1 gives fun climbing, but struggles to find new ground. P2 is very good, taking a bold, if not serious line up the clean groove left of the main *The Big Groove* corner. It gets E5 for the bold nature of P2. Start as for *The Big Groove*.
P1 5b 39m Follow *The Big Groove* up and right along the juggy, steep flake line to the ledge system below the corner at 12m. Leave *The Big Groove* here by continuing to traverse diagonally rightwards to the steep groove of *Graduation Ceremony* and follow this to *The Big Groove* belay ledge. Belay on the left side of the platform in the 1st corner to the right of the left edge of the platform (1 new peg). This is directly below the main continuation corner groove.
P2 6a 34m Start as for *The Big Groove* P2 moving left from the belay, then climb up from the left side of the ledge to surmount a small black wall and gain a corner with a spike at its top (thread). Continue up the black wall right of the thread for 4m until your hands are on a sloping shelf where the rock starts to become brown. *The Big Groove* heads off right from here, but you are climbing straight up the groove above. This is quite technical and bold. Once standing on the shelf arrange some uninspiring 'RP' protection and then commit to the crux; technical moves hopefully gain a finger jug in the corner after 3m. Climb quickly up to good undercuts and gear in the steep wall above. Traverse left along the undercuts to their end, at a small corner (junction with *Wastelands*). Move 3m left to a thin crack and climb up this on good edges to a small right facing corner. Up this on good holds, pull onto the wall above on good holds then trend easily up rightwards to a belay stance on the arête by some solid flakes, making sure you choose the ones that really are solid.
P3 4b 18m Continue up the arête in good position and reach easy ground where the terrain becomes more broken. Head up diagonally right to the belay blocks 5m above the finishing groove of *The Big Groove*.
P4 18 *The Big Groove* P4.
[B Wyvill, R Evans 26.05.73]

▶ **48. Pentathol HVS 5a** ∗∗ 103m
Early memories from the pioneers: "...I can remember going along that traverse, thinking 'God, we are going to die if we are not careful', then struggling on the first pitch of *Pentathol*, watching the tide come in and wondering if we were going to drown?"
The 2nd route to be established on the Main Cliff, and the first of many significant contributions from Pete Crew. Start as for *The Big Groove* 12m right of the large, high square block below an indistinct, rightwards trending line of flakes. This position is just after the lowest point of the approach traverse where it gains about 1.5 m in height by moving up and over a large sea washed flake with three distinctive spiked teeth on its top. This position can be hit badly by the swell from the high speed ferry as it comes into port.
P1 5a 32m Climb up steeply from the toothed flake for 4m to reach a line of rightward trending flakes; follow this flake system strenuously rightwards to a ledge beneath a short corner. Go up the corner for 5m until forced left along the easiest line to gain another left facing corner, which leads to a very sloping ledge on the right. Belay here on the right of the ledge.

The Big Groove Area • **Main Cliff**

P2 4c 24m This pitch traverses more than it heads upwards and it is easy to get lost if you do not see the line – you are aiming for the base of the big, blocky groove that lies about 18m to the left and 6m higher than the belay ledge, The 2nd half of the route follows the line of massive flakes that run across the face and lead up to the base of the groove; these are clearly visible from the belay ledge. Reverse back down from the belay ledge for 2m to gain a traverse line that leads 4m left to a wide corner crack. Ancient sling and krab at the top left of the crack. Climb up on to the top of this and move diagonally left along the stepped ledges and big flakes to gain the base of the wide groove. Belay here on a large block and large wires.

P3 5b 24m. A very traditional pitch. Climb up into the recess above the belay and after 4m move left into the groove and then climb it to the inconvenient bulge that blocks the way; a hard, yet slightly precarious mantel over this onto a very polished shelf gains easier ground. Continue up the groove to exit onto the massive platform above. Scramble up to the top right corner of the slab to belay next to a very large fallen block that lies below and left of the finishing groove.

P4 4b 20–40m. Climb up behind the belay on easy ground to reach the broken, slabby groove that lies straight above. Climb this with decent gear and exit onto the slope above. After pulling onto the finishing slope it is possible to reach belays at the top of the slope below the final wall, but if rope drag proves too much then there are plenty of belays on the side walls to the right. Exit on to the heather slopes above via the pinnacle that lies against the left side of the back wall and reach belay blocks that sit 10m above. (Un-rope here.)

The easiest way to reach the return path is to move rightwards and slightly upwards from the blocks following an often very vague path for 35m before hitting the much better defined paths that contour up the hill from *The Big Groove* finishing area. You can gain the return path by heading straight up the hillside, but the gorse is often quite deep.

[P Crew, B Ingle 24.04.64]

▸ **49. Peepshow E1 5b** * 96m

Unfairly dismissed in the last guide, this route offers good, open climbing on the wall left of *The Big Groove*. P1 is great, whilst P2 is pleasant pulling on big holds, and P3 starts well, but quickly becomes a green scramble. It is possible to get back down to the ground from the second belay on 50m ropes and thus you could do both *Peepshow* and *Jaborandi* in one session, maximising the good climbing.

Start as for *Pentathol* and *The Big Groove* on the toothed flake 12m right of the 4m high platform that blocks horizontal progress along the traverse. Immediately above the toothed flake is a crack system that runs vertically up the wall – this is the substance of the P1. (Low to low/mid tide needed.) This position can be hit badly by the swell from the high speed ferry as it comes into port. There are higher belays available either on the higher block 2m to the left or in more dire situations on a good spike 4m up the initial wall.

P1 5b 28m The crack is steeper and harder than appearances suggest. Climb strenuously up the grey crack (small cams useful) to better holds below an impasse where a short, steep section of red rock blocks progress. Undercut rightwards to its right edge then pull back up and left on jugs to gain a wide crack directly above the initial crack. Climb this awkwardly on pinches and slopers to a belay at the base of the wide crack on P2 of *Pentathol*. There is an ancient sling and krab on the top left of the crack.
P2 5a 19m Climb up the wide crack and at its top move rightwards for 2m. Climb up the wall above trending gradually leftwards to gain the continuation crack after 7m. Follow this for 5m to belay on a small platform – junction with *Jaborandi*, which comes in from the left. The best belay is actually just below the block using large slings over top of the block. There are several untrustworthy, old slings and krabs already in place.
P3 5b 34m P3 of *Jaborandi*.
P4 4b 15-20m P4 of *Jaborandi*.
[B Wyvill, R Evans 12.05.73]

50. Jaborandi E2 5b/c * 97m

A fine route that is worthy of attention. It has 2 great pitches of very varied climbing and may be worth 2 stars. The only disappointment is P3, which starts well, but quickly becomes a green scramble. It is possible to get back down to the ground from the second belay on 50m ropes and thus you could do both *Peepshow* and *Jaborandi* in one session, maximising the good climbing.

Start 4m right of the 4m high block that blocks the traverse. This should position below a red corner and under a large block/platform that sits above the traverse. Start either below or on the large block. The high block is a haven of safety from the sea if you can reach it.
P1 5b 34m Climb up into the corner and move up its right hand side until the holds seem to run out. There should now be a small (15cm) flake ear up and right; gain this using an excellent hidden incut and pull rightwards onto the ramp line. Romp up this and at its end step up into the crack line above. Delicate climbing on sloping and hidden hold leads up to the *Pentathol* traverse. Follow *Pentathol* leftwards along the massive flake line to its block and sling P2 belay below the groove.
P2 5b/c 14m There is a small, bottomless corner up and right of the belay; climbing it is easy, but getting there is not. The easiest option seems to be moving back down the flake line for a couple of metres until level with footholds on the wall above. Balance up, then delicately move right into the corner. Climb this and belay at its top on a small platform. The best belay is actually just below the block, using large slings over the top of the block. There are several untrustworthy, old slings and krabs already in place. It is also possible to protect the initial section by placing a high runner in the groove above the belay.
P3 5b 34m Move up from the top of the block and climb the steep crack on the left to another small ledge after 5m. Climb the wider continuation crack for another 5m until it is possible to step left around the arête to a broken ledge, just before the wide crack becomes overly green and vegetated. Climb up easily, with care, from the right side of the broken ledge to gain a vague groove on the right. Climb this, then take the easiest line up the open funnel above. Belay on the terrace from one of the many spikes and flakes.

49
46
44
47
46a
42
58a
59
48
57
51
60
58
56
55
54
53
52
50
49
48
46
45
44

138 Main Cliff • The Big Groove Area

P4 4b 15-20m Finish as for *The Big Groove* or climb straight above the exit funnel to the wide rectangular recess in the back wall; take the easy angled groove on the right side of the recess and exit on the slopes above. Belay on the rocky blocks as you exit and then move up and diagonally right to gain one of the paths that lead up the ridge to regain the return path.
[P Crew, D Alcock (4pts) 11.06.66]

▶ **51. Morphine E2 5c** ∗ 97m
An interesting way up the cliff that has some entertaining climbing. The route starts (as for *Syringe)* on the prominent, square cut block that blocks the sea level traverse once past *The Big Groove/Pentathol* area. The block lies above the high water line, but access to it may be difficult at high tide.
P1 5b 23m From the top of the block climb the centre of the wall quite boldly (as for *Syringe)* until it is possible to move right to the crack in the right edge of the wall. Continue up this to a position just below and right of an obvious fin of rock, below the sentry box on *Syringe*. Now trend slightly up, but mostly rightwards, for 7m on a series of natural weaknesses to a recess below a crack. Belay.
P2 5a/b 14m Move diagonally leftwards up the flake line to gain the smooth corner. Climb this, which is surprisingly bold and technical by using flat holds on the right wall and bridging. This brings you directly at the *Pentathol* P2 belay. Belay as for *Pentathol* below the continuation groove on a large block with additional large nuts and medium cams.
P3 5c 45m This pitch, which takes the right hand crack line above the belay, runs almost parallel to and 2-3m right of *Pentathol*. Move up above the belay into the recess as for *Pentathol* and then continue straight upwards into the awkward crack; fight over the initial bulge to a rest and then tackle the 2nd bulge to get onto a polished sloping shelf that is shared with *Pentathol*. Move more easily up the continuation corner groove and exit onto the broken ledge (junction with *Peepshow* and *Jaborandi*). Climb up easily, but with care, from the right side of the broken ledge to gain a vague groove on the right. Climb this, then take the easiest line up the open funnel above. Belay on the terrace from one of the many spikes and flakes.
P4 4b 15-20m P4 of *Jaborandi*.
[B Wintringham, M Wintringham 05.05.79]

▶ **52. Syringe E4 6a** ∗∗ 76+m
A very fine route that requires a wide repertoire of skills and a cool head if a clean ascent is to be made. The route starts on the prominent, high, square cut block that blocks the sea level traverse once past *The Big Groove/ Pentathol* area. The block lies above the high water line, but access to it may be difficult at high tide.
P1 6a 31m From the top of the block climb the centre of the wall to the overhangs. Move right past a fin into the bottom of a sentry box. The next section is hard, particularly for the short, but the gear is good. Climb tenuously up the sentry box and pass the bulge with difficulty to gain the groove above. The groove lacks positive holds and is hard to protect and loose in places. Stay cool and teeter upwards to gain a small (1.5m x 1.5m) ledge on the left with a peg and some remnants of others. Belay here with relief.

P2 6a 25m Climb up the left hand corner of the belay to gain the wall that lies above. Move right delicately to the thin crack that leads through the bulge into the corner/groove above. Alternatively and harder, climb the fin above the right side of the belay ledge to gain the same position. The crack is insecure, but then offers better jams as it gets steeper. The crux lies on the lip of the bulge where it helps to move slightly left before pulling into the corner itself. Easier ground leads up the corner to a belay on the top right side of the massive ledge next to a very large fallen block that lies on the slab.
P3 4b 20-40m P4 of *Pentathol/Hypodermic*.
[D Scott, R Gillies (7 pts) 11.06.66]

53. The Camel E4 6a ** 84+m
A good old-fashioned fight, where the combination of a stubborn refusal to lose and a thorough 'trad' apprenticeship will pay great dividends. The route can be started in two ways depending on the time or how wet the initial crack is. The original start is via the crack that starts below and 1m left of the high, square topped block that blocks the sea level traverse (start of *Syringe*). If it is early or very greasy this sea-washed start can be desperate. It is possible to start from the top of the square topped block and climb up the wall above the block for 5m before stepping left into the crack. This alternative start is also ideal if the tide is in.
P1 6a 35m Once established in the crack follow it, easing with height, until 3m below the overhangs. Move leftwards and up to gain the enclosed rectangular bomb bay chimney that lurks menacingly above. Summon your primeval self and pull rightwards past the fang of rock that encloses the front of the chimney to gain the steep crack/groove that runs upwards through the roof. The next 7m is a fight, but leads to an easing in angle where *Hypodermic* comes in from the left. Continue up more easily to the top of the groove which forms a large flake with a blunt, spiky top. Drop down past this for 4m then right to the small belay stance on *Syringe* (peg).
P2 5c 25m Head back the way you came to regain the top of the flake and then trend up leftwards to the arête and a junction with the crack of *The Needle*. Pull onto the sloping ledge and contemplate the crack going through the bulge. Yes, it goes there, up the bulging wide crack immediately above that has a jammed hex at 3m. This is brutal to start and needs big gear, but once over the bulge things get easier, if looser and greener. Continue with care to the massive ledge above. Pull up onto the platform and head left to belay below the twin cracks on the left side of the headwall.
P3 5a 25-50m The left hand of the 2 cracks looks green, but is well worth doing. Interesting moves off the deck lead to bigger holds and fun climbing. After pulling onto the finishing slope it is just possible with 50m ropes to reach belays at the top of the slope below the final wall, but if rope drag proves too much then there are plenty of belays on the sidewalls to the right. Exit on to the heather slopes above via the pinnacle that lies against the left side of the back wall and reach belay blocks that sit 10m above. Un-rope here. The easiest way to reach the return path is to move rightwards (looking in) and slightly upwards from the blocks following an often very vague path for 35m before hitting the much better defined paths that contour up the ridge from *The Big Groove* finishing area. You can gain the return path by heading straight up the hillside, but the gorse is often quite deep
[A Sharp, J Zangwill 01.07.74]

140 Main Cliff • The Big Groove Area • The Needle Area

▶ **54. Hypodermic E2 5c** ✱✱ 85+m
A very good route that weaves its way between *Syringe* and *The Needle*. It is not easy for E2, but it is well protected and is a good introduction to the Main Cliff extremes. For the start, in the perfect square cut corner below and to the left of the *Syringe* block, a low to mid tide needed.
P1 5b 25m Take care with drag on this pitch. Climb up the corner for 10m and then quickly follow the horizontal line of incuts out to the left arête: rest. Move horizontally left for 5m until below a rib/small corner and pull up onto a small ledge; now move diagonally leftwards for 2m until below the line of weakness in the upper wall and climb it onto a small ledge. This is the same small (1m x 3.5m) belay ledge as used on *The Needle* and *Assassin*. Although it would be preferable to belay on the right the most substantial belays are on the left.
P2 5c 40m From the right side of the belay ledge move rightwards and make committing moves to get established in the crack that shoots straight up the cliff. Climb the crack for 3m until you reach the perfect jug on the right of the crack and use this to swing rightwards to the bottom of a small right facing corner. Up this and at its top step right into the bigger left facing groove, which becomes a large flake with a blunt, spikey top. Step onto this and pull straight up over the bulge with difficulty to reach a massive hidden jug; a long move off this gains small incuts on the slab above. Pull up on improving holds to enter the big corner groove on the right (*Syringe*). Climb the groove more easily to gain a comfortable belay stance on the slab above on the right side of a large fallen block.
P3 4b 20-40m P4 of *Pentathol*. Climb up behind the belay on easy ground to reach the broken, slabby groove that lies straight above. Climb this with decent gear and exit onto the slope above. After pulling onto the finishing slope it is possible to reach belays at the top of the slope below the final wall, but if rope drag proves too much then there are plenty of belays on the sidewalls to the right. Exit on to the heather slopes above via the pinnacle that lies against the left side of the back wall and reach belay blocks that sit 10m above. Un-rope here.
The easiest way to reach the return path is to move rightwards (looking in) and slightly upwards from the blocks following an often very vague path for 35m before hitting the much better defined paths that contour up the ridge from *The Big Groove* finishing area. You can gain the return path by heading straight up the hillside, but the gorse is often quite deep.
[L E Holliwell, L RHolliwell 20.07.68]

Needle area • Routes 55–59 *The Needle* to *Nightprowler*.

A brilliant area that is full of classic routes of great quality. The routes are all based on the front of the buttress immediately beyond *Hypodermic*. This area is more badly affected by high tides, rough seas and the wake from the incoming high speed ferries and the initial cracks can be damp in the mornings.

The traverse and starts of the routes need a calm sea and a low/low-mid tide. *Scavenger* starts slightly higher on a small stance, but the rock architecture means the stance is subject to a lot of sea spray in all but calm seas. The traverse past the *Scavenger* stance gets a lot more difficult for a short section before easing just before the large bay where *Nightride* starts.

50
46a
42
62a
58a
59
51
48
57
62
63
47
61
60
58
56
55
54
53
52
50
45
44
41
49
48
46

All the routes start up the cracks that run up the lower face of the buttress; the starts are identified by counting the number of cracks along from the right arête of the buttress.

55. The Needle E3/4 5c *** 83+m
Another very good route that has a varied P1 and a very sustained P2 that together really define the top of the E3 grade. Whilst not overly technical or bold, this is a route that keeps on coming and throws in some hard moves at the very top. It starts by climbing the front of the buttress that lies to the left of the *Hypodermic* corner via the 2nd crack to the left of the right arête. In calm seas this should be accessible from mid tide.

P1 5b/5c 22m Pull into the crack strenuously and climb it in the same manner to an easing in angle. Continue directly up to the small, steep groove line that lies immediately above and pull into it. Continue up this to where it steepens and becomes a mini corner; get some gear in and then sprint up it with a long final move to reach the belay ledge (5c version). This is the same small (1m x 3.5m) belay ledge as used on *Hypodermic* and *Assassin*. Although it would be preferable to belay on the right the most substantial belays are on the left. It is also possible to skirt the steep final corner on the left, but this is not really in the spirit of things (5b version).

P2 5c 34m From the right side of the belay ledge move rightwards and make committing moves to get established in the crack that shoots blindly straight up the cliff. Climb the crack with continued interest and excellent gear to a final impasse just below a large sloping ledge. Layback the crack wildly on sloping footholds to gain the ledge and, at last, some respite.

There are 3 ways to finish the pitch:

a Up the bulging wide crack immediately above that has a jammed hex at 3m. This is brutal to start and needs big gear, but once over the bulge things get easier if looser and greener. The enthusiast's choice and also the finish of *The Camel*.

b Up the disintegrating left facing corner 2m left of the wide crack. The original finish, but not recommended.

c Move 4m left and climb the weakness on good, but furry holds. This leads easily to the large belay ledge after a further 10m. The easy option.

Belay under the twin cracks in the back wall, left of a large fallen block.

P3 5a 25-50m The left hand of the 2 cracks looks green, but is well worth doing. Interesting moves off the deck lead to bigger holds and fun climbing. After pulling onto the finishing slope it is just possible with 50m ropes to reach belays at the top of the slope below the final wall, but if rope drag proves too much then there are plenty of belays on the sidewalls to the right. Exit on to the heather slopes above via the pinnacle that lies against the left side of the back wall and reach belay blocks that sit 10m above. Un-rope here. The easiest way to reach the return path is to move rightwards (looking in) and slightly upwards from the blocks following an often very vague path for 35m before hitting the much better defined paths that contour up the hill from *the Big Groove* finishing area.

You can gain the return path by heading straight up the hillside, but the gorse is often quite deep.

[R Evans, C Rogers 19.05.73]

Needle Area • **Main Cliff** 143

▶ variation: **The Needle Alternative Finish**
P3 5a 25-50m Climb the right hand crack (if you have already ticked the left hand one).
[A Evans, J Moran 05.07.78]

▶ **56. The Assassin E3 5c** ∗∗ 79+m
An excellent route with interesting and varied climbing. The 2nd pitch, although not desperate, demands composure and ideally some micro wires.
The route starts below the 6th crack left of the right arête of the buttress. It is possible to belay on a low platform just below the crack or slightly higher on the left. The lower platform is better, but can easily be swamped even at low tide. In general the route can be climbed at mid tide, although the high speed ferry or rough seas can cause a bad swell here.
P1 5b/c 21m Start up the crack, which initially is a little rounded and awkward, before nice, big positive holds arrive. Continue up the crack until it opens out into a niche at around 10m and move diagonally right for about 4m until just past a horrible flared crack. Don't worry it doesn't go there. Climb the steep wall that lies just to the right with interest to reach a small (1m x 3.5m), sloping belay ledge with some rotten pegs. Belay on the left hand side on a variety of small/medium gear.
P2 5c 33m Go diagonally leftwards up the strangely featured wall and pull over the small bulge that has a miniature corner on its left side. Clip the peg that lies above and move diagonally right and up into an open scoop. Climb this and the short wall above with some hard moves on small flatties to reach good holds on the left in a short slanting crack, Follow this crack rightwards for a couple of metres to reach a sloping ledge. Go up the scoop above and continue into the easy, but lichenous cracks to reach a palatial belay on a huge ledge below 2 cracks in the headwall to the left of a large fallen block.
P3 5a 25-50m P3 of *The Needle*.
[J Moran, G Milburn, A Evans 11.06.78]

▶ **57. Hyena E3 5c** ∗ 79m
A good, hard eliminate based between the 2 variations of *Scavenger*. It does borrow a bit from *Assassin* and it gets a bit close to *Scavenger* at one point, but these are not bad routes to have as close neighbours. P1 is a direct on the initial crack of *Assassin* that lands you at a belay on the traverse line of *Scavenger* and P2 heads straight up the wall that separates *Scavenger* and *Scavenger Direct*.
The route starts, as for *Assassin*, below the sixth crack left of the right arête of the buttress. It is possible to belay on a low platform just below the crack or slightly higher on the left. The lower platform is better, but can easily be swamped even at low tide. In general the route can be climbed at mid tide, although the high speed ferry or rough seas can cause a bad swell here.
P1 5b/c 21m Start up the crack, which initially is a little rounded and awkward before nice, big positive holds, arrive. Continue up the crack until it opens out into a niche at around 10m. Move around the niche on the right and the head back into the crack, which is followed easily for 4m. The rock now becomes less featured and the final 6m to the belay are quite technical, with delicate moves on sloping sidepulls. Belay on the sloping ledge above at a point marked by 2 pegs on good cams and nuts.

P2 5b 21m This pitch heads straight up above the belay, weaving around the thin crack that runs up the centre of the wall. Climb straight up from the pegs on good holds until a couple of harder moves gain a perfect, parallel break. (cam #2). Go rightwards along this for 1.5m, until just left of the *Scavenger* groove and then move up and left into crimpy territory. Boldly climb the centre of the wall on positive edges until a reach left gains a good pocket and the better holds above. Continue up the wide crack for 5m to reach the *Scavenger* belay on the sloping (1.5m x 1.5m) ledge. Sling and cam belay.
P3 4b 18m As *Scavenger* P3a.
P4a 4c 21m As *Scavenger* P4a.
[B Wintringham, M Wintringham 19.05.79]

▶ **58. Scavenger HVS 5a** ★★★ 85+m
A brilliant route in every sense: superb rock, fantastic positions, interesting moves. A Gogarth classic; P2 is pure magic!
Start below the 7th crack from the arête. This starts from a small ledge that marks a 1m step up in the level of the traverse and leads to the right side of the ledge that is just visible 10m above. Although the start platform is at a higher level than *Assasin, Hyena* or *The Needle*, sea spray does hit it more than expected because of the rock architecture.
P1 4c 10m Climb the steep crack on excellent holds to a large sloping ledge. Belay on the right hand side in the corner (peg) on good wires.
P2 5a 36m Go up into the crux corner with some hard bridging at the 5m mark and then at 10m break out right past the arete onto the obvious yellow and black ledge system. Move across this past 2 pegs (*Hyena*) to the base of the grey open corner groove on the right. The wonderfully exposed groove is climbed on good holds to reach a small (1.5m x 1.5m) sloping ledge that also marks the point where *Scavenger Direct* comes in from the left. Good sling and cam belay.
There are 2 main ways of finishing:
P3a 4b 18m Continue up the easier groove above with care until it ends after 14m. Move up onto the long, narrow ledge above and move forward along this for 4m to reach block belays opposite a short chimney in the side wall.
P4a 4c 21m On the side wall next to the block belay is a 11m high chimney recess filled with a couple of blocks. It all looks a bit green and loose, but is actually OK. Climb it with much cam protection and exit onto an easy slab. Move straight forward across the slab to spike and cam belays.
P3b 4c 25m Follow the continuation groove until possible to stride rightwards and climb into the base of the narrow chimney on the right after 5m (this requires a bit of care as there are several large, perched blocks sitting at a point directly above your belayer).Traverse right past a flake crack, then continue along a ledge until the big, easy angled slab is reached. Scramble rightwards under the large block to belay below the corner/groove. This is the final pitch of *Penthathol*.

Phil Dowthwaite on the exposed P2 of **Scavenger** HVS 5a   photo: Jethro Kiernan   >

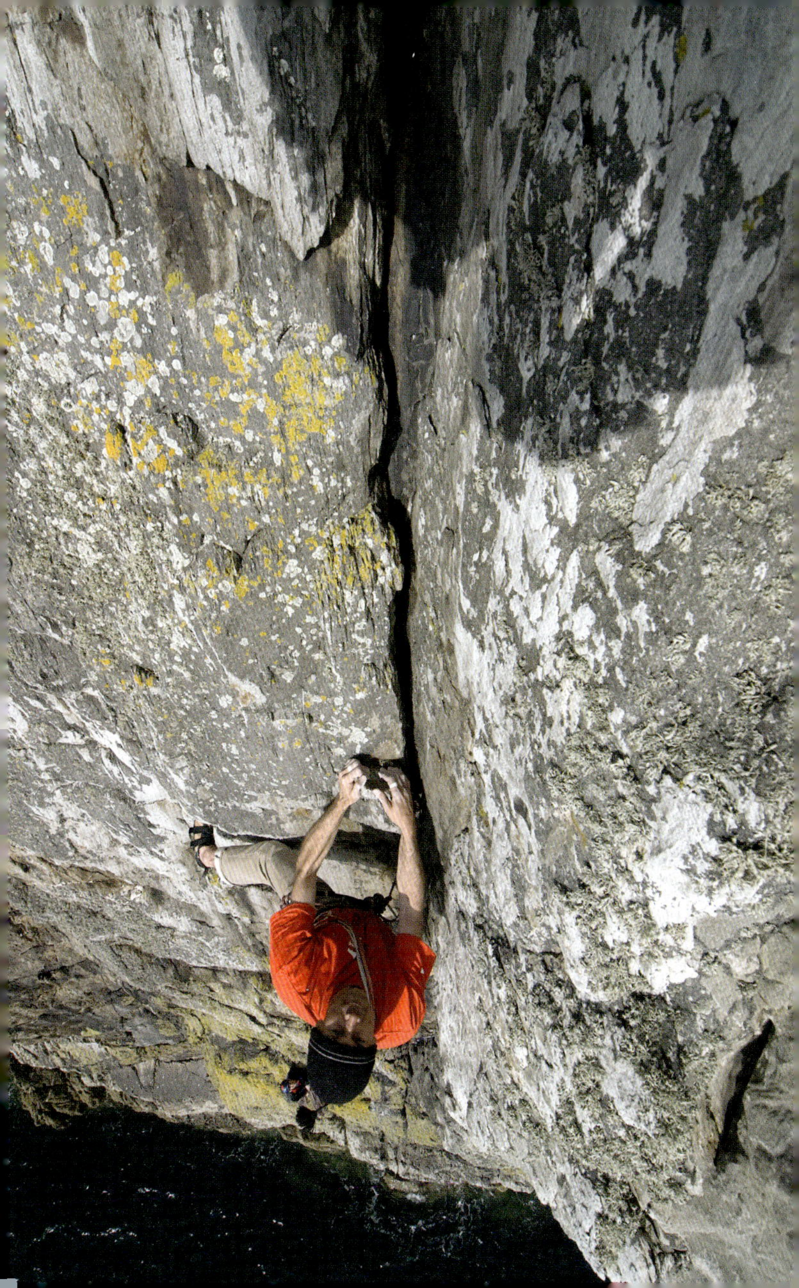

146 Main Cliff • Phaedra Area

P4b 4c 20-40m P4 of *Pentathol*. Climb up behind the belay on easy ground to reach the broken, slabby groove that lies straight above. Climb this with decent gear and exit onto the slope above.
The finish for both variations is as follows: exit on to the heather slopes above via the pinnacle that lies against the left side of the back wall and reach belay blocks that sit 10m above. Un-rope here. The easiest way to reach the return path is to move rightwards (looking in) and slightly upwards from the blocks following an often very vague path for 35m before hitting the much better defined paths that contour up the hill from *The Big Groove* finishing area. You can gain the return path by heading straight up the hillside, but the gorse is often quite deep.
[M Boysen, J Jordan 14.05.66]

▶ Variation: **58a. Scavenger Direct HVS 5a** ** 80+m
A fine alternative to the main pitch on *Scavenger*. Very good gear.
P2a 5a 31m Go up into the crux corner and do the crux move of *Scavenger* at 5m, but then continue straight up the corner groove above. This has brilliant and sustained moves on a wide variety of holds. The hardest section is passing the ledge system at 10m and this involves some thoughtful moves on slightly unhelpful holds. Continue up on increasingly big grips to a point where the route curves back right to re-join the original route at a small (1.5m x 1.5m) sloping ledge. Good sling and cam belay. Continue as for *Scavenger*.
[R Evans, D Cuthbertson 05.74]

▶ **59. The Night Prowler E1 5b** * 86m
A short variation based on *Scavenger Direct* that connects that route to the top section of *Nightride* on the left via a steep crack. Sustained, steep climbing on the main pitch.
P1 4c 10m As for *Scavenger* P1.
P2 46m. 5a. Follow *Scavenger Direct* for 16m to an overlap. (This is the second overlap on the pitch). Yard leftwards on good holds to reach the base of a steep crack, which is followed on more good holds until it is possible to step, left into the bottom of the wide crack on the P3 of *Nightride*. Finish up this to belay above the broken grass slope against the back wall.
P3 4c 30m Finish as for *Nightride* P4.
[P Greening, N Sharp 05.07.95]

Phaedra Area

This area is based around the deep bay situated just beyond *Scavenger*. The deep bay seems to consist mainly of overhanging rock, massive hanging flakes and deep chimneys that give the routes an intimidating aura. However don't be put off because they are actually a lot easier than appearances suggest.

The traverse past the *Scavenger* stance gets more adventurous and is physically strenuous for a few moves. Care should be taken here. 10m from the *Scavenger* stance you reach the right arête of the bay from where *Nightride* starts. All but the very intrepid will need a low/low-mid tide to get to this area, however once here the routes start from a relatively high level that is safe at mid tide.

The best way off for routes 61–65 is either as for *Scavenger* P4a (the 11m high chimney that forms the substance of this pitch is 15-20m up on your right as you pull onto the slopes) or via scrambling up the lines of weakness on the rear right of the bay.

▶ **60. Nightride E1 5b** ∗∗ 92m
A superb route with a steep and pumpy main pitch. This route is top end E1 and may be considered E2 by some. Start from the right arête of the bay. Low to mid tide and calm seas needed.
P1 4c 14m Climb up diagonally rightwards to gain the large ledge on *Scavenger*. Belay on the right below the corner.
P2 5b 21m Climb up the corner for 3m, then follow the traverse line out left to the overhanging arête. Step up and right to reach a steep crack and race up it with a sense of urgency. A perched stance on the arete is soon reached. It is also possible to combine the first 2 pitches by starting further towards the back of the bay and then heading diagonally right to the arête, joining it just below the steep, crux crack.
P3 4c 27m Head up right to gain and follow a wide crack to the broken, grassy slope. Belay on the back wall.
P4 4c 30m Scramble up right to gain a series of blocks on the left of a long, narrow ledge (*Scavenger* belays here at the end of P3a). On the sidewall opposite the block belay is an 11m high chimney recess filled with a couple of blocks. It all looks a bit green and loose, but is relatively okay. Climb it with much cam protection and exit onto an easy slab. Move straight forward across the slab to spike and cam belays.

Exit on to the heather slopes above via the pinnacle that lies against the left side of the back wall and reach belay blocks that sit 10m above. Un-rope here. The easiest way to reach the return path is to move rightwards (looking in) and slightly upwards from the blocks following an often very vague path for 35m before hitting the much better defined paths that contour up the hill from *The Big Groove* finishing area.

You can gain the return path by heading straight up the hillside, but the gorse is often quite deep.
[J Brown, G Rogan 26.02.67]

▶ **61. Dream Seller E1 5b** ∗ 47m
A nice, long pitch that just needs a little traffic. In the back of the bay lies a large chimney (*Heroin*). *Dream Seller* takes the bubbly wall to the right of this chimney in quite a bold fashion before attacking the steeper bottomless corner groove that guards the exit.
P1 5b 47m The initial wall can be climbed in a variety of ways. There are plenty of holds, but the gear can be a little spaced on the lower wall – thin slings useful. The natural lines of weakness will lead you an amazing diagonal flake line that leads leftwards to a point right of a steep bottomless corner groove with a thin crack running through the back of it. Enter the groove and then make some difficult moves to gain easier ground. Continue carefully up the groove to gain the slopes above. The last 5m leading to the grass slopes are quite loose and it is best to trend right away from the groove itself towards the right arête and finish up this.
[J Moran, G Milburn 10.02.76]

148 Main Cliff • Phaedra Area

▶ **62. Heroin E1 5b** ∗∗ 52m
A great little trad adventure that finds an amenable line through some steep territory. It climbs the steep chimney in the very back of the bay and packs a lot of different climbing into the first pitch.
P1 5b 37m Start below the chimney and climb up into it wildly using a variety of techniques – thankfully the right wall is quite featured. When the chimney closes pull steeply up into the continuation crack and left facing corner groove; continue delicately up this until a very thin horizontal overlap is on your left - this is the middle of 3 such overlaps crossing the brown wall. Traverse 5m leftwards across the slabby wall at this level to reach a prominent blunt flake that lies on the left hand side of the brown wall just short of a slabby groove. Belay here or on spikes 5m higher on the left of the groove.
P2 5a 15m Continue up the left trending corner groove which becomes increasingly fluffy to reach a good platform on the edge of the grass slopes. Good spike belays 4m up and left.
The best way off is either as Scavenger P4a (the 11m high chimney that forms the substance of this pitch is 15-20m up on your right as you pull onto the slopes) or via scrambling up the lines of weakness on the rear right of the bay.
[P Crew, J Baldock 19.03.66]

▶ Variation: **62a.** It is also possible to continue to forego the traverse on P1 and continue up the obvious groove line to the top in a single pitch at a similar grade.

▶ **63. Horse Above Water E3/4 5c** 48m
Fancy a battle? Well, step this way sir (or madam). This route takes the short, flared, bottomless chimney to the left of the larger chimney that runs up the back of bay (*Heroin*). It is really quite hard to grade and possibly harder to climb. A Vedauwoo, Wyoming grade of 5.10d may be most accurate.
P1 5c 35m Climb up into the back of the bay and then move steeply up into the bottom of the chimney. Improvise upwards with the aim of trying to get established in the chimney itself – no mean task. Once there continue to thrutch upwards for a few moves until things get a bit easier. Relax and head up the lichenous crack to a belay. There are several places where a belay can be taken, but the most obvious is on the blunt spike just to the right of the groove (*Heroin* comes in fro the right to share this belay.) This belay is level with the middle of 3 thin horizontal overlaps that runs across the brown wall on the right.
P2 5a 15m Finish up the corner groove as for *Heroin*.
[A Sharp, C Dale 03.07.75]

58
way
off
71
70
73
62a
59
68
72
57
58a
74
62
71
64
63
71a
61
69
67
66
73
65
75
60
58
56
routes 65-75

150 Main Cliff • Hustler Area

▶ **64. Phaedra E1 5c ∗ 45m**
A great little route that is well worth seeking out. It has two contrasting sections with an initial technical crux followed by an ominously wide crack that is actually quite straight forward.
A small sea level rift marks the left edge of the *Phaedra* area belay platform; above this rift are two grooves capped by overhangs at 10m. The right hand groove has by far the widest wall on its right hand side. The route gains this right hand groove and at its top moves left into the wide crack. Start by scrambling up the platform to belay on the right of the right hand groove.
P1 5c 33m Move up into the groove with difficulty and climb it to its top before moving left around the arête to gain the wide crack that is a bit green, but perfectly climbable. Thus climb the crack with less difficulty to a stance in the recess formed as the crack widens out to body width. Various spike belays in the bottom part of the recess.
P2 5a 12m Continue up to the top of the recess and then climb easily in the same line to the grass slopes. Good spike belays 5m up the slope,
[M Howells, B Whybrow 18.06.66]

▶ **65. Zed HVS 5a 45m**
A good pitch, bold in places. Start a little left of *Phaedra*. Climb up the blunt arête to reach the roof, thread. Step left and go up the wall above for 10m. Move right around the arête and follow a crack to the top.
[D H Jones, J Brown 07.87]

Hustler Area

This amazing area lies beyond the *Phaedra* recess and provides the adventurous with splendid routes in a setting that epitomise the Gogarth experience. There are very few crags in the UK that can give teams operating in the lower extremes the exposure and positions that will be encountered in the days exploring these small crags.

Accessing the area involves making a roped traverse pitch leftwards from the *Phaedra* bay. All of the routes except *Hud* and *Piglet's* start perched below a large, hidden corner that is 17m from the *Phaedra* bay. The corner has a comfortable belay ledge on its left hand side. The traverse can be done at mid tide and the belay ledge is quite high so should be safe at a high/medium tide in calm seas. The main problem is that getting to the *Phaedra* bay is difficult other than at low tide. There is a fixed sling belay at the top left of *Hustler* that you can use to get back down to sea level after completing the main pitches. This way you can maximise the number of routes that you can do in a day.

The best way off for routes 66–75 is either as for *Scavenger* P4a (the 11m high chimney that forms the substance of this pitch is 15-20m up on your right as you pull onto the slopes) or via scrambling up the lines of weakness on the rear right of the bay.

Alex Williams on P2 of **The Hustler** HVS 5b photo: Al Leary >

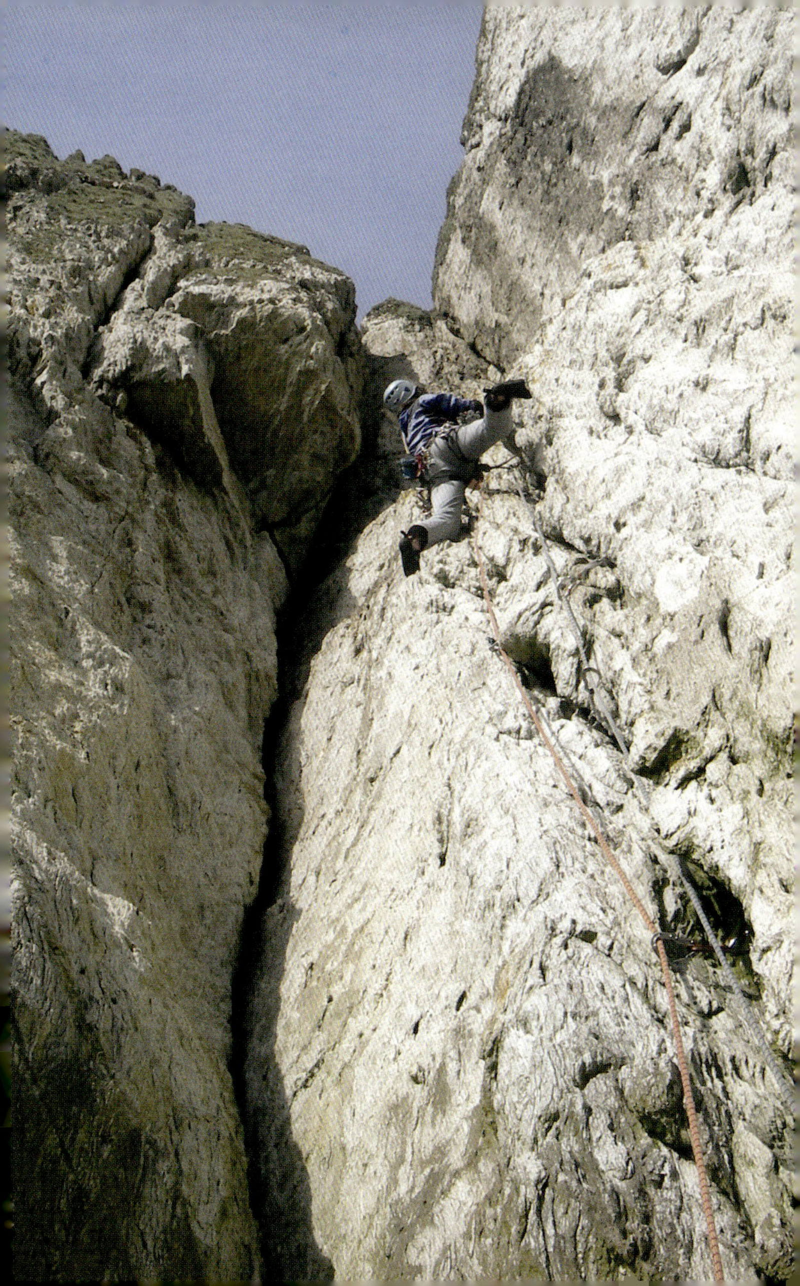

152 Main Cliff • Hustler Area

▶ **66. Hud HVS 5a** * 50m
A superb route that gives interesting climbing based around a steep groove and corner system. Well protected with the hardest climbing in the first third of the route.
P1 4c 8m Make an exposed traverse left out of the bay past some good, high spikes on the left arête onto the front face; drop down with a couple of long moves and move along until you are below a small groove and just right of the arête. Belay on good nuts in the rear of the groove in an exposed position, hoping the high speed ferry does not come into port…
P2 5a 42m Pull up onto the right wall of the corner groove and continue to climb up the line of the groove mainly using its right wall until at a point about 8m below the capping roof and 4m below a white fang of rock that hangs down from the right side of the roof. Now make a 3m traverse right using an obvious huge foothold before heading upwards again into the continuation groove. Easier, but slightly greener ground leads to the slopes above and a good flake belay 6m above the edge of the cliff.
[J Brown, H Drasdo 14.06.66]

▶ **67. Piglet's Left Boot E5 6b** * 48m
A bold, modern offering that climbs the arête to the right of the big corner (*Hustler*). There is no gear for the first 10m on the second pitch and so a confident approach and the ability to swim are prerequisites for any prospective candidates. Low tide and calm seas are also mandatory.
P1 5a 8m Make an exposed traverse left out of the bay past some good, high spikes on the left arête onto the front face; drop down with a couple of long moves and move along until you are below a small groove and just right of the arête. Hope the high speed ferry does not come into port, as you belay on a sling and nuts in an exposed position
P2 6b 40m Climb up and left from the belay and continue boldly straight up to gain a thin a thin crack and gear just to the right of the flake crack of *Mestizo/Mulatto*. Continue relatively easily for a few more metres up the incipient cracks in the wall right of *Mestizo* until the headwall kicks back and life gets harder. Blast up the steep wall to a hard finish with pumpy climbing and fiddly gear in flared cracks. Good large cam belays on the platform at the edge of the slopes or good spike belays 7m above the cliff edge.
[M Turner, A Townsend 1998]

▶ **68. Mulatto HVS 5a** 53m
This route is a bit redundant now with *Mestizo* sharing the same start and then taking the obvious challenge that this route avoids. It does not help that the second pitch is also largely overgrown.
P1 5a 18m A great little appetiser for the main pitch that feels adventurous – take plenty of long/thin slings. Make an exposed traverse left out of the bay past some good, high spikes on the left arête onto the front face; drop down with a couple of long moves and move past the a small groove and arête. You are now out of sight of your belayer, but in sight of the belay ledge at the base of the large corner. A couple more long moves gain the ledge and a good belay on slings.

P2 4c 17m Step from the belay ledge on to the right wall of the corner and make a rising traverse rightwards across the wall to pass a flake crack at 4m (*The Three Musketeers*); continue for another 4m to a second flake crack and move up this for 6m before gradually crossing rightwards to the arête and a poor stance. This is slightly above the relatively palatial stance on *Mestizo* which is on the large 1m² flake 5m to the left.

P3 5a 18m 'Agent Orange' in hand, move up and right into the cracks above and climb them for about 7m. Move into *Big Furry* (the wide crack on the right) and swim up this to the top. Good spike belays 5m above.
[J Brown, G Rogan, A Wright 09.67]

69. Mestizo E1 5b ✸✸ 55m
A terrific route and a great adventure. (Combine this with *Hustler* for a great day out.) P2 and P3 can be run together and the route is, perhaps, best done this way. Belay in the *Phaedra* bay towards the left hand side if possible.

P1 5a 18m A great little appetiser for the main pitch that feels adventurous – take plenty of long/thin slings. Make an exposed traverse left out of the bay past some good, high spikes on the left arête onto the front face; drop down with a couple of long moves and move past the a small groove and arête. You are now out of sight of your belayer, but in sight of the belay ledge at the base of the large corner. A couple more long moves gain the ledge and a good belay on slings.

P2 4c 17m Step from the belay ledge on to the right wall of the corner and make a rising traverse rightwards across the wall to pass a flake crack at 4m (*The Three Musketeers*); continue for another 4m to a second flake crack and shoot up this to belay on a large 1m² flake below a well defined crack that widens in its upper section.

P3 5b 20m Move into the main left hand crack and climb this. This proves to be quite sustained and as the headwall steepens towards the top, increasingly pumpy. There are good spike belays 7m straight above the lip of the wall.
[T Taylor, P Jones 07.09.70]

70. The Three Musketeers E5 6a ✸✸ 55m
A throw-away gem from Fawcett who must have been going well since this was originally graded E2 5c. The initial section is glorious 4c climbing on the best Gogarth quartzite, but the top pitch mutates into a bold man-eater with blind, run-out climbing on positive side pulls. P2 and P3 can be run together and this may be the best way of doing this route, especially as it is quite possible to take a 'factor 2' fall onto the second belay if you don't use side runners. A Cam #1 and RPs are very useful on the top pitch.

P1 5a 18m As for P1 of *Mestizo*.

P2 4c 16m Step from the belay ledge on to the right wall of the corner and make a rising traverse rightwards across the wall to gain a flake crack at 4m. Easily up this for 12m to its end, step right 1m to gain a belay on a large flake (belay shared with *Mestizo*).

P3 6a 21m Up and slightly left of the belay is a thin crack that leads to the top of the crag; climbing the crack is not easy and gaining it is harder. Step back down left from the belay and climb the wall directly below the crack on positive side pulls, but without gear to a point where things get harder. (There is crucial cam #1 placement just out of reach and a possible skyhook on a good incut at shoulder height.) A long reach and high step gains the cam placement; carry on in the same vein with long reaches and high steps on positive, but slightly crispy holds to gain the crack and more substantial gear. Up this to the top and a belay either very close to the edge of wall (cam #2 and 2.5) or 7m further back and right on spikes.
[R Fawcett unseconded 21.10.79]

71. The Hustler HVS 5b ** 56m
A great, well protected route and one of Gogarth's hidden delights. The main pitch is quite sustained and seems to go on forever. The route climbs the obvious line of the big corner by the crack on its right hand wall.
P1 5a 18m As for P1 of *Mestizo*.
P2 5b 38m Bridge up the corner for 3m until it is possible to step right into the crack in the right wall. Climb this crack quite steeply on jugs until level with the small overhang in the corner itself. Things get a bit more difficult now and thoughtful bridging is required to make progress up the continuation chimney/corner system. This gradually eases and leads to a sling belay on the left – the in situ slings are in a bad way so back them up.
[M Howells, B Whybrow 11.06.66]

Variation: **71a.** The corner crack itself has also been climbed at E2 5b with a crux section passing the bulge.

72. The Third Man E2 5b ** 56m
A marvellous action packed route. The main pitch takes the right trending miniature groove and crack that bends slightly rightward to join the mid height break and then continues up the right hand crack to finish. Start 2m left of the corner from the comfortable belay ledge that lies to the left of the corner (*Hustler*).
P1 5a 18m As for P1 of *Mestizo*.
P2 5b 38m Climb straight up the left wall of the corner at a point 2-3m left of the corner aiming for a very slim, short rightwards trending groove/crack that runs to the mid height break. This is initially bold – take thin slings – but on very good holds. Once at the start of the groove things get more difficult with a couple of especially trying moves on undercut sidepulls to reach a good hold on the left just below the break and then jugs in the break itself. Swing athletically right into the continuation crack and follow this to the top with sustained interest. Belay on the (backed-up) in-situ slings at the top of the route or move 8m up and right to a good spike belay.
[J Moran, A Evans 14.05.78]

58
way off
71
70
73
62a
59
68
72
57
58a
74
62
64
63
71
71a
61
69
67
66
73
65
75
60
58
56
routes 65-75

156 Main Cliff • Girdle traverses

▶ **73. Gringo E1 5b** * 59m
Despite some strange and indirect route finding, a good and worthwhile climb, which takes the vertical crack that runs up the wall 7m left of the big corner of *Hustler*. The crack starts above a 4m high black/dark coloured streak that runs up the lower part of the wall. The route veers left at the mid-height break. It is also possible, and easier, to fire straight up the continuation crack that is actually the finish of *High Noon*.
P1 5a 18m As for P1 of *Mestizo* to belay on the ledge left of the corner.
P2 5b 23m Start 4m left of the corner and trend up and left to the start of the crack; slightly bold, but on mainly on good holds. The crack leads steadily to the halfway break from where an awkward traverse leads leftwards to the arête and a comfortable belay on a small stance.
P3 5b 18m Pull back right to climb the crack to the right of the arête and after 4m move back left to the hanging crack that lies directly above the belay. Climb strenuously up this before reaching easier ground just before top.
[J Brown, J Cheesemond 09.67]

▶ **74. High Noon E1 5b** 54m
Essentially a variation on the theme of *Gringo*.
P1 5a 18m As for P1 of *Mestizo* to belay on the ledge left of the corner.
P2 5b 18m Climb up *Gringo* until it is possible to move left into the overhanging groove. Follow this up to the stance on *Gringo*.
P3 5b 18m Traverse right and climb the crack directly above *Gringo* P1 to the top.
[B Wintringham, M Wintringham 09.06.79]

▶ **75. Wrangler E2 5c** 66m
The most leftward line on the cliff tackles the steep crack and easier upper groove left of the *Gringo* wall. Low tide essential.
P1 5a 18m As for P1 of *Mestizo* to belay on the ledge left of the corner.
P2 5c 30m Go left to the arête and climb up for 6m to place a runner. Return to sea level and traverse left until below an overlap. Move up with difficulty to gain the overhanging crack on the left. Follow the crack up to a good stance. The route *Swastika* in the Easter Island Gully area lies just to the left.
P3 18m Easier climbing leads up the groove above to the top.
[J Brown, I MacNaught-Davies 14.05.67]

Girdle Traverses

To paraphrase Elvis: "If you're looking for trouble, you've come to the right place." The girdle traverses of Main Cliff provide big, exhausting days out with plenty of potential for navigational errors. A good knowledge of the cliff is probably a wise starting point for any would be suitors. Or you could just dive in at the deep end and maximise the potential for a character building epic. The choice, as ever, is yours.

76. The Girdle Traverse HVS 5b * 192m

A fine expedition, linking the initial pitches of *Cordon Bleu* into the upper pitches of *Pentathol*. The difficulties are sustained, and there is a fairly committing abseil on P3. In fact, quite an undertaking for a HVS! Start as for *Cordon Bleu*.

P1 4a 38m Descend to an obvious traverse line leading out left onto the slabby face. Keep going until an arête is reached. Pass the arête and climb down a short chimney to a ledge. Belay on the far side beneath P4 of *Gogarth,* at the base of a 20m crack formed by a house sized flake leaning against the cliff. Good sling belays. (This is P1 of *Cordon Bleu*.)

P2 4b 37m Climb down and move around the base of the massive flake to reach a corner on the other side. Go up this and traverse out left along the top of the flake traverse line to belay just beyond its apex. (This is P2 of *Cordon Bleu*.)

P3 31m Climb down to the left edge of the massive flake. From a block, abseil down the steep and impressive wall of *Mammoth* until ledges in the middle of the wall can be gained (i.e. the first belay on *Mammoth*). Care should be taken to ensure that the ropes can be retrieved after the abseil.

P4 4c 12m Make a traverse left to climb up a short steep wall, passing a large spike, to gain a big ledge and the 1st belay on *The Big Groove*.

P5 4c 6m Climb down to belay at the 1st belay on *Pentathol*.

P6 4a 24m This pitch traverses more than it heads upwards and it is easy to get lost if you do not see the line; you are aiming for the base of the big, blocky groove that lies about 18m to the left and 6m higher than the belay ledge, The second half of the route follows the line of massive flakes that run across the face and lead up to the base of the groove; these are clearly visible from the belay ledge. (This is P2 of *Pentathol*.) Reverse back down from the belay ledge for 2m to gain a traverse line that leads 4m left to a wide corner crack. Ancient sling and krab at the top left of the crack. Climb up on to the top of this and move diagonally left along the stepped ledges and big flakes to gain the base of the wide groove. Belay here on a large block and large wires.

P7 5b 24m A very traditional pitch! Climb up into the recess above the belay and after 4m move left into the groove and then climb it to the inconvenient bulge that blocks the way; a hard, yet slightly precarious mantel over this onto a very polished shelf gains easier ground. Continue up the groove to exit onto the massive platform above. Scramble up to the top right corner of the slab to belay next to a very large fallen block that lies below and left of the finishing groove. (This is P3 of *Pentathol*.)

P8 4b 20–40m Climb up behind the belay on easy ground to reach the broken, slabby groove that lies straight above. Climb this with decent gear and exit onto the slope above.

After pulling onto the finishing slope it is possible to reach belays at the top of the slope below the final wall, but if rope drag proves too much then there are plenty of belays on the side walls to the right.

Exit on to the heather slopes above via the pinnacle that lies against the left side of the back wall and reach belay blocks that sit 10m above. (This is P4 of *Pentathol*.)

[P Crew, G Birtles 28.05.66]

158 Main Cliff • Girdle traverses

▶ **77. Trunk Line E3 5c ∗∗ 142m**
Another very sustained journey crossing the impressive central wall of the cliff. Start as for *Resolution Direct*.
P1 5b 25m From a point 3m right of the base of the *Gogarth* pinnacle (the start of *Gogarth*) scramble up 5m to a sling belay on a large flake in a recess. This is on the left side of a bay of overhanging, creaky looking rock. From this belay move 3m left to gain the crack line in the arête. Follow the crack in the arête with sustained climbing until a pull into a corner system yields a junction with *Gogarth* P2. Continue up and left to take a belay at the left side of the ledge.
P2 5a 22m Follow the obvious line trending left (as per the first part of *Falls Road* P3), rising slightly across a broken area, until it is possible to gain a narrow ramp which is followed down to a good stance below the chimney of *The Rat Race*.
P3 5c 18m Climb down the upper section of the slanting groove line of *Alien* until an obvious traverse line leads leftwards. Follow this and move up to a resting place. Continue leftwards to reach the 1st belay on *Dinosaur*.
P4 5b 15m Traverse leftwards into *Mammoth* and follow this up the crack slightly left of the red groove. Belay on the right side of the thin ledge 3m above.
P5 5c 15m From the left hand end of the belay climb the steep diagonal crack leftwards until, at 12m, it is possible to move left over a bulge to belay on *Citadel* P2 at a large flake.
P6 5c 22m Continue up the sustained crack of *Citadel* P2 past some ledges on the left, and belay 5m further up the crack at an indistinct sitting belay, in a slight niche on the green slabs.
P7 4c 30m Climb directly up from the belay into the broken continuation groove (it looks worse than it is), then continue straight up to join the large, slabby corner line that comes in from the right. Follow this until an impasse where the corner is stopped by a steep wall. Pull steeply onto the right wall of the corner and follow this on hollow jugs for 6m to gain a fine sling and cam belay on the rock saddle above. (This is *Citadel* P3.)
Finish by dropping down the opposite side of the saddle and scrambling up the sidewall of the ridge. Continue upwards along its side until the ridge becomes less rocky and more rounded; follow indistinct steps leftwards onto the crest of the ridge and less steep ground. Un-rope when you feel safe and follow well-worn steps directly up the heather covered ground to join the return path.
[M Fowler, J Stevenson 09.76]

▶ **78. The Horizon E4 ∗∗ 331m**
"The best traverse in the world" according to Chris Parkin! An incredibly long and sustained girdle of the left hand side of The Main Cliff and Easter Island Gully area. Initially done in sections, it has been completed in one day. Great care is needed with the ropes on many sections. No pitch is harder than E3, but worth E4 for the full trip. Start as for *Syringe* on top of the prominent, high, square cut block that obstructs the sea level traverse once past *The Big Groove/Pentathol* area. The block lies above the high water line, but access to it may be difficult at high tide.

P1 22m From the top of the block climb the centre of the wall to the overhangs and move left beneath these to cross the wall left of the groove. Move up onto the arête and continue left until it is possible to step down onto the 1m x 3.5m belay ledge (as used on *Hypodermic*, *The Needle* and *Assassin*). Although it would be preferable to belay on the right the most substantial belays are on the left.

P2 37m Climb the wall on the left continuing leftwards to beneath overhangs. Cross the smooth slab on the left and go around the steep wall into *Scavenger*. Follow the obvious flake to good ledges.

P3 43m From the end of the ledges go around left into *Heroin*, then climb the wall slightly left to the big overhang, and climb this. Move slightly left, and then traverse left to a hidden peg under a small overhang. Descend 9m to a small ledge in the middle of the wall. Move left across the top of the steep groove of Hud, and onto the arête where a crack leads to a good spike. Climb leftwards to the top of a huge flake, in the middle of the wall right of *The Hustler* and belay.

P4 18m Go left to a ledge, on *The Hustler*, then move left past the chimney crack and across the steep left wall (skyhook in horizontal crack to start). Reach the arête and move left again to a good belay ledge, on *Gringo*.

P5 31m From the left hand end of the ledge climb the wall to a peg, then step down and climb leftwards to spikes on the steep wall. Follow these leftwards until, using a rock fang, it is possible to gain a resting place on the arête. Go left again, on spikes, to take a hanging belay on the arête.

P6 9m Traverse left around the arête to the good ledge in the next corner on *Big Gut*.

P7 31m Cross left, through *Rotten Gut*, then semi-hand traverse beneath the obvious ledge, moving down to a good ledge, below the top pitch of *Tape Worm*.

P8 12m Drop down a little and traverse left, across the arête of *Phagocyte*, on a line of quartz holds to reach the top of a good crack. Carry on passing a further 2 cracks to a ledge and belay in the corner, on *Volcano*.

P9 31m Climb the corner above and move left into a small cave under the huge arch. Chimney down behind the arches until it is possible to move left into the corner at a pod (*Exit Groove*). Cross the wall on the left, with difficulty, to a point just short of the arête, and climb up (peg for aid) to a ledge. A long reach gains a crack above, on *Sex Lobster*, then step left to a hanging belay on the arête.

P10 9m Go down left to a spike on the arête, then descend into the steep corner on *Belial*, and take a hanging belay at the foot of this.

P11 12m Descend again and move across to a crack on the left. Climb this until moves left gain the arête of *Drag*. Take another hanging belay here.

P12 12m Move across the wall (skyhook tension) to gain a good flake, and continue more easily to large belay ledges on *Exit Chimney*.

P13 15m Climb the chimney a little way, and then take the steep wall above to a good flake in the right hand corner. Traverse left to a small corner and move down to a ledge. Move around the corner to belay in the chimney on *Ormuzd*.

P14 18m Move left and go up before climbing down and across to thin flake ledges on the wall. Move left to a spike on the arête, and climb up and then leftwards to belay ledges on *Ahriman*.

P15 31m Go leftwards up the wall and follow a line of shelves, slightly leftwards, to the top. [E Drummond, B Campbell-Kelly originally done with 8 pts spread over five separate days spread over several months 24.03.69]

Main Cliff • Girdle traverses

Steve Long and Chris Parkin get the prize for the most epic link up: they started via *Cordon Bleu*, abseiled down *Mammoth* and finished up *A Dream of White Horses* via *The Horizon*, adding a couple of straightforward linking pitches. "A long day: finished by lighthouse lights!" according to Steve.

Connecting *Trunk Line* into *The Horizon* would give an amazing connection. This would certainly be the longest E4 in the UK; it would also probably be the 'best traverse in the world......'

Above the routes at the left hand side of Main Cliff is a neglected upper wall of more broken rock, which at its highest point provides some worthwhile exit routes from the Main Cliff. Directly above the finish of *Mulatto* a scramble leads to a wall, with an obvious crack in the centre, right of a big corner directly above *The Hustler*.

79. The Fast Buck HS 4b 37m
The obvious big corner on the left is the line of *Minnesota Fats*. Right of this is an easier corner, followed by a steeper wall containing a wide crack starting at 5m. Take a short corner for 5m, and then go 2m left to reach the crack, which leads to a platform. A continuation crack then leads to a second sloping platform. Go into the corner and climb the crack to finish.
[G Milburn, A Evans 05.11.78]

80. Minnesota Fats S 4a 30m
This big corner provides an obvious and direct way off from this area of the cliff. Scramble up to the base of the corner and enter it from the left. This leads pleasantly to the top.
[A Evans, G Milburn 08.07.78]

81. The Finisher E1 5b 30m
This is the crack around the last arête of the previous route, exiting right onto a slab and finishing up a wall at the top.
[S Reid, J Roberts 17.06.83]

Adam Wainwright heading into wild territory on **Alien** E6 6b   photo: Jethro Kiernan   >

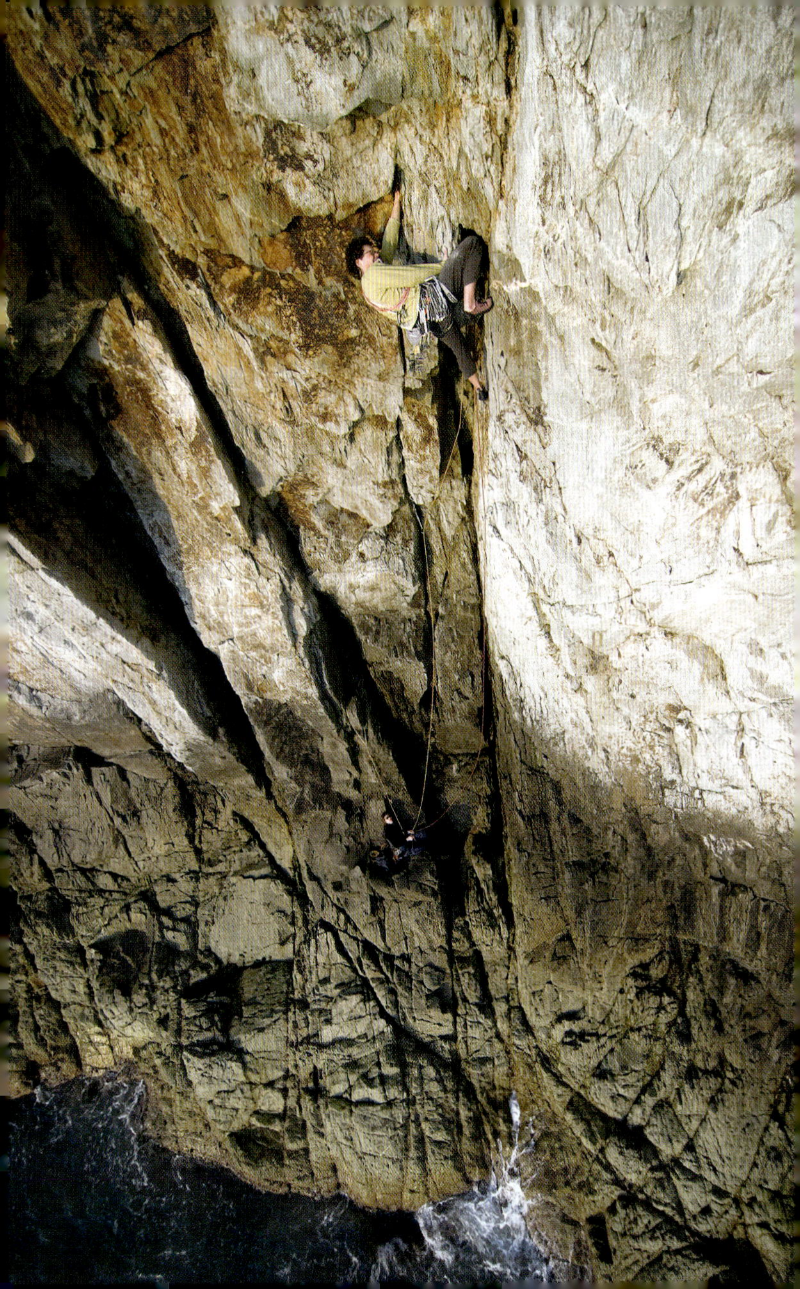

Easter Island Gully

Area: North Stack
Style: Trad (1-4 pitches)
Aspect: West
Rock type: Quartzite
Approach: 25 minutes
Altitude: Sea level – tidal
OS ref: 215 836

For Mad Men Only	E6

The Red Sofa	E5
Annihilator	E5
The Ancient Mariner	E5
I Wonder Why	E5
Ormuzd	E4
Wonderwall	E3
Sex Lobster	E3
Vicious Fish	E3
Tumbling Dice	E3
Pequod	E3
This Year's Model	E3
Supercrack	E3

Belvedere	E2
Merchant Man	E1
Swastika	E1
Hombre	E1
Drag	E1
Shagger's Start	HVS
Exit Groove	HVS
Phagocyte	HVS
Ahriman	HVS
Gazebo	HVS
Belial	HVS
Tape Worm	HVS

This fine section of Gogarth is sandwiched between the ever-popular Main Cliff and Wen Zawn. The name of the area is derived from the rock pinnacle, which marks the start of the gully proper and resembles its namesakes on Easter Island in the Pacific Ocean. Although often overlooked it contains many fine routes in the HVS to E5 range. It is also a place where solitude can normally be found. Indeed, on a warm sunny day Easter Island Gully has a very chilled out atmosphere.

Elfyn Jones firing up the steep and pumpy P1 of **Merchant Man** E1 5b
photo: Streaky Desroy

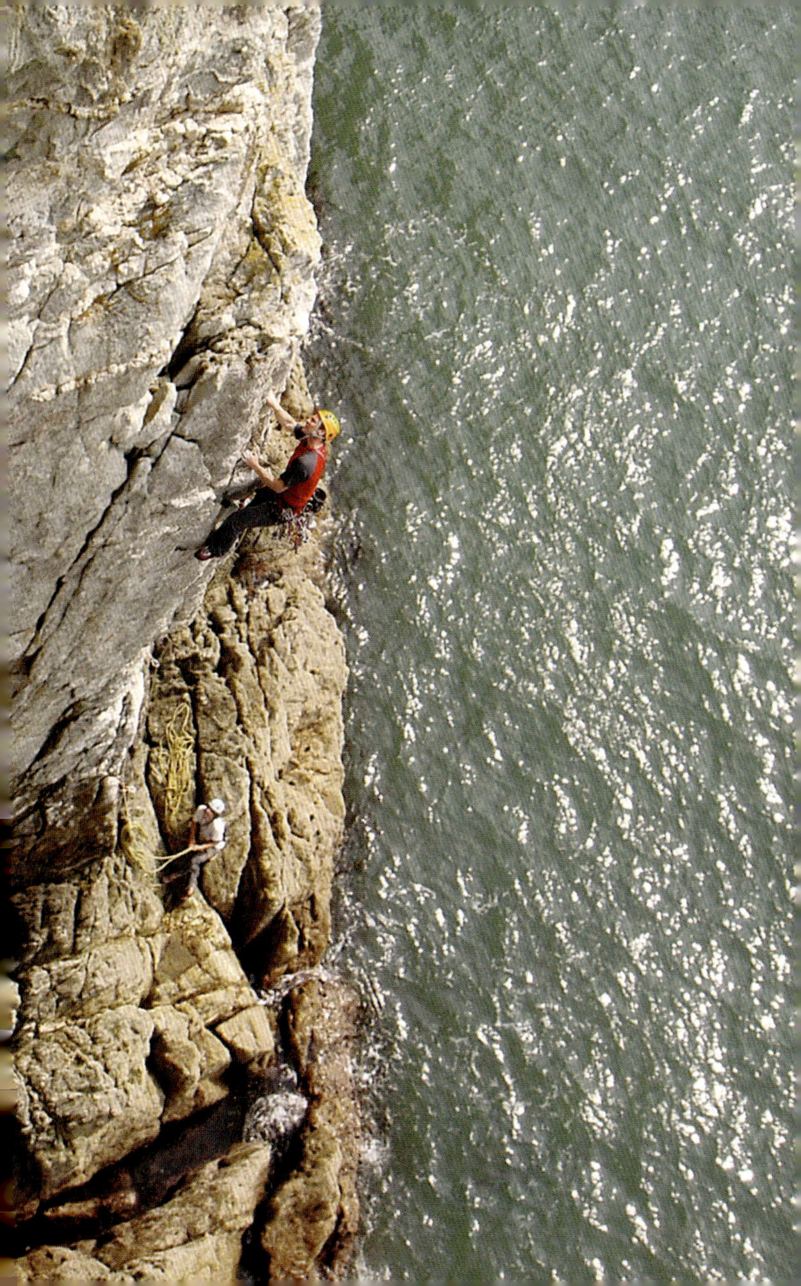

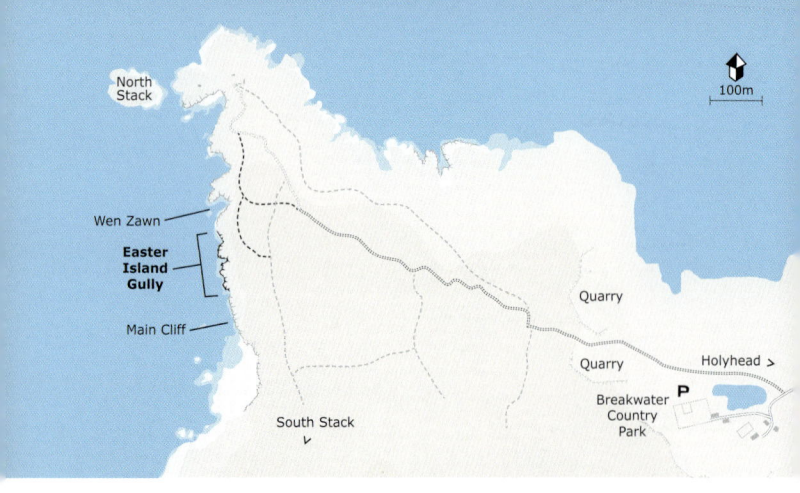

Although the cliff is quite short in comparison to its neighbours, a degree of competence is still required (both on the descent and on the typically loose exits). While the routes are generally on solid rock with good protection, the rock, as with most areas at Gogarth, does deteriorate towards the top.

Conditions: As a west facing suntrap, the crag does dry quickly. However damp soapy rock is common (particularly at the base of the routes) in the morning, before the sun has had the chance to burn the moisture off. The best combination for a visit is a low tide and a calm sea, as access to the routes is via a sea level traverse from the base of the abseil, which is obviously compromised by lively sea conditions or an incoming tide. Routes outside the *Supercrack* zawn are inaccessible at high water.

Approach: The cliff can be approached from South Stack via a path leading past Holyhead Mountain and over the top of Main Cliff, but is easier to locate from the top of Wen Zawn, the approach gully being the first one south of Wen Zawn. From the Breakwater Country Park car park gain the rough Landrover track 50m to the north of the small lake. Follow this for 750m up the hill and then down the other side to where the overhead electricity poles cross the track (Pole No. 8168 18). 50m to the left are two cols/dips beyond the Coastal Path on the skyline. Gain the left hand dip which marks the start of the approach to Easter Island Gully (The more pronounced one to the right marks the start of the descent into Wen Zawn). Descend the faint path down into the gully to just beyond a large block 10m in front of the prominent pinnacle (said to resemble the Easter Island statues). From here a 35m abseil (trend to the left, facing in) will take you down steep grass to a belay on a small rock platform at the top of *Supercrack*. (NB. There is a risk of causing stonefall into the zawn when pulling through the ropes on this section.) Some people choose to scramble unroped down the upper grass section, although this is particularly treacherous if the grass is wet. A further 30m abseil will land you at sea level. If possible leave an abseil rope in place here, in case of a forced retreat.

Easter Island Gully South • **Easter Island Gully** 165

▶ **1. Watership Down VS 4c** 34m
A fun route which is to be found just to the right (looking out) when descending the upper part of the approach gully en route for the Easter Island climbs. Start at the foot of the buttress where there is a slab on the right. Climb a steep crack in the slab to an overhang at 6m, and then move left and make a hard move right to enter a chimney groove, which is climbed more easily, then go up leftwards to a ledge on the nose. A tricky step up right on dubious holds gains the finishing groove.
[A Evans G Milburn 05.11.78]

The main crag is described in 2 sections. The **Easter Island Gully South** area includes the zawn at the bottom of the approach abseil and all the routes running rightwards (facing in) to the edge of Main Cliff. The routes are described left to right from the line of the abseil. **Easter Island Gully North** is the area to the left of the abseil line running leftwards to the edge of Wen Zawn. The routes here are described right to left.

Easter Island Gully South

▶ **2. Supercrack E3 5c** *** 30m
The striking crack line, following the abseil line, is hard to on sight! Start to the left of the abseil line below the steep crack – this start is on the highest part of the platform and is reasonably protected from the tides and rough seas – it stays climbable when the start of *Wonderwall* on the other side of the zawn under is being drenched by high tide or rough seas. Pull into the crack and climb it with sustained interest for the first 7m until the angle eases. Continue up the crack more easily on positive holds until an impasse just below the top when you least expect it. A short technical section leads to big holds and the top.
[L E Holliwell (2 pts) date unknown, FFA: A Sharp, C Rogers 17.08.74]

▶ **3. Exit Groove HVS 5a** * 30m
A good climb up the left hand corner crack at the back of the zawn. Start beneath the corner and gain the vertical slot by the chimney and crack. Leave this at its top by a step left into the niche below the corner crack proper. Jam and bridge your way to near the top where moves left allow the abseil block to be reached.
[J Brown, P Crew 22.01.67]

▶ Variation: **Shagger's Start HVS 5b** * 30m
A better version of the original. Climb directly into the niche of *Exit Groove* by way of the obvious crack to the right of *Supercrack*.
[P Trower, I Wilson 04.89]

▶ **4. Supercak E4 5b** 33m
The obvious wide and crumbly crack that takes the wall to the right of *Exit Groove*. Large cams and a steady head will be found useful. Start as for *Exit Groove* and follow it to the niche. The sanctuary of the corner has to be left at some point, at which point the fun begins. The finish is also insecure and it is wise to leave the upper abseil rope in place as a belay.
[N Bullock, G Desroy 2007]

166 Easter Island Gully • Easter Island Gully South

▶ **5. Wandering Wall E2 5b** (1pt. aid) 48m
A curious route taking the back wall of the *Wonderwall* zawn. Start beneath a chimney, at the back of the zawn.
P1 4b 15m Go up the inside of the chimney for 10m to reach an overhang, then using a 'weighted line', thread a rope through the hole above and use this to gain a small stance.
P2 4b 8m Traverse left beneath the overhang to belay in *Exit Groove*.
P3 5b 25m Climb the crack for a couple of moves then make a rising traverse rightwards to reach a small ledge. Step right then go up a couple of metres before moving left onto the wall and climbing straight up the centre of it to the top.
[J Brown, D Howard Jones, P Jewell (1pt) 09.05.78]

▶ **6. The Ragged Runnel E5 6a** 50m
A good adventure through 'territory'. Ascend the first pitch of *Wandering Wall*, free climbing past the fishing rod manoeuvre (possible stance here). Arrange some protection and battle with the roof. Place some more good gear on the wall above before the legs collapse, then go up the shattered dyke to a rest on a tiny ledge. Continue up the disintegrating scoop above past a possible spike belay. The top requires some care. (It would be possible to escape onto the *Wonderwall* side of the zawn after the easier ground is reached). Belay well back on the descent path. The route in no way supersedes *Wandering Wall*, it is merely an alternative exploit for those without fishing rods.
[G Smith 28.08.91]

▶ **7. Volcano E3 5c** 45m
A very strenuous but worthwhile route which follows the overhanging crack in the corner at the back of the zawn before trending rightwards to join *I Wonder Why*. Start beneath a short crack to the right of the base of a groove.
P1 5a 8m Climb either crack to a ledge and belay.
P2 5c 35m Gain the overhang and continue to reach the thin crack. Follow this for a few metres over another overhang then climb rightwards to finish carefully up *I Wonder Why*.
[J Brown, P Crew (3 pts) 15.01.67, FFA: A Sharp, S Humphries 1970s]

▶ **8. Wonderwall E3 6a** ** 45m
A splendid pitch weaving up the steep wall immediately opposite the abseil. Climb the central crack in the wall; until an obvious transfer is made to the parallel crack on the left, which leads up to overhangs. Pull past the steepness then swerve right to the base of a groove. Climb the groove with difficulty until good holds lead leftwards to a narrow ledge. Move back right to the arête and follow it to the top.
[L E Holliwell, D S Potts (2 pts) 19.04.69, FFA: A Sharp, J Pasquil 1973/4]

▶ Variation: **I Wonder Why E5 6a** ** 40m
A strenuous direct finish; the difficulties are short, but feel committing and some of the crucial holds are slightly fragile. The E5 grade is generous in retrospect, but at the time feels warranted. Once at the overhang on *Wonderwall* follow a thin crack to a hard section on creaky undercuts; span upwards from these to gain a series of finger ledges. Climb up these to gain a crack in easier ground, before moving left to belay.
[M Crook, C Smith 06.86]

Abseil scramble/approach
Abseil approach
Main Cliff
Mestizo
Easter Island Gully North
6
7
8
9
10
11
12
13
14
16
17
18
19
20
21
22
23
24

9. Phagocyte HVS 5a ** 45m
A fine and popular jaunt.
P1 5a 20m Jam your way up the steep right hand crack until a quartz ledge leads to a belay just round the arête.
P2 5a 25m Climb the short groove above and to the right. Move back left and teeter up the faint arête on the left until a belay can be arranged in the blocks well above.
[J Brown, P Crew 30.04.67]

10. Merchant Man E1 5b * 45m
Pumpy, out there climbing on the initial arête, and a bold 2nd pitch: in fact, it could be E2! Start just right of the arête below the steep buttress.
P1 5b 20m Climb the wall just right of the arête to where it steepens. Launch boldly up left onto the arête with knowledge that good holds will arrive. Moves then up and right lead to the belay of *Phagocyte*.
P2 5a 25m Climb the short groove above and to the right. Step left and follow the arête to the right with interest until a belay can be constructed in blocks well above.
[J Moran, G Milburn 06/07.05.78]

11. Tape Worm HVS 5a * 52m
A direct line up the groove to the right of the right arête of the buttress with a steep top pitch.
P1 4c 22m Climb up the groove for 10m to a sloping ledge. Follow the thin diagonal crack on the left to a small ledge. Step back right to another ledge and spike belay.
P2 5a 30m Climb the steep cracked wall to the left of an obvious groove (*Small Gut*) to the top. Belay well back on blocks.
[J Brown, P Crew 15.01.67]

12. Small Gut HVS 5a 60m
Start as for *Fluke*, beneath the groove a few metres right of *Tape Worm*.
P1 4a 20m Climb the groove to a ledge with spike belays.
P2 5a 10m Take the clean-cut groove above.
P3 4a 30m Go right along ledges for 12m then finish up a thin crack.
[J Brown, D Alcock 08.01.67]

13. Fluke HVS 5b 50m
Strenuous climbing up the wall between *Rotten Gut* and *Small Gut*. Start beneath a groove, a few metres right of *Tape Worm*.
P1 4b 15m Climb the overhanging groove diagonally rightwards to a small ledge then move left to climb a short crack to reach a belay ledge on the left.
P2 5b 20m Move back right and go up the wall to a short overhanging crack. Go over the bulge above then step left and ascend to another ledge. Belays higher up.
P3 4a 15m Step right (as for *Small Gut*) to climb a crack to the top.
[P Crew, A Alveraz (2 pts) 14.01.67]

14. Rotten Gut HVS 5a 45m
The yellow faultline is not as disgusting as it looks (which is a good job really). Start directly beneath the fault and climb the groove by its right wall to reach the overhang. Step right then move back into the fault above the overhang. Follow the deteriorating yellow gunge to the top. [1967]

Easter Island Gully South • **Easter Island Gully** 169

▶ **15. Catalogue Man's Big Adventure E3 5c** 33m
Essentially a left hand finish to *Rotten Gut*. Climb up *Rotten Gut* to the overhang then break left and make a gnarly move over a roof. Continue on suspect rock for 7m and step left before a wall of green lichen. Finish up *Fluke*.
[M Smith, R Saunders 21.05.94]

▶ **16. Crossover VS 4c** 50m
Start beneath the corner right of *Rotten Gut*.
P1 4b 15m Climb the corner to belay on a good ledge on *Big Gut*.
P2 4c 10m Take the crack in the right wall, then the shallow groove which leads back into the main corner, to belay as for *Big Gut*.
P3 4b 25m Climb steeply up the slab on the right of a thin crack in the right wall, then take the groove and a flake on the right to finish.
[J Brown, P Crew 22.01.67]

▶ **17. Rock Island Line HVS 5a** 45m
This climb takes the obvious arête between *Crossover* and *Big Gut*. Start at the foot of *Crossover*.
P1 5a 23m Go right and climb the fine open arête to a ledge, then take the short corner crack, as for *Big Gut*, to the ledge.
P2 5a 22m Take the thin flake crack in the wall left of *Big Gut* until an easier wide crack leads to the top.
[J Moran, A Evans 13.05.78]

▶ **18. Big Gut VS 4c** 52m
A varied and interesting climb, reasonable for its grade. Start at the base of the last corner groove where the scrambling sea level traverse ends.
P1 4c 15m Ascend the corner/groove to a ledge.
P2 10m Amble up the broken corner on the left to another ledge.
P3 4c 27m The slabby groove leads to a small ledge; continue up the broken corner to the top.
[J Brown, D Alcock 08.01.67]

▶ **19. Boil All Irishmen E5 6b** 60m
This again follows the wall to the right of *Big Gut*, starting as for that route.
P1 6b 30m Climb the wall left of *Hombre*, by 2 thin seams, to reach a dubious hold on the left at 25m. Span right and move up to a sloping ledge and belay.
P2 4c 30m Step left and follow the groove, on its right side, aiming for a crack and finish up this.
[C Smith, M E Crook 06.86]

▶ **20. Hombre E1 5b** *** 47m
A superb and well protected classic.
P1 5b 15m Start in the obvious corner groove (*Big Gut*), just before the cliff juts out runs steeply straight into the sea. From a few metres up the corner groove a line of quartz holds leads out right to the arête. A small groove leads steeply to a belay ledge on the right.
P2 5b 26m Climb the groove, then finish up the steep crack above.
P3 6m A straightforward saunter up the wide cracks leads to the top. A roped scramble above follows.
[J Brown, I G MacNaught Davis (1 pt) 14.05.67]

21. Lost In Space E4 6a 50m
The wall right of *Hombre* yields a worthwhile route.
P1 5c 15m From the base of the obvious corner groove (*Big Gut*), drop down a metre or so and traverse right round the arête onto the front of the buttress. Move up and right to a flake before descending rightwards to a stance below the steep wall.
P2 6a 20m Traverse back out left for a few metres and climb up the shallow crack system to the right of the blunt arête guarding *Hombre*. At the top of the blunt arête trend up rightwards around the rib and onto the lichenous hanging slab. Move up to belay in the corner.
P3 4b 15m Continue up leftwards to a ledge, finishing up wide cracks above.
[M Turner, L Thomas 1990s]

22. This Year's Model E3 5c ** 50m
An excellent route taking the leaning wall right of the arête of *Big Gut*.
P1 5c 15m From the base of the obvious corner groove (*Big Gut*), drop down a metre or so and traverse right round the arête onto the front of the buttress. Move up and right to a flake before descending rightwards to a stance below the steep wall.
P2 5c 15m Bear back left to ascend a shallow steep crack/groove, then following a line of holds rightwards across the steep wall to gain a belay at the base of a ramp.
P3 5a 20m Finish directly up the crack.
[J Moran, P Jewell 13.06.78]

23. Praetor E1 5c 57m
Another committing proposition, again with one tricky move at the start. Start as for *This Year's Model*.
P1 5c 15m As for *This Year's Model* P1.
P2 5a 21m Gain the shallow chimney and follow this and the crack above to a peg belay.
P3 5a 21m Continue, following the obvious line to the top.
[J Brown, I G MacNaught-Davis (1 pt) 14.05.67]

24. Swastika E1 5c * 62m
A roving, but strangely satisfying excursion. Start as for *Big Gut*.
P1 5c 15m As for *This Year's Model* P1.
P2 5a 10m Move out right from the base of the chimney (*Praetor*) and climb to a flake. Continue up rightwards to a ledge.
P3 5a 15m Climb straight up, then slightly right to a ledge on the arête, then up again to another ledge. From its left end pull decisively over a bulge and trend leftwards to belay in the groove (*Praetor*).
P4 5a 22m Traverse left for 3m and move onto a small slab. Ascend the 2nd steep crack to the left, stepping right to finish up a short corner.
[L E Holliwell, L R Holliwell 17.05.69]

Easter Island Gully North

These climbs are all to the north of the *Supercrack* abseil and extend to Wen Zawn. The routes are described right to left (facing in) from the abseil.

▶ **25. Sex Lobster E3 5c *** 30m
This takes the arête left of *Supercrack*, starting directly below it.
Climb up past a peg to reach large pockets. Go left around the arête (possible belay to the left) and gain the steep slab above. Climb up to the overlap and move right round the arete to gain a fine hairy crack in the wall left of *Supercrack*. Follow the crack to the top.
[C Smith, M E Crook 07.86]

The next 2 routes take the steep front face of the buttress left of *Sex Lobster*.

▶ **26. Belial HVS 5a *** 30m
A good route with a steep finish. Start below the overhanging groove on a platform. Gain the groove and climb it until it steepens. Strenuous and spacey moves lead to easier ground and the abseil point.
[P Crew, A Alveraz 05.02.67]

▶ Variation: **Belial Direct HVS 5a**
A better start, especially if a sea is running or the tide encroaching. Climb the crack just left of *Sex Lobster* to gain the groove of the original route.
[A. Boorman, P. Bailey 21.12.98]

▶ **27. Pequod E3 5c *** 30m
A deceptive route, which climbs the steep crack in the scooped wall left of *Belial*. Start just right of the left hand arête of the buttress. Climb the wall to reach the flake crack and follow this to the bulge. Continue rightwards up the ever-steepening crack to reach easier climbing and the abseil point.
[J Moran, A Evans 23.04.78]

▶ **28. Drag E1 5b *** 30m
A fine climb, but care is needed to avoid one's ropes realising the route's name. Start as for *Pequod* and ascend the short wall until undercuts lead left round the arête. Follow the crack leftwards to easier ground and the abseil point.
[L E Holliwell, L R Holliwell (1pt) 07.12.68]

▶ **29. Vicious Fish E3 6a *** 30m
Good steep climbing up the arête. Start just left of the arête and climb the pillar stepping right to the undercut crack. Launch up the arête initially on its right side, following it to the abseil point.
[C Waddy, P Pritchard 06.05.88]

▶ **30. Neutrino E4 6a/b** 30m
This bouldery little test piece is hard and initially lacking in useful protection. Climb the thin crack to the left of the arête to join and finish up *Drag*.
[A P Rouse, B Hall 1976]

▶ **31. Exit Chimney VS 4c** 30m
This route follows the obvious slabby chimney in the rear right-hand corner of the zawn, on rock that leaves a little to be desired. It is the easiest way out of the area. Start by a short scramble up to the foot of the chimney, then follow the slab to the overhang and move right to easy ground, which leads to the abseil point. [P Crew, B Ingle 14.07.68]

Easter Island Gully • Easter Island Gully North

The remaining routes finish on steep grass. Ascend with care, heading diagonally up and right to reach the descent above the Easter Island pinnacle.

▶ **32. The Real Keel E5 6b** 23m
The hanging prow to the right of *Annihilator* is serious for the grade. Start up *Exit Chimney*, and from 6m up it make an obvious traverse to gain the keel. Climb up it, peg, to a rest on a plinth, before taking the wall direct past 2 portholes to a big spike, belay. Abseil off, or scramble up to the top.
[P Pritchard, C Waddy 06.05.88]

▶ **33. Annihilator E5 6a** ** 30m
Classic, steep, well protected, but uncompromising climbing up the leaning wall left of *Exit Chimney*. Scramble up to start on a good ledge on *Exit Chimney*. Step left across onto the hanging wall. Move left around the bulge into the groove. Struggle up this to a nestling place at the base of a wide cracked groove with a steep wall to its right. Tricky moves up the right wall precede a step left to be made back to the groove. Easier but still unnerving ground leads to a belay well back.
[A Sharp, S Humphries (1pt) 08.03.75, FFA: S Haston, S Andrews 1986]

▶ **34. For Madmen Only E6 6b** * 30m
A pumpy, strenuous beast, thankfully with good protection. Follow *Annihilator* to the nestling place, and swing wildly left into a flake line. Layback heading for a keel, then make a hard move onto on a sloping ledge, and finish just left of *Annihilator*. Old bolt belay.
[C Smith 06.86]

▶ **35. Ormuzd E4 6a** *** 33m
A fantastic character building exercise, tackling the daunting cleft. A couple of large cams may be found to be useful.
P1 5b 18m Start from a small ledge below the steep wall left of the chimney. Ascend the left side of the wall for a few moves then traverse right into a shallow groove. Move up this a little way before slipping into the chimney on the right above the lower overhang. Continue up to a good stance. Watch out for the hidden cavern on this pitch.
P2 6a 15m Continue up the chimney then bridge out across the roof, eventually moving out on to the front face and finishing up the wide crack.
[J Brown, G Birtles, P Crew (1 pt) 04.02.67]

▶ **36. The Red Sofa E5 6b** * 37m
A fine route with interesting climbing on good rock. Start as for *Ormuzd*, and climb up the continuation groove left of the chimney of *Ormuzd*, until a difficult traverse left gains a hand-and-finger crack. Finish into a flake line, and then go out left to a crack on the arête. This leads to the top.
[J Dawes, N Craine 28.04.87]

▶ **37. The Ancient Mariner E5 6b** * 37m
Climbs the wall and hanging groove between *Ormuzd* and *Ahriman*.
P1 5c 15m Climb up the wall then boldly traverse leftwards, past an old wire, to gain the arête. Move left again to the belay on *Ahriman*.
P2 6b 22m Climb up the left side of the arête until difficult moves lead into the groove. A pocket near the top of the left arête provide a welcome exit onto a ledge. Finish up the groove above. [M E Crook, J Silvester 26.06.86]

Wen Zawn
Exit line from top of routes
Abseil scramble/approach
Easter Island Gully South
47
46
45
41
44
40
39
39
38
37
36
35
34
33
32
28
27
26
25
6
8
9

Several metres to the left is an arête:

38. Ahriman HVS 5a * 35m
Worthwhile climbing starting to the left of the arete below a crack in the scooped wall.
P1 5a 15m Climb the wall, keeping left of the crack, until holds lead right round the arête to a belay ledge beneath the groove.
P2 5a 20m Follow the bulging groove to the top.
[J Brown, P Crew 22.01.67]

39. Gazebo HVS 5a * 30m
A good companion route to *Ahriman*. Start as for *Ahriman*, below the diagonal crack and follow it for 8m (leftwards) before moving right to a spike. Gain the bottomless groove above and follow it to a short corner. Go up again to a ledge below a second corner, swing left onto the wall and finish up this.
[L E Holliwell, L R Holliwell, D Mossman 01.12.68]

40. Tumbling Dice E3 6a * 30m
A good steep pitch. Start as for *Gazebo*. Follow the crack until holds lead up right to the small overhang in the middle of the wall. Surmount this on the right with difficulty and after a further move up left, head up right to a flake. Move left and climb the steep open corner, finishing up a final short corner/crack.
[J Moran, G Milburn 29.04.78]

41. Perpendicular VS 4b 33m
A contrived but reasonably interesting route, starting as for *Gazebo*.
P1 4b 15m Follow the crack until it is possible to move left to a ledge on the arête.
P2 4b 18m Go left into the groove on *Diagonal*, and then take the obvious flake crack out across the left wall and finish straight up.
[A Evans, J Moran 23.04.78]

42. An Unimportant Wave E4 6b 30m
This takes the overhanging wall, and crackline, left of *Perpendicular*.
[J Dawes 22.05.88]

43. Belvedere E2 5c * 30m
This route follows the obvious arête left of *Perpendicular*, starting at its base. P1 is technical, whilst P2 is fairly bold.
P1 5c 15m Climb the arête, using the thin crack on its left-hand side, to a good ledge and belay (rusty peg).
P2 5b 15m Climb the groove above to finish up a crack in the arête.
[J Brown, F Corner, D Jones (1pt) 02.01.78]

44. Diagonal VS 4c 30m
Confusingly this doesn't take the obvious diagonal break at the left side of the cliff. Instead, start beneath the shallow groove left of *Belvedere*, and climb it, finishing up the wall on the right near the top.
[J Brown, D Alcock 08.01.67]

The Easter Island Pinnacle, in full view from the abseil approach photo: Al Leary >

Easter Island Gully North • **Easter Island Gully** 175

43. Diatom VS 4c 25m
Start as for *Diagonal*. Climb the groove of *Diagonal* for 6m then take the lower line of holds leading diagonally left to the arête. Climb the arête on its right side to join and finish up the last few moves of *Perpendicular*.
[A Evans, J Moran 23.04.78]

44. Micron HVS 5a 25m
This follows the diagonal crack left of the groove of *Diagonal*, and gives a short section of strenuous climbing. Start as for *Diagonal*, taking the awkward wide crack up leftwards to reach easier ground and the top.
[1976]

45. Microdot HVS 5a 25m
Climb the slab left of *Micron* to reach a short steep crack. The challenge is to use it to gain the ledge and upper crack with style. Finish up a short easy corner.
[J Moran, G Milburn 29.04.78]

A Dream of White Horses, Gogarth
For Boz & Chris

I'd wanted the line of this legend
for so long. Near any sea (in Cornwall,
or maybe in Greece, or perhaps Corsica)

if I thought of it hooves drummed
in me – galloped a lather or just cantered
prickly across my palms:

from the sea-horizon beasts snorting white
came at me with my fears; crashed
into the coast of my imagining being
on Drummond's climb. The thought

of Hard Very Severe quartzite
hundreds of feet above sea made

brine seep
from my fingers.

Years on in mist, smoothly
and at peace, up early for low tide, no longer
apprentice to longings, I enjoyed

the Dream's sweet hints of terror;
the sun's hung ball faint in cloud;
sea-wind gently tampering with my balance;
a seal's & guillemots' natural nonchalance;
the fog-signal's gentle melancholic bleep;

the brilliant shatter of water when sun
momentarily broke through –
Wen Zawn's narrow vastness dim then
lit then dim again;

the crazed bone-white slab a tilted
land, a tilted life, a tilted
remembrance. Crisp

moments to cling to. One

long surge of white excitement. Then the crash

afterwards of tiredness; the boil
of some sort of voyage done, lying
next to the tent on grass in the sun.

The wet stable of the heart occupied
by a shimmering liquid beast

galloped & ready for sleep.

by Mark Goodwin

The final pitch of **A Dream of White Horses** HVS 5a photo: Gill Lovick

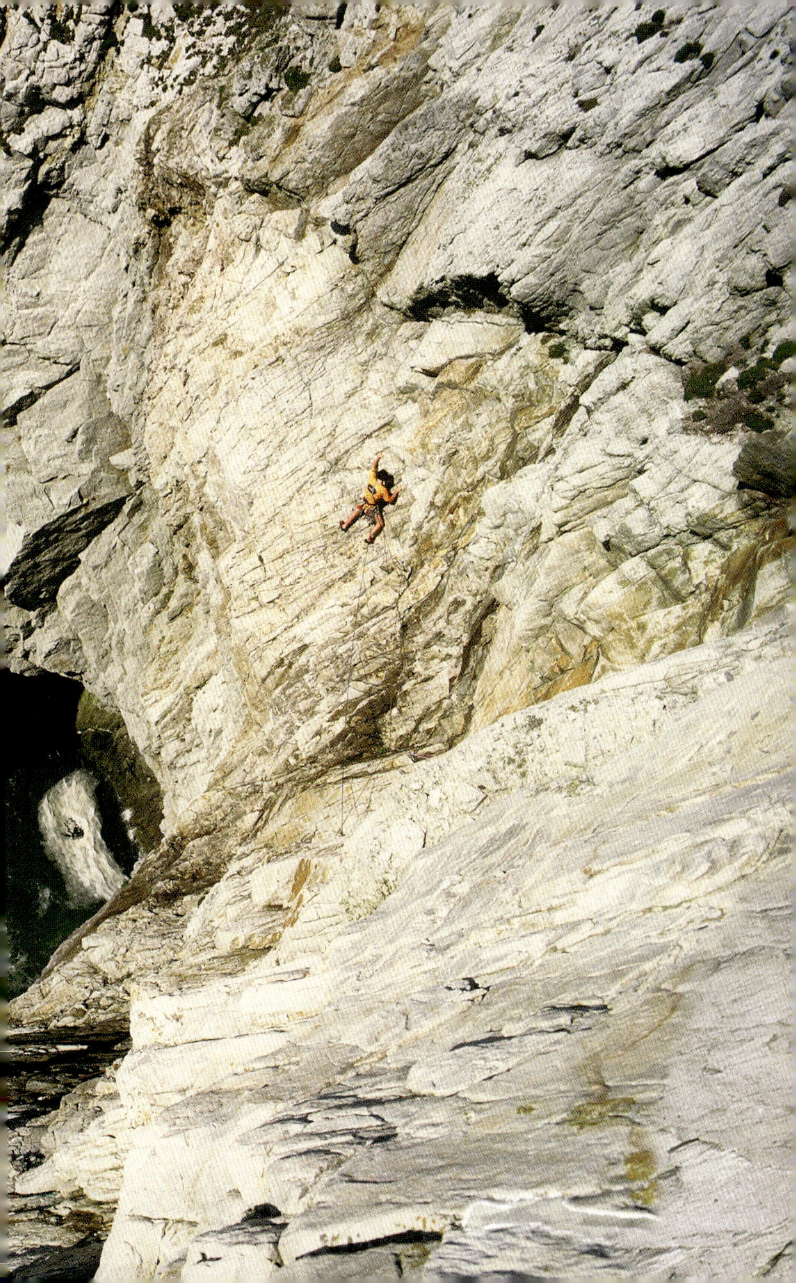

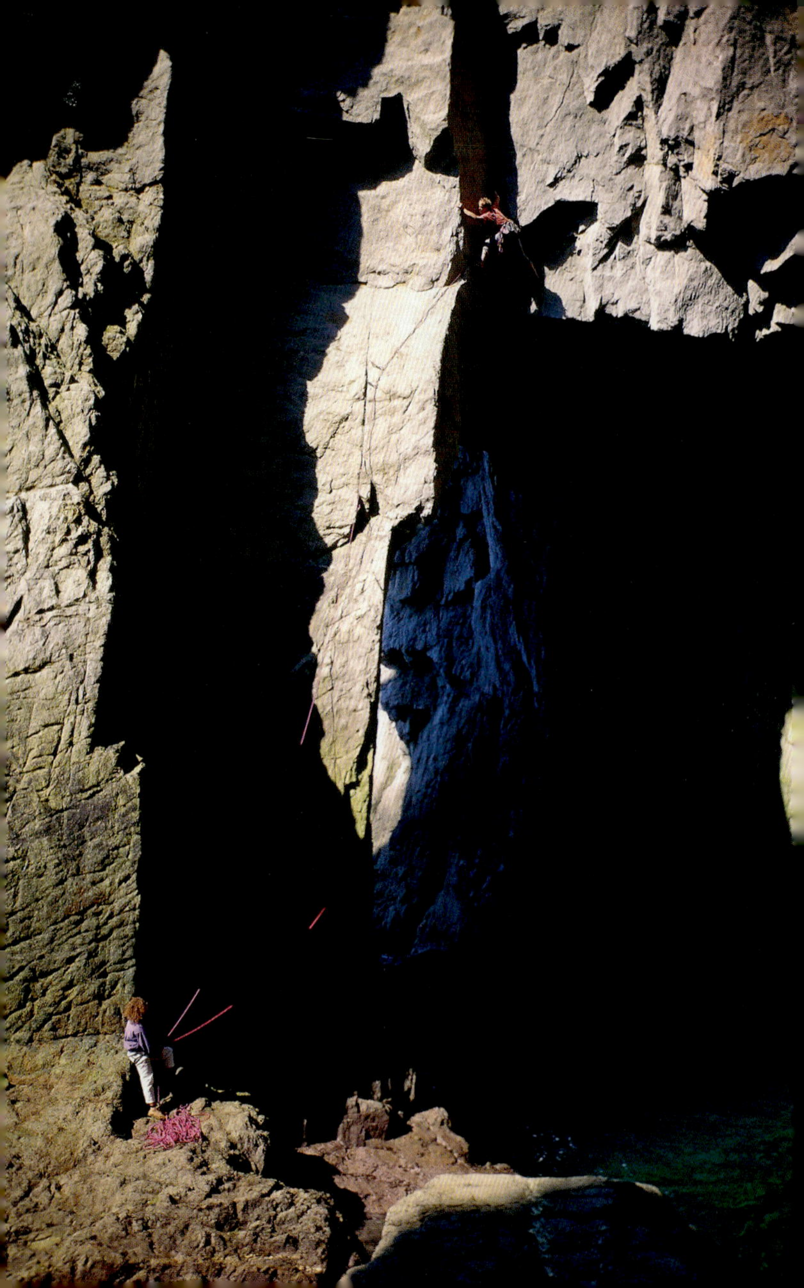

Hardback Thesaurus	E7
Heinous Flytrap	E7
The Wild Underdog	E7
The Mad Brown	E7
The 4th Dimension	E7
The Collection Plate	E7
The Undertaker	E7
The Unrideable Donkey	E7
Rubble	E7
Bar Fly	E6/7
(It's a) Broad Church	E6/7
Mister Softy	E6
Billy Bud	E6
Conan the Librarian	E6
Games Climbers Play, Original Start	E6

The Boston Struggler	E5
Spider's Web	E5
Instant Van Goch	E5
Evidently Chickentown	E5
Forgery	E5
Metal Guru/ The Golden Bough Finish	E4
T. Rex	E3
Dislocation Dance	E3
Gobbler's Arête	E3
The Tail	E3

The Quartz Icicle	E2
Genuflex	E2
Toiler on the Sea	E2
Zeus	E2
Vend-T	E2
Blow Out	E2
Echo Beach	E2
Archway	E2
The Bluebottle	E2
Spider Wall	E1
The Concrete Chimney	HVS
The Trap	HVS
A Dream of White Horses	HVS
Sprung	HVS
Wen	HVS
Flooze	HVS
Dde	HVS
Britomartis	HVS
Mr Seal	HVS
Maverick	VS

Wen Zawn

Area: North Stack
Style: Trad (1-5 pitches)
Aspect: Varied
Rock type: Quartzite
Approach: 20 minutes
Altitude: Sea level – tidal
OS ref: 215 837

Wen Zawn is one of the key sections of Gogarth, with classic challenges both old and new. Its most famous route, *A Dream of White Horses*, which strikes a sweeping line up and across the huge Wen Slab, is a much photographed and celebrated adventure. This brilliant and ingenious route has captured the hearts of climbers for generations. Wen Zawn is also home to some of the most outrageous sea cliff routes in Britain. During the late '80s and early '90s the impending back wall of the zawn and the steep underside of the arch provided a radical playground for a new breed of Gogarth activists, namely Johnny Dawes, Craig Smith, George Smith, Crispin Waddy, Adam Wainwright, Steve Mayers, Paul Pritchard, Noel Craine, Leigh McGinley and Nick Dixon. The fruit of their labours over this 10 year period is a series of mind-blowing and imaginative routes.

Throughout the zawn the rock quality is generally good, but the final sections of all routes, and most of the back wall, fall into the 'loose and challenging' category.

George Smith and Adam Wainwright on **Conan The Librarian** E6 6b, quite possibly the best route in Britain photo: Dave Kendall

180 Wen Zawn

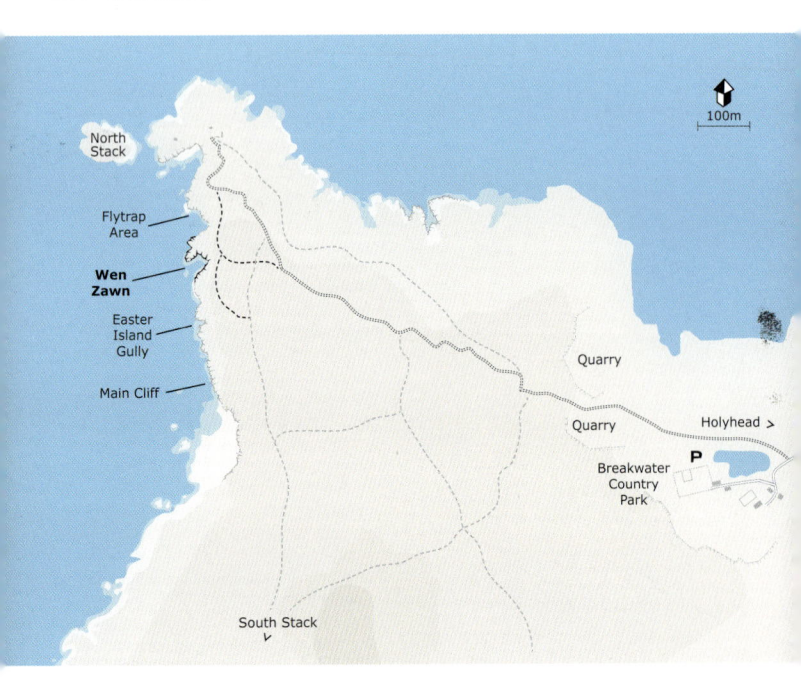

- North Stack
- Flytrap Area
- **Wen Zawn**
- Easter Island Gully
- Main Cliff
- South Stack
- Quarry
- Quarry
- Holyhead >
- Breakwater Country Park

Conditions: The crag is mostly northwest facing and does dry quickly once the afternoon sun swings around and burns the moisture off. Damp soapy rock is common on the first pitches of many of the routes. This is always worth bearing in mind, for example the chimney/layback on P1 of *T. Rex* can be very traumatic if at all wet. For routes starting at the bottom of the zawn a low tide and a calm sea are essential. The zawn is also particularly vulnerable to the high speed ferry wake, so make sure you have checked the times of the incoming ferry before you descend to sea level; see page ? for more details.

Approach: From the Breakwater Country Park car park gain the rough Landrover track 50m to the north of the small lake. Follow this for 750m up the hill and then down the other side to where the overhead electricity poles cross the track (Pole No. 8168 18). 50m to the left are two cols/dips beyond the Coastal Path on the skyline. The more pronounced one to the right marks the start of the descent into Wen Zawn. A path leads down from the col to the promontory under which *Spider's Web* arch runs. The vast Wen Slab, which defines the right side of the zawn, can be viewed from this convenient grandstand position. For individual approaches to the different parts of the crag see the introductions for each of the sections.

Wen Slab • **Wen Zawn** 181

Mustang Wall

The Promontory

The Back Wall

Wen Slab

Wen Slab

This huge sheet of bleached rock presents an impressive front, its scale and apparent steepness overwhelming the first time visitor viewing it from the promontory. On closer inspection it soon dawns that the angle is in fact friendly and the distribution of holds quite accommodating. The climbing is bold in places, and the difficulties increase significantly at its undercut left edge as the menacing back wall of the zawn is reached.

Approach for routes 1-11: Follow a narrow path, which leads over the top of the slab, and scramble carefully down close to its edge to reach some blocks and an obvious abseil point on the right shoulder of the slab. (Please remember that any rocks dislodged from the approach path are likely to endanger teams already climbing on the slab below!) It is normal to start from a series of ledges approximately 20m above the sea and level with the belay at the top of *Wen* P1. If there is a low tide, the sea is calm and you have the urge, the first pitches can be accessed via a second abseil from the 'ledges'. Leave a belay, pull your ropes and collect the belay as you climb past later.

Approach for routes 12-29: Abseil from the top of the promontory down the *Uhuru* face immediately opposite Wen Slab. At low tide it is possible to skip across boulders at the base of the zawn to your chosen route. (N.B. It is only possible to reach the start of *Dream* via this approach at very low spring tides.)

Helen John negotiating the bend at the back of the zawn on P4 of **A Dream of White Horses** HVS 5a photo: Jethro Kiernan

Wen Slab • **Wen Zawn** 183

▶ **1. Hydrophobia HVS 5a** 45m
An alternative approach to the upper slabs of *Dde*. Start at sea level round the arête right of *Dde*, at the foot of a square-cut chimney. Climb the chimney and exit right at its top. Move left onto the right hand edge of Wen Slab then go up left into *Dde* up which the route finishes, belaying as required.
[C Jones, S Hoste, S Smith 10.81]

▶ **2. Dde HVS 5a** ∗ 105m
This enjoyable climb is low in its grade and a good alternative when the more popular routes are busy. It takes the right-hand side of Wen Slab, to finish via the obvious layback crack. At low/mid tide, start at sea level by a boulder, beneath a steep groove capped by an overhang. This is just right of the arete of the first pitch of *Dream*. At high water, start from the first stance of *Dream*.
P1 5a 45m Move right and climb a thin crack to a good ledge 5m short of the arête.
P1a 4c 35m Variation: From the first stance on *Wen* go right along easy flakes and ledges then climb a thin crack to a good spike. Move right and go up to the sentry box belay.
P2 4c 15m Climb the slab to a sentry box and a belay.
P3 5a 45m Follow flakes up to the left to below a small overhang where an awkward move up around the corner gains a groove, which is followed to finish with care onto the approach path.
[J Brown, B Sharp 13.05.66]

▶ **3. Monday Club Blues E1 5c** 65m
A well-protected and direct line. Follow the finger crack in the corner just right of *Dream*, up to the roof. Move left through the roof and then wander up the slab back to the abseil point, belaying as required.
(T O'Rourke, S Omebody 1990]

▶ **4. A Dream of White Horses HVS 5a** ∗∗∗ 150m
The classic Gogarth adventure, demanding similar levels of proficiency from all members of the team. Do make sure that all runners on the final pitch are properly extended; failure to do so will result in hideous rope drag and the possibility of key runners popping out! It is vital that both leader and second(s) are carrying prussik loops, as a fall from this pitch may leave the climber swinging in space. (N.B. It is common to start the route from the ledges near the top of P1.)
P1 5a 45m Start beneath a steep groove topped by a roof. Follow the left edge of the groove to ledges on *Wen*, mentioned above. Continue up to a spike, and then trend up right to a small corner.
P2 5a 25m A horizontal traverse line leads leftwards, past a difficult section, to a hanging belay in *Wen*.
P3 4c 35m Trace a line of flakes up left, passing a decent ledge at 15m. When the flakes run out, move across to good holds, then climb down and across a short broken chimney, to gain a belay ledge on *Concrete Chimney*.
P4 4c 45m Move out left and up to a roof. Traverse left beneath it and descend to make a nerve-wracking move around a rib to gain better holds. Climb up to some spikes then traverse left to reach the final slab. Cross it daintily and climb up a bottomless groove, exiting leftwards. Scramble carefully up left to finish. There is a block belay well back from the edge.
[E Drummond, D Pearce 18/19.08.68]

A variation start for *Dream* is possible. However it involves a dangerous scramble approach down the edge of the slab from the traditional abseil point to reach the notch in the arête:
P2b 5a 35m From the notch on the arête, climb down the groove and out onto the slab. Follow the traverse line leftwards across the slab, past the rusty pegs, to gain the crack of *Wen* after a couple of difficult moves. Hanging belay.

5. Echo Beach E2 5b * 80m
Interesting and bold climbing, traversing the upper part of Wen Slab from right to left (looking in). Start at the belay at the top of P1 of *Dream*.
P1 5b 40m Boldly follow the quartz band up and leftwards across *Zeus* to a hanging stance in *Wen*; protection good but well-spaced.
P2 5b 40m Go up left under a roof, then cross *High Pressure*, and continue leftwards to finish up the *Original Finish* to *The Quartz Icicle*.
[M Duff, T Dailey 1980]

6. If HVS 5a 62m
Another bold route taking the slab right of *Wen*, starting as for the variation start (P2b) of *Dream* at the notch on the arête. The exact relationship between *Echo Beach* and this route is not clear, and they may share a portion of the climbing.
P1 5a 40m Climb down the groove and across the traverse line for a little way, then follow quartz holds diagonally leftwards, into shallow scoops, to climb over the small roof on *Zeus* at the right side. Climb up a crack, then go right to belay in a small bay to the right of *Dde*.
P2 5a 22m Climb the cracks to a spectacular overhanging finish.
[E Drummond, B Whybrow, J Rogers 25.05.69]

7. Zeus E2 5b ** 85m
A good route, both bold and delicate for the grade, taking the slab between *Wen* and *Dde*. Start at sea level below a groove, immediately right of the chimney of *Wen*.
P1 5a 25m Move left onto the wall and go straight up to where it steepens. Move left to a small niche then move up and bear rightwards to good ledges just right of *Wen*.
P2 5b 45m Climb the line of cracks behind the stance to a bulge at 10m. Cross this rightwards, tricky, then go up to a junction with *Dream* at a rusty peg. Continue bearing up to the left for a further 10m until it is possible to move right, and then go up to a line of small roofs. Step right and pull through these at the widest point, then go straight up, to a poor stance and dubious peg beneath the final wall, junction with *Dde*.
P3 4b 15m Go up right and climb a friable thin crack to the top.
[L R Holliwell, L E Holliwell 05.09.70]

8. Wen HVS 5a ** 100m
The striking chimney/crack line, that splits the slab, provides a fine and historic route, albeit one that sensibly deviates away from the loose upper reaches of the fault line.
P1 5a 25m Ascend the chimney, moving through the 'hole' to continue up a shallow groove. Belay just right of the crack line on ledges.

P2 4c 40m Follow the crack to a hanging belay at its widest point.

P3 5a 35m Surmount the bulge on the left to gain a cracked corner leading up left. Make a tricky move left to a ledge, then follow it leftwards to belays on the back wall. (NB. The final section of the crack can be climbed direct, but be warned, it is loose – neither your second nor any other team is likely to thank you!)
[J Brown, M A Boysen 08.05.66]

9. High Pressure E4 6a 55m
An eliminate line wandering up the slab between *Wen* and *The Quartz Icicle*. Start from the good ledges at the top of *Wen* P1.

P1 5c 30m Follow *The Quartz Icicle* for 8m, and then step right and climb up past the left side of the small overlap, continuing straight up the pink slab above to belay on the decent ledge mentioned on P3 of *Dream*.

P2 5b 25m Follow the flakes for 3m then climb straight up to a prominent crack, and climb this to where it closes. Step right to a 2nd narrow crackline and follow this to an undercut section. Pass this to join the top ledge traverse on *Wen*, a couple of metres right of *The Quartz Icicle*, and belay as for that route.
[P Livesey, R Fawcett 19.07.76]

10. The Quartz Icicle E2 5b *** 87m
This stunning open route is both immaculate and classic.

P1 5a 25m As for P1 of *Wen*.

P2 5b 37m Climb up left to the start of the attractive diagonal quartz vein. Follow it past some thin moves just before it opens out into a crack. Continue to a belay in a broken chimney 6m right of *The Concrete Chimney*.

P3 5b 25m Trend diagonally rightwards through the *Dream* traverse, and then traverse right to gain a small curving groove. Go up this and pull out right to reach a thin diagonal crack on the right side of a smooth slab. Climb up leftwards and finish up a crack leading to the traverse at the top of *Wen*. Traverse leftwards to belays on the back wall.
[E Drummond, B Campbell-Kelly P1: 09.11.68, P2: 31.08.69]

Variation: **The Original Finish E2 5b** 25m

P2a From the belay go straight up then move left into a crack. This leads to a jutting overhang and a step left onto its lip. Carry on up the slab, move right and take the crack to the top. A slightly easier finish, that some may find less trying to locate.

11. The Concrete Chimney HVS 5a *** 95m
A contender for the best route on the slab, although the last pitch lets it down slightly. Combining P2 with the last pitches of *Dream* gives a real 'four star' trip.

P1 5a 25m As for P1 of *Wen*.

P2 5a 45m An obvious rising line leads leftwards to the arête overlooking the conglomerate-packed chimney. Move up the slab to a thin crack, and then ascend the wall on positive holds. Move left above the overhang and climb up the slab and short crack to belay in the chimney (as for *Dream*).

P3 5a 25m Trend up left across overlapping slabs to gain an overhanging groove. Go up the groove and exit right at its top join the final bulge of the chimney proper. Scramble up to gain the *Wen* belay on the back wall.
[P Crew, J Brown 12.02.67]

186 Wen Zawn • Wen Slab

▶ **12. Rubble E7 6a** * 83m
The 'concrete' chimney that *Concrete Chimney* manages to avoid is arguably the most obvious line at Gogarth. It also features perhaps the 'softest' and most challenging rock on the crag – you have been warned!
P1 6a 33m Super steep climbing leads out of the cave at the bottom on the very finest pebbledash conglomerate. Continue up with appalling protection, eventually making a left exit from the rubble to reach the belay at the end of *T. Rex* P1.
P2 6a 27m Follow *T. Rex* to the huge ceiling and go through the right end of this past the hanging flange of death (apparently a crucial RP #1) to join *Concrete Chimney* and belay.
P3 5a 23m Continue up the chimney in a sensational position.
[L McGinley, P Pritchard 10.91]

▶ **13. Games Climbers Play, Original Start E6 6b** ∗∗ 30m
A brave and very strenuous lead, which follows a streak of unusual bubbly rock left of *Rubble*. The initial moves are the hardest, with no gear and a horrible landing. The protection slowly improves as the climbing gets easier but the poor old arms have to fight hard to keep up. Belay as for *T. Rex*. This pitch formed the original aid climbing start to *Games Climbers Play*. The niche on P2 was reached via a long pendulum from the corner of *Metal Guru*.
[D Pearce, E Drummond (aid) 27.09.70, FFA: R Fawcett, G Kent 12.79]

14. Hardback Thesaurus E7 6b ✶✶ 30m
A fierce and historically important route. Climbed ground up, it set the ethical standard for all future routes in the zawn.

Climb the crack in the wall right of *T. Rex* to a crucial cam slot, move rightwards onto the wall, pulling on little 'stuck on' flakes. Then trend back leftwards above a vague bulge to reach the overlap. Arrange runners (small cams essential), then surmount the overlap before running it out up the twin right-slanting shallow cracks. A final hard move left reaches the sanctuary of the *T. Rex* traverse line.
[J Dawes, B Drury 15.05.88, after seven days of attempts!]

15. T. Rex E3 5c ✶✶✶ 115m
A brilliant route and a classic challenge, with an infamous layback sequence on P1.
P1 5c 40m Start 10m left of the rubble-jammed chimney. Wriggle up inside the flake (making use of the large cams you have remembered to bring), until forced to make a difficult and committing switch into a layback position on the outside. Head quickly up to a small overlap and 'thank god' runner. Continue up, a bit pumpy, but well protected, to reach an obvious juggy traverse line leading out right across the open wall to a stance on the slab.
P2 5b 35m Climb up left passing a short steep wall to a slab. Cracks lead up left to a large overhang. Climb down and move leftwards, awkwardly and blindly at first, until easier ground leads to a stance.
P3 4c 40m Climb up to, and then follow the traverse on the final pitch of *Dream*.
[E Drummond, L E Holliwell, D Pearce, J Rogers (2 pts) 08.06.69, FFA: P Littlejohn 1971]

Variation: The Original Finish E3 5b 35m
P1a Climb up to the traverse on *Dream* and move left along this a few metres, then take the steep groove above before stepping out right onto the wall. Follow a vague right-trending crack to a ledge in a niche. Poor rock leads to the top. Not as good as the *Dream* finish.

16. Metal Guru/The Golden Bough Finish E4 6a ✶✶ 65m
A superb, strenuous direct on *T. Rex*.
P1 6a 40m Start as for *T. Rex*, but continue directly up the corner with further interest, to join and follow the final section of P2.
P2 5c 25m Climb up to gain the traverse on the final pitch of *Dream*, then blast up the golden groove above, trending slightly left, and exiting right onto the finishing slab.
[S Long, C Parkin 13.08.89/E Drummond C Dale 1973]

The Back Wall

The huge steep wall at the back of the zawn is an extremely impressive and challenging place to climb, providing some of the finest adventures that can be found on British rock. The rock is a good deal less than perfect, and the routes are both hard and committing. A large rack is essential - two full sets of cams is ideal although one set and a good selection of long extenders will help stack the odds in your favour!

Approach: At mid/low tide it is possible to abseil from the top of the promontory down the *Uhuru* face immediately opposite Wen Slab. Skip across boulders at the base of the zawn to your chosen route.

▶ **17. Games Climbers Play E4 5c** (1 pt aid) 72m
A strenuous climb taking the obvious flake/groove system left of *T. Rex* although the rock in parts is dubious. The direct start has been combined with the original finish to provide the most logical route. Start in the groove just left of *T. Rex*.
P1 5c 20m Follow the groove to the overhang, and then pull over this to holds leading up left to a spike. Enter the groove above and step right to a small ledge and belay.
P2 5b 30m Climb steeply up the cracks on the left to reach an obvious niche. Carry on up, past the roof to a small rib, peg, and climb the steep wall above to a ramp which is followed leftwards to small ledges, pegs.
P3 5a 22m Use a sling for aid to gain the final slab on *Dream* and finish up this.
[D Pearce, E Drummond (via original aided start) 27.09.70/ P1: P Littlejohn, R Harrison (1 pt) 29.05.77]

▶ **18. (It's a) Broad Church E6/7 6b** ** 77m
An amazing adventure with hard struggling interspersed with loose rock and in situ gear. If the pegs look good, the route is safe and worth E6. Future generations may feel E7 more accurate.
P1 6a 17m Start at a groove left of the start of *Games Climbers Play*. Go up the groove to a bulge. Swing left and climb diagonally left to a peg belay.
P2 6b 12m Hard work allows progress up the groove directly above the belay, past a peg and a warthog, to a rest in a chimney. Reluctantly leave the rest, swinging right to a belay on *Games Climbers Play*.
P3 5c 33m Climb up over a bulge and continue up to eventually reach a belay on the slab above – *Dream* traverses across at this height.
P4 6a 15m Go up left and pull through a roof (just left of *The Golden Bough Finish*), and continue up to the top.
[N Dixon, N Craine 02.05.97]

▶ **19. The Collection Plate E7 6b** * 15m
A direct start to *Broad Church*. Start left of P1, and climb the wall to the roof. Traverse right and pull over into a shallow groove (peg); climb up to the *Broad Church* belay.
[N Dixon, N Craine 1997]

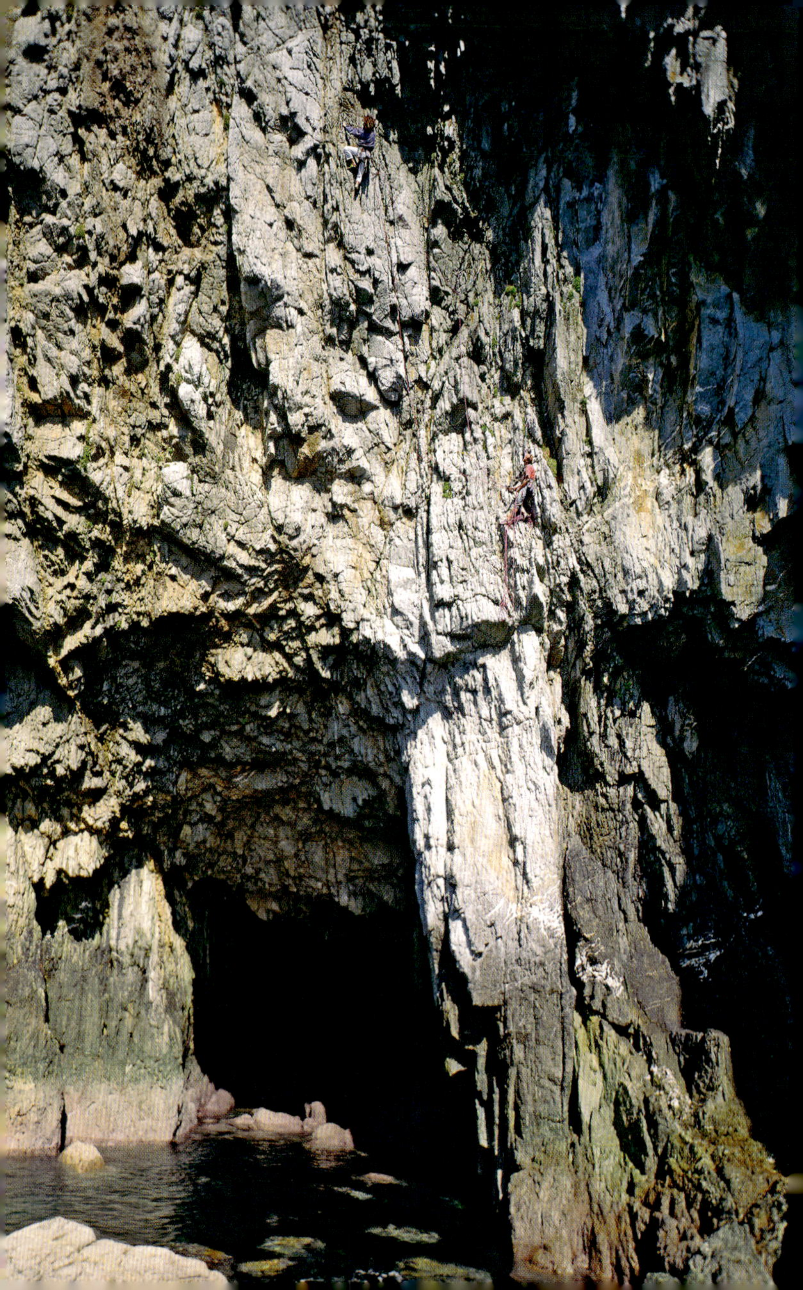

The Back Wall • **Wen Zawn**

20. Mister Softy E6 6b ✶✶✶ 80m
A 'once-in-a-lifetime' experience climbing the line of least resistance up the back wall of the zawn. Start at the base of the obvious pillar approximately 10m left of *T. Rex*.
P1 5b 15m Climb the pillar to a small overlap. Pull over this into a decomposing groove and follow this to a stance.
P2 6b 40m Move left into a groove (passing two old pegs) and climb up and right onto a hanging slab. Follow this to more old pegs and a rest. Commit to the wall above (ice stakes and a 'warthog') then move left with difficulty round an arete into a shallow groove. Follow this "where angels tread to fear" to join *The Janitor Finish*. Traverse right to easier ground and a semi hanging belay (old in situ thread).
P3 6a 25m A much more solid 'normal' pitch (worth E5). Climb the obvious crackline and groove up and rightwards to a deep slot. Traverse blindly leftwards to a short hanging groove. Struggle up this strenuously and exit rightwards at the top onto the *Dream* slab and finish leftwards along this.
[G Smith, A Wainwright 30.08.94]

21. The Mad Brown E7 6b ✶✶ 80m
A fabulous expedition up the looseness left of *Mister Softy*. None of the pitches is excessively serious or difficult, but the cumulative effect is fairly debilitating. Be aware that failure on the crux needs a low spring tide to escape from whilst staying dry.
P1 6a/b 20m Climb the initial pillar of *Mister Softy* to a large fin. Swing round left and cross the wall on good holds to gain a straight crack leading to a roof. Surmount this to gain a wide crack and good resting holds. Traverse left across the hanging slab with difficulty and enter the huge hole. Belay on in situ 'warthogs' and a #4 cam.
P2 6b 35m Move left past a suitcase-shaped 'thread' block. Good holds lead up and left to the base of a steep brown crack - the 'mad brown' itself. Climb this (pegs and good cams) until difficult moves lead left round the arete and into a shallow groove. Follow this to the *Conan* traverse (possible poor belay). Follow the *Conan* traverse to belay on the in situ thread, as for *Mister Softy*.
P3 6a 25m Follow the top pitch of *Mister Softy* for 7m, up the wide-open groove to a good spike and arrange protection. Step down and swing left round a fin to gain diagonal cracks. Go up to an obvious hand jam and left into a niche, peg runners. Exit the niche, left to attain a sloping boss. Cross the headwall leftwards for 5m to better holds in the mosaic choss. Go straight up the shallow groove on obscure holds to the roof. Surmount this in a position of sensational rope drag.
[G Smith, A Wainwright 07.96]

< Adam Wainwright and George Smith crossing the crux wall of **Mister Softy** E6 6b, and about to enter the groove "where angels tread to fear" photo: Dave Kendall

Wen Zawn • The Back Wall

To the left of the back wall of the zawn is a huge natural arch. The next route takes an amazing left-to-right sweeping line across this.

▶ **22. Conan the Librarian E6 6b** ✶✶✶✶ 95m
A stunning adventure tracing a compelling line. Difficult climbing combined with some friable rock makes this a route for a strong team. Start at the foot of the obvious open corner at the base of the arch. (Accessible at all but high tide.)
P1 6b 28m Climb the crack, just right of the corner, diagonally up right, then use this and the arête until the hanging corner on the right, peg at base, can be gained. Climb this with difficulty, on perfect rock, to a peg. Traverse right and go up to a hanging stance left of the groove. (Small but good cams.)
P2 6a 15m Climb the friable groove passing numerous pegs to a semi-hanging belay on blocks.
P3 5b 30m **The Janitor Finish**: Follow the obvious traverse line rightwards across the back wall of the zawn, passing in situ pegs and 'warthogs', crossing *The Mad Brown* and *Mister Softy* to join *T. Rex*.
P4 5c 22m **The Golden Bough Finish** beckons. If your arms are unwilling, then escape along *Dream*.
[J Dawes, C Smith 08.86]

Variation: **P2a E7 6b** 36m The original 2nd pitch was climbed by finishing up leftwards from the top of the groove with an aid peg. This was subsequently climbed free, but with a slightly leftwards finish to avoid an area of rockfall. If you wish to repeat this it is probably best to utilise the stance on *The Unrideable Donkey*, which has now been cleaned up.
[J Dawes, S Donahue (1pt) 1986, but prior to the ascent of the 'normal' way/FFA: S Mayers, M Tompkins 1992]

▶ **23. The Undertaker E7 6c** ✶✶ 30m
A direct start to *Conan the Librarian*, starting 7m around to the right of the original, under the arch. Belay on a ledge, accessible approximately 2 hours after high tide. It takes the obvious wide crack until a swing left on a spike can be made to a peg, which can be backed up by RPs. Swing out wildly across the roof to gain the base of the *Conan* groove and continue as for that route.
[S Mayers, G Farquhar 1992]

▶ **24. The Unrideable Donkey E7 6b** ✶ 60m
A stubborn little number, taking the huge corner groove just left of *Conan The Librarian*, with some desperate climbing and a portion of suspect rock thrown in for good measure. Start at the base of the groove in a sort of cave area.
P1 6b 38m Climb up into the groove proper and follow it, and the slab, to the overhangs. Desperate moves past 3 pegs, poor, gains a niche and a rest on the left. Move back to the lip of the 2nd roof and climb the groove again to a 'warthog' peg below the 3rd roof, before exiting left to a rubble-covered ledge and belay. (RPs are useful)
P2 5c 22m Climb right of the belay until diagonal progress can be made to the base of a hanging groove, where the 2 walls of the zawn meet. Finish up the talc groove in a fine position. A serious pitch, part of which fell into the sea some time after the first ascent, although not apparently affecting the climbing!
[P Pritchard, N Dixon 12.07.87]

The following 2 routes appear to share much common ground, and their relationship is not totally clear.

25. Igdrazil E2 5c 53m
This follows the steep wall opposite Wen Slab, crossing *Uhuru* at half-height, and starts at a group of isolated pinnacles at the base of the wall.
P1 5c 28m Head up rightwards towards a cave then go straight up a groove for 6m. Go left then up the wall, peg, and then trend up leftwards to a ledge and peg belay, (shared with *Uhuru*).
P2 5b 25m Work left a few moves, then climb a short groove and ramp back up right until above the belay, and continue straight up the wall passing a peg halfway to the top.
[L E Holliwell, L R Holliwell (1 pt) 18.05.69]

26. Broken Mirror E3 5c 45m
Serious climbing up the middle of the *Uhuru* wall, starting at a ledge at the centre of the base of the wall.
P1 5c 25m Climb cracks bearing slightly rightwards to a ledge on the right after 10m, step left and climb up to a peg belay, (shared with *Uhuru*).
P2 5c 20m The obvious crack leads directly to a ramp. Cross this then climb thin cracks to the top.
[R Fawcett, P Livesey 19.07.76]

27. Uhuru E1 5a 60m
The climbing is well positioned, but marred by a loose and serious top pitch. Start at a small stance, with a big flake, about 6m above the boulders.
P1 5a 30m Move right and climb diagonally, as the line dictates, to gain a small ledge on the right. Move up, then go back left to regain the slanting line and follow this to a stance with peg belays.
P2 4c 30m On the right is a shorter corner. Ascend this, exiting left to climb the loose groove, moving left just below the top.
[D E Alcock, G Rogan 12.02.67]

28. Boogie Woogie VS 4b 45m
Start right of *Thor*. Climb the sharply defined rib, and the overhanging flakes above.
[C J Phillips, M Wallis 08.08.88]

29. Thor VS 4c 56m
This route takes the slanting diagonal break on the left-hand side of the wall, and starts from the nose to the right of *The Trap*, or from the bottom of the chimney. The top pitch has some loose rock.
P1 4c 28m Go around the arête on the right to the start of the wide chimney. Climb this to a small cave, then take the steep crack on the right, and go up a short chimney through the overhang to a stance and peg belay.
P2 4b 28m The obvious crackline, trending rightwards, leads to the top.
[J Brown, P Crew 06.01.67]

The Cryptic Rift

The next 6 routes explore the atmospheric wonders of the hidden cleft behind *Thor*. The rift is a great place to find shelter from the sun on those blazing hot days.

Approach: To reach the start of the routes bridge into the rift behind *Thor* for 10m, to a sloping ledge on the right (not high tide). Alternatively abseil down *Thor* until a boulder choke leads into the depths of the rift. Then abseil again to the same tidal, sloping ledge (using the end of the same rope).

30. The Escapegoat E1 5b 15m
Start at the near end of the ledge, and chimney up until forced deeper into the rift. Continue up to the boulder choke. Scramble off.
[C Waddy, J Dawes 29.07.87]

31. Agrophobia E4 5c 60m
Interesting positions on this route, which samples the atmosphere of the rift.
P1 5c 15m Climb the strenuous leftward-slanting crack to gain a block, lunge out right to hidden leftward slanting flakes and follow these to a hanging belay.
P2 4c 9m Traverse right then bridge across the zawn top to a boulder choke and belay.
P3 5c 18m Climb the wall on the right, initially hard and serious, to a thread. Continue easily straight up the crack and belay below an overhang.
P4 5b 18m Go round right up blocks to the top.
[C Waddy, C Malem 29.05.86]

32. Dislocation Dance E3 5c ** 27m
Great climbing, starting as for *Agrophobia*.
P1 5c 18m From the middle of the ledge at the base of the rift, step down to a square foothold, then cross the zawn, and climb easily up holes and flakes to a chimney formed by a huge thin flake. Climb up the back slab of this to a roof. Move around the right-hand side of this, and into the continuation. Step down and right to a foothold on the rib, and lean across the zawn using a down-pointing spike as a balance, to gain holds and swing wildly across and climb to a belay, as for *Agrophobia*.
P2 4c 9m As for *Agrophobia* P2. Scramble down to finish.
[C Waddy, D Holmes 26.07.86]

33. Evidently Chickentown E5 6b ** 35m
A brilliant, but tricky route with some amazing positions. Start as for *Agrophobia*, on the ledge in the zawn. Climb down from the inside end of the ledge and traverse at sea-level, to gain and cross a boulder-dam leftwards, only possible at lowish water. Climb diagonally outwards and up to gain a flake chimney, below *Dislocation Dance*, and climb this to the roof. Neck and foot, (this bit's wide!), rightwards and inwards until it is possible to layback around the roof to an apparent rest on an apparent slab! Step up left, outwards, and lean against the underside of a protruding slab behind. Swing up backwards and right, to gain a good rest in a huge niche. Step right, outwards, to gain the hanging stance as for *Agrophobia*.
[C Waddy, D Holmes 26.07.87]

The Cryptic Rift • **Wen Zawn**

▶ **34. The Wild Underdog E7 6b/c** ★★★ 30m
A remarkable route tackling the flake line right of *Evidently Chickentown*. Start up that route, following the chimney to the bulge at its crux. Step down and right for 3m to a ridiculous $1m^2$ slab on the arête. Grasp the huge flake and bar relentlessly into the hanging groove. Ascend this to a large thread in the roofs above and almost in the centre of the arch itself. Lower off.
[G Smith 07.96]

▶ **35. Instant Van Goch E5 6b** ★★ 23m
A delightful trip up the north-facing painted wall, underneath arch at the landward end of the Cryptic Rift. Magnificent varied climbing. From the 'dam' (low tide needed), step onto the wall and climb diagonally left on magnificent holds to a good rest. Venture up and right, past two pegs, to gain an enormous undercling. From this, lunge for the very dubious looking block and continue in the same line leftwards to a huge spike. Lower off.
[G Smith, J Harrison 1996]

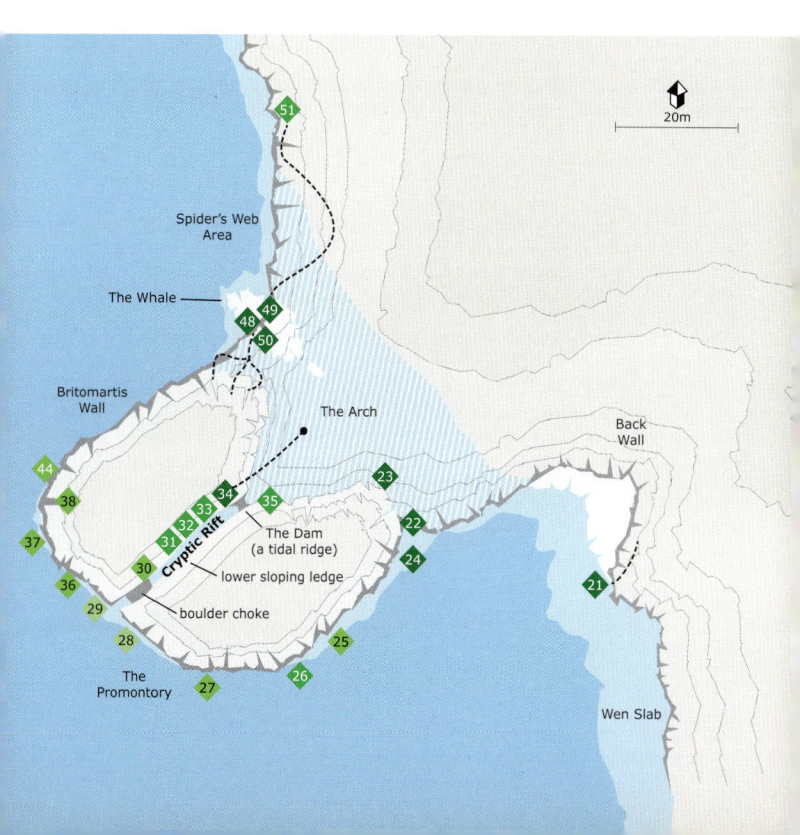

Britomartis Wall
The clean west facing side of the arch yields a range of excellent routes.

Approach: Abseil down the line of *The Trap* chimney on the seaward end of the promontory. For routes 48–50 see the abseil line on the topo and the description listed above the route descriptions.

36. Minute Man HVS 5a 50m
This follows the nose of the buttress between the clefts of *The Trap* and *Thor*. Start at the base of a groove in the front of the buttress.
P1 4b 25m The groove leads to a large ledge with peg belays.
P2 5a 25m Go right and up to an overhang. Traverse right below this to gain a chimney, which is followed a little way before stepping onto the right wall and going up to the top.
[L E Holliwell, L R Holliwell, J Rogers 25.08.70]

37. Sprung HVS 5b * 45m
Start beneath the arête, right of the start of *The Trap*.
P1 5b 25m Climb the steep wall, keeping just left of the arête and move right near the top to the good stance on *Minute Man*.
P2 5a 20m Climb the groove of *Minute Man* to the overhang. Move left, surmount the overhang and finish up the arête on the right.
[D Howard Jones, J Brown 19.10.78]

38. The Trap HVS 4c ** 40m
A route with a great line and much character, and one that has caused more than a few epics. This is the left-hand of the 2 chimneys on the end of the promontory, down which the abseil approach is made. Larger frame climbers may find the final squeeze on P1 to be nigh on impossible.
P1 4c 25m Enter the chimney and levitate up to the overhang before tackling the narrow vice above. Thankfully gain the wider section above and move left to a good belay ledge.
P2 4a 15m Climb up the shattered groove on the right. Finish up the final wide cleft.
[D E Alcock, G Rogan 04.02.67]

39. Friday's Extendable Arms E2 5c 30m
An exciting alternative entry onto the *Britomartis* wall. Start in the base of *The Trap*.
P1 5c 30m Move left to a hold on the left arête and continue steeply on good holds to the ledge (joining *Gobbler's Arête*). Continue up to the 2nd diagonal ledge and move left around the arête to find an immaculate hand traverse leading across the face to join *Britomartis* about halfway up P1. Continue up this to the belay.
P2 5b 25m P2 of *Toiler on the Sea* to finish.
[N Arding, D Pearce 10.10.03]

40. Star of the Sea E2 5c 40m
This route follows the outside of the chimney of *The Trap*.
P1 5c 25m Climb the outside of the chimney and crack moving left to the large sloping belay ledge.
P2 5a 15m Take the groove on the left to join and finish up the final few moves of *Britomartis*. [D Durkan, S Omebody (1 pt) 01.11.70]

Britomartis Wall • **Wen Zawn** 197

41. Gobbler's Arête E3 6a 40m
Follows the wall and arête left of *The Trap*. Start just left of *The Trap*.
P1 6a 25m Gain a diagonal ramp on the wall from the left, and follow it to the foot of a short wall, which is climbed to gain a series of diminishing steps below twin cracks on the left. Climb steeply up the cracks to the good sloping ledges.
P2 5a 15m Climb the crack on the left to join and finish up *Britomartis*.
[B Wyvill, R Evans 10.09.77]

42. Vend-T E2 5b 55m
A good addition that takes a parallel line of weakness across the wall above *Britomartis*. Start as for *Gobbler's Arête*.
P1 5b 37m Swing left around the arête onto the wall right of *Britomartis*, just above a small overhang, and make a bold move to gain huge holds at the start of a line of craters leading up leftwards. Follow these to the left-hand end of the large sloping belay ledge.
P2 5a 18m Move right and climb the steep crack to the top.
[G Gibson 04.04.80]

43. The Sad Cow E3 6a 35m
A direct version of *Vend-T* P1, striking a line up the obvious pink wall to the ledge. Follow *Vent-T* to the start of the line of craters. Step right on small flakes and climb directly, crux, to reach better holds and a little crack. Finish slightly left to the large ledge.
[C Waddy and G Smith 05.91]

44. Britomartis HVS 4c *** 58m
This popular jugfest provides a superb outing, assuming you can get past the tricky entry section at its base.
P1 4c 36m From the ledge beneath *The Trap*, climb down and make a difficult traverse left into the diagonal groove. (NB. At low tide it is possible to make a more pleasant direct start from below the good ledge.) Follow it up as it turns into a fine jug-ridden diagonal crack, all the way to a small stance high on the wall.
P2 4c 22m Move right and climb over a bulge to gain a good ledge. Traverse right around an arete to finish up a steady groove.
[D E Alcock, G Rogan 11.02.67]

45. Toiler on the Sea E2 5b ** 62m
A splendid open route tackling the wall left of *Britomartis*.
P1 5b 37m Start as for *Britomartis*, but break out left from the groove/crack after a few metres, heading diagonally leftwards above the lip of the steepness to gain the base of a steep crack. Blast up the crack to the *Britomartis* belay.
P2 5b 25m Ascend the thin crack above the stance, and then weave a line upwards, first left, then back right across the upper slab to reach easy ground.
[G Gibson, D Beetlestone 03.04.80]

Britomartis Wall • **Wen Zawn**

▶ **46. Spider Wall E1 5a ** 60m**
Another superb excursion onto this fine wall.
P1 5a 45m Follow *Toiler on the Sea* to the base of the crack. Move up the crack for 4m then head out left for 2m and up to a flake, before stepping right and climbing a shallow groove up to the *Britomartis* belay.
P2 4c 15m Trend diagonally leftwards across into the groove, and follow it past some creaky holds to a ledge on the left.
[L E Holliwell, D S Potts, L R Holliwell 29.06.69]

▶ **47. The Bluebottle E2 5b ** 80m**
A very good route, which goes across the top of the arch in a fine position, before finishing direct.
P1 5a 45m Follow *Spider Wall* until below the steep crack, above the arch, and then carry on traversing to reach a small stance shared with *Spider's Web*.
P2 5b 35m Move up to the roof and climb round it to the right to gain the crack above. Follow this to the groove above and finish up the steep crack. However, stepping left as for *Spider Wall* can make a more pleasant finish.
[E Drummond, B Campbell-Kelly 30.08.69]

Approach to routes 48–50: Abseil straight down to 'The Whale' island, clipping a crucial thread (marked on the topo) on the steep ground. With a belay constructed on The Whale for your second, pendulum into a short leftwards-facing groove on the cliff. Place some gear and transfer your weight to it. Detach yourself from the abseil rope and start climbing. The Whale remains above water at high neap tides. Spring high tides, and/or choppy seas should be avoided, unless you don't mind getting wet.

▶ **48. Billy Bud E6 6b *** 27m**
A good steep pitch with perfect rock and protection. From the pendulum point, go rightwards under the roof for more gear. Surmount the roof and climb up the leaning crack above. Pull over a bulge and grab the 'handle' (don't use this feature for a runner as it will break – there are good wires instead). The next bulge is easier and gains the upper wall; continue up *Spider Wall* to a belay, or retreat from the abseil rope.
[G Smith, C Waddy 1991]

▶ **49. The 4th Dimension E7 6c *** 27m.**
A quality pitch on excellent rock; steep and safe too. From the pendulum point follow *Heinous Flytrap* leftwards for 3m until obvious good holds lead rightwards through steep rock to a thread. Difficult moves lead leftwards to another thread. A flake on the left side of a roof leads to good holds and a vague easing of angle. It is possible to step left here into the niche belay on *Heinous Flytrap* and get a good shake out. Once rested climb up rightwards to a large undercut block, which provides runners and kneebars. Clip a peg on the right and make hard moves past this rightwards (crux) to gain the upper wall; continue up *Spider Wall* to a belay, or retreat from the abseil rope.
[A Wainwright 16.07.96]

50. Heinous Flytrap E7 6b ✶✶✶ 60m
This magnificent route searches out a remarkable line of weakness through some very impressive territory. According to Steve Mayers, "the best route on the entire cliff!" (N.B. This route was first climbed using lower offs to belay on *The Whale*, rather than long hanging belays.)
P1 6b 17m From the pendulum point, climb the groove to its top, and then move out left along the obvious undercuts to a technical kneebar crossover crux (with a 'Greek kick' if you want) and on up large flakes to belay where it eases at jugs in a slight recess with a small spike.
P2 6b 10m Continue up a short crack on the left, then swing out left onto a huge flake and duck round and under. Continue up to belay at the left hand end of the obvious large roof crack.
P3 6b 13m Follow the roof crack rightwards (beneath and parallel to the *Barfly* pitch) round the lip to reach the *Spider's Web* belay.
P4 4c 15m P4 of *Spider's Web*.
[C Waddy, G Smith 23.07.92]

Spider's Web Area

The next routes are situated on the landward side of the arch, although some of the routes finish on the Britomartis Wall. Here we have more wild and wacky adventures up inside the arch itself, and a series of interesting routes to the left.

Approach: From the top of the promontory, trend down and rightwards (facing out to sea) on a faint path to a small level section just above a gully; several old pegs mark the abseil point (good wires as back up). A 50m rope will easily get you down the gully and to the non tidal ledges at the base of *Ipso Facto*. Traverse left (facing out) to gain all the routes in the following section.

51. Spider's Web E5 6b ✶✶✶ 58m.
A thrilling, and well protected trip with some awkward moves. Start at the base of the large chimney.
P1 5b/c 18m Circumnavigate the bulge rightwards and climb up a shallow groove. Move right again for 2m, then ascend the steep and difficult wall, trending right at the top to reach a small cave tucked up within the darkest innards of the arch.
P2 6b 25m Bridge the chimney to its top. Extend the web with slings and bridge down to the lip. Reverse arm bar a slot, good #1 wire. Swing out across the lip and layback vigorously and gain the small stance up right.
P3 4c 15m Step down to the right and ascend a crack to a ledge in the groove. Move awkwardly leftwards into another crack which leads up and out to an easier finish. A loose pitch.
[J Brown, P Crew (some aid) 08.68, FFA: G Smith, T Bonner 06.91]

The route is still possible in spectacular but 'traditional' style as an 'atmospheric' E2 5b/c/A1 expedition.
P2a 5a/A1 25m Ascend the chimney in to the bowels of the roof, and move up and out over the sea to reach a cluster of decaying pegs at its top. Easy but impressive. Using 2/3 points of aid on good nuts, traverse across the downward pointing spikes in the roof to reach the seaward lip. A further point of blind aid around the lip enables a small stance to be reached. Beware of rope drag on the lip. Seconds

need to be competent in following A1 overhangs. Double ropes are essential while prussiks are useful in the event of a fall.

52. Bar Fly E6/7 6b *** 13m
Another outrageous roof crack from Smith. From a belay at the base of the *Spider's Web* chimney, swing out across the straight crack leading towards the lip of the *Web*. Finish at the *Spider's Web* belay. E6 in bone dry conditions, E7 if damp. Best visited at the end of the day, when it comes into the sun.
[G Smith 06.91]

53. Archway E2 5b * 48m
Another atmospheric route, which escapes the lefthand side of the *Spider's Web* arch by an airy traverse. Start at the base of the large chimney, as for *Spider's Web*. This is reached by a short sea level traverse from the sloping ledge on the arête.
P1 4a 15m Go around right into the chimney, climb right again then bear up rightwards to gain a second chimney and good belay below the overhangs.
P2 5b 18m Drop down leftwards for 3m before climbing up left beneath the overhangs. Move left to the arête and a poor stance.
P3 4c 15m Take the wall above before going rightwards and over a bulge to easy ground.
[J Brown, B A Fuller 18.09.67]

202 Wen Zawn • Spider's Web Area

▶ **54. Blowout E2 5c** * 45m
A fine, steep route which climbs diagonally right through a series of capped overhangs on the wall at the left hand edge of the *Spider's Web* arch. Start immediately to the right of the wide chimney of *Genuflex*.
P1 5c 30m Climb the overhanging groove to the overhang, then step right and cross the slab to its right edge. Gain the roof above and cross it rightwards to a steep crack leading to the belay on P2 of *Archway*. Sustained.
P2 5a 15m Go up right into the groove and climb this until it is possible to move right onto the arête. Climb this easily to a belay overlooking *Spider's Web*. Loose in places.
[M Wragg, G Hardhill (1 pt) 01.06.77]

▶ **55. The Boston Struggler E5 6b** ** 46m
A fantastic route, comparable to South Stack's *Free Stonehenge*.
P1 5c 23m Climb P1 of *Archway*, then layback flakes leading out leftwards from the huge wide chimney to reach a belay at the arête.
P2 6b 10m Swing into the wild roof slot and jam round the lip with more gambling bars than Monte Carlo. Belay in the groove above.
P3 5c 13m Swing round right and climb the gently overhanging scoop of knobs and flakes above the *Web*, finishing rightwards.
[G Smith, D Kendall 06.91]

▶ **56. Genuflex E2 5b** * 40m
A tricky wide crack provides the meat of this route, taking the edge of the wall left of the arch. Start as for *Spider's Web*, at the sloping ledge on the arête. Go around the corner into the deep chimney and climb this past the overhang, to reach, and follow, steep cracks to below loose bulges near the top. Go right and over a bulge to easy ground.
[P Crew, B Ingle 18.02.67]

▶ **57. (Will Mawr gets the) Vulcan Lip Lock E4 6a** 40m
Left of *Genuflex* is a North Stack-like wall, ochre-coloured in its upper part. Start in the middle of the wall. Gain a ledge at 3m and climb a short left facing corner to a thin flake, which leads quite boldly to a square roof (thread). Go right around this, crux. Make a hard step right then finish directly past an easy flake.
[S Haston, C Bull 06.88]

▶ **58. Forgery E5 6b** 34m
Follow *Vulcan Lip Lock* around the roof, and then traverse left across the lip to a groove (bold). Climb this and a vague rib, and then trend left to a peg on the first belay of *Annie's Arch*.
[C.Waddy, J,Vlasto 07.89]

▶ **59. Ipso Fatso E1 5b** 30m
The chimney line and corner to the right of the *Ipso Facto* wall.
Climb the chimney to the overhang, pull up into a loose corner and continue to the top.
[A Morley, D Ferguson, M Rowlands 21.12.97]

Patch Hammond and Will Perrin making a pendulum from The Whale during an attempt > on **Billy Bud** E6 6b photo: Adam Wainwright

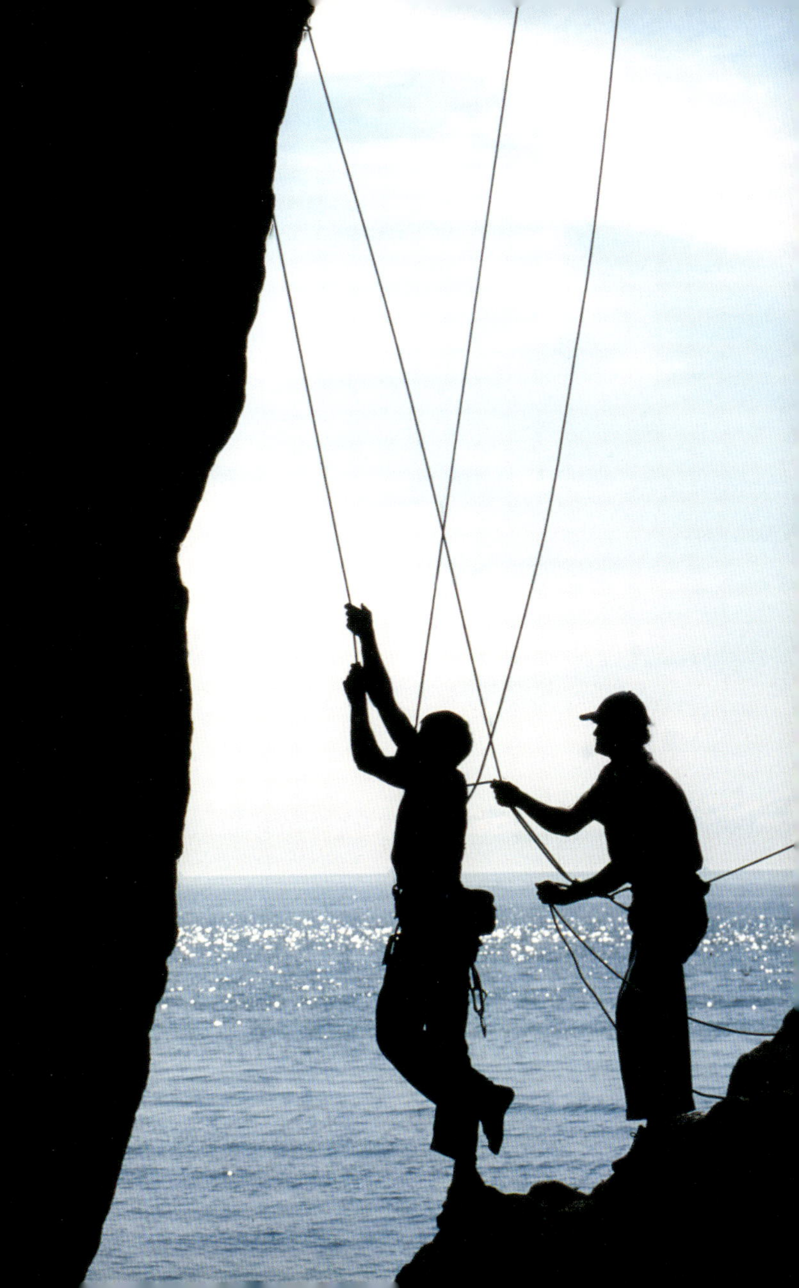

60. Ipso Facto VS/HVS 4c 30m
Gives steep, positive climbing on slightly friable/hollow rock. It takes the wall to the left of a shallow groove, about 15m left of the huge arch, and just to the right of the descent. Climb up the crack, and then move right to a small roof. Pull over this, then continue steeply up rightwards to a small ledge on the arete. Step left and follow the slanting crack to finish at a clean ledge. From here either:
a traverse up and left for a few metres to belay in the gully, just before a prominent block (30m). A short traverse across the gully will re-gain the abseil rope.
b pull through the bulge and continue up the short slab to the hillside (40m to this point).
[M Howells, B Whybrow 18.02.67]

61. Kraken VS 4c 30m
An obvious line and a good route taking the straight crack line to the right (looking in) of the abseil descent. Follow the crack until near the top where a step right gains a short flake which leads onto the clean ledge of *Ipso Facto*. Finish up this.
[P James, A Leary 04.08]

62. Annie's Arch E2 5b 103m
A girdle of the cliffs between *Ipso Facto* and *Britomartis*, crossing over the huge arch of *Spider's Web* on the way and providing some well positioned climbing on intimidating ground. Start as for *Ipso Facto*. A recent rockfall has added spice to the start of P3.
P1 4c 30m Follow *Ipso Facto* to the arête, which is climbed for 3m before swinging right around into a groove to belay at some pegs.
P2 5b 12m Step down right and go across the wall to a peg. Carry on to the arête passing a hole/hollow, and then move down and right to a green slab, which is descended for 3m to a belay.
P3 5b 18m Go down right across the slab to a corner, and move up onto the right wall to gain the arête, peg. Step down and traverse to a large fin, which is climbed to a peg, before descending across for 5m to the corner and a belay, on *Spider's Web*.
P4 4c 25m Enter the flake crack down on the right and go up this for 3m, then make a descending traverse to an obvious flake. Move up to a good spike and traverse across the wall to a junction with *Britomartis*. Descend this a little until a traverse gains a huge ledge, and good belays at the top.
P5 5a 18m Move right and climb the steep crack to the top. (P2 of *Vend-T*)
[B Campbell-Kelly, A J D Ferguson (1 pt) 11/12.06.70]

62a. The Archie Gemmell Variant E2 5b 25m
An alternative to P1/2 of *Annie's Arch* which avoids the need to climb to the top of the cliff, before descending back down to regain the traverse line as the original line does.
Start from an uncomfortable hanging belay constructed around the small ledge on the arete of *Ipso Facto*. From the ledge, step down and stride right into the slanting groove and follow this (common with *Forgery*) to join the traverse line of the original route to the left of the hole. Continue as for P2 of *Annie's Arch*. [A Leary, H Jones 05.98]

Mustang Wall • **Wen Zawn**

▶ variation: **62b. Stanley's Arch E2 5b** 81m
Annie's Arch is equally good and possibly a more natural line, in reverse. Also on the arch section, the tasty moves to gain the rockfall area are better protected.
P1 5a 45m P1 of *The Bluebottle* to the belay of *Spider's Web*.
P2 5b 18m Reverse P3 across the arch.
P3 5b 18m Reverse P2 around the arete, past the hole and across the now rising traverse line to the top. Scramble up to belays.
[S Lowe, R Cully 2005]

Mustang Wall

Although relatively short by local standards (the atmosphere is more akin to Cornwall than Gogarth), the crag provides good quality climbing that is much steeper than appearances first suggest. As you look out to sea all the routes to the right of the abseil line finish on a grassy terrace, approx 2/3rds of the way up the cliff. Easy traversing along this ledge regains the abseil rope, thus allowing several routes to be climbed in a day (a similar situation to Easter Island Gully). Despite their mostly amenable technical grades, the majority of these routes are rather bold and require a bit of cunning and guile to adequately protect. A range of micro wires and thin slings can be put to good use. The enclosed nature of the bay and the small off-shore island/block offer a certain amount of shelter from the high speed ferry's wake. However the wall has a tendency to stay damp until the sun comes around. The best conditions are a calm sea, a gentle breeze blowing and low water around mid/late afternoon. (NB. The nearby *Ipso Facto* and *Kraken* routes catch the sun a couple of hours earlier than the other routes.)

Approach: From the top of the promontory, trend down and rightwards (looking out to sea) on a faint path to a small level section just above a gully; several old pegs mark the abseil point (good wires available as back ups). A 50m rope will easily get you down the gully and to the non tidal ledges at the base of *Ipso Facto*. The routes are all accessed via the sloping and rather slippery ledge which is gained by scrambling down and rightwards (looking out) from the base of *Ipso Facto*. All the routes require calm seas and a low-ish tide; especially beyond *Mr Seal*.

▶ **63. Mustang VS 4c** 30m
Steep climbing up the wall to the left of the descent. Start below the 1st groove along the ledges, and climb it to the top.
[T Taylor, D Garner 04.04.70]

▶ **64. Carol VS 4c** 30m
Climbs the vague crack 5m right of *Mr. Seal*. Go up the crack to a ledge and bear left. A step right gains a quartz jug and the top.
[J Dalton, F Williams 11.04.90]

▶ **65. Mr. Seal HVS 4c** * 30m
A very good little pitch, albeit a touch bold towards the top. Start left of *Mustang*, at the next groove along the ledges. Follow the ramp until steeper moves up the left arete lead in a fine position to a ledge. Use a break line in the slab to traverse rightwards until it's possible to pull up to the base of a steep groove; finish up this to various spike belays on the main ledge.
[A Newton, A Howells, C Parry 25.08.81]

66. The Tail E3 5c * 32m
Start at a pointed block on the traverse along the ledges left again from *Mr Seal*, and beneath the 3rd groove. Climb the groove direct to the top.
[J Brown, D Howard Jones 19.10.78]

67. Miura VS 4c 37m
An easier way of climbing the previous route. Start as for *The Tail*. Follow the groove until it gets hard, and leans leftwards. Traverse left and go over a bulge, and up, loose, to a small overlap which is passed on the left. Climb up leftwards and then rightwards to the top.
[T Taylor, M Barraclough 05.05.70]

68. Huncho E2 5b 32m
Quite a serious pitch. This takes the shallow groove 3m left of *The Tail*. Climb the groove (bold) to a bulge, lots of poor runners. Move up carefully to gain easier ground. Finish up left, blind but on excellent rock.
[M Crook, A Newton 18.04.94]

69. Maverick VS 4c * 45m
A fine route, the longest on the wall. Start where the ledge traverse peters out, just left of *Miura*.
P1 4c 25m Climb diagonally up and left on unusual rock, passing a small spike (thin sling is useful) until a long stride leftwards gains a large spike. Either belay here or move up for a few metres to a more comfortable stance.
P2 4c 20m The steep groove can be a touch damp in the back, however this doesn't affect the pitch which is climbed via spectacular wide bridging. At a prominent leaning spike, swing right and continue up easier rock to spike belays at the back of the ledge (a further 10m or so). [T Taylor, D Garner 04.04.70]

70. Flooze HVS 4c * 37m
An excellent pitch; technically reasonable, but some of the holds are not beyond suspicion. Start as for *Maverick*. Climb up directly from the initial traverse of *Maverick* to gain a band of well featured rock. Various blobs and chickenheads lead steeply past a flake to the terrace. [D Ferguson, C Brown 1993]

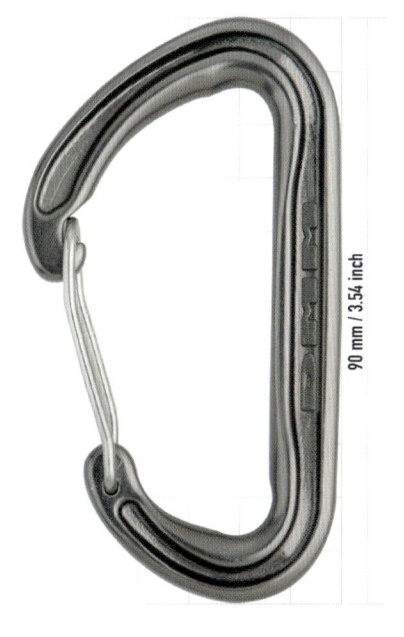

25.5 GRAMS
0.8994 OZ

90 mm / 3.54 inch

DMM PHANTOM IS THE LIGHTEST, FULL SIZE CARABINER AVAILABLE

The quest for the combination of strength and lightness continues! The Phantom is the lightest snap gate carabiner in our range, and now the lightest in the world We have retained a sensible overall size, so the carabiner is still easy to operate, but have used our I Beam system to massively reduce the weight. This carabiner is a must for Alpinists wanting to carry less weight or Trad climbers in search of the ultimate lightweight rack. Outrageously light, stylish and yet fully functional.

BENEFITS

- Ultra light 25.5 grams
- Integral rope groove
- Very strong gate open strength 9kN
- Compact and useable size
- I Beam construction for strength & lightness
- Hot Forged

DMM — CLIMB NOW · WORK LATER

HOT FORGED

PHANTOM TECHNICAL SPECIFICATION

STRENGTH [GATE CLOSED]	STRENGTH [GATE OPEN]	STRENGTH [MINOR AXIS]	WEIGHT	GATE OPENING	CATALOGUE Nº
23 kN	9 kN	7 kN	25.5 G	20 MM	A318

www.dmmwales.com

MADE WITH THE ORIGINAL I BEAM TECHNOLOGY
COPIED BUT NEVER BETTERED

Flytrap Area

Area: Gogarth Bay
Style: Trad (1-4 pitches)
Aspect: South-West
Rock type: Quartzite
Approach: 20 minutes
Altitude: Sea level – tidal
OS Grid ref: 215 838

Roof Rack	E7
The Ultraviolet Exterminator	E7
The Porcelain Arena	E6
Flytrap Roof	E5
Bury My Knee	E5
The Shadowy World of the Nemotodes	E5
Holyhead Revisited	E5
Seal's Song	E5
Dai Lemming!	E3/4

20,000 Leagues Under the Sea	E3
In the Next Room	E3
Flytrap	E2
The Hitcher	E1

A fascinating section of the main sea cliffs, situated between Wen Zawn and Parliament House Cave. This little visited area is home to the classic E2 adventure route, *Flytrap*. In and around the atmospheric cave - through which the aforementioned route passes - a number of superb challenges will be found. Indeed, *The Ultraviolet Exterminator* is one of Gogarth's best hard routes, at least according to George Smith (aka: the patron saint of upside down offwidths). On the periphery there are a number of neglected routes, where peace and quiet, and not a little adventure can be savoured.

George Smith busting a gut on the lip of the awesome **Ultraviolet Exterminator** E7 6b
photo: Ray Wood

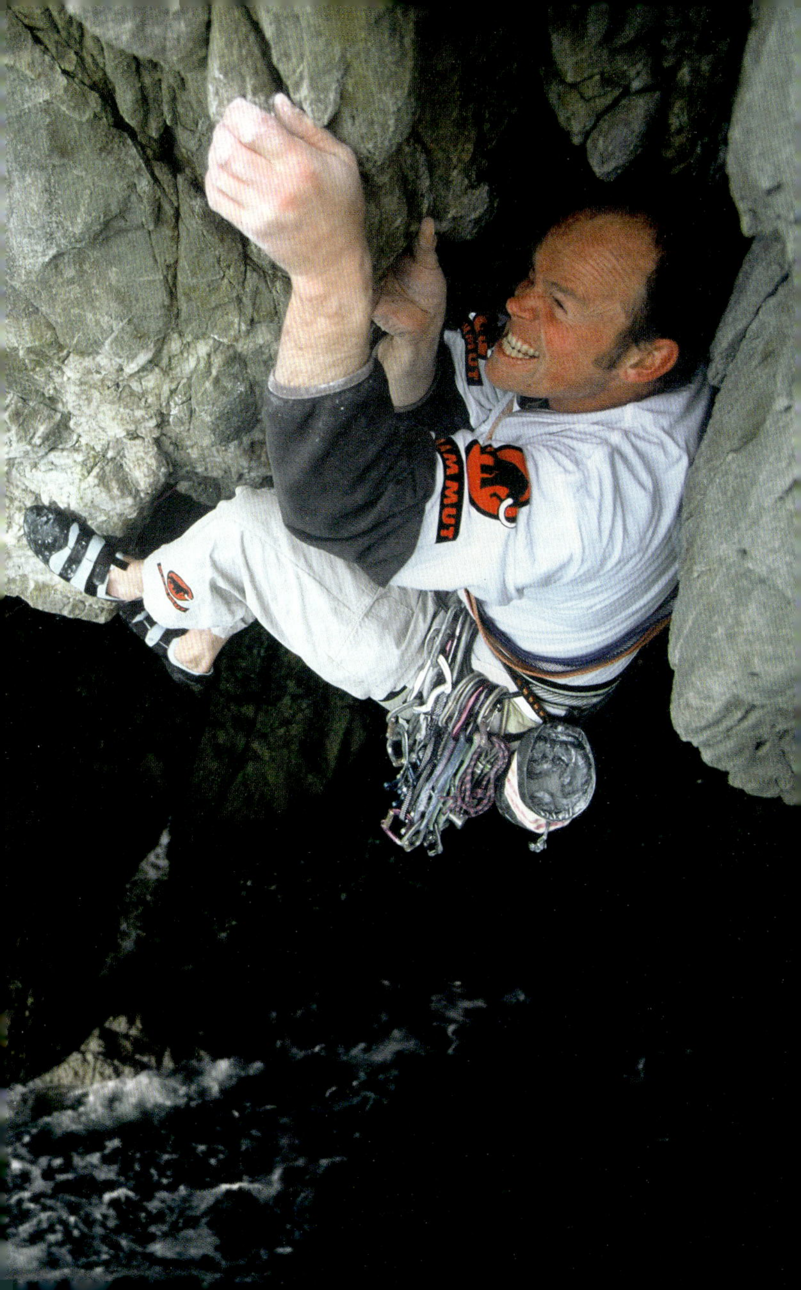

Flytrap Area • Approach

Conditions: The crag has a sunny aspect and does dry quickly. However the inner sections of *The Flytrap* cave are often quite damp. Lowish tide and a calm sea are desirable for all of the routes.

Approach: From the Breakwater Quarry car park, follow the path up, taking the left fork where it divides. Further up hill the path divides again; follow the right fork down by some telegraph poles to reach the fog warning station on the North Stack promontory. From here walk over the top of Parliament House Cave and traverse the hillside to reach the promontory marking the southern entrance into the North Stack Wall zawn. Alternatively the promontory can be reached by walking across from the top of Wen Zawn.

Once at the cliff top, the approaches to sea level are as follows:

• Prom Buttress routes are reached by abseiling directly down the buttress.

• For routes 5-14 descent is via a short gully on the North Stack side of the Mordor Wall. Initially scramble down broken ground to a platform containing some blocks. Abseil 45m down to sea level, and then traverse right or left to reach your chosen route.

• Routes 15-28 can be reached by scrambling down to the ledges at the top of *20,000 Leagues Under the Sea*, and then abseiling directly down the wall left of the *Flytrap* cave. Once at sea level, traverse across to reach the base of the routes. Access is also possible via a slightly tricky sea level (low tide) traverse from Parliament House Cave.

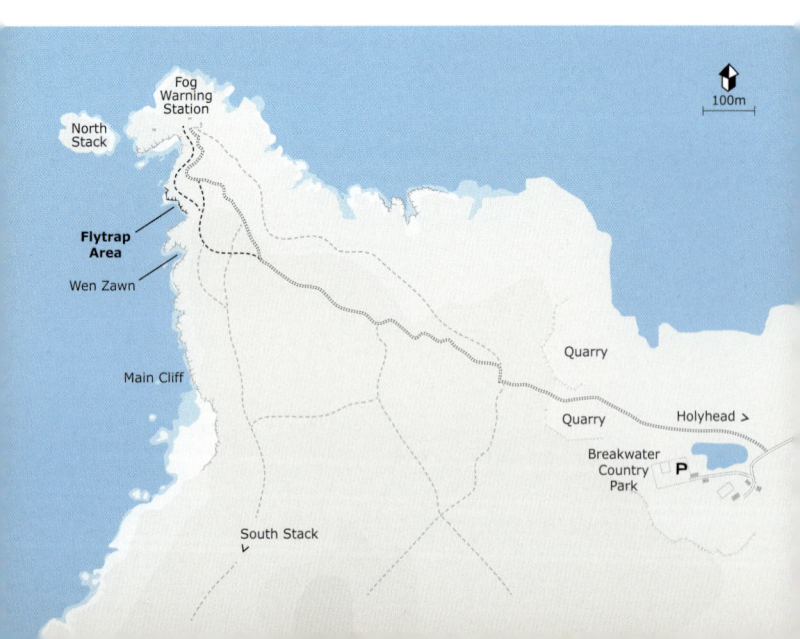

Prom Buttress

This is the promontory on the far right (south east) side of the Flytrap Area, where the cliff abuts the Mustang Wall on the edge of Wen Zawn.

1. Bullitt HVS 5a 45m
Reasonable climbing, but the quality of the rock is not good, taking a line of grooves up the right-hand side of the buttress. Start right of the foot of the abseil, at a small cave. Gain the slabby groove, via a steep initial crack and move up this to the overhang. Move up into a 2nd groove on the right then exit left onto a ramp. Ascend this then go left round a small overhang and go up to the top.
[L E Holliwell, D Mossman, L R Holliwell 13.09.69]

2. Prom HVS 47m
The route is quite often damp, and as with the previous route, the rock could be better. The route follows the crest of the buttress and is gained by an abseil to the foot of the rib.
P1 17m To the left of the rib is a groove which leads to a stance.
P2 30m Move left then go up for 5m until moves can be made to gain the obvious groove to the right of the rib. This leads to the top.
[J Brown, B Fuller, D Alcock 07.04.68]

3. The Dope HVS 5a 47m
Follow a shallow V-groove in the arête between *Prom* and *Hash*.
[K Glass, D Martin 1981]

4. Hash HVS 5a 48m
Another fairly loose climb, this time following a groove-line above a large cave on the left hand side of the *Prom* buttress. Start at the left-most side of the buttress.
P1 5a 10m A scramble leads to a good stance overlooking the cave.
P2 5a 38m Go leftwards across a short wall then ascend a steep slab to a short wide crack. Climb this and the broken groove above, stepping right to finish over broken ground.
[L E Holliwell, L R Holliwell 27.09.69]

Mordor Wall

The steep cracked wall left of the cave, which marks the left edge of Prom Buttress.

5. Seal's Song E5 6b * 50m
A most peculiar excursion, which includes a rather shocking leap of faith. Start beneath the large slanting chimney on the outside edge of the large cave that sits between Mordor Wall and Prom Buttress.
P1 6b 20m Climb the left wall of the large slanting chimney (as per *Mordor*) for 6m until opposite a collection of jugs near the bottom of the fang hanging from the roof of the zawn. Arrange some protection higher up the chimney, before descending and leaping across the zawn to gain the jugs. If you land the jump, scuttle around the overhanging arête, and up to a belay.
P2 5b 30m Surmount the roof above, at the easy left hand section, and traverse right to the good crack, which leads past loose rock, to the top.
[S Haston, C Bull 05.05.88]

Variation: **6. Roof Rack E7 6c** ✴✴ 30m
P2a 6c 30m The roof above *Seal's Song* provides a spectacular route. Well protected (mostly pegs) From the *Seal's Song* belay on the outer face of the fin, go up to the break. Tug across the roof, passing good pegs ('average' peg near the lip). The crack above is about 8 grades easier but seems very difficult nonetheless.
[G Smith 1995]

7. Mordor HVS 68m
A neglected route accessing the striking crack line in the headwall via the large slanting chimney.
P1 43m Ascend the left wall of the chimney (as per *Seal's Song*), moving over an overhang onto a steeper wall. Go up the wall to a flake, and then climb up right to a crack in the overhang. Follow the crack to a stance and belay.
P2 25m Head left for 3m to reach left-trending cracks that lead to the top.
[J Brown, D Alcock (1pt) 31.03.68]

Variation **Mordor Newydd E3 5c** 41m
P1a 5c 41m A strenuous direct version of *Mordor*. Start up *Mordor*, but head straight up the overhanging squeeze chimney/crack to rejoin *Mordor* for the upper crack.
[T Hodgson, S Haston 1986]

8. Six White Boomers VS 4c 33m
Start between *Mordor* and *Colditz* just right of some black spikes. Climb easily up cracks to a ledge, move steeply left to a left slanting niche and pull over a bulge into the groove above. Follow this and move left at the top to finish up the front of the buttress.
[D Ferguson, J McQueen 07.05.94]

9. Colditz VS 4c 30m
The traditional escape route starting 6m right of the arête marking the edge of the *Flytrap* zawn. Ascend the crack to a break, traverse this leftwards onto the arête, then climb this and a flake before scrambling up to the top.
[A Newton, J Peart 03.09.82]

Variation: **10. Mistaken Identity HVS** 35m
This curious route makes a traverse across the top of the *Flytrap* zawn, and was in fact the first exploration of the *Flytrap* cave. Approach via an abseil to the ledge on the arête of *Colditz*, or abseil to sea level and start up *Colditz*.
P1 10m From the ledge on the arête head left along the ledge, belaying at a point almost in the cave.
P2 14m Traverse to the back of the cave and chimney down to a ledge and belay on top of the *Flytrap* chockstone.
P3 11m Traverse left along the folded cracks leading from the bottom of the belay ledge. 6m out a niche is reached; go up over a bulge then follow a cracked groove to the top.
[M Royle 1973]

If you're still hungry for adventure after that little excursion, more 'fun' can be had by continuing the traverse line along *Route 66*.

Parliment House Cave

Absell approach

Absell approach

Mustang Wall (Wen Zawn)

214 Flytrap Area • Mordor Wall

▶ **11. Flytrap E2 5b** ✶✶✶ 82m
A wild and adventurous journey into the cave. The route passes through some exciting territory, and is best suited to an experienced party of balanced ability. Calm seas and a lowish tide are advisable.
P1 4a 12m From the base of the arête left of *Colditz*, head up left on large holes to gain a ledge.
P2 5a 25m Descend for 5m from the left side of the ledge. Traverse left (slightly descending) on small but positive holds until the bottom of a black groove is reached.
P3 5b 25m Ascend the groove, which is often damp, then follow an obvious traverse rightwards. This is straightforward at first, but then becomes steep with a hard section passing a peg to gain juggy holds on the back face of the huge jammed chockstone at the top of the cave. The stance is just above.
P4 4b 20m Climb the right wall for 6m, and then traverse the break rightwards for 6m to reach a crack – finish up this.
[J Brown, P Jewell, D Cuthbertson (1 pt) 16.04.78]

▶ **12. In the Next Room E3 5c** ✶ 50m
A fine addition, which gives *Flytrap* veterans another reason to head back to the cave.
P1 4a 12m P1 of *Flytrap*.
P2 5c 12m Climb diagonally out leftwards through the overhung cave above the belay ledge. Pull into the crack above and traverse left to the ledge above the chockstone (*Flytrap* belay at end of P3). Belay at the left hand end.
P3 5b 25m Traverse left - as for *Mistaken Identity* - along the folded cracks leading from the bottom of the belay ledge into the hanging groove just before the finishing groove of *Mistaken Identity*. Climb the groove and belay on the ledge at its top.
[A Lole, B Anderson 14.08.06]

▶ **13. Bury My Knee E5 6b** ✶ 82m
A variation on *Flytrap* climbing around the front right side of the chockstone roof. The action is centred on a short-lived struggle through the obvious hanging niche. Take large cams.
P1 4a 12m P1 of *Flytrap*.
P2 5a 25m P2 of *Flytrap*.
P3 6b 25m Ascend to a ledge (possible belay) below the roof. Gain a prominent niche in the roof up right and exit boldly to good holds in a wide crack leading to the ledges at the end of P3 of *Flytrap*.
P4 4b 20m P4 of *Flytrap*.
[G Smith 2004]

▶ **14. Flytrap Roof** (AKA: **The Nemotode Strikes Out**) **E5 6a** ✶ 18m
A ludicrous excursion lapping the *Flytrap* chockstone. From the top of the chockstone (end of *Flytrap* P3) descend (!) at the inland end. A hidden hand crack leads you back under the 6m roof and round the lip in a fabulous position to regain your starting position. (NB. It is possible to belay at sea level on the *Flytrap* side of the zawn.)
[G Smith 2005]

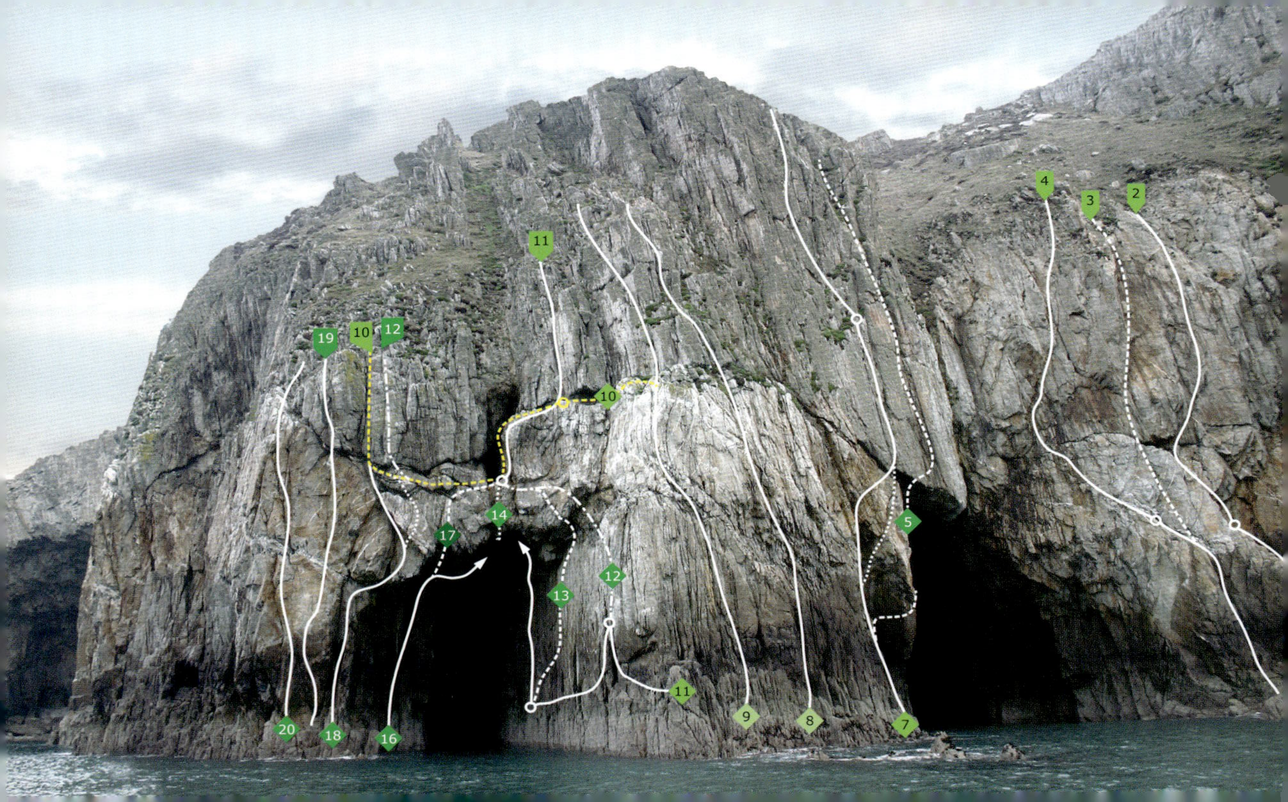
19
10
12
11
10
14
17
13
12
11
20
18
16
9
8
7
5
4
3
2

216 Flytrap Area

▶ **15. The Porcelain Arena E6 6b** * 50m
An exceedingly traditional route, exploring the back of the *Flytrap* cave. Start on the left wall of the zawn.
P1 6b 20m Ascend the initial V chimney of *The Shadowy World of the Nemotodes*, and then traverse right to the arête. Gain a slanting crack around to the right with difficulty. This widens to a strenuous and awkward vice/pod, which in turn leads to the roof of the cave. Belay.
P2 5c 10m Either throw yourself into the sea, or arrange protection and traverse the wall outwards to a point where it is possible to bridge the width of the zawn (or cross the west wall without bridging) to the top of the *Flytrap* chockstone. An atmospheric pitch.
P3 4b 20m P4 of *Flytrap*.
[G Smith, S Melia 2003]

▶ **16. The Shadowy World of the Nemotodes E5 6b** ** 40m
A disorientating trip into the weird and wonderful world of the *Flytrap* cave. The gear is good and the rock solid, if a little sharp.
P1 6b 20m Ascend the V chimney on the left wall of the zawn and arrange protection before pulling up and right through bulges until a steep wall leads to the inland end of the *Flytrap* chockstone.
P2 4b 20m P4 of *Flytrap*.
[G.Smith, T Briggs 2002]

▶ **17. The Ultraviolet Exterminator E7 6b** *** 45m
The perfect pitch for the seasoned Gogarth roof connoisseur.
P1 6b 25m Ascend the V chimney and arrange protection. Head out across the big roof on undercuts and pull into a niche on the lip. The short wall above leads to a break. Move right onto the *Flytrap* chockstone belays.
P2 4b 20m P4 of *Flytrap*.
[G Smith 2004]

▶ **18. Arachnid E5 6a** 30m
Although once a fairly classic pitch (steep and pumpy and well protected), rockfall on the lower section has rendered this route a bold and relatively nasty undertaking. If you still fancy a go after that warning, climb the cracked groove in the arête to the break. Swerve right, then chimney up underneath the roof, emerging on its left side to finish up the cracked groove of *Mistaken Identity*, on the left.
[G Smith, G Hughes 05.05.88]

▶ Variation: **E5 6a/b** 30m Climb the original route up to the roof, but pull out right and follow a crack up to the *Mistaken Identity* break.
[J Dawes 1988]

▶ **19. Holyhead Revisited E5 6a** * 30m
An absorbing route, which climbs the wall between *Arachnid* and *20,000 Leagues Under the Sea*. Start up the steep groove just right of the latter, gaining a ledge on the right below an obvious nose. Move up the wall on the left, stepping into a slabby groove, which leads to a break where the main difficulties end. Follow the groove to the top.
[C Waddy, B Pritchard 04.88]

George Smith brings 'LPT' strength to Gogarth with the first ascent of **Roof Rack** E7 6c
photo: Glen Robbins

> **20. 20,000 Leagues Under the Sea E3 5c ∗∗** 30m
> A fine and strenuous burn up steep ground. Ascend the groove in the lower wall, and then blast up the overhanging crack in the arête.
> [M Crook, D Kendal 29.07.87]

> **21. Dai Lemming! E3/4 5c/6a ∗** 30m
> A worthwhile addition starting 6m to the left of *20,000 Leagues Under the Sea*, just right of *The Hitcher*. Climb up and right to gain a small triangular ledge, then follow slim grooves to overlaps, which lead to easier climbing and a break. Finish up the obvious compact headwall.
> [D Lampard, M Turner 1994]

> **22. The Hitcher E1 5a/b ∗** 30m
> This enjoyable pitch, starting 7m left of *Dai Lemming* below an obvious crack, is the ultimate elevated boulder problem in the sky. Ascend the crack and groove onto the slabby wall, which leads via cracks to the top.
> [C Waddy 1988]

> **23. Jug Patrol E1 5b** 43m
> This takes the flake crack some 3m left of *The Hitcher*, starting about 15m right of the highpoint on the traverse from Parliament House Cave.
> **P1** 5b 23m Climb the steep pink flake to reach good holds and a ledge beneath the less steep wall. Move left and surmount the bulge, climbing gradually left to reach a niche on the *Route 66* horizontal break.
> **P2** 4c 20m Climb the crack above the belay with care to reach the grassy slopes above. Belay on the abseil rope or blocks above.
> [M Crook, A Newton 17.04.94]

Flytrap Area

▸ **24. Touching Cloth E1 5b** 45m
The exact line of this route is not known for certain. Crispin could not confirm the precise details so the line shown on the topo is our best guess! Start up the south-facing chimney a 5m left of *Jug Patrol*. From 7m up the chimney go right to a crack, which leads to a niche in the *Route 66* horizontal break common with *Jug Patrol*. Continue from the left hand side of this up a crack to the top.
[C.Waddy 05.90]

▸ **25. Oijee Wall E1 5b** 45m
A tricky looking prospect, but take heart; there are some hidden jugs up there. Start 10m left of *The Hitcher*. Move up to the large lump of odd rock, and then head up rightwards on decent holds through a bulge. Continue up the slabby wall to a large ledge. Finish up the obvious crack, right of the chossy corner (P2 of *Point Blank*), and belay well back.
[C Waddy, G Percival 03.88]

▸ **26. Point Blank VS 5a** 40m
A tough route starting a few metres left of *Oijee Wall*.
P1 5a 25m Go up the crack leftwards to reach a flake, and then head up right to a good crack in a shallow groove. The groove leads to the large recess on *Route 66*; move right to belay.
P2 4c 15m Go right, into the chossy corner, and climb the crack to the top.
[J Brown, T Peck 09.67]

▸ **27. Skippy E1 5b** 45m
Start 3m left of a left-slanting chimney, between *Jug Patrol* and *Point Blank*.
P1 5b 25m Climb the wall left of the chimney to a groove. Climb this to an overlap and make steep moves over it to reach the P2/3 belay of *Route 66*.
P2 4c 20m The slab above, via big flakes, leads to a grassy finish and a belay on blocks.
[T Morley, D Ferguson 08.04.97]

▸ **28. The Walls of Jericho E1 5b** 73m
The prominent arête, above the hard section, on the traverse around from Parliament Cave. A good P1, followed by steep rubble (a clue is the name).
P1 5b 28m Ascend the arete direct to a ledge.
P2 4b 45m A lethal scramble leads to the top (alternatively abseil off).
[C Waddy 1988]

▸ **29. Route 66 VS** 82m
This adventurous girdle (of the wall opposite North Stack Wall) will appeal to those who revel in the more esoteric end of the sea cliff experience. Expect plenty of guano and loose rock. Start by scrambling down to the ledges at the top of *20,000 Leagues*...
P1 30m Traverse the ledge leftwards, over much guano, to belay in a large recess below a steep crack.
P2 15m Step down and traverse along the narrow ledge, which soon runs out below an overhang. Continue for a few more moves then head leftwards up the steep wall to reach a belay in a grassy bay.
P3 37m Follow the obvious diagonal break to the top passing some loose rock on the way.
[J Brown, P Crew, B Ingle 20.02.67]

North Stack Promontory

Area: North Stack
Style: Trad (1 - 2 pitches)
Aspect: South
Rock type: Quartzite
Approach: 15 minutes
Altitude: Sea level – tidal
OS Grid ref: 215 839

The Hollow Man	E7/8
The Bells! The Bells!	E7
The Angle Man	E7
The Clown	E7
The Demons of Bosch	E7
A Wreath of Deadly Nightshade	E6/7
Stroke of the Fiend	E6/7
Flower of Evil	E6
The Long Run Direct	E6
The Cad	E6

The Long Run	E5
Not Fade Away	E5
Sarah Green	E4
Blue Peter	E4
South Sea Bubble	E3

Talking Heads	E2
Green Gilbert	E1
Nice 'n' Sleazy	E1

Black Rod	A4
L'Affreuse	A4
The Big Overhang	A3

For many years North Stack Wall was seen as emblematic of the bold and adventurous Gogarth style. Indeed for a time, in the late 70s and throughout the following decade, this distinctive sweep of white quartzite occupied centre stage in British climbing culture. It is here that a series of dramatic, and sometimes controversial ascents took place. In 1978 Fawcett climbed *The Cad*, but only after placing two bolts, then in 1980 Redhead established Britain's first E7 with a lonely soul searching lead of *The Bells! The Bells!*, and in 1986 Pollitt made his mark with *The Hollow Man*, at a possible grade of E8. By the end of the 80s attention had shifted elsewhere, but this run of serious climbs remained intact; to this day they still present a formidable challenge to those with aspirations towards the top end of the bold wall climbing game.

Regardless of the sunny aspect and easy access, this is a serious crag. On the harder routes protection is typically spaced, and/or marginal. Moreover, the rock is not beyond suspicion, snappy holds are common, and ground falls a possibility should the unthinkable happen.

For those with more modest ambitions there are a number of excellent mid grade routes following strong feature lines, where meaningful protection tends to be more abundant. There are also the esoteric joys of hardcore aid climbing to be savoured, should you ever tire of the conventional climbing opportunities hereabouts. The humungous roof of the adjacent Parliament House Cave is crossed by a selection of impressive, but nowadays neglected, aid routes.

∧ The mercurial John Redhead stepping out on his own creation, the groundbreaking and unspeakably bold **The Bells! The Bells!** E7 6b photo: Andy Newton

222 North Stack Promontory • Approach

Conditions: A quick drying suntrap catching the morning sun and therefore a great place to do a morning route whilst waiting for the afternoon sun to dry out the rest of the Main Cliff or Wen Zawn area. All routes left of *Blue Peter* are affected by high tides.

Approach: From the Breakwater Country Park car park gain the rough Landrover track 50m to the north of the small lake. Follow the track all the way to the fog warning station on the North Stack promontory. Access to the routes is via a 40m abseil from the telegraph pole stump by the side of the white wall. This takes you down a short groove, onto a slab, and then down the line of *Birth Trauma*. It is advisable to leave this rope in place for emergencies, as the easiest way out of the zawn is E1. At low tides it is possible to reach (or escape) from the bottom of the zawn via a tunnel that runs underneath the promontory from sea level on its north side to emerge in the back left corner of Parliament House Cave. This normally involves some wading or swimming - watch out for seals in the dark!

Several large ring belays can be found at the top, on both sides of the white wall, but these are old and potentially unreliable.

Access: Parliament House Cave hosts breeding seals for about a month after the autumn equinox (i.e. late September until the end of October). Please do not go into the cave at this time. Your presence will disturb the seals, and they may respond in an aggressive fashion.

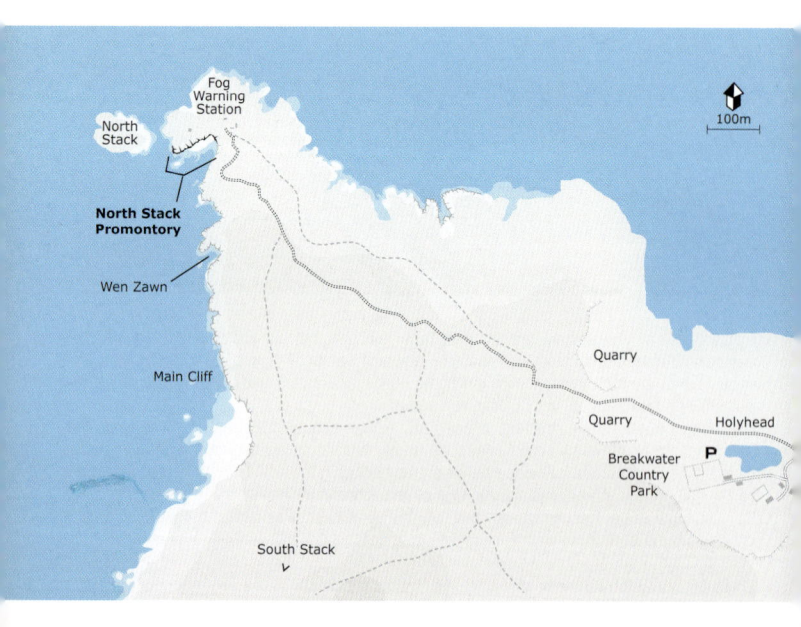

Parliament House Cave

The aid routes in Parliament House Cave see little traffic these days; however they are recorded here should anybody fancy a change of style, or some practice for a Yosemite visit. Be warned though, the topo lines given are approximate and that the grades are very dependent on the amount and quality of fixed gear in place at the time of an ascent; obviously this varies from time to time. The artificial grades given are old style European grades (i.e. A3: many difficult placements, but there will be the odd good piece, A4: several 'nothing-more-than-bodyweight' placements in a row). It should be noted that these grades are easier than modern American aid climbing grades.

▸ **1. Black Rod A4** * 55m
Takes a line through the vast roof just right of centre. Some of the rock is dubious and needs careful handling. Start at a pedestal, to the right of the start of *The Big Overhang*.
P1 18m Climb the pedestal and wall to a hanging belay at the roof.
P2 25m Follow the obvious line across the roof to reach the lip and belay in a hanging corner.
P3 12m Go round the lip and up to an ice peg. Free-climb to the top.
[M Barnicott, C Remy, Y Remy 17/18.03.75]

▸ **2. Pigs in Space A4** 55m
A direct start to Black Rod from *The Big Overhang* pedestal. Traverse from the top of *The Big Overhang* start pillar to the old tat below the belay of *Black Rod*. "Bloody desperate and total death should one placement fail... ropes, hooks and bottoming KBs behind loose blocks." [J Howel, D Anderson 1992]

3. L'Affreuse A4 * 58m
Another long and difficult aid route through the huge ceiling of the cave.
P1 18m As for P1 of *Black Rod*.
P2 40m Go straight up and across the roof to the obvious hanging slab midway out. Follow this to its end, over a bulge and gain an upside down groove. Continue for 6m to a possible hanging stance on the lip, and climb the wall rightwards to the top.
[D Williams, J Williams 14/15.11.82]

4. The Big Overhang A3 *** 55m
An excellent expedition, full of character and excitement for those who are not used to swinging about on gear. Many pegs are usually in place but it does tend to vary. The rock could be better on the first 10m or so, but the rest is not as bad. Long slings are needed to prevent rope drag. Start beneath a buttress in the back wall of the cave.
P1 12m Free-climb the buttress, via a crack, to a shattered stance beneath the roof.
P2 43m Aid up to the roof and follow 2 vague parallel cracks through the roof to the lip and a possible stance. Climb the final headwall to finish.
[D Scott, B Palmer 11/12.67]

Another aid line was recently bolted up in Parliament House Cave. This was quickly de-geared by local climbers; it was felt that the drilled bolt placements were out of step with the adventurous Gogarth ethic and that even an aid route should not be bolted.

North Stack Wall

5. Wall of Horrors E2 5b 45m
This takes the wall left of the huge cave entrance, and is serious in the easier upper part. Start at the foot of the arête, which comes down from the left side of the lip of the huge roof. Climb the arête rightwards onto the face. Go up to a small ledge, peg, then move up into the yellowish groove above to a second peg. Step right and climb the wall until moves back left over the top of the groove lead to the large flake crack above, go up the groove and exit left onto the upper slab. Ascend leftwards over this to a niche, move left on flakes and finish up a groove at the top (loose as for *The Whip*.)
[C Phillips, N Horne 02.05.70, FFA: P Whillance, D Armstrong 27.08.78]

6. Birth Trauma E6 6a 43m
A serious proposition due to poor, spaced protection and some dubious rock. The route starts steep and burly, and then gradually leans back to become less strenuous, but increasingly technical. Start 6m left of *Wall of Horrors*, a couple of metres left of a small cave. Move steeply up, with some difficult moves, passing a short flake to reach a 'handrail'. Traverse right to a peg then follow the obvious thin crack up the wall, transferring to a 2nd crack on the left, peg, and climb this to finish up an easy slab and wall.
[J Redhead, A Pollitt 27.05.84]

33
31
28
25
24
18
12
27
26
20
10
Abseil approach
32
30
29
25
23
22
19
17
9
8
7
6
5
Routes 35 -37
Parliment House Cave

7. The Whip E1 5a 44m
A worryingly loose and bold route taking the long groove to the left of *Birth Trauma*. Start on the sloping platform at the foot of the groove.
P1 5a 22m Ascend the groove via a selection of friable holds and with increasingly poor runners to reach a stance on the right at half height.
P2 5a 22m Follow the groove to the top, steering clear of a block on the right. Poor protection.
[D Scott, B Palmer 05.68]

8. Headbutt E6 6a 40m
An uninspiring pitch on dubious rock. Start a couple of metres left of *The Whip*. Climb up leftwards to a peg at 10m and pass this before stepping left after 3m. Ascend the open scoop passing a poor peg to gain progressively easier climbing up to a shattered roof. Climb through this leftwards, dangerous, and finish on creaking holds.
[N Dixon, C Smith 18.07.86]

9. Tom's Shredded Slippers E4 6a 40m
A bold pitch at the top of its grade. Start beneath the slim groove just left of *Headbutt*. Climb the groove and a thin crack, loose in places, to join *Headbutt*. Move left into *Green Gilbert* and finish up this.
[J Redhead, B Drury, M Boater 18.07.86]

10. Green Gilbert E1 5a * 40m
The obvious flake crackline is the traditional escape route, but it also provides a decent route. The rock is slightly friable (particularly the footholds), although the associated risk is to some extent alleviated by the presence of a reasonable crop of runners – none are that bomb proof, but there are plenty of them.
[M Boater, S Johnson, R Perry 1970]

11. Art Groupie E6 6a 40m
The gap between the grooves of *Green Gilbert* and *Blue Peter* is plugged by this wandering pitch - low in the grade, but serious nonetheless. Follow *Blue Peter* until it moves left. At this point a hidden hold provides the key to gaining the wall above. Once ensconced on the wall, trend slightly rightwards to a 'hands off' ledge and small wires (from here it is possible to escape up *Green Gilbert*). If you wish to continue move back up leftwards, tracing the obvious line up the wall to a junction with *Blue Peter*; finish up this.
[A Pollitt, J Redhead 27.05.84]

12. Blue Peter E4 5c ** 40m
A strong line with some fine climbing. That said, this is a fairly serious route that requires a steady lead. Move up to the overhang and pull through to the wall above. Trend up left to gain the flake crack, and follow it to a small ledge near the top of the wall. Step left and finish up the short groove.
[P Whillance, D Armstrong 02.09.78]

Variation: Sarah Green E4 5c * 37m
A good and worthwhile variation, and one that is more involved than you might expect. Take the obvious direct groove leading into *Blue Peter*.
[D Hersey, A Haynes 1983]

13. The Angle Man E7 6b * 45m

This rising counter line to *Stroke of the Fiend*, crosses some impressive territory, but has little in the way of independent climbing. Also, the belay relies upon a combination of an insitu abseil rope and the old bolt on *The Cad*. The bolt stud can be threaded with a wire, but it hardly constitutes a reliable antidote to any significant sideways pull, this being the likely scenario should the leader or second fall off either pitches. Start as for *Blue Peter*.
P1 6b 25m Follow *Blue Peter* then *Wreath,* round onto the wall to traverse across past the peg on *The Bells!* (crux), to belay on *The Cad's* old bolt (abseil rope back-up).
P2 6b 20m Climb *The Cad* for a little way, before traversing left from the large foothold above the bolt. Climb up to a runner then traverse left, reversing the crux of *The Long Run* to finish up the obvious direct finish.
[D Towse, J Redhead 07.87]

14. Flower of Evil E6 6b * 37m

Often confused with *Wreath*, this is actually an easier proposition, taking a higher traverse line out of *Blue Peter* to reach the edge of the main wall. Still, a serious undertaking, and not one to be taken lightly. Start up *Sarah Green* and continue up *Blue Peter*. Several metres after the junction of the 2 routes, break out left on a line of crimpy edges to reach the arête. Move up, and then bear left, to reach the upper traverse on *The Bells!*. Climb straight up with difficulty, and then head slightly rightwards to a sloping ledge and the top.
[J Redhead, D Towse 05.86]

15. A Wreath of Deadly Nightshade E6/7 6b ** 40m

A superb pitch with a hard and blind crux pulling out on to the left wall of the arête. Climb *Sarah Green* to the junction with *Blue Peter*, and then follow the obvious series of overlaps out leftwards, until it is possible to move around the arête and onto the edge of the wall. Climb straight up, left of the arête, to reach easier ground on the upper traverse of *The Bells!*. Finish straight up with sustained difficulty as for *Flower of Evil*.
[A Pollitt, A Hughes 20.05.88]

16. The Hollow Man E7/8 6b *** 43m

This brilliant direct version of *The Bells! The Bells!* yields the most taxing pitch on the wall; both physical and harrowingly bold. The strenuous start of *The Clown* leads straight into the bold crux of *The Bells..*, which is topped by an independent direct finish. Follow *The Clown* through the overlaps to join *The Bells..*, taking advantage of the good rest near the right arete of the wall. Climb up through the crux section of *The Bells..* to reach easier ground at the start of the upper traverse line. From here move up and left to a good pocket and crucial small cam placement. Continue directly to the top.
[A Pollitt, J Dawes 02.10.86]

17. The Clown E7 6b ✱✱✱ 45m

The big counter diagonal line to *The Cad* weighs in at bottom end E7. It is often cited as the best hard route on the wall. The climbing is excellent, albeit sometimes difficult to read. The hard sections are 'relatively' safe, but do expect to run it out in between.

Start below a left facing flake crack/groove, with double overhangs at 8m. Climb up the groove to the first overlap (peg and size 1.5 cam) and make hard moves through to gain the next overlap (small wire out right). Surmount this and emerge onto the upper face where a decent rest can be found near the right arete of the wall. Traverse left (a reverse of *The Bells! The Bells!*) and move boldly up to the undercut flake on *The Cad*, which thankfully can be laced with gear (a small thread is sometimes insitu). Step left onto the wall and move up to some undercuts. Make committing and reachy moves up to gain easier ground and a junction with *The Long Run* at the horizontal break. Finish up this.

[J M Redhead, D Towse, J Silvester 25.04.84]

18. The Bells! The Bells! E7 6b ✱✱ 45m

An historic landmark route (the first British E7), albeit one that was later outshone by its neighbours, at least in terms of quality. Although relatively steady in physical terms this is a very serious and arduous lead, weaving a tortuous and complex diagonal line across the face.

Follow *The Cad* up the initial shallow groove, surmounting the small overlap and gaining a reasonable spike runner in the wall above. From here traverse horizontally right on the lip of the overlap to the resting position common with *The Clown/Hollow Man*, near the right arete of the wall. In the wall above is an old protruding peg runner; this is what you are aiming for. Climb the wall with difficulty (crux). The old peg is much easier to clip if there is a sling on it but the new peg just above cannot be clipped until after the crux in any case. Continue up the slightly easier wall above until and a rightwards traverse can be made to a 'no hands' rest on a ledge on the arete. The crack/groove in the arete leads to a sloping ledge and then the top with much relief.

[J Redhead, C Shorter 30.06.80]

19. The Cad E6 6a ✱✱✱ 37m

A classic route with a colourful history featuring the placement and subsequent removal of 2 bolts. What remains today is a bold and sustained wall climb. Thin slings are useful for protecting the lower section.

Start 10m left of *The Clown* below a faint cracked groove running up onto the wall. Move up the crack and head up rightwards to some spike runners at 8m. Climb carefully up and right to gain the undercut flake (a small thread is sometimes insitu here). Lace with gear, then make difficult moves rightwards across the flake to reach a good foothold by the old bolt stud (which can still be looped with a small wire). Compose yourself, and then head boldly up the wall past a blind break to reach a ledge. Easier climbing leads to the top.

[R Fawcett, C Gibb 17.09.78]

8
9
10
11
12
14
15
16
17
18
19
19a
20
20a
22
23
24
25
26
27
28
29
30
31
32
33

Nicolas Favresse living the dream on
Blue Peter E4 5c photo: Ray Wood

North Stack Wall • **North Stack Promontory** 231

▸ **19a. The Cad Direct Start E6 6b** 35m
The crux moves at the flake can be gained directly by starting a couple of metres left of the start of *The Clown*, and climbing over the overlap with difficulty to gain the wall above and join the parent route.
[J Redhead 11.88]

▸ **20. The Long Run E5 6a** *** 38m
Another classic, bold wall climb, offering fairly sustained difficulties. The protection is never great, but the route can be made relatively safe if the effort is made to search out runners. Start up *The Cad*, but break out left at 5m and move up to a thin flake crack. Climb this and the wall directly above to reach good holds at a point where the wall becomes steeper. Traverse right for 3m and surmount the bulge on dinky holds, before trending more easily up left to the top.
[P Whillance, R Parker, D Armstrong 30.09.79]

▸ Variation **20a. The Long Run Direct E6 6a** ** 35m
A direct start and finish to the parent route; well worth doing if you've already ticked the classic original (or even if you haven't). Start left of *The Cad* and climb up over the roof to join the E5 version. Continue up this to the horizontal break where *The Long Run* goes right. With good runners placed, forge a line directly up the seam above to reach the cliff top, somewhat wide-eyed.
[D Towse, J Redhead 11.88]

▸ **21. Stroke of the Fiend E7 6b** * 40m
A sustained and serious girdle going from left to right across the face, with some superb delicate climbing. Start as for *South Sea Bubble*. This route relies on the same hanging belay set up as the *Angle Man*, and as such the possibility of an ascent is similarly open to question. Start as for *Blue Peter*.
P1 6b 20m As for *South Sea Bubble* for about 5m then go rightwards across the wall and up to *The Cad* flake. Pass this to a hanging stance on the bolt above, an abseil rope back-up would be prudent, if not essential.
P2 6b 20m Traverse directly rightwards on a vague break, which is 3m beneath the upper traverse of *The Bells!*. This leads to the arête of *Flower of Evil*, wire runners. Step down and reverse the traverse of *Flower of Evil*, descending slightly, to reach the sanctuary of *Blue Peter*. Finish up this.
[P1: D Towse, M Crook, J Redhead/P2: J Redhead, D Towse 28.05.86]

▸ **22. South Sea Bubble E3 5c** ** 35m
The striking flake crack gives a fine route. Move up to the bulge and climb boldly leftwards through it to reach the bottom of the flake crack. Scoot up this to a large ledge. The remaining short wall provides an awkward finish (or sneak off left).
[J Moran, S Horrox, A Evans, G Milburn 30.07.78]

▸ **23. The Demons of Bosch E7 6b** * 35m
A very sustained, fingery and serious line taking the wall between the cracks of *South Sea Bubble* and *Nice 'n Sleazy*. Start between the crack, and beneath a small overhang at 5m. Go up to and over the overhang, then up the middle of the wall for 8m. Pass a poor peg above, before embarking on a very sustained few metres, which lead to an exit rightwards onto the sloping ledge, just below the top. Finish up leftwards easily.
[J Redhead, D Towse 11.06.84]

24. Nice 'n' Sleazy E1 5a * 35m
A fine pitch taking the obvious crack line 7m left of *South Sea Bubble*. Climb steadily at first up the crack, until it steepens and the difficulties become more pressing. Where the crack closes, move left to large flake and continue more easily to the top.
[A Evans, G Milburn, J Moran 29.07.78]

The next routes are only reachable at very low tides:

25. Talking Heads E2 5b ** 37m
An excellent route, with a memorable crux stride. Start just left of *Nice 'n' Sleazy*, and traverse left just above the water until directly beneath the overhang higher up the wall. Ascend the wall, and then follow a crack up to reach the right side of the overhang. Pull over and make an eye-popping stride out left to gain the final crack. The crack, although initially troublesome, soon eases.
[J Moran, G Milburn, A Evans, S Horrox 30.07.78]

26. Pulling For Two E6 6b 40m
This route is less strenuous if you are good with your foetus. Climb *Talking Heads* to the roof a long reach left gains a strenuous pull up over a roof via an obvious crack. Peg up left. Traverse left on the quartzy vein and follow the quartz vein and holds to join the finish of *Live at the Witch Trials*.
[M Turner, L Thomas 2005]

27. Live at the Witch Trials E6 6b 38m
A hard route, filling a gap between 2 older routes. Start as for *Talking Heads*. Step left and climb direct to the left side of the large roof above, cross this on undercuts, then climb straight up the wall, sustained and poorly protected, to reach a good break 3m from the top. Move right a metre or so and climb a short crack to the top.
[C Waddy 09.88]

28. Not Fade Away E5 6a * 40m
A sustained pitch, serious in places, up the wall left of *Talking Heads*. Start as for *Talking Heads*, tide allowing. Traverse left, just above the low tide mark, until below the top crack of *Talking Heads*. Climb the wall on the left for about 8m then traverse left (not obvious) with difficulty, for 3m to reach the arête. (Big roofs down left of here.) Ascend steeply to a peg beneath the bulge above, move up left to a flake then bear up leftwards again before moving back up right to a flake crack. Climb this, moving rightwards to good footholds and finish direct up some cracks in the wall.
[J Moran, G Milburn 28.10.78]

29. Penelope Undercling E5 6b 35m
A direct approach to *Not Fade Away*, starting from the foot of the groove below the roofs to the left of that route, gained by traversing in, or by abseil. Climb the groove towards the roofs until desperate moves right and up, passing the remains of an RP, lead into *Not Fade Away* and finish up this.
[M Crook, D Kendall 04.08.87]

North Stack Headland • North Stack Wall • **North Stack Promontory** 233

▶ **30. Le Bon Sauveur E3 5c** 30m
Start 12m left of *Not Fade Away* at a small ledge just above sea level at the base of a big roof-capped groove, gained usually by abseil. Climb the obvious steep groove to reach the roof, and then traverse right 3m to surmount the roof via a crack. Continue up this to the top.
[J Redhead, K Robertson 08.84]

▶ **31. Sincerely El Cohen E3 5c** 30m
This takes the left-hand exit from the groove, starting as for the previous route. Climb the groove, over the first roof, and then move diagonally left up the golden-coloured wall to reach the arête. Finish up the hidden groove.
[M Crook, F Lowe 15.08.86]

▶ **32. The Wrath of Deadly Lampshade E5 6a/b** 27m
The obvious cracks left of *Le Bon Sauveur* provide a hard tussle up to the 17m mark; above the standard eases, and shortly after the left hand side of the large overhang is reached. Finish up *Le Bon Sauveur*.
[A Hopkins, G Smith 05.91]

234 **North Stack Promontory** • North Stack Headland

The starts of the next 3 routes are gained by abseil.

▶ **33. End Game VS 4c** 30m
Interesting, but a little contrived. From sea level on the slab around the corner, follow the left hand arête of the North Stack Wall as closely as possible, past one steepish section to the top.
[A Newton, J Peart 1982]

▶ **34. Pawn HS 4b** 27m
Climb the narrow chimney and the continuing crack just left of *End Game*.
[N Jones, B Jones 05.90]

▶ **35. Bank Holiday Bypass VS 4c** 27m
A nice route, if a little slight in the broader context of Gogarth. Ascend the deep chimney left of *Pawn* until it is possible to pull onto the slabby wall on the left. Follow the wall and corner groove to the top.
[B Jones, N Jones 05.90]

In 1998 a pair of routes was climbed on the section of cliff to the left by Glenda Huxter and Howard Jones, however the exact lines taken are not known. **Rickety Fence Route (HXS 5c/6a)** started from a hanging belay on an arête; **The Jigs Up (E5 6a)** started in the same place but took a different line: move up the groove in the arête to holds below the 1st bulge. These lead leftwards onto the overhanging face. Climb a fragile flake to a rest at its top, then sprint straight up to the top.

Tsunami Zawn

Area: North Stack
Style: Trad (1-4 pitches)
Aspect: West/East
Rock type: Quartzite
Approach: 15 minutes
Altitude: Sea level – semi tidal
OS Grid ref: 220 838

| Tidal Wave | E2 |
| The Groove | VS |

A peaceful and largely forgotten area, situated between North Stack and Breakwater Country Park. Tsunami Zawn, the largest of the zawns hereabouts sports a collection of interesting routes, varying from the attractive single pitch lines at the mouth of the zawn, to the harrowing adventure that is *Tsunami*.

Elsewhere along this stretch of coast there is potential for more development, however, exploration thus far has been limited to a lone deep water solo by the ever-intrepid Crispin Waddy.

Conditions: The crag has an open aspect and dries quickly. Low tide and a calm sea are desirable for most of the routes.

∧ Follow the yellow brick road..... photo: Simon Panton

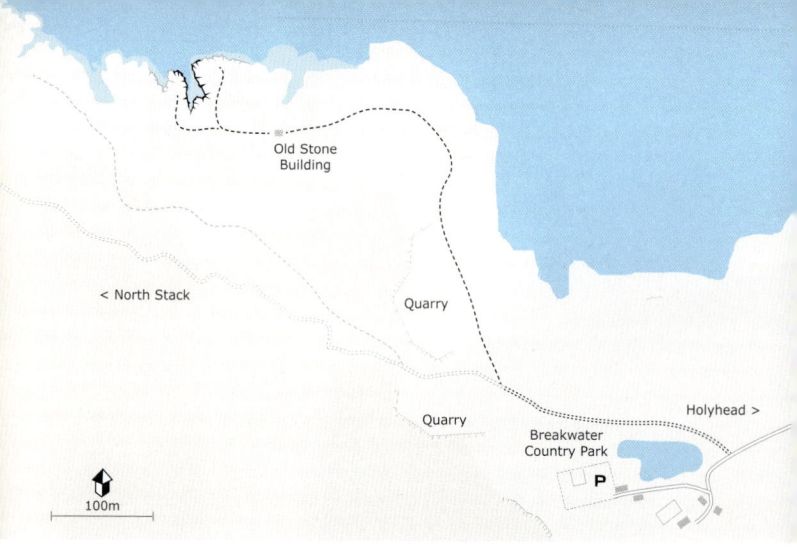

Approach: From the car park in the Breakwater Country Park, take the path past the western end of the small lake, and then turn left onto the main path. After 30m the path heads up the incline; turn off rightwards and follow the coastal path across below some quarried walls, and then round onto the hillside above the coastal cliffs. Continue along the stone pitched path (Follow the yellow brick road…) until a small, dilapidated stone building is reached. Contour across for a further 50m, before descending the steep hillside to the east of the main zawn. Once sea level is reached traverse west into the base of the zawn. (NB. Back in the 1980s this hillside was destabilised by a heath fire. The vegetation has become established once again, but care should still be exercised.)

East Wall • **Tsunami Zawn** 237

East Wall

To the left of the first couple of routes there is a slab. The obvious crack lines have been climbed at Severe and V Diff.

1. A Groove VS 4c 23m
Climb the lefthand of the twin grooves just left of the entrance to the zawn.
[J Entwistle, L Wood 07.10.67]

2. Another Groove HVS 5b 25m
The right hand groove provides a bold pitch. Ascend to the overlap, then step left to a ledge on the arête and move over the overlap. Continuing up the groove to the top.
[L Wood, J Entwistle 07.10.67]

238 Tsunami Zawn • East Wall

▶ **3. Tsunami E5 5b** 102m
A terrifying traverse across the wall, culminating in a particularly horrific groove on the final pitch – a good view of this is from the top of the opposite side of the zawn. There is some solace for those hell bent on repeating this exceptionally adventurous route: the belays are said to be good (just don't expect anything too reliable in between on the last 2 pitches). Start at a rock pedestal beneath the bulging wall right of *Another Groove*.
P1 5a 25m Go right then up the groove, through overhangs, trending rightwards to the brown slabs. Ascend the slabs heading diagonally rightwards to a hanging belay left of an overhung corner.
P2 4c 18m Gain the corner beneath the overhang and climb up to reach slabs on the right. Belay by some loose blocks.
P3 5b 25m Traverse rightwards towards the overhangs, stepping down under a sharp fang, then continue traversing along a hanging slab belay in a wide crack below the final groove. Loose and serious, and worth E3.
P4 5b 34m Scary moves up the groove then escape out right onto a ledge. Move right then make an ascending traverse until it is possible to top out. Very loose and very serious, and worth E5! Use three pegs to climb the groove and on the right. Use a peg to and go up overhanging heather to belay higher up.
[C Jackson, K Myhill (5pts) 14.11.71/FFA W Perrin, P Robins 06.01]

▶ **4. Charlie Don't Surf E2 5b** 35m
Start right of *Tsunami*, below the *Shell Shock* crack. Climb up to and over the initial overhang, then take the obvious diagonal line across a groove to reach the edge of the slab, peg in pocket. Follow the arête and groove just left to reach good ledges. Finish up rightwards.
[M Crook, A Newton 09.04.85]

▶ **5. Shell Shock HVS 5b** 35m
The prominent crack at the left hand side of the brown slab. Climb up past the overhang at 6m, and continue more easily via the upper section of the crack. Move up right to find a block belay on the ridge.
[J Moran, G Milburn 28.08.78]

▶ **6. Reptile HVS 5a** 38m
A direct route through overhangs right of *The Amphibian* Slab. Start below a thin crack, just left of *The Amphibian*. Climb the thin crack to the large roof then exit right around this to finish up the continuation crack in the slab.
[J Moran, G Milburn 28.08.78]

▶ **7. The Amphibian HVS 4c** 43m
A serious climb up the brown slabs between grooves and roofs, in the back of the zawn. Start, at low tide, at blocks at the back of the zawn. Trend left across the slab to the overlap. Surmount this on the right then make moves back left and continue to the top.
[L E Holliwell, L R Holliwell 21.04.68]

The exact lines of the following 2 routes are not clear. If you try to repeat them, good luck!

▶ **8. Too Cold for Comfort HVS 5b** (5 pts) 55m
Start beneath a ledge at 10m, in the back left hand side of the zawn.
P1 5b 25m Ascend the slabs for 6m then aid right on 3 pegs to a bottomless groove. Go up this with the aid of 2 more pegs to a hanging stance where the angle eases.
P2 5a 30m Move up for a couple of moves, then go left under a fang of rock onto the slabs. Climb the thin central slab to easier ground and belay at some blocks. [R Conway, C Jackson 09.10.71]

▶ **9. Sue P. E2** (1 pt) 82m
This truly terrible, loose and dirty route, up the back of the zawn, is included only as a warning to would-be explorers. Start at the back right-hand side of the zawn.
P1 35m Climb the left hand groove to the top, gain a ledge on the right, and climb a short wall to gain a grass field. Cross this diagonally rightwards to reach another field and belay (poor) on a ridge at the top of this.
P2 22m Climb up loose flakes, and use a peg (not in place) to gain a ramp, which leads up right to a flake crack. Avoid this by a ledge traverse leftwards to the base of a groove.
P3 25m Climb the groove a little way, then step onto the left arête and follow it to the top. [M Lynden, D Towse 10.10.82]

West Wall

On the opposite side of the zawn to *A Groove* and *Another Groove*, there are 2 attractive slabby walls broken by a large vertical overlap which hides an ominous looking chimney cleft (*Tidal Wave*) at its back edge. A number of good routes can be found here. Approach, either by traversing across the zawn from the east side, or by descending the slope above down to a broken area to the right of the climbs leading down to sea level, and then traversing back left to the base of the routes. A low tide is recommended. Belays at the top of this section of the zawn are scarce.

▸ **10. Cracked Slab HVS 4c** 28m
Start at a crack, left of the chimney on the left side of the left hand wall. Climb the main crack, and then head up leftwards via a flaky crack, finishing on poor rock. Take care on the last section.
[J Brown, C E Davies 1987]

▸ **11. Chimney Climb VS 4c** 25m
The obvious chimney on the left side of the left hand wall.
[J Brown, M Anthoine 1987]

▸ **12. Overlapped Groove E1 5b** 25m
Follow the crack just to the right of *Chimney Climb* until it divides. The right fork takes you into a small groove, which leads to the top.
[J Brown, M Anthoine 1987]

▸ **13. Crackers VS 4c** 25m
Just left of the right arête of the left hand wall, there is an obvious crack and groove system. Climb this trending rightwards to a blocky vegetated finish.
[J Brown, D H Jones 1987]

▸ **14. Sirplum E2 5c** 25m
Climb the crack in the narrow overhanging wall just left of the *Tidal Wave* chimney cleft, to finish near *Crackers*. [J Brown, D H Jones 1987]

West Wall • **Tsunami Zawn**

▶ **15. Tidal Wave E2 5b** ∗ 30m
The large chimney cleft marking the left corner of the right hand slabby yields a route of much character. Traverse out from the back to finish steep groove.
[1987]

▶ **16. Cracked Up E1 5b** 25m
Start just right of *Tidal Wave*, and follow a crack up the wall, moving under the overlaps at the top, until it is possible to exit directly.
[J Brown, C E Davies 1987]

▶ **17. The Crack VS** 21m
The crackline 5m left of *The Chimney*.
[J Brown, C E Davies 1987]

▶ **18. The Groove VS 4c** ∗ 21m
The slanting groove, just left of *The Chimney* provides a fine route.
[J Brown, C E Davies 1987]

▶ **19. The Chimney S** 21m
The obvious chimney cleft 16m right of *Tidal Wave*.
[J Brown, C E Davies 1987]

Immediately west of Tsunami Zawn is a small zawn with an intriguing feature. There are no routes in here (yet), perhaps because sections of rock look a little suspect? Further west towards North Stack there is ano bay, and right again is a tibia shaped arête, left of a roofed square groov

▶ **20. God's Bone XS 6b** 10m
The tibia shaped arête, which is climbed on its left side, has no relevant Although at high tide it is a 'safe' deep water solo.
[C Waddy 1996]

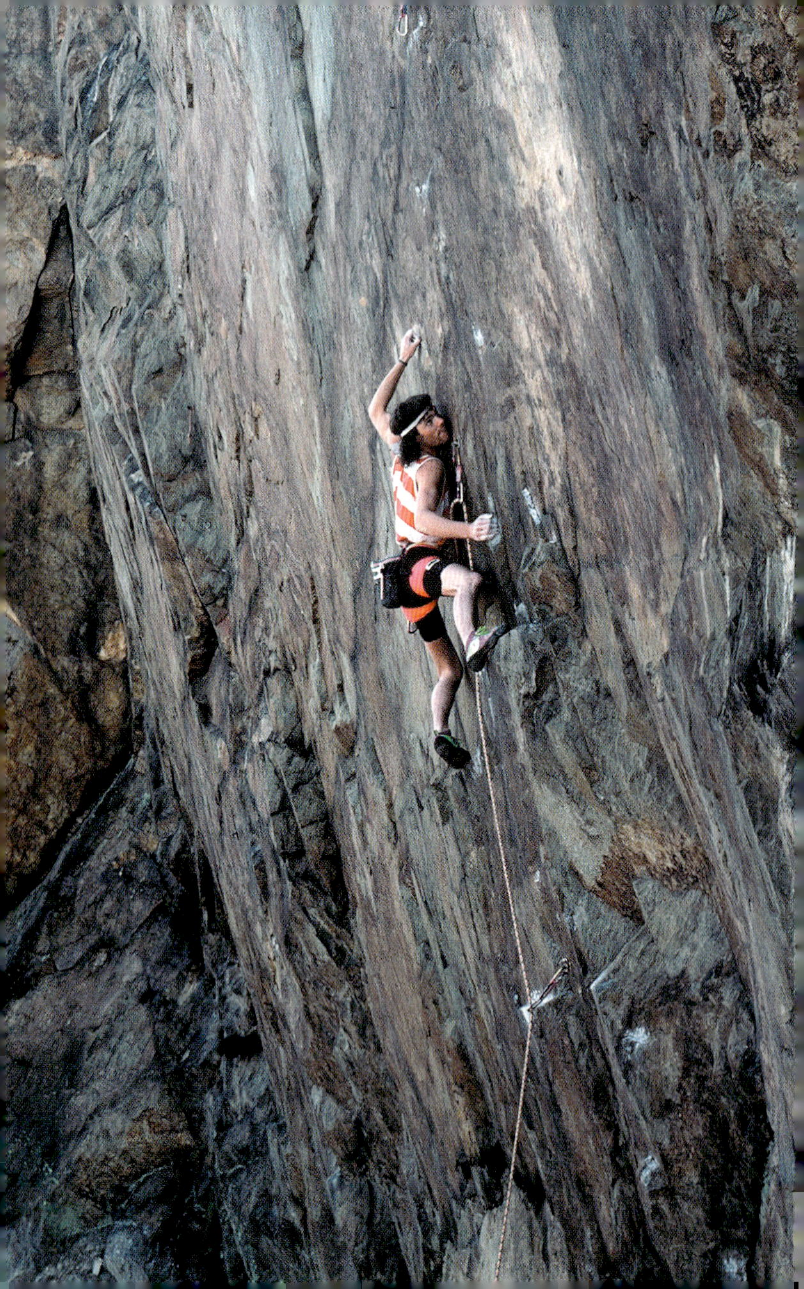

Breakwater Quarry

Area:	Holyhead Mountain
Style:	Sport/Trad (1-3 pitches)
Aspect:	North-East
Rock type:	Quartzite
Approach:	1 minute
Altitude:	30m
OS Grid ref:	225 834

- The Mustapha Twins E4
- The Terrible Thing F7c+
- The Crimson Crimp F7b

The main attraction in this old quarry situated on the Holyhead side of Holyhead Mountain is a pair of cracking sport routes on the impressive Physical Face. Once the site of an operating brickworks, the area has now been developed into the Breakwater Country Park; it is also the starting point for the main approach to the North Stack Wall, Wen Zawn and other cliffs in this area. The development of the Country Park has meant that all the routes have been affected to some degree by earth-moving operations. The owners of the quarry do not formally permit access for climbing; however climbers continue to enjoy the routes here. That said, a low-key approach should be adopted; if you experience any problems contact the BMC.

The older routes are not particularly recommended and have lost significant portions of their original starts under an earth bank. Their descriptions are included for the historical record.

Andy Pollitt making an early repeat of
The Crimson Crimp F7b photo: Glenn Robbins

Breakwater Quarry

ditions: The developed section of the quarry doesn't get much sunshine, ugh it is fairly sheltered. The Physical Face is steep enough to stay dry in, and thus provides a good option for strong teams retreating in bad her from the nearby sea cliffs.

roach: Take the A55 dual carriageway directly into Holyhead. Once in town, follow the road straight through passing the large clock tower on ght side. Continue until you reach a left hand turn signposted for South k (Prince of Wales Road). Follow this road to a mini roundabout; go ght across, and then straight across the next mini roundabout, before g the next turn immediately on the left (signposted: Breakwater Country). Follow the narrow road along over numerous speed bumps to the car on the right at the end. The developed section of the quarry lies just to eft of the car park.

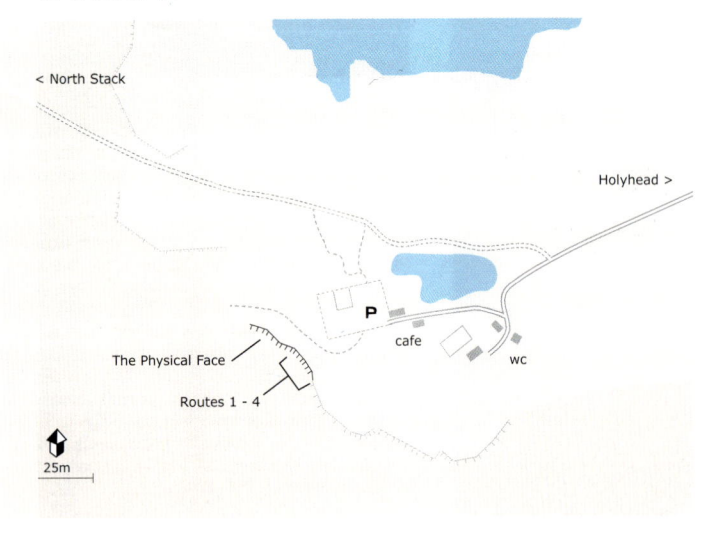

first 4 routes take the slabs and walls to the left of the steep red wall (The ical Face).

erontion VS 4c 68m
e left-hand side of the main (right hand) wall is an obvious rib of light-red rock, also a small barred tunnel entrance.
c 25m Ascend the rib then after 12m head up right to the edge of the ress. Climb this to a block on a ledge.
b 43m Go easily up the rib to an obvious crack in the upper buttress. right and climb this crack moving right at its top to finish up short walls grassy ledges.
acnair, J Gosling, E Thurrel, T Brooder 04.10.69]

Breakwater Quarry 245

▶ **2. Dementia E3 5c** 73m
Loose and dangerous especially on the last pitch. Start beneath the right hand of the 2 slabby grey ribs.
P1 5b 45m Go up to a ledge on the left at 12m then go left to the pale rib. Traverse left onto its front and ascend this to a ledge. Gain a big detached block below the overhang then traverse right and move up onto a slab. This leads up leftwards to a big grassy ledge with a peg belay 5m to the left.
P2 5c 28m Step right a couple of moves then move up to an obvious crack forming the left hand side of a pedestal. Climb this to a peg on top of the pedestal then ascend the short green corner on the right to a sloping ledge. Go 3m to the right and move up to an overlap. Carry on a few metres to finish up a short rib on the left.
[J Gosling, T Brooder 04.10.69]

▶ **3. Progeria E1 5a** 70m
Again unpleasant and dangerous especially at the top. Start beneath the right hand of the two slabby grey ribs. Climb the right side of this rib.
P1 5a 45m Follow the rib to a small recess on the right at 12m. Go left to grass then move up right to a detached block. Pass this, and once above, go up left to more grass in a small recess. Ascend the grass to a ledge. On the right is a short corner crack which leads to a ledge.
P2 5a 25m Gain the top of the shattered pillar on the left, peg. Step left then go up a steep rib to another ledge. Ascend right, past a peg, to a spike then carry on, over loose rock to another recess. Finish up this to a high belay on the right.
[J Gosling, T Brooder 28.09.69]

The following route seems to cover very similar ground to *Progeria*, although the last pitch appears to be independent:

▶ **The Mad Hatter** E2 (1 pt) 81m
Takes a line up the central buttress, via its right-hand edge with some loose rock at the top.
P1 5a 31m Climb directly up the right edge of the grey slabby buttress to a loose-looking block. Gain the ramp above, then go over the next ramp using a peg. Grassy ledge stance above.
P2 5b 25m Move up onto the short rib above then go left for three metres. Go up right to a gorse ledge then climb the wall on the left, past a spike, and go right to a loose ledge with peg belays higher up.
P3 5a 25m Gain a yellow pillar on the left, then a scoop on the right, which is just left of a hanging flake. Pull over a bulge then climb the loose corner and easier ground to the top.
[R Mallinson, A Green 28.07.74]

▶ **4. The Twilight Zone** E4 6a 25m
About 20m left of the steep red wall (The Physical Face) is a square light-coloured buttress bounded on its left by a slabby grey rib and protected at its base by a thicket of brambles. Start below the steep wall with an overhanging crack in its centre. Gain and climb the thin crack and when this runs out traverse right to the arête. Climb this to a ledge then climb the upper wall past a bolt, first left then back right to finish. Abseil descent.
[P Jiggins 09.08.88]

The Physical Face

This is the impressive steep red wall. Approach from the path at the right hand side of the wall.

▶ **5. The Mustapha Twins** E4 6b * 22m
The corner at the left side of the steep wall provides a difficult and technical climb. Finish at *The Terrible Thing* belay.
[C Waddy 1988]

▶ **6. The Terrible Thing** F7c+ * 20m
This takes an imposing line up the left of the wall, with a desperate start and only slightly easier climbing above. Superb climbing.
[G Smith 03.88]

▶ **7. The Crimson Crimp** F7b * 20m
Another sustained route striking a daunting line up the right hand side of the wall, with a tricky move to stand up on the ledge at 6m.
[P Pritchard 09.02.88]

▶ **8. Lord Snooty** E3 5c 23m
This takes the clean slab right of *The Crimson Crimp*, starting from the apex of the heather mound. Climb directly then slightly left to below an overlap. Pass this rightwards to reach a sloping ledge, traverse right, and then with difficulty, climb a right-facing ramp to its end. Belay stakes a long way back. [P Jiggins, G Stamp 13.06.88]

Nick Bullock caught mid crux on **A Wreath of Deadly Nightshade** E6/7 6b (Yes, he made it!) >
photo: Ray Wood

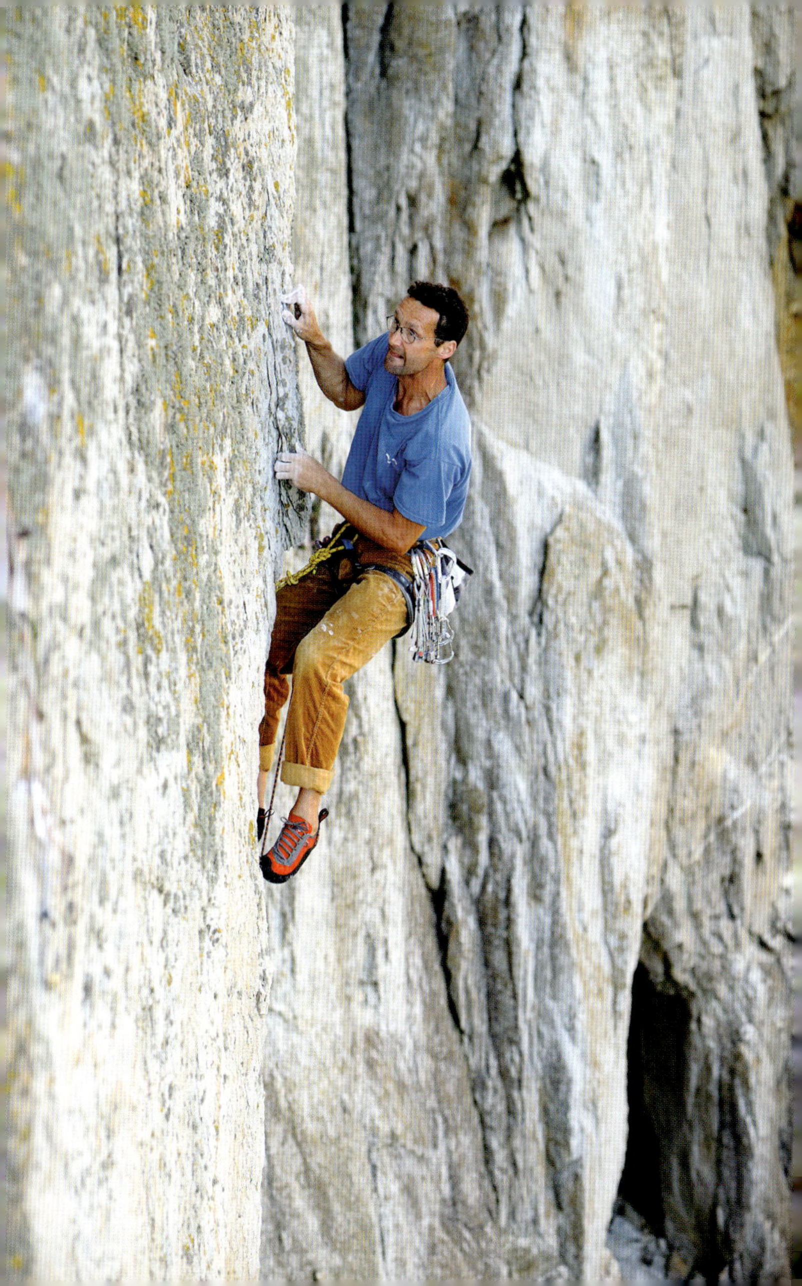

Craig Badrig (Craig y Sbliff)

Area: North coast
Style: Trad (single pitch)
Aspect: North
Rock type: Sandstone
Approach: 20 minutes
Altitude: Sea level – tidal
OS ref: 382 951

An interesting, yet little visited sea cliff with a series of quality routes in the VD–E3 range. The rock is a metamorphosed sandstone/conglomerate offering glorious frictional qualities. It is seemingly solid, save for the usual deterioration towards the cliff top. The location is both pleasant and quiet; if you are looking for an escape from the crowds this could be the place for you. The only awkward aspect of the crag, apart from its tidal nature, is that the belays for most routes are situated well back from the edge and require a bit of creativity to set up.

Idris Mad Dog	E3
North by North West	E3
Skerries Wall	E3
Ibby Dibby	E2
Sneaky Seal	E1
The Paranoid Duck	HVS
Caught by the Skerries	HVS
Pebbledash	S
Hardcore Prawn	VD
Away With the Fairies	VD

Looking down to the crag from the approach path photo: Graham Desroy ^

Conditions: The cliffs are tidal and accessible from mid to low tide. Seepage is an issue on all sections except Mellow Wall and Pebbledash Wall, so a dry period of weather is advisable.

Approach: The cliff is situated approximately 2km north-east of Cemaes Bay, directly south of Ynys Badrig (aka: the island of Middle Mouse). Park at Llanbadrig Church, and walk through the churchyard, turning right onto the coastal path footpath. Follow the path, through a gate at 400m, and then down some steps at 500m until a coastal footpath marker post is reached going up a hill at 800m. The old coastal footpath contours left at this point – the new coastal footpath continues up the hill. Follow the old path for 170m where a prominent undercut boulder meets the path.
Craig Badrig is directly below and the descent ramp for Sneaky Seal Wall and Skerries Wall is just visible.

Sneaky Seal Wall

Go down the descent ramp; Sneaky Seal Wall is the black wall 30m to the right (facing out to sea).

▶ **1. The Paranoid Duck HVS 5a** * 20m
Climb the obvious crack line.
[H Jones, G Huxter 1991]

▶ **2. Sneaky Seal E1 5b** * 20m
Start 3m right of *The Paranoid Duck*. Follow the thinner crack which heads slightly leftwards into a hanging corner at 12m. Finish up this.
[H Jones, J Biddle 1991]

▶ **3. Hazy Memories HVS 5a** 20m
2m to the right of *Sneaky Seal* is a large, low and left facing hanging corner. Gain this and follow it to its top. Finish up and right.
[G Huxter, J Biddle 1991]

Skerries Wall

Skerries Wall is situated directly above the descent ramp.

▶ **4. Skerries Wall E3 6a** * 20m
Start 2m right of the lowest point of the ramp below a small overlap at 3m. Climb the thin crack to the overlap where a move or 2 left leads to another short thin crack. Follow this and step right onto the upper wall. Go directly up the wall until the broken arête above leads to the top.
[J Biddle, H Jones 1991]

Craig Badrig 251

▶ **5. Ibby Dibby E2 5b** * 20m
2m right again is another short crack. Climb this and step left into a short right facing corner. Surmount this and continue up the groove above to the top.
[J Biddle, H Jones 1991]

▶ **6. Caught by the Skerries HVS 5a** * 20m
Climb the steep 'ledgey' wall 2m to the right to gain a flake crack at 5m. Continue up this, through a small overlap to the top.
[G Huxter, H Jones 1991]

▶ **7. North by North West E3 6a** * 20m
Climb the large but thin corner 2m to the right to the overlap at 12m. Cross this leftwards to reach broken rocks and the top.
[I McNeill, A Hall 1996]

Mellow Wall/ Pebbledash Wall

To access Mellow Wall descend the steep grass 10m to the left (facing out to sea) of the undercut boulder (mentioned in the main approach) until an old metal spike is found 5m below the path. Scramble carefully down the small ramp below, which leads under Pebbledash Wall. Mellow Wall is the yellowish wall to the right of Pebbledash Wall, facing out to sea.

▶ **8. Molesting Mollusc VD** 10m
Start at the left side of the wall at a slabby short corner. Climb up this, step right at the diagonal break and then follow the crack above.
[H Jones 1991]

▷ **9. Hardcore Prawn VD** * 12m
Climb the central right trending crack system.
[H Jones 1991]

▷ **10. Away With the Fairies VD** * 12m
Climb the corner at the right side of the slab on its left side.
[M Hill, J Biddle 1991]

▷ **11. Boulderdash HVS 5a** 12m
Climb the steep crack just right of the corner until the easier crack of Pebbledash is reached. Continue up this.
[J Biddle, M Hill 1991]

▷ **12. Pebbledash S 4a** * 12m
Start halfway up the ramp and access the slab at its easiest point. Move up and left to reach a wide broken crack. Follow this to the top.
[M Hill, J Biddle 1991]

▷ **13. Diagonal Dash VD** 30m
Start as for *Molesting Mollusc*. Gain the diagonal break which is traced across the Mellow Wall; continue by following the same line across the Pebbledash Wall until rubble bars the way and an exit upwards is advisable.
[H Jones 1991]

Boot Zawn

This is accessed by descending down the west face of the Pebbledash Wall ramp. Belays can be found at sea level where the traverse into Boot Zawn starts. Both routes start from here.

▷ **14. Idris Mad Dog E3 5c** ** 50m
Traverse right rising gradually until the black rock below the roofs is reached. Climb up into the short hanging corner below the 1st roof. Traverse out right on the hanging slab to its right edge. Make a tricky step right and up round the arête. Follow the corner to the top.
[H Jones, J Biddle 1991]

▷ **15. Boreal Boot Tester E1 5b** 25m
Follow *Idris Mad Dog* for 5m until a direct line can be taken up the wall.
[H Jones, J Biddle 1991]

Ynys Badrig (aka: the island of Middle Mouse) photo: Graham Desroy ∧
Nick Bullock on the brilliant **Captain Mark Philips** E5 5c photo: Graham Desroy >

Porthllechog (Bull Bay)

Area:	North coast
Style:	Trad
Aspect:	West/north
Rock type:	Quartzite
Approach:	15 - 30 minutes
Altitude:	Sea level (non tidal,
OS Grid ref:	(varied: see crag ir

Sunset Wall
Stable Wall
Baby Zawn
Equestrian Walls
Porthllechog Arch

Gate

< Porth Wen

Bull Bay Hotel

P

Porthllechog
Bull Bay

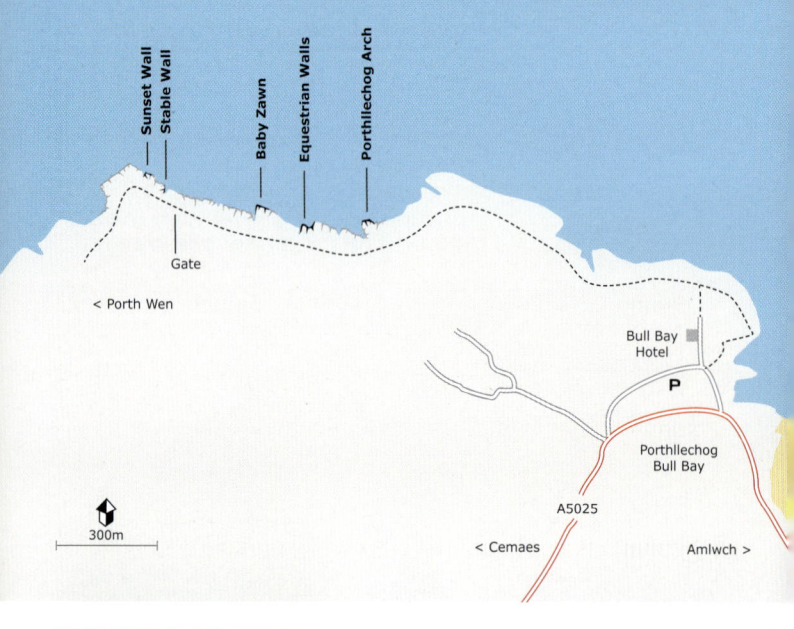

A5025

< Cemaes   Amlwch >

300m

A Limpet Trip	E5
Captain Mark Phillips	E5
The Crossing	E4
Three Day Event	E4

| Faller at the First | E2 |

| Bull Rush | VS |
| Nautical Mile | HS |

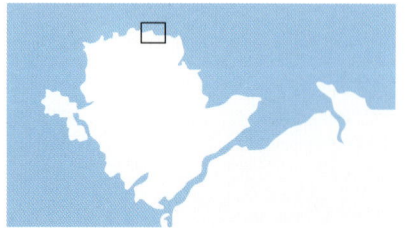

A quiet backwater with a range of intriguing routes awaiting the attention of the sea cliff connoisseur. From the west side of the bay, cliffs of varying height and quality run west towards Porth Wen, the best of which are a kilometre or so along the coast path. Initially developed in the mid-late 80s, the area saw a minor resurgence of interest in the summer of 2008.

Conditions: Quick drying crags with no major seepage issues. Some routes are tidal, some aren't.

Approach: Park on the sea front or in the car park. Walk up the hill past the Bull Bay Hotel until the road turns into a track. Follow this until it joins the coast path. Follow the coast path west wards, referring to the introductions of each section for specific approach details.

Porthllechog Arch • OS Grid ref: 419 947

1km from the hotel an arch will be seen looking back towards Porthllechog. A descent can be made leftwards to gain sea level and then a traverse back towards the arch leads to the first steep wall split by an obvious chimney at the bottom. Both of the described routes are tidal.

▶ **1. Big Wednesday E1 5b** 21m
Start up the chimney, and continue up the rightward-curving crack, with interest, to a step left at the top. Belay well back.
[M Murray, R Austin 06.88]

▶ **2. Aliens Ate My Bewick E1 5b** 18m
Ascend the same chimney, then step left and move up the wall to a break. Gain the line of disjointed grooves and follow them to the top, passing some loose rock.
[M Crook 05.88]

A further 130m just at the bottom of a dip past some stone steps is a bay (41726 94605) which contains: **3. Bye Bye Sunday Blues VS 5a** an obvious ramp gained by a bulge with a finish up a steep cleaned corner. [B Kemball, A White, G Jordan 22.06.88].

Porthllechog

estrian Walls • OS Grid ref: 416 946

ther 140m on at the top of the rise is the most important crag hereabouts. main steeper wall faces west, so it is good to go slightly past the crag g the coast path and then to look back to identify this very obvious face. access to this wall is down a steep grass ramp which leads directly to its . The routes here are steep, hairy (in more than one sense of the word) on thought provoking rock. The in situ pegs that remain are old enough arrant suspicion. The harder routes take lots of cams; large sizes being icularly useful.

razy Horse E3 5b 28m

obvious wide decomposing crack on the right side of the wall provides emorable route. Follow the crack into a cave and out to the top via an hang and offwidth.
llock, G Desroy 10.09.08]

Limpet Trip E5 6b * 30m

ant, technical wall climbing, with spaced kit and a wild finish. Ascend the left of *Crazy Horse* for 6m, moving left to a pod (#3 cam), and then make ained moves past some pegs to a rest on the left. The steep groove above ts the leader upwards with huge holds, bomber kit, and a peg to a thought oking finale which guards access to the crag top. Belay well back.
nith, G Hughes, M Crook 06.05.88]

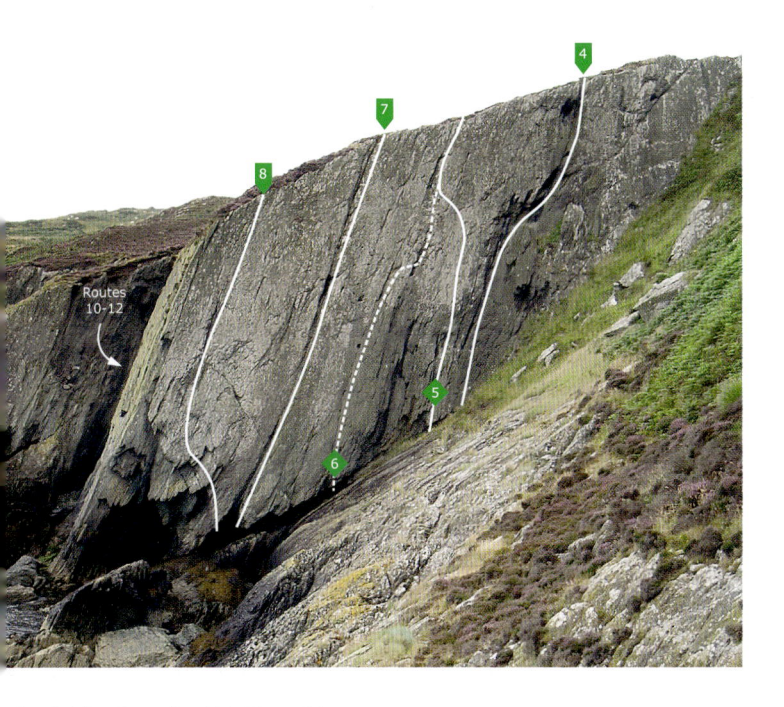

▶ **6. The Crossing E4 6b ∗∗ 34m**
A fine sustained route tackling the crack system running parallel to and right of *Captain Mark Phillips* to a finish common with *A Limpet Trip*. The crack has 3 distinctive pods which take large cams; climb it to the 3rd pod, and then make some great moves right into another, larger pod. A knee bar rest here allows some composure to be regained. Steep airy moves out of the top of the pod lead to a junction with *A Limpet Trip* at its 2nd to last peg. Finish up the steep groove as per *A Limpet Trip*.
[N Bullock, D MacManus 12.09.08]

▶ **7. Captain Mark Phillips E5 5c ∗∗ 34m**
An excellent adventurous route tackling the line of the crag. The compelling diagonal cleft swallows cams, so make sure you're packing plenty.
[E Stone, M Campbell 06.86]

▶ **8. Three Day Event E4 6a ∗ 34m**
A sustained, but well protected line (particularly if large cams are carried) gaining the thin face crack 3m right of the arête. Start at the base of the crack line of *Captain Mark Phillips* where an awkward step gains the wall to the left. Continue diagonally leftwards, via 2 overlaps, to reach the wall below the thin crack. Hard moves up and left lead to sustained climbing up the crack to the top.
[M Campbell, E Stone 06.86]

The seaward facing slab has more amenable routes and is accessed by following the easy hillside and rock down to sea level 50m to the east of the top of the crag. In the slabby-backed bay, a wall at right angles to the slabs, and encountered at the base of the descent, provides an interesting pitch:

9. Derek and Clive E1 5b 18m
Takes a cleaned crack line on the slabby wall.

The next routes described lie on the bigger slabs forming the back wall of the little bay.

10. Camel Crack HVS 5a 18m
The obvious corner line at the left hand side of the slabby wall.
[M Murray, R Austin 06.88]

11. A Sea Change E1 5a 30m
This takes a central line up the slab through the small half-height, overlap. Follow a vague corner up the lower slabs boldly up to the overlap. Surmount this, using a flake on the right, and step left to a crack. Follow this for 5m, then move left to another crack, which leads to a tricky rightwards finishing move. Belay well back.
[R Brookes, M Murray 04.87]

12. Free Bourn E1 5c 30m
A bold start leads to well-protected crack climbing. Start at the bottom right-hand side of the slab. Climb up to an overlap and small corner. Go over this, on the left, then move up and back right to the bottom of the left-hand of two cracks. Go up this until it is possible to pull into the right-hand crack, and finish up this with fingery moves. Belay well back.
[M Murray, B Wisheart 04.87]

Baby Zawn • OS Grid ref: 414 947

A further 200m on is a large steep west ward facing wall on uncompromising rock of dubious quality. The short seaward facing slabs on this wall's headland provides a few short routes. These can be accessed by scrambling down to the east.

13. The Dark Side of Growth E4 6a 12m
Start just right of the prow, and climb the overhanging spiky wall for 6m (#2 cam), and make difficult moves over the lip, to finish up an easy wall.
[G Smith, I Sherrington 05.88]

14. Fatty on Sight VS 4c 12m
5m right of the previous route is a crack line. Make an awkward move to gain the crack on the left, and climb it to the top.
[I Sherrington, G Smith 05.88]

15. Gumshoe HVS 5a 12m
A good climb up the crack right of *Fatty on Sight*.
[M Crook 05.88]

16. Babes in Consumer Land E1 5c 12m
The crack, right again.
[M Crook 05.88]

Stable Wall • OS Grid ref: 410 948

After 250m a gate is reached. Immediately down to its right is a west facing wall with a very undercut prow. Another 150m brings an east facing short steep wall where a brace of punchy little routes can be found. A mid to low tide is preferable.

17. The Trots HS 4c 6m
The obvious crack on the extreme right is over all too soon.
[G Desroy, D Simpson 16.08.08]

18. Horse Play E1 5b 8m
Start 3m left of *The Trots* below the overhanging arête. Gain the steep shattered corner, which is followed with care until a move out right to the arête enables an airy exit.
[G Desroy, D Simpson 16.08.08]

19. Neigh Bother HVS 5a 10m
Take the short steep corner to the left and gain the large ledge. Follow this rightwards up the ever steeping corner to finish.
[G Desroy, D Simpson 16.08.08]

20. Nagging Doubt E1 5b 10m
Layback moves immediately to the left of *Neigh Bother* access the large ledge. Continue up the widest brown broken crack on the right, until a diagonal crack leads up and right. Finish safely to the right. [G Desroy, D Simpson 16.08.08]

21. Faller at the First E2 5c * 12m
Start at the left hand end of the large ledge. Gain the ledge and follow the fine left hand crack to the top [G Desroy, N Bullock 22.08.08]

Sunset Wall • OS Grid ref: 409 948

This delightful triangular wall (a bit like a smaller Equestrian Walls) has a small selection of worthwhile routes. It can be found a few hundred metres further on from Stable Wall, and just before Trwynbychan, the eastern headland of Porth Wen (the large bay containing the brickworks). Access is by obvious grassy slopes west of the wall. The crag, which is semi tidal, is composed of sound and generally clean rock. The routes all use a handy block belay on the grassy top of the crag.

▸ **22. Le Cadeau de Vacances HVS 5a** 22m
An enjoyable pitch with sound rock and good protection. Start at the seaward toe of the wall and climb awkwardly up the short arête and over a bulge to gain the flakey chimney line. Move up a little then traverse left on good holds into the open right-facing groove. This leads to a straightforward left-facing groove and so to the top.
[M Crook, A Newton 14.09.08]

▸ **23. Bull Rush VS 4c** * 20m
A good start leads to a blocky finish. Nice moves up the short groove and bulge 3m right of the toe of the buttress gain a good crackline. This leads to a grassy ledge and a finish up the corner and crack above.
[M Crook, A Newton 07.09.08]

▸ **24. Nautical Mile HS 4a** * 18m
A delightful pitch on good slabby rock. Start 10m right of the toe of the buttress and follow the crackline past a diagonal break to the top.
[M Crook, A Newton 07.09.08]

Miscellaneous crags on the north coast of Anglesey

There is much esoterica to be found along the north coast of Anglesey. Some crags are of little worth, beyond giving you an excuse to go for a walk in the area, but others are actually worth climbing on and may be ripe for future development potential (or possibly not?). The crags are described clockwise (west-to-east) along the northern coast line of Anglesey.

Porth Swtan (Church Bay)
There is a stretch of short, but eminently fascinating cliffs in this area. A tight water worn corridor in the bay 500m south of Porth Swtan provides some bouldering potential.

Ynys Y Fydlyn/Carmel Head
A trio of interesting routes in a little visited area. Turn off the A5025, following signposts to Llanfairynghornwy. Drive through the village and continue for 1.5km until a triangulated T junction is reached. Turn left and follow the road for 500m until it is possible to park in the obvious parking area on the apex of the bend. Walk westwards on the obvious path for approx 1km keeping the plantation on your right. An ornamental lake is reached just before the shingle beach at the back of the prominent Ynys Fydlyn.

▸ **The Lost Pillar of Scheiser XS** 18m • OS Ref 292 917
The cliff is largely decomposing but with a single 'magnificent' vein of quartz. This is of course *The Lost Pillar*. Start just right of the biggest sea cave at the northern end of the aforementioned shingle beach. Quest upwards to the top, taking care with the rock [G Smith, M Crook 18.11.92]

▸ **Jam Yesterday, Jam Tomorrow,
but Never Jam Today E4 6a** 20m • OS Ref 292 918
This route is best approached by a tunnel through the headland which begins in the cave to the left of *The Lost Pillar of Scheiser*. More boringly, or if the tide is in walk north over the headland from the beach to a tall concrete post. (NB. The approach route over the top is subject to a seasonal access ban, which operates here from September 15th to January 31st). Go down left and find the clean slot left again at the mouth of the through cave. The route takes the clean central line up the wall, past a tied off peg at 2/3rds height. [G Huxter 1998]

Grass Tripper S 60m • OS Ref 290 923
Follow the coastal footpath northwards and contour north westwards towards the point of Carmel Head. After 250m a very prominent V groove feature can be seen. Reach the base by descending easy rocks on the north side of the groove. The route was originally climbed in 2 pitches with a peg belay at half height. [D Durkan, W Owen, D Edwards, D Williams date unknown]

Traeth Lligwy • OS Ref 504 873
At the south-west end of the beach a low limestone cliff juts into the sea. It is not however as impressive as it appears from the car park.

Miscellaneous Crags

Moelfre • OS Ref 514 858
The best thing here is a clean vertical limestone wall above a wave cut platform. There is a selection of thin technical problems best appreciate with the comfort of a bouldering pad. Approach in a few minutes by following the edge of the bay out rightwards (facing out to sea).
There is also a stretch of long low cliffs running north west from the headland on the other side (OS Ref 517 869).

Mynydd Bodafon • OS Ref 464 849
Nice spot... shame about the climbing. The best crag lies at the roadside near the church, but it is dirty and rather overgrown. Good views!

Red Wharf Bay • OS Ref 532 816
The main feature here is large rock island, Castell Mawr, the remains of an old quarry situated on the west side of the bay. Access to this is currently banned and the information is provided for historical record. The rock castle is an SSSI, in respect of its geological interest.
The top can be gained at the north west corner but it is covered in man-eating gorse bushes. Also, a band of tightly bedded limestone provides a nasty loose finish to most routes. The landmark feature is a small through cave, at the nearest corner to the car park. Here an overhung and partially overgrown bay provides a couple of interesting routes.

▶ **1. Old Wedge Route E3 6a** 37m
Take the obvious left hand crack, although retreat from below the overlap might be prudent. The right hand start to the route is HVS.

▶ **2. S W Arête HS 4b** 30m
This starts as for the previous route, and takes a rising line to reach the arête on the right. Climb the wall around the arête to the top, loose. The direct starts have been aided.

▶ **3. Red Wharf Groove VS 4c** 28m
Around on the east face is a faint groove, halfway along the wall. Climb the right hand side to ledges, then move left on an easier wall, before moving back right across the groove to finish. It has been climbed direct with some aid.

▶ **4. Enchanter's Nightshade HVS 5a** 25m
This is the greenish wall right of the previous route, and it is climbed via ledges and the arête. [1967]

▶ **5. Brown Split VS 4c** 18m
The groove system, some way right of the previous route, is climbed on loose rock. [1967]

▶ **6. North Face Route VS 4c** (2 pts) 37m
Around on the north face, a line over the obvious overhang, with 2 points of aid, and up to the top via a large ledge on the right. [1967]

▶ **7. Mobil XS** (2 pts) 30m
A little way right of the easy way up, on the west face, is a groove. This is taken direct over bulges with some aid. [1964]

Miscellaneous Crags

White Walls • OS Ref 58 82
The cliffs in this area contain an old quarry and a long stretch of sea cliffs stretching eastwards for some distance. Both the quarry and the natural crags are dirty and loose in huge chunks, and although interesting have little or no climbing potential.

Penmon Area
Another limestone area with some neglected routes and some potential for further development, particularly in the tidal bays west of Trwyn Dinmor (OS Ref 629 817). The large disused quarry at Trwyn Dinmor (known as Penmon Quarry) did see a spurt of development in the early 90s. However, there is now a large fish processing plant located in the quarry and it seems unlikely that access for climbing will be tolerated. The record of the existing routes is slightly confused, it is not entirely clear of the precise relationship between the following:

1. Quirky Hip Gyrations E3 6b 8m
On the seaward edge of the quarry a horizontal crack leads to a large ledge. Pull out to large holds trending leftwards. Steep moves up a corner lead to a triangular block. Move right around this to gain the top. [M Breialt 12.07.93]

2. Elephant Talk E2 5b 21m
A reasonable route that lies on the seaward end of the quarry. Climb friable rock to the base of the obvious crack, and follow this to a niche at 14m, pegs. Traverse left onto the exposed upper wall, peg, and finish straight up with a long reach, crux. Belay well back at an iron stake. [1988]

3. Hamamatsu Flies Again E3 5c 27m
An interesting varied route through big roofs on solid rock. Good gear. Ascend the scree slope directly below the cliffs to largest roof. Climb suspect rock until a groove leads directly to a corner and ledge underneath the first roof. A long sling can then be attached to an iron nail here. Traverse out, turning the roof on its left and make a hard move up to get both feet on the lip and a rest. Ascend the crack to a second roof and make a strenuous traverse left under this. [R Durnford, M Boater 07.08.91]

4. Driller Killer (grade unknown) ?m
A delicate route on mainly sound rock. Start below the obvious drill line and ascend shattered rock to an obvious crack at 5m. Good gear. Pull round the bulge with difficulty and onto the main face and the drill line where the rock becomes solid. Follow the drill line on small positive holds to a good peg at 13m. Move right to a line of flakes. Move back into the drill line, and carefully trend left to gain the arête just below the obvious ledge. From the ledge, make delicate moves left on suspect rock and pull up an overhanging finish. [R Durnford, M Boater 22.08.91]

5. Passions of Fools HVS 4c 33m
Takes the slab and corner left of Driller Killer. Finish moving right from the ledge of Driller Killer. [M Boater, M Raw, R Durnford 22.07.91]

6. ?? Dee HVS 5a 40m
Hanging crack 12m left of Passions of Fools. [M Boater, R Durnford 28.03.92]

A few old quarry faces close to the Priory and running south from Penmon Point provide some potential for development.

Benllech Crags

Area: North Coast
Style: Sport/trad (single pitch)
Aspect: East/north
Rock type: Limestone
Approach: 10 - 20 minutes
Altitude: Sea level (semi-tidal)
OS Grid ref: Varied (see crag intros)

Gone Fishing	F7b

Trigonometry	F6c+
Boys From the Black Stuff	F6c
Puppy Power	F6c
Waking the Witch	F6c
Six Blade Knife	F6c
Costa Del Benllech	F6c
Sportingly Pocketed	F6b+
Down to the Waterline	F6b+
Crackpot Crack	F6b+
Vi Et Armis	F6b+
Wind of Change	F6b
Christmas Cracker	F6b
A Quiet American	F6b
Contraflow	F6b
Hit me like a Hammer	F6b
A Pocketful of Pockets	F6a+
Fossil Zone	F6a+
Cracking Sport	F6a+
Sporting Crack	F6a+
The Song Remains the Same	F6a+
Hard Shoulder	F6a+

Escape Route	F5+
Carousel Ambra	F5+

The Seventh Wave	E2
Ramble On	E2
Trampled Underfoot	E2
The Whispers	E1
Registration Blues	HVS
Heulwen	HVS

Carlsberg Crack	VS

Pete Robins on the steep **Christmas Cracker** F6b, Craig Dwlban   photo: Rachael Barlow

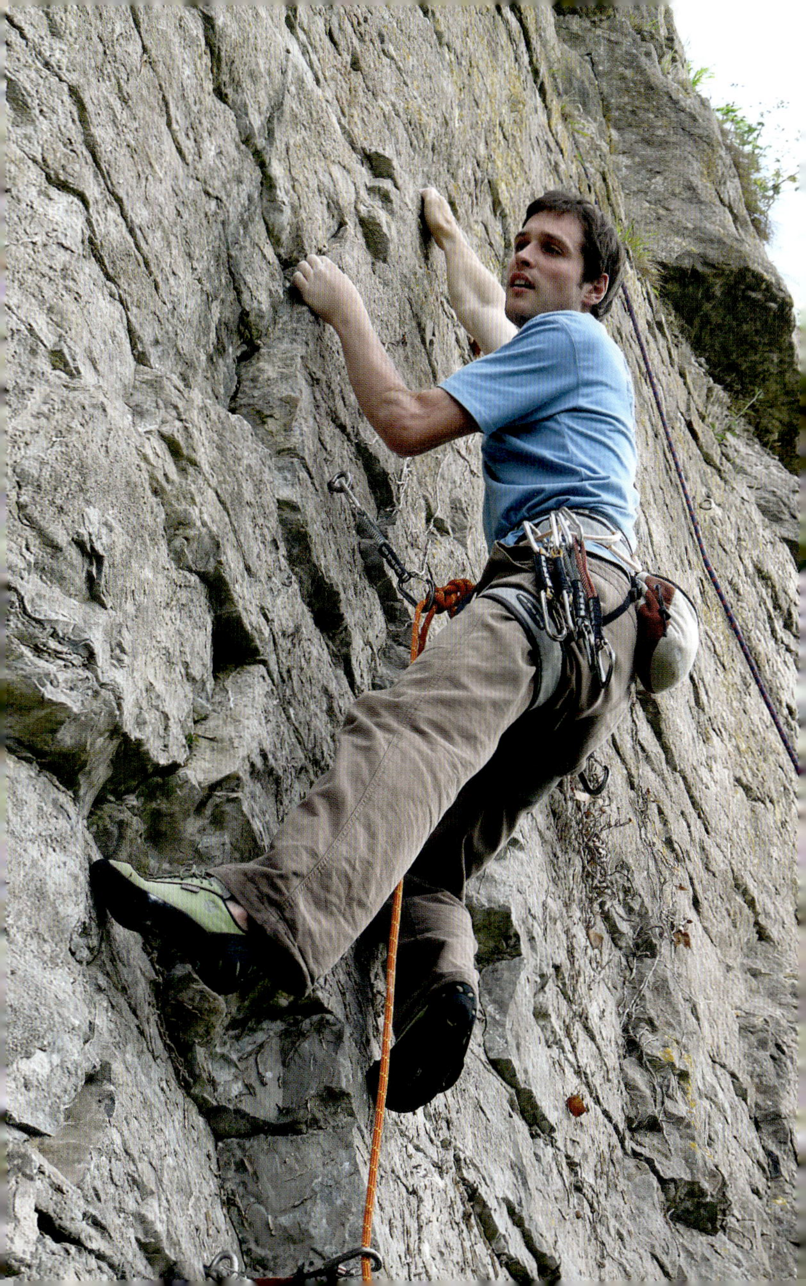

A series of easy access limestone cliffs running along the coast from Benllech offer an appealing spread of sport and trad routes throughout the F5+ - F7b and VS – E3 grade range. Many of the routes were originally climbed in 1991, and the whole area was re-equipped over the winter of 2007/08.

None of these crags is a major venue, but the seaside resort ambience, ease of access and generally non-serious nature of the routes all add up to an attractive prospect, if only as a pleasant diversion from the more committing Gogarth sea cliffs.

The rock is compact and tightly banded limestone, giving rise to clean open walls, typically dotted with numerous horizontal edges and cleaved by the occasional vertical crack or narrow groove system. Most of the routes, including some of the trad routes, are equipped with bolt lower-offs or bolt belays.

Conditions: Craig Dwlban is non tidal, but all the crags running north from Benllech are tidal to some degree or other. It is possible to reach the base of Leaning Wall and Angler's Wall Upper Tier at all but high spring tides, but access to Angler's Wall is restricted to a few hours around low tide. Craig Dwlban is north-east facing and receives some morning sun. Leaning Wall Area and Angler's Wall face east and also receive morning sunshine. Hidden Wall is north facing and shady.
All of the crags are quick drying, and seepage is rarely a problem. The barnacled lower sections of the tidal crags do stay annoyingly damp, although on a breezy day this is less of an issue.

Looking past the Benllech Isaf café towards the start of the coastal footpath ∧
photo: Simon Panton

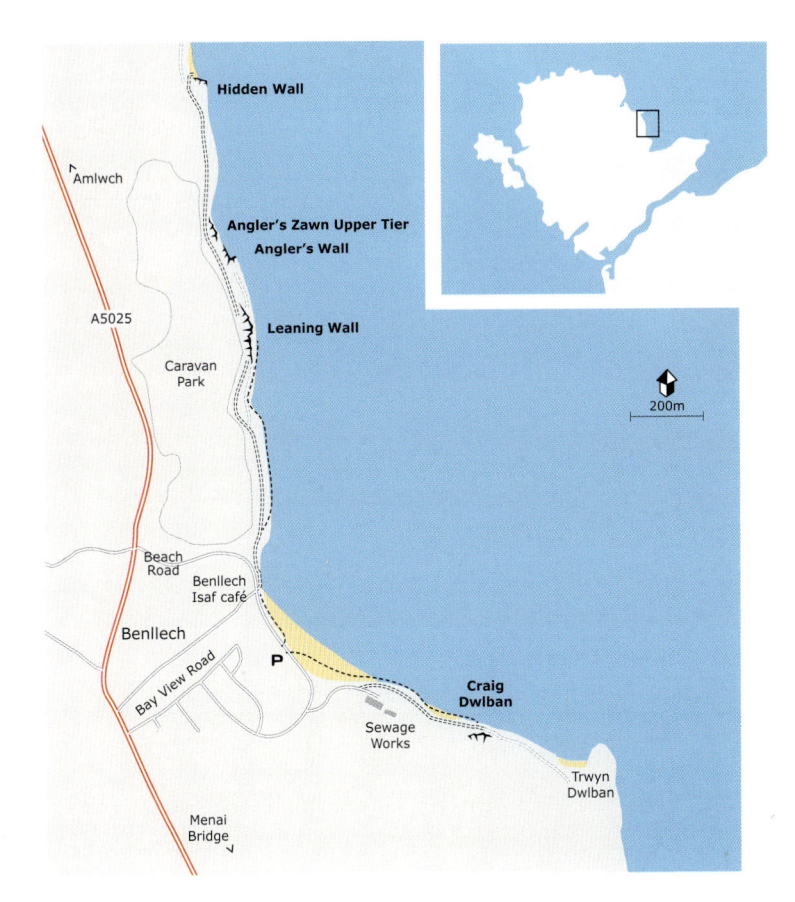

Approach: To reach Craig Dwlban from the public car park, in front of the Benllech beach, walk southwards along the beach (or if the tide is in along the coastal path), passing the sewage works to reach the crag in 10 minutes. The other crags can be reached by walking northwards towards Moelfre along the land side of the beach, joining the coastal path by the side of the Benllech Isaf café. Leave the coastal path just after a large metal 'kissing gate' entrance to the caravan site. Go down the steps with a brick supported handrail. Walk round a small bay (with some minor bouldering potential) and follow the wave cut platform to reach the first crag (Leaning Wall). Angler's Wall lies a small distance on from the Fossil Zone wall. To reach Hidden Wall follow the coastal path above the cliffs for about 5 - 10 minutes until it is possible drop into a pebble beach bay (Borth-wen), via some wooden steps.

268 **Benllech** • Craig Dwlban

Craig Dwlban OS Grid ref: 528 822

This small disused quarry located next to the Benllech beach, with a mixture of sport and trad routes, gives pleasant open wall climbing on good limestone. The crag is non tidal, and as such is a good option if you have arrived at high tide.

Main Wall
The first section of rock, at the bottom of the wooden steps.

▶ **1. Poison Ivy F6a** 12m
Follow the crack line on the right side of the face. A steep lower section gains the upper wall and a bulge (crux).
[T Peers 2007]

▶ **2. Central Reservation F6b** 14m
An easy lower section leads to the steep upper wall. Climb this heading left at the top and make a committing move (crux) to gain jugs and the lower off shared with *Hard Shoulder*.
[T Peers, D Peers 10.07]

▶ Variation: **Central Reservation - Diversion Finish F6b** 13m
Finish rightwards to the *Poison Ivy* lower off
[T Peers, D Peers, J Cuff 16.03.08]

▶ **3. Hard Shoulder F6a+** * 13m
A suprisingly awkward lower section leads to nice open wall climbing and a shared lower off of with *Central Reservation*. [T Peers, D Peers, J Cuff 16.03.08]

4. Christmas Cracker F6b ∗ 9m
A good steep route which follows the obvious crack on the left of the main wall to a lower off. Nice but short-lived climbing. From the ledge, strenuous moves gain a block. Continue on positive crimps (crux) to gain a jug where the difficulties end. Lower off. [T Peers, D Peers 26.12.07]

5. Contraflow F6b ∗ 9m
A test of wing span. Start at the base of the wall next to the block and make sidepull lunges to gain the easier climbing above and a lower off shared with *Escape Route*. [T Peers, D Peers 25.07.08]

6. Escape Route F5+ ∗ 9m
A good route which follows the big crack on the far left of the main wall. Pleasant steep climbing on positive holds and jugs throughout. There is a lower off shared with *Contraflow*. [T Peers, D Peers 25.07.08]

Left Wall

7. Greaseball E1/2 5b 8m
The route follows a faint crack-line splitting the face. An easy start leads to the upper wall, passing to the left of a grease-like stain. Side runners (small wires) on the left protect the upper section. [T Peers, D Peers 10.07]

8. Dwlban Arete HVS 4c 8m
Start on the left of the arête and climb up on good holds. Pass the half-height bulge and climb the upper arête on its left. [T Peers, D Peers 10.07]

270 **Benllech** • Leaning Wall Area

Leaning Wall Area OS Grid ref: 523 833

This collection of clean walls provide a series of good sport routes in the F6a+ - F7b range. Access is possible during most tidal states, so a typical visit to the area will often be focussed here.

▶ **9. Costa Del Benllech F6c** * 12m
Takes the line of resin bolts on the left hand side of the wall to a lower off.
[P Targett, I Lloyd-Jones 1991]

▶ **10. Trigonometry F6c+** * 12m
Start by climbing the 'trigonometrical' feature then continue steeply on small holds up the line of bolts to a lower off.
[I Lloyd-Jones, P Targett, C Davies 1991]

▶ **11. Crackpot Crack F6b+** * 12m
The crack right of *Trigonometry* to the same lower off.
[C Davies, P Targett, I Lloyd-Jones 1991]

▶ **12. The Tide is Turning F6b** 12m
The shallow V groove just left of the large corner crack provides a powerful and sustained route, which only eases on the final section leading to the lower off. The start requires a little care and there is some loose rock higher on the route.
[I Lloyd-Jones 20.12.07]

Leaning Wall Area • **Benllech** 271

▶ **13. Gone Fishing F7b** ∗ 12m
Relentlessly overhanging, yet varied in character, this route has the advantage of staying dry in light rain. A steep start gains a ledge; continue up the groove/crack to reach the small roof. Launch up the headwall to finish on a thank god jug just over the final little roof. Lower off.
[J Ratcliffe 31.07.08]

▶ **14. Fossil Zone F6a+** ∗ 12m
A sustained little number; technical and fingery all the way, although the hardest climbing is on the lower section. 50m right of *The Tide is Turning* a narrow strip of clean rock presents an obvious challenge. Move carefully up the ledgey start, and then zig-zag upwards using numerous small fossil holds to reach a lower off.
[I Lloyd-Jones 20.12.07]

272 Benllech • Angler's Wall

Angler's Wall OS Grid ref: 522 834

Walk along the wave cut platform from Fossil Zone for 50m to reach an obvious right angle tidal zawn. If approaching directly from the car park in Benllech, follow the cliff top coastal path for 10-15 minutes until the path drops down into an opening; the zawn lies just below.

The base of the crag is only accessible 1 or 2 hours either side of low tide (3-4 hours in total). Access is either by abseil or by walking over beyond the top of the *Wind of Change* wall and scrambling down to the pebble/boulder beach passing one awkward, and often slimy, step which requires care.

The routes are all quite short, but they do pack a lot in. The barnacled lower section tends to be damp, and can make for some awkward feet cleaning scenarios once the dry rock is reached.

▶ **15. Carlsberg Crack VS 4c** * 10m
Takes the deep crack line left of the cave.
[I Lloyd-Jones, P Targett 1991]

▶ **16. Trampled Underfoot E2 5b** * 10m
The obvious bow shaped crack just right of *Carlsberg Crack*, finish direct.
[I Lloyd-Jones, P Targett 1991]

▶ **17. Candystore Rock E2 5c** 10m
Follow *Trampled Underfoot* until it is possible to traverse rightwards and finish up the headwall. [I Lloyd-Jones, P Targett 1991]

Angler's Wall • **Benllech** 273

▸ **18. Mother Ship F6b** 10m
The right edge of the cave provides a steep little route. Climb up the blunt arête to gain the crack, which leads quickly to the top.
[I Lloyd-Jones, P Targett 30.08.08]

▸ **19. The Song Remains the Same F6a+** * 10m
A good route. Start up the crack to the blow hole then fire directly up the steep wall just right to a lower off/belay on the ledge above.
[I Lloyd-Jones, P Targett 1991]

▸ **20. Ramble On E2 5b** * 10m
The thin crackline with a small roof at the bottom to the right of the previous route.
[I Lloyd-Jones, P Targett 1991]

▸ **21. Dazed and Confused F6a+** 10m
Right again after a blocky start a line of 3 bolts leads the way up the wall to a belay on the ledge above.
[I Lloyd-Jones, P Targett 1991]

▸ **22. The Whispers E1 5a** 10m
The thin crackline in the centre of the wall passing through the obvious inverted triangle at half height.
[P Targett, I Lloyd-Jones 1991]

▸ **23. Registration Blues HVS 5b** * 10m
The thin crack right of *The Whispers*. [P Targett, I Lloyd-Jones 1991]

▶ **24. Reflections E3 5c** ∗ 10m
The thin crackline right again with a small overlap on its right.
[P Targett, I Lloyd-Jones 1991]

▶ **25. Pencil Crack VS 5a** 10m
Follow the thin but well protected crack line just right of *Reflections*.
[P Targett, I Lloyd-Jones 30.08.08]

▶ **26. Paper Moves F5+** 10m
The easy corner direct to the shallow groove in the arete.
[P Targett, I Lloyd-Jones 1991]

▶ **27. Carousel Ambra F5+** ∗ 10m
Climb the initially blocky arete via 3 bolts to a thinner finish which gains the belay.
[I Lloyd-Jones, P Targett 1991]

Angler's Wall • **Benllech** 275

▶ **28. Guitar Solo F6a** 10m
The thin crack line to a blocky finish just left of *Vi et Armis*. Lower off.
[I Lloyd-Jones 1991]

▶ **29. Vi Et Armis F6b+** ∗ 10m
A barnacled boulder problem start gains the first horizontal break... small holds and 3 bolts lead the way to the top and a shared belay on the cliff top block.
[P Targett, I Lloyd-Jones 1991]

▶ **30. Wind of Change F6b** ∗ 10m
Another barnacled boulder problem start gains the first horizontal break... small holds and 3 bolts lead the way to larger holds and the top (to the same shared belay).
[I Lloyd-Jones, P Targett 1991]

▶ **31. Drum Solo F5+** 10m
The thin crack line to a blocky finish right of *Wind of Change* finishing just left of the hanging arete. Lower off. [I Lloyd-Jones 1991]

Benllech • Angler's Zawn Upper Tier

Angler's Zawn Upper Tier

The series of cliffs extending northwards from Angler's Zawn have the best routes at Benllech. The attractive adjacent walls of The Grey Bay and The White Wall are the only sections developed so far. Plans are afoot for further development – check **www.groundupclimbing.com** for updated topos.

The routes can be accessed at virtually all states of tide (except perhaps a high Spring tide) by scrambling down the left hand end of Anglers Zawn (as you look out to sea) and walking/scrambling over boulders a short distance (approximately 50m) northwards. This descent is slimy and does require care; a knotted rope has been placed here to reduce the potential for accidents – if in doubt abseil from the top of the *Wind of Change* wall (this latter option is only available at lowish tides). It is also possible to reach the crag by following the wave cut platforms and boulder jams south from the top of Hidden Wall.

The Grey Bay

▶ **32. Heulwen HVS 5a** * 16m
The obvious traditional line that defines the left side of the Grey Bay. Start up the groove before doing battle with the continuation crack. Well protected with a steep and strenuous finish leading to a lower off.
[I Lloyd-Jones, Phil Targett (both lead) 28.09.08]

▶ **33. A Quiet American F6b** ** 16m
The thin line of weakness right of Heulwen provides a superb sport route. A balancey crux section on pockets leads to a wonderful finishing jug. Shared lower off with *A Pocket Full of Pockets*.
[P Targett, I Lloyd-Jones (both lead) 28.09.08]

▶ **34. A Pocketful of Pockets F6a+** * 16m
Another good route climbing direct to the *A Quiet American* lower off.
[I Lloyd-Jones, P Targett 08.11.08]

The White Wall

▶ **35. Sportingly Pocketed F6b+** ** 18m
A fine climb of Pen Trwyn quality and hard for the grade. Ascend the left hand of the 3 crack lines on the clean white wall; once the crack ends move right to gain a pocket. Continue up via 2 undercut pockets to gain the scoop; an excellent sequence of moves using pockets, side pulls and crimps will eventually gain the lower off. [I Lloyd-Jones, P Targett (both lead) 23.09.08]

▶ **36. Sporting Crack F6a+** ** 18m
The middle crack line yields a steep and strenuous challenge. Follow the impressive crack line to a scoop, surmount the bulge on thin holds and continue up to lower off. [I Lloyd-Jones, P Targett (both lead) 21.09.08]

▶ **37. Cracking Sport F6a+** ** 18m
The right hand crack line of the trio gives more steep and strenuous climbing; a series of interesting formations and pockets lead to a lower off.
[I Lloyd-Jones, P Targett (both lead) 19.09.08]

278 Benllech • Hidden Wall

Hidden Wall OS Grid ref: 521 838

Hidden Wall lies on the edge of a pebbley bay 8 minutes walk further along the coastal footpath from Angler's Zawn. It is also possible to reach the crag by following the wave cut platforms and boulder jams north from Angler's Zawn Upper Tier.

The climbing takes place on the north facing black wall on the right (facing out) of the bay. The wall bulges slightly in its middle third and then lays back to just off vertical in its upper third.

The climbing is typically intense, fingery and sometimes blind (just where, in that sea of black rock, is the next hangeable hold?). In an unchalked state the routes can be tricky to onsight; often a degree of zig-zagging around is required before the solution becomes apparent. The rock is mostly solid and well fused, but the odd sugary edge is prone to breakage – this minor issue will presumably clean up over time.

The barnacled base of the wall does retain dampness and it pays to carry a small beer towel with which to clean off your rock shoes once the cleaner, dry rock of the wall proper is reached.

There is only 1 cliff face lower off on the wall: at the top of *Hit me like a Hammer*. There is however a natural thread at the top of *Waking the Witch* and a double bolt belay on the ledge above the finish of *Boys From the Black Stuff*.

▶ **38. Hit me like a Hammer F6b** ∗ 12m
A fine route, taking the obvious line of blocky grooves on the right side of the wall. Pull steeply through the initial steepness on large friendly holds until, moving onto the upper wall, things turn a touch more technical. The rampy ledge system leads quickly to a lower off.
[I Lloyd-Jones, P Targett 1991]

▶ **39. Waking the Witch F6c** ∗ 12m
The slight line of weakness left of *Hit me like a Hammer* provides an intense outing. It shares a bolt with *Puppy Power* just above the ¾ height ledge. There is large thread belay on top and/or a shared bolt belay at the top of *Puppy Power*.
[P Targett, I Lloyd-Jones 1991]

▶ **40. Puppy Power F6c** ∗ 10m
An even slighter line forcing a path up the centre of the wall. Work up the wall, trending slightly right, to reach the 3/4 height ledge; clip the bolt (shared with *Waking the Witch*) above this, and then trend left to gain the top. Bolt belay.
[I Lloyd-Jones, P Targett 1991]

▶ **41. Boys From the Black Stuff F6c** ∗ 10m
Another intense route with some blind and fingery pulls. Once above the barnacles gain an obvious good hold, then zig left to use a good edge shared with route 25, before zagging back up right past small crimps to reach a large flatty. A tricky and gripping rock-up must be executed before the next bolt can be clipped. If successful, cruise onwards via small, but positive edges to the top. Bolt belay.
[I Lloyd-Jones, P Targett 1991]

▶ **42. Six Blade Knife F6c** ∗ 10m
A good route with a devious and hard start leading into a steadier finish. Crunch up the barnacles to the right side of the large ledge, but swerve off right, making some hard moves to gain the good edge shared with *Boys From the Black Stuff*, before kicking back up left to reach the sanctuary of a small ledge. Rock up and gain the upper overlap, and a finish common with *Down to the Waterline*.
[P Targett, I Lloyd-Jones 1991]

▶ **43. Down to the Waterline F6b+** ∗ 10m
Action packed moves around the bulge precede a nerve wracking teeter up to the top bolt and an easier finish common with *Six Blade Knife*. Gain the ledge, shuffle leftwards and power through the bulge, continuing up and rightwards past the overlap feature.
[P Targett, I Lloyd-Jones 1991]

▶ **44. The Seventh Wave E2 5c** ∗ 10m
The hanging crack is the best line on the wall; the climbing isn't bad either. Start as for *Down to the Waterline*, but shuffle further leftwards along the ledge, before climbing through the bulge into the easier upper section of the crack, which leads quickly to the top.
[P Targett, I Lloyd-Jones 1991]

A pair of coastal limestone crags close to the National Trust Fedw Fawr site. The first cliff, White Beach Crag is a west facing non tidal single pitch sport crag that was originally developed in 1990/91 by Chris Parkin, Nick Biven, Frazer Ball and George Smith. It was re-equipped in 2007 and offers a dozen routes in the F6a – F7b+ range. Style wise it is reminiscent of the Marine Drive Pen Trwyn crags at Llandudno, albeit with a more crystalline rock.

In early 2008 the less accessible Fedw Fawr crag was developed by Ian Lloyd-Jones and Phil Targett. This offers 12 short sport routes on superb quality, compact limestone with a grade range of F5+ - F6c. There is also some bouldering potential at the right side of the crag. There is a 3rd area too: a good tidal bouldering venue located on a wave cut platform further west along the coast (it is visible from the Fedw Fawr crag). There are around 50 problems with a grade range from V0-/Font 4 – V8/Font 7b. The landings are generally flat rock. Unfortunately there is no official cliff top access at the moment.

Finally, there is a pillar of curious rock on the main White Beach (just beyond the point at which the steps open out onto the beach) which provides some bouldering interest.

Fedw Fawr

Crane Fly	F7b+/7c
The Wasp Factory	F7b
Hip to be Square	F6c+
Statement of Roof	F6c
Sir Lobalot	F6c
River of Steel	F6b+
Sexy Garcon	F6b+
Mike's Glory	F6b
42 Moves	F6b
Tricky Fruitbat	F6a+
Bunty	F6a+
Mr Hulo	F6a

Area: North-East coast
Style: Sport (single pitch)
Aspect: West/North
Rock type: Limestone
Approach: 10/20 minutes
Altitude: Sea level (non tidal/tidal)
OS Grid ref: varied (see crag intros)

↑ Gemma Powell on **Bunty** 6a+ photo: Rob Lamey

Fedw Fawr • Approach

Access note: The area is already popular with both walkers and the fishing fraternity. Parking is limited and the approach road very narrow, with few passing places. Weekends can be busy, particularly during the summer holidays. Consequently, the smart thing to do, especially in the summer, is to avoid weekend visits.

Conditions: With the exception of *42 Moves*, White Beach Crag is non tidal. It has a pleasant westerly aspect with a plentiful quota of sunshine. It dries quickly and doesn't suffer from any significant seepage.
Fedw Fawr is tidal and north facing. It can be accessed 2 - 3 hours either side of low tide (approximately 4 - 5 hours in total). Some seepage lines should be expected after rain, although these don't have much impact on the existing lines. As with all sea level crags, a light breeze is preferable to dry off any remaining dampness once the tide has receded.

Approach: From Beaumaris follow the B5109 north to Llangoed. At the far end of the village turn left and follow the road to Glanrafon (1.5kms). The road starts to rise up a hill; turn right at the triangle junction before the top of the hill is reached, and then take the first left turn after 70m. Follow the narrow road for 700m past a left hand bend (hoping that you don't meet someone driving the other way!) to reach the small National Trust car park above White Beach. See the crag introductions for the rest of the approach details.

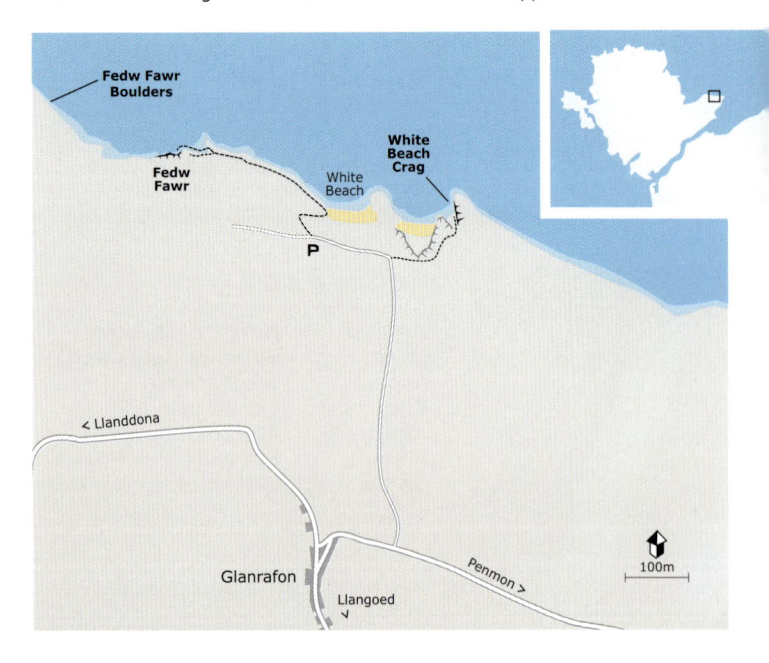

White Beach Crag OS grid ref: 608 818

A good selection of routes on an attractive sweep of limestone. The rock is generally good, but a little care is required with the calcite crystals which form the business end of many of the holds.

Approach: To reach the crag from the car park walk back along the approach road and cross the stile in the wall at the apex of the bend in the road. A vague path contours eastwards across the field for around the top of one depression and then quickly to arrive at the top of the zawn with the crag clearly visible on the right (facing out). Drop down steep grass to reach the base of the wall. (5-10 minutes)

The routes are described from right to left.

1. The Man Who Would be String F6c+ 8m
A short line just left of the large ivy patch on the right side of the crag. Start on big crozzley holds and finish on small crozzley dinks at a 'middle of nowhere' lower off.
[T Taylor, A Barton 29.06.91]

2. Crane Fly F7b+/7c * 15m
An intense and sequency line meandering up the wall. A fine route, but hard to on sight.
[G Smith 1990]

3. Sexy Garcon F6b+ * 16m
A hard start followed by easier, but still sustained climbing. Attack the steep initial wall to gain the hanging flake, and then follow its crystal edge to the roof. After a final pull on the widening flake the route ends at a lower off on the upper wall.
[C Parkin 1990]

4. Hip to be Square F6c+ * 18m
Boulder out the steep wall directly below the 1st bolt (or cop out with an easier start on right) and gain the base of the hanging groove. Pull through this and move up to the overhang; climb over this and move left with difficulty to a lower off. The original finish went up right to the *Sexy Garcon* lower off.
[T Taylor 1991]

5. Project line
An apparently unclimbed line with 2 very old bolts with aluminium hangers (1st snapped) leading to a blank section 1.5m below the overhang/break.

6. Tricky Fruitbat F6a+ ** 22m
Climb straight up the impending wall on large holds, pulling on to a ledge after the 3rd bolt. Tackle the bulging head wall using a short crozzly crack and continue to the lower off.
[N Biven 21.08.91]

7. Bunty F6a+ * 15m
Fancy some more steep jug pulling? Use the hanging flake to gain good horizontals, and then continue to a lower off below the headwall. The route originally traversed right to finish up *Tricky Fruitbat*.
[N Biven 24.08.91]

▶ **8. Frazer's Direct F?** 15m
A single old bolt (not re-equipped) marks the line. It needs a proper finish through the bulging headwall.
[F Ball 1990]

▶ **9. The Wasp Factory F7b** * 22m
Start right of the 1st bolt and climb up and diagonally left then right passing the 2nd bolt to where the climbing eases. Don't relax yet though as the final headwall provides a taxing crux section before the sanctuary of the lower off is reached.
[N Biven 24.08.91]

▶ **10. Mike's Glory F6b** ** 24m
The longest offering on the crag provides a fine jug haul, in fact its almost 'Riglos comes to Anglesey'. Start up the not-too-steep section on the final land bound section of the crag. Climb up then leftwards before switching back right to finish with a short bulging head wall leading to the lower off. The obvious steep crack provides an alternative and difficult way around this final section.
[Mike from Bangor Uni 1990]

White Beach Crag • **Fedw Fawr** 285

▸ **11. River of Steel F6b+** ** 18m
Superb technical climbing up the crack line. A thin and slightly gripping start (where's that clip stick when you need it?) leads to the base of the crack line where the angle gets steeper. Follow the crack to a lower off.
[F Ball 1990]

▸ **12. Albin & Co. F7a** 18m
A potentially good climb spoilt by crumbly rock. Expect some loose holds, some powerful, blind reaches and a thin technical crux just when you thought it was all over. Start just right of arête and climb diagonally rightwards passing 2 bolts (1st crux) to gain a short flake where the angle eases. Continue gently on the brown holds midway between the arête and the crack line of *River of Steel* to a tricky 2nd crux high on the wall. There is a lower off on head wall, or alternatively finish over the top and belay on large blocks and take in some sun.
[C Parkin 1990]

▸ **13. 42 Moves F6b** * 18m
This is the obvious bolted line 8m left of *Albin & Co.* A fun, steep route with an entertaining crux at the top. Climb up through steep ground on horizontal breaks to reach the blanker headwall above. Some thin moves gain a grassy ledge and the lower off above. [I Lloyd-Jones, P Targett 17.02.08]

286 Fedw Fawr • Fedw Fawr

Fedw Fawr OS grid ref: 602 822

A short, tidal crag with a selection of neat sport routes on excellent rock. All routes top out. Alternatively set up a lower off using slings etc on the large blocks on the ledge.

Approach: To reach the crag from the car park descend the steps to White Beach and head left (facing out) following the coast west (towards Red Wharf Bay), moving over boulders on the rock platform. After about 10 minutes scramble down a ledge and short corner to reach a lower level and keep going until you reach an open bay with a distinctive bright green band of algae covering a rock step. Scramble down via easy steps 15-20m left of the bright green algae band and walk across the sea weed covered wave cut platform, or walk round scrambling over blocks at the top of the algae band to scramble down ledges (tricky at the bottom) 15-20m beyond the algae band. The initial routes wall is just around the other side of the promontory. Alternatively, abseil from blocks to reach the base of the crag. (15-20 minutes)

The routes are described from left to right.

The first 4 lines lie on the wall left of the main roof. Belay on/lower off large blocks on the ledge above.

▶ **14. Les Vacances F6b** 8m
Takes the wall left of *Mr Hulo*. From the barnacle covered ledge make steep moves up the wall just right of a seepage line.
[I Lloyd-Jones, P Targett 13.05.08]

Fedw Fawr • **Fedw Fawr** 287

▶ **15. Mr Hulo F6a** ∗ 8m
The steep wall left of the deep hole at ¾ height provides a fine route. A reachy start gains positive pockets leading to the top.
[P Targett, I Lloyd-Jones 06.05.08]

▶ **16. Unclimbed F6c** 9m
Right of the deep hole at ¾ height, follow the rightwards trending diagonal line passing a small sloping ramp feature.

▶ **17. Sir Lobalot F6c** ∗ 9m
A great little route with some funky rock. A steep start gains the horizontal break, good holds and foot jams, followed by large pocketed holds and cracks which lead to the top. [I Lloyd-Jones 13.05.08]

The main roof section to the right is currently unclimbed, although some obvious hard project lines do exist.

▶ **18. Statement of Roof F6c** ∗ 10m
An action packed route forcing a line of weakness through the right side of the main roof. Climb up steeply on the left, and then trace the thin crack rightwards through the roof (really steep!) to reach easier angled rock. Continue more easily to the top and belay on/lower off the bolt on the large block on the ledge above.
[I Lloyd-Jones, P Targett 13.05.08]

▶ **19. Scream to a Sigh F6c** 9m
Start by pulling through the initial roof and continue up, overcoming the final problematic roof. Top out and belay on/lower off the blocks on the ledge.
[I Lloyd-Jones, P Targett 06.05.08]

The next 3 lines lies 5m right of *Scream to a Sigh*. Top out and belay/lower off the blocks on the ledge (large slings).

▶ **20. Back in Black F5+** 9m
A steep start gains a shallow groove, move right out of this and climb the wall above past some large holds.
[I Lloyd-Jones, P Targett 14.03.08]

▶ **21. For those about to Rock... F6a** 9m
Start just left of the obvious groove of *We Salute You!* A steep start gains a shallow groove; move right out of this and climb the blunt rib/wall above.
[I Lloyd-Jones, P Targett (both led) 14.03.08]

▶ **22. We Salute You! F6a+** 9m
The attractive leftwards trending groove line. A steep start leads to the easier groove line above.
[I Lloyd-Jones, P Targett (both led) 14.03.08]

Fedw Fawr • **Fedw Fawr** 289

The last 3 routes can be found a 5m to the right, just beyond the bulging prow. Top out and belay/lower off the bolt on the ledge.

▶ **23. The Missing Link F6b** 8m
Start below a ledge with a rusty chain wedged in a break to the left of *Rockferry*. 2 bolts lead the way.
[I Lloyd-Jones, P Targett (both led) 13.05.08]

▶ **24. Rockferry F6a+** 8m
Balancey climbing up the middle of the wall.
[I Lloyd-Jones, P Targett (both led) 13.05.08]

▶ **25. Rock Monster F6b** 9m
The last line on the wall has a bouldery start. Pull through the initial roof with conviction and continue more easily to the top.
[I Lloyd-Jones, P Targett (both led) 13.05.08]

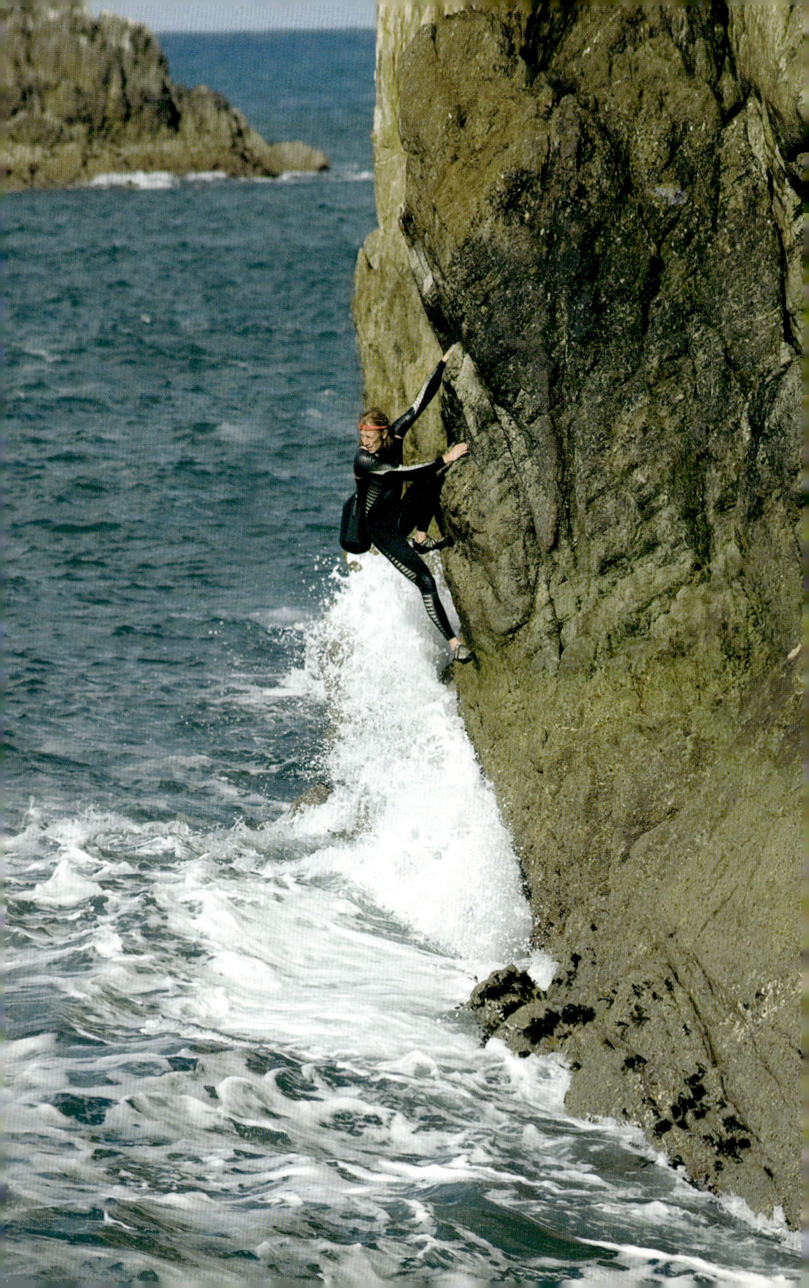

Sea Level Traversing

To a twisted and aquatically inclined minority this perverse activity is at the heart of the Gogarth adventure experience, mazimising as it does the time spent in the magical zone of perfect sea washed crozzle, between the sea and the leaning walls. The tides, waves and temperature will make or break the experience, and in less than ideal conditions you have an epic on a plate. Traditionally done with a rope for the Tyroleans, the traverses are now more commonly soloed, with short swims across unclimbable sections. Confident swimming ability is essential. Some prior knowledge of the cliffs, tides, key descents and main routes is very useful. A wetsuit is strongly recommended on all but the hottest days. They also provide good protection against the abrasive rock. A small dry bag is also useful; pack some food, water and this guide in it (information is power) and consider carrying some or all of the following: a throw line and waist belt, a buoyancy aid, a helmet, a mini day and night flare. If you are thinking of taking a chalk bag, you have seriously misunderstood the deal.

The traverses are best attempted on a falling Neap Tide. This means that generally the traverses become easier and less committing as the tide falls and more holds, boulders and ledges become exposed. Consider also the direction of tidal flow if traversing on exposed headlands. The tidal race which forms at North Stack on an ebb tide is especially powerful/dangerous. Never underestimate being in, or just above, the Irish Sea at the bottom of Gogarth. In less than calm conditions some of these traverses are impossible, and several fatalities and rescues have occurred. In 1980 Scottish climber John Cunningham died on a low level traverse at South Stack after being swept out to sea while trying to rescue someone. Escape routes are often well spaced, or, in the case of the Main Cliff, non-existent, without confident soloing abilities. Spring high tides and choppy seas should be avoided. Even on calm days you should be sensitive to the risks associated with the ferry wake (see the Safety on the Crags section on page 15).

Some indication of the number of swims necessary is provided. Varying water levels, critical barnacle locations, and personal ability all contribute to the degree of difficulty and extent of baptismal antics experienced. The same traverse can provide varied experiences at different water levels and in different directions.

Deep Water Soloing

The Gogarth North crags do not provide an ideal venue for deep water soloing. There are plenty of cliff sections that are directly above deep water; the problem is that they are generally too far above it. If you fall from a height greater than 12m whilst soloing, the fact that you are above deep water doesn't mean that you're not in very real danger. Even a fall into water from less than 12m could end in disaster, especially if you consider the potential for collisions with under water rock protrusions.

There are a few suitable, albeit potentially serious, DWS propositions at Gogarth, however it wouldn't be appropriate to list them here. They are best scoped out by experienced activists who know well the inherent risks of this exciting, but ultimately dangerous game.

< Streaky Desroy fully kitted out with wetsuit and dry bag, keeping an eye out for the incoming ferry wake, on the Main Cliff section photo: Jethro Kiernan

The Main Cliff to North Stack

A Gogarth classic, with amazing scenery and a degree of commitment (there is only one easy escape point between Upper Tier and North Stack.). Between 3 and 5 short swims are normal, and it is a much easier proposition at low tide.

Tidal issues: Gogarth Bay is generally sheltered from strong tidal flows, but not from big seas. Wen Zawn has at least 1 or 2 swims, and huge boulders in the zawn can make this a wild place in rough conditions and/or incoming tides. However, in calm conditions and on a falling tide you will wonder what all the fuss is about.

Access: Follow the Main Cliff descent path below the Upper Tier. Traverse below the Main Cliff to a compulsory 6a/b section, or a short swim, just after *Hustler*, to get to Easter Island Gully, reversing the low-level 5c traverse on *Swastika*. Continue to Wen Zawn (6a or swim), which presents an amazing sight from the sea. A number of possibilities exist here, including: traversing outside the arch to *Britomartis*; traversing the Cryptic Rift and exiting 'The Dam'; swimming through the arch; or traversing the back of the zawn from *T-Rex*. All end in a swim, which can be broken using The Whale boulder (the exposed rock under *The Fourth Dimension* wall). In extremis, it is possible to escape here by VD standard climbing between *Miura* (Mustang Wall) and *Ipso Facto*, then steep grass rightwards to reach the Wen Slab promontory. Pass through the Seal's Song zawn (swim) and *Flytrap* cave (good climbing, with a hard exit from zawn, or a swim). North Stack beckons, with perhaps one short final swim. From Parliament House Cave, either traverse the base of North Stack Wall with difficulty (calm conditions), or exit via the through tunnel, with wading or a short swim. This tunnel is in the back left hand corner of the cave, below where North Stack Wall meets the main cave. In adverse weather or seal breeding periods, the seaward end of the tunnel can be 'interesting'. There is a left hand exit tunnel branching off from the main tunnel – this is much more challenging prospect.

Egress: Scramble up on to North Stack from either side of the tunnel exit.

An enticing prospect: the main section of the traverse from Main Cliff to North Stack ∧
photo: Jethro Kiernan

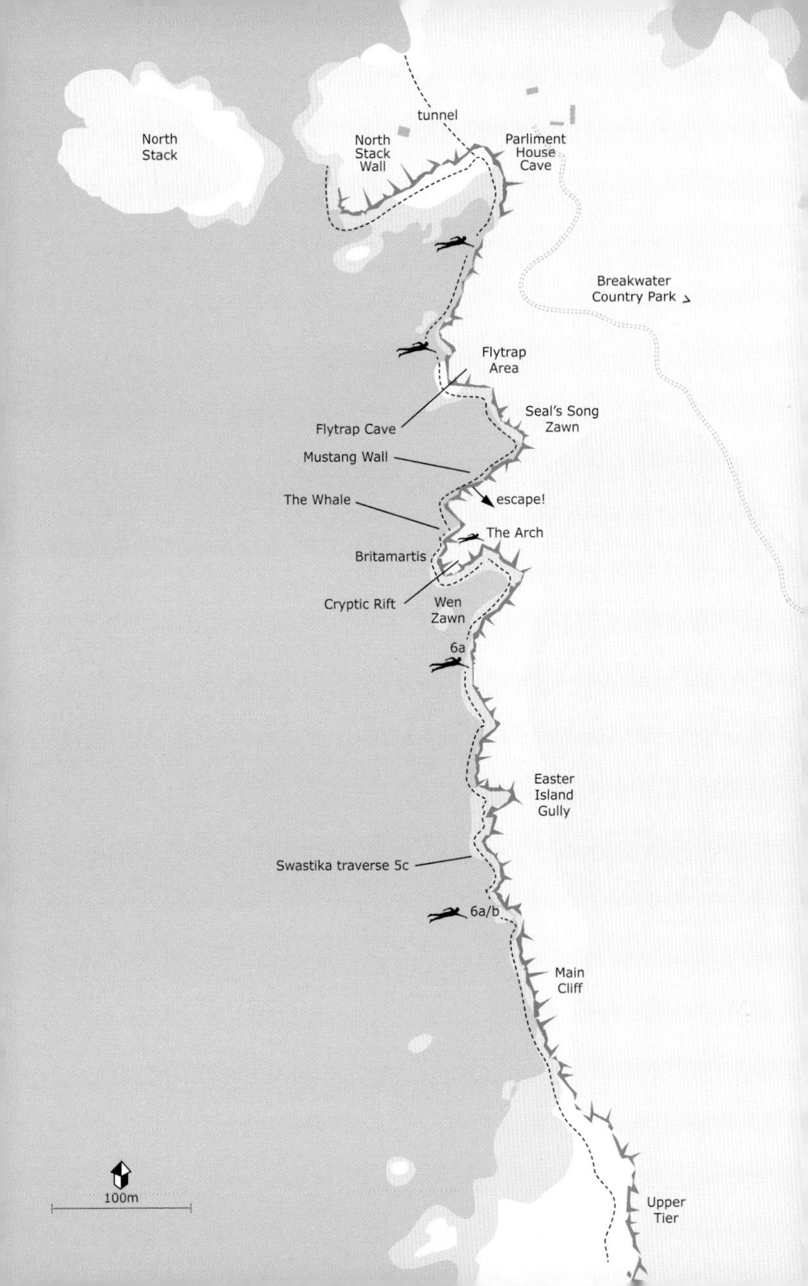

tunnel
North Stack
North Stack Wall
Parliment House Cave
Breakwater Country Park
Flytrap Area
Flytrap Cave
Seal's Song Zawn
Mustang Wall
escape!
The Whale
The Arch
Britamartis
Cryptic Rift
Wen Zawn
6a
Easter Island Gully
Swastika traverse 5c
6a/b
Main Cliff
Upper Tier
100m

North Stack to Holyhead Breakwater Quarry • The North Face Traverse

Highly recommended. A long traverse, with continuously interesting climbing and a variety of possibilities, including a hidden through-tunnel halfway along. Five swims are likely, and as with the previously described trip this is a much easier proposition at low tide. Because of the northerly aspect this is a cool, isolated and sunless proposition; thus a wetsuit is advisable in all but the hottest weather. It takes in many esoteric little zawns and deep, dark caves, which are crossed by excellent climbing, or several short swims. The indented nature of the cliffs make this a longer expedition than the Main Cliff traverse, with which it is ideally combined to make a fascinating day trip.

Tidal issues: Very exposed in adverse weather and tidal conditions, particularly in the North Stack area.

Access: From North Stack there are three options:
1: abseil in to Parliament House Cave, and use the through tunnel to gain the north side of North Stack.
2: easy scrambling down the north side of the headland from the Lighthouse, to arrive at the seaward end of the tunnel.
3: descend to sea level at the extreme point of the headland, directly opposite North Stack Island.
The traverse is escapable in several places by short scrambling, then steep grass slopes leading up to the North Stack approach path.

Egress: Up a steep grass gully after the boulder beach, to reach the Breakwater Country Park car park.

Looking along the heavily indented coastline running from North Stack, past Tsunami Zawn ∧ and round towards Breakwater Quarry   photo: Si Panton

North Stack

- North Stack Wall
- tunnel
- Parliment House Cave
- Breakwater Country Park
- Through tunnel
- High water swim (or 5c)
- Tsunami Zawn
- Easy, but interesting ground (no swims)
- Breakwater Country Park

100m

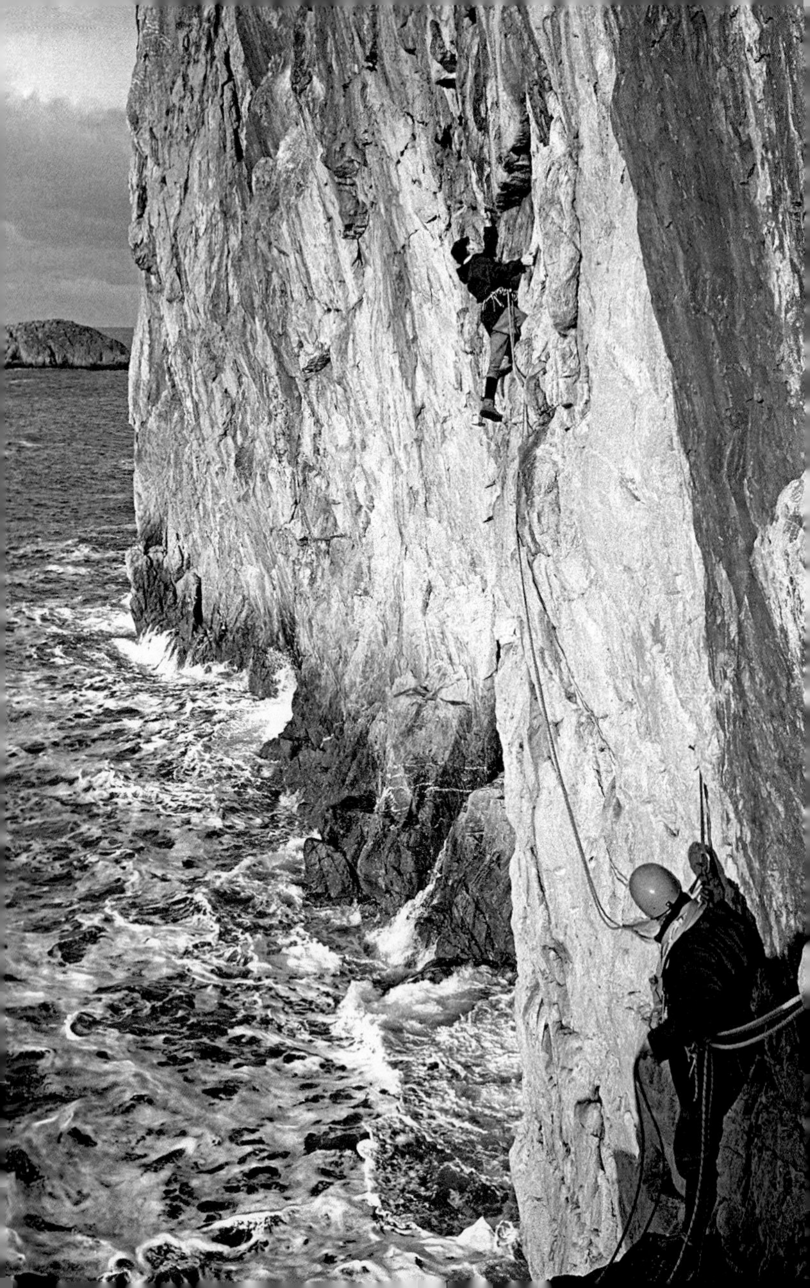

Gogarth North History

On April 4th 1964 two Alpha Climbing Club members, Martin Boysen and Baz Ingle, embarked on a journey which took them away from traditional climbing areas in rain-lashed central Snowdonia, across Anglesey towards Holyhead Mountain. Here could be found some fine outcrop climbs, largely unrecorded and stemming from exploration by RAF Valley climbers in the 1950s. Boysen and Ingle's interest lay someway below these relatively miniature crags with the much larger cliffs, rising one hundred metres from sea level towards disintegrating, gorse-spattered heather slopes. These lovely white quartzite walls had apparently been noticed years earlier by Trevor Peck whilst travelling via the Irish ferry. After making preliminary investigations Peck decided, perhaps wisely, to leave for future generations now represented by Boysen and Ingle. They arrived at the cliff's base after contouring below what became known as the Upper Tier, then descended to just above sea level, where they were confronted by acres of unclimbed rock at dizzying angles. With no idea how difficult, loose or feasible their undertaking might be, they set off on a five pitch adventure, emerging some hours later, having completed a landmark Welsh rock climb, **Gogarth**, now E1 5b, then HVS. Boysen recalls:

*"The tide was out when we went down. We just walked along and picked **Gogarth** as an obvious line, which we could get to in any sort of tides. In fact it was an unfortunate choice because it was incredibly loose at the time – the second pitch had a tremendous number of big loose flakes, and the top pitch was really incredibly dangerous, absolutely littered with eight-foot-long slivers of rock. You just didn't dare pull them out – Bas climbed that top pitch magnificently – it really scared us silly."*

This, then, was an inaugural ascent on arguably Britain's finest sea cliff. Although the same team climbed Upper Tier's **Shag Rock** during their visit it was **Gogarth** which took pride of place whilst also becoming the collective name adopted by climbers for the various cliffs, caves and zawns between North and South Stack. A week later Ingle returned with Peter 'kid' Crew. They went further along the sea level traverse, then climbed out via **Pentathol** (HVS 5a) - another exploratory probe - this time directly above the waves and vulnerable to the ebb and flow of a tidal range that might cut climbers off from retreat, in the event of failure. This was to be the Gogarth ethos and set a tone for the climbing experience; namely adventurous on-sight ascents, often beyond Very Severe standard, for which climbers trained in the pub and came armed with rudimentary racks consisting initially of slings and pegs together, on occasion, with home made chockstone nuts on line or tape. Returning in April, then early May, Crew and Ingle probed the sea grass carpeted Upper Tier, doing **Bezel** at VS, the deceptively easy looking **Gauntlet** HVS. They then visited Main Cliff's flank for **Simulator** (VS 4c) and **Emulator's** magnificent corner crack/groove; HVS with one point of aid. Boysen did **Ampitheatre Wall** on Upper Tier's left side at HVS, whilst Williams and Royal contributed **Pantin** (VS 4b), also on Upper Tier.

After nine routes this activity dropped to zero as if someone had planted a crop then left it for a year to bear fruit. Crew having been self admittingly, *"absolutely bloody frightened by the sea"* turned his attention, along with his contemporaries, towards more traditional areas.

< Pete Crew belays Joe Brown on an early ascent of **Rat Race** E3 5c on Main Cliff in 1966
photo: John Cleare

1966 was an altogether different matter and one in which Gogarth came into the climbing limelight as Robin Collomb put it in *Sea Cliff Climbing in Britain* "*with a loud fanfare of trumpets*", and was much enhanced in time by an emerging climbing media championed by photographic talents including Leo Dickinson, John Cleare and Ken Wilson.

Initially Crew revisited the cliff whilst conducting guidebook work for a proposed *Snowdon West* volume, which would include Gogarth. Checking over an initial nine routes he considered the cliff worked out. This attitude did not prevail for long as his accomplices in these sojourns, including Wilson, Llanberis impressario Al Harris and no less talented climber Jancis Baldcock, began to realize the vast potential. Cementing this view early in March, Claude Davies and Ali Cowburn did **The Rift**; a VS chimney on Upper Tier which whilst not an overly important route proved to be a particularly significant event. It kick started further development, which intensified from that point on, so that by the years end Gogarth would be synonymous with serious, hard climbing imbued with quality and drama. Crew recalls:

"*It struck us like a bombshell: 'Bloody hell, if people like Ali can do a route on* **Gogarth***, there must be thousands of damn things there.' So we went the following weekend with a very big party...*"

April saw teams engaged in various lines all over the cliffs; a trend that continued into May when Crew, climbing with Dave Alcock, eventually managed **Central Park,** after a marathon cleaning session. Joe Brown, having initially visited the South Stack area for a Television extravaganza at Easter, now made his first real appearance on the Gogarth scene and immediately found, then climbed with Martin Boysen, the hitherto hidden Wen Slab. **Wen** (HVS 5a) was the result. Brown comments:

"*We went to North Stack for a walk, and I was with Martin Boysen, hanging back behind the others. We looked back and saw the top of Wen Slab. All you could see was about forty feet of slab sticking out of grass. We walked back and we were absolutely pop-eyed when we saw the thing. We only had a little bit of climbing gear with us, so we borrowed odd karabiners and slings that other people had got, and went and did it.*"

In June Brown did the legendary **Winking Crack** which folklore decrees winked at him every time he walked underneath it. Shortly after Jack Street made an impressive free ascent at E3 5c (Brown had used 6 pts of aid). Another major line fell to Crew and Alcock when they climbed **Big Groove**, the magnificent left facing corner nestling above **Pentathol's** first pitch. Perhaps inevitably Crew was to join forces with Brown and he did so on 19th June for **Dinosaur** on the great leaning central wall of Main Cliff. So named pre-emptively by Crew since he claimed that anyone who did it would have to have a "long neck and no brains".

Dinosaur proved an epic undertaking, which saw Brown and Crew, pushed to their limit on the first pitch, then utterly gripped on the second whilst cleaning loose rock from a long overhanging groove. Brown later recalled feeling more nervous seconding this pitch than on many other harder leads, showing that at times the Gogarth atmosphere can get to anyone.

Laurie Holliwell on the first ascent of **Park Lane** E2 5b, Upper Tier in 1967 photo: Leo Dickinson >

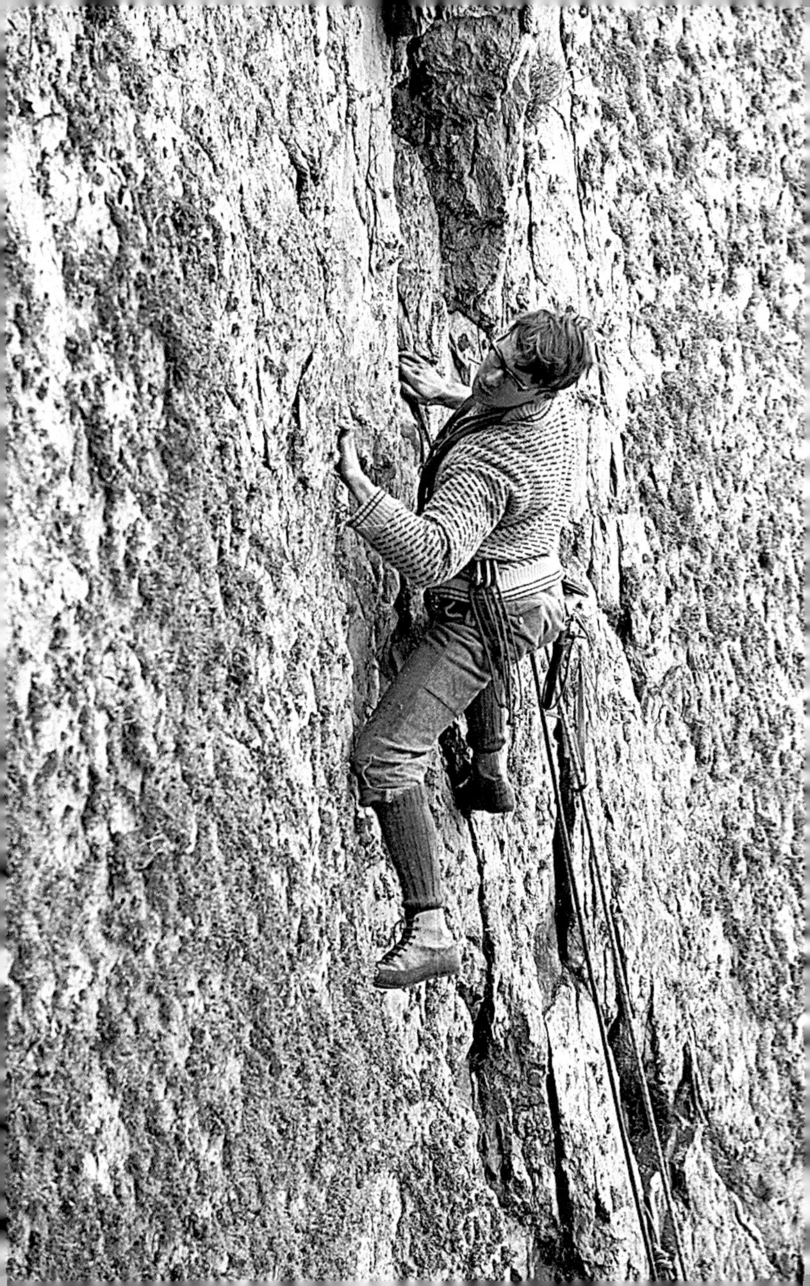

Crew had, in his own words, *"frigged"* his way up it whilst leading because at that time it was extremely loose, the entire route requiring ten aid points. It was clearly a tour de force and, in common with other ground up first ascents hereabouts, much of the aid was due to cleaning loose rock. It should also be noted that the entire line was not climbed completely free until 1980 by Ron Fawcett at its current E5 6a grade. Next came **The Rat Race**, so named because many different teams had tried it before Brown and Crew's complete ascent.

Thus by autumn thirty new routes had been added to the original nine and Crew had prepared an interim guide to the cliff which he published later in the year. Indeed much of the opening up of Gogarth can be credited to Crew, who, aside from his impressive first ascents on the crag, was very generous with information, even to climbers capable of taking project lines from him. Arguably he did more than anybody to push Gogarth into the public domain, although credit is also due to Ken Wilson and Mountain magazine which gave coverage to the wave of new routes.

1967 saw the discovery, and then exploration of Easter Island Gully, initially by Brown and Alcock, then by Brown and Crew. Alcock teamed up with Gerry Rogan to explore possibilities on the outer seaward face projected by the flying buttress opposite Wen Slab. Here they found **The Trap** (HVS), which essentially followed their abseil line back up a fine chimney, while the main challenge lay on an open wall reached by moving leftwards below **The Trap**, which they addressed a week later to give a high quality classic two pitch HVS: **Britomartis**. The same team, with Brian Fuller, became crag-fast whilst attempting a line on Main Cliff's left side and when they failed to show in Llanberis, at their usual haunt The Padarn, Brown enlisted a rescue party. In an effort that should not be understated they managed to abseil in from above to find the marooned trio bivouacing on a ledge fifteen metres above sea level and lapped by massive waves. There then ensued a long prussiking epic up what would subsequently and not surprisingly become **Nightride** (E1 5b), by Brown and Rogan.

Clearly much attention was focussed on Gogarth at this time and new faces began making their mark, particularly Ed Drummond and the Holliwell brothers, Les and Lawrie. Drummond's introduction was particularly severe i.e. 'burnt off' by Crew during **Mammoth's** first ascent; an incident that did not however exclude him returning to lead **The Strand** on Upper Tier later that year. A few weeks after Drummond's ascent of **The Strand**, Laurie Holliwell made an impressive ground up ascent of the neighbouring **Park lane** (E2 5b). Leo Dickinson explained the scene:

"Laurie told me in the Padarn the night before what he had in mind, so we went over to watch the ascent. Ron Prior & myself climbed up vertical grass to get level with Laurie as he climbed the lower cracks. Once I was in position I realized the significance of where I was and what I was watching. Laurie was one of the most underrated climbers of his generation. For a couple of years he did not mix with the 'in team' as he had no idea how good he was. He was a genius, in fact both he and Les were. To be in their company after a first ascent was an experience I have yet to equate. It was like a blitzkrieg – both would speak at once in totally incomprehensible cockney accents as if giving a stereoscopic

DAVID DURKAN.
NEWRY FAIR.
HOLYHEAD.
ANGLESEY.

CRAIG GOGARTH

1st edition July 1966
2nd edition February 1967
Produced by Peter Crew
Diagrams by B. Whybrow
© Peter Crew 1966, 1967

Available only from :

Joe Brown
Menai Hall,
Llanberis

Price 5 shillings

Cover. Dave Edwards on 'Dirty Corner', Rocky coast.

Back. DJD on the 'White slab', Rocky coast.

version of what they had experienced. This was '3D' before it became popular, but just so invigorating. It was the 60's after all. The line looked so beautiful I wanted to go and do it immediately. I'd seen all the holds! Ron, holding me back, suggested it might be tactful if I waited a few days. Three weeks later I led it easily, but I would not have had the balls to do it first."

These very real events were in stark contrast to the fantasy that became known as 'The McAllum Affair', or 'The Great Gogarth Hoax', which centred on claims by a certain Mr X that he had done four new routes on Upper Tier. It was the Holliwells who first alerted the climbing fraternity to Mr X's apparently bogus climbs. After much gardening during their ascent of **Yellow Scar** on Upper Tier they were surprised to learn that Mr X had recently claimed a route which more or less covered the same territory, so Les wrote to Mr X and received a very detailed reply. Suspicion was soon backed by hard evidence when it was revealed that the same day the Holliwells made the first ascent of **Park Lane**, Mr X claimed **Gael's Wall**, a route easily scrutinised from **Park Lane** and on which they saw no climbers all day. Enquiries were made amongst Mr X's Apollo Club members, none of whom had witnessed the Gogarth climbs, nor seen Mr X climb particularly hard. Supposed seconds named by Mr X could not accounted for, deepening the subterfuge and fuelling a general view that **Heilan' Man** (HVS), **Tam Dubh** (HVS), **A'Bhaister** (XS) and **Gael's Wall** (XS) were all spurious inventions climbed only in the imagination. Nevertheless Mr X claimed he was telling the truth and threatened libel action against anyone who claimed otherwise. Meanwhile descriptions to the aforesaid routes had now appeared in a new climbs bulletin as the year passed. Eventually the main climbing magazines published a cautionary note for twenty six routes claimed by Mr X throughout Snowdonia and the matter was investigated by none other than Sunday Times journalist Peter Gilman. He gave a sensitive, objective overview pointing out the threat to authentic, taken on trust, climbing records and the clearly dangerous implications concerning faking climbs in this way. Nothing has been heard from Mr X since 1968.

Tam Dubh (HVS) is now recorded as the **Eternal Optimist** (E2 5b) [A Sharp]. **Gael's Wall** (XS) is now recorded as **Afreet Street** (E5 6a) [E Drummond]. **A'Bhaister** (XS) is now recorded as **Yellow Scar** (E2 5b) [Holliwells]. **Heilan' Man** (HVS) was recorded as **Sceptic** (XS) [Holliwells] – the whole route fell down shortly after its ascent in 1967/68!

1967 also saw Doug Scott and Brian Palmer establish a challenging aid route through Parliament House Cave at North Stack, done in three weekends with over forty pegs at A3. Aid was also employed during Joe Brown's significant 1968 solution to the sea arch opposite Wen Slab, **Spider's Web**, though in spectacular and unorthodox fashion (prussiking upside down etc.) between hard face climbing, which at times involved the climber suspended in air above the sea, and the use of three ropes, hence the name.

Joe Brown in action during the second ascent of his own route **Spiders Web** E2/A1, Wen > Zawn in 1970 photo: John Cleare

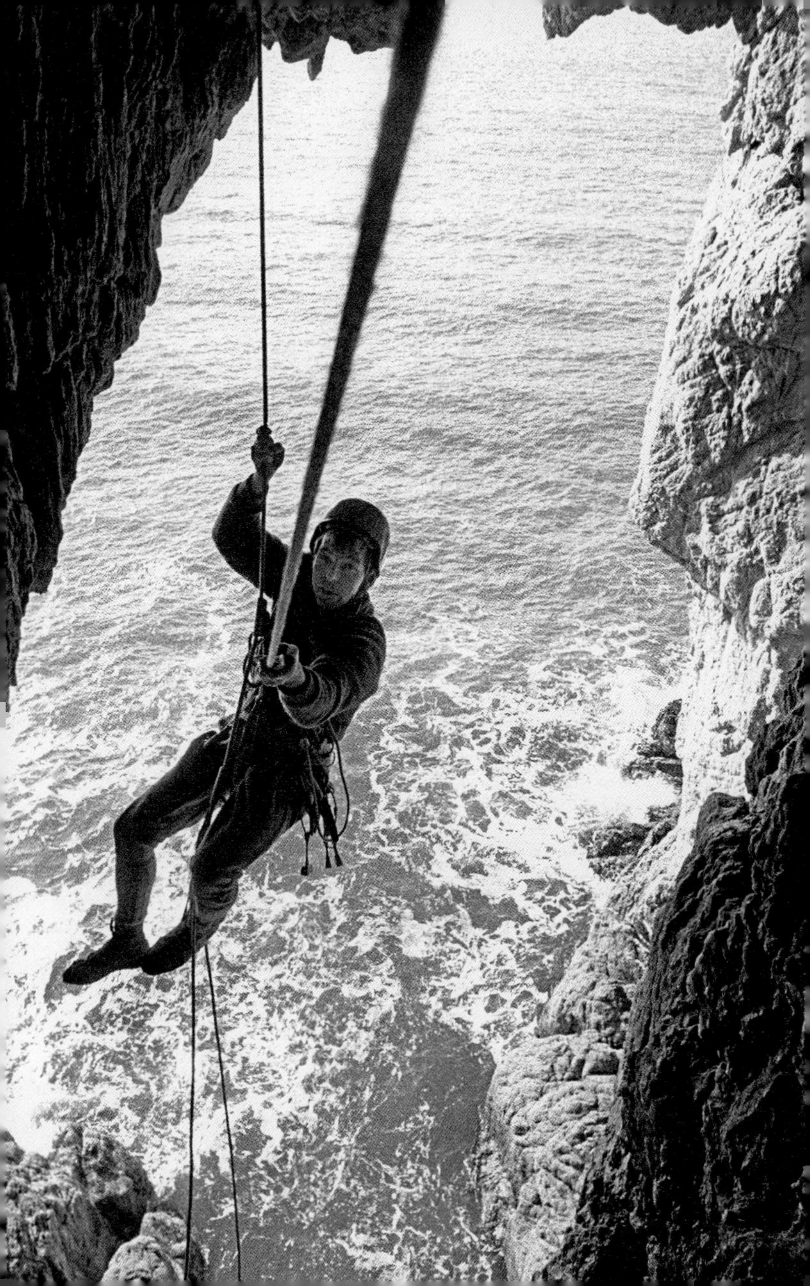

Earlier in July the Holliwells had put up **Hypodermic** on a painfully hot day, but it was Drummond, now clearly over his '**Mammoth**' episode, who in August lead Dave Pearce across Wen Slab's utterly unfeasible looking **Dream of White Horses** with Leo Dickinson on hand to provide the now iconic photo. At HVS **Dream** remains one of the great British rock climbs. Returning in November Drummond, with Ben Campbell Kelly did **Quartz Icicle**, the poorly protected thin white vein between **Concrete Chimney** and **Wen** at XS, another aesthetic and atmospheric quality find. Late in November Jack Street succeeded on **Citadel** with Gordon Hibberd though he had previously climbed the first pitch with Geoff Birtles who had become soaked to the skin whilst belaying so was unable to follow. The next weekend Street returned with Hibberd, climbed **Cordon Bleu** until above the final crack, and then abbed using slings as a makeshift harness. Realising that he would spiral into space and miss the stance as well as alarmed by the crack's crumbly width (making it difficult to protect with available gear in the 60s) he resorted to placing several aluminium etrier rungs, both to keep himself in rock contact and subsequently use as protection or aid depending on how difficult the climb turned out.

By 1968 **Citadel** was considered a 'last great problem', which would finally tackle Main Cliff's overhanging central wall and thus be superior to **Dinosaur** and **Mammoth**. Crew had tried it but gave up short way up the first pitch on a baking hot summer's day, *"Just looking at Citadel used to frighten us."*, he had said. Such a route invited fierce rivalry and competition, yet in a generally sociable atmosphere. For example, after **Citadel** was done Street recalls being criticised by the Holliwell brothers only for his in-situ abseil rope (which in any case hung out in space, so could not be reached). It was an undoubtedly unorthodox ascent, but his gripping rappel down pitch two, together with the etrier rung action was unfairly maligned in subsequent guides (albeit, not in Crew's original in 1969). According to fellow Gogarth activist, Joe Brown, Street deserved more respect for his groundbreaking ascent, and it should be noted that despite the hoo-ha, he had only used three to four aid points per pitch. In 1976 Pat Littlejohn climbed **Citadel's** top crack free whilst its first pitch, despite various free attempts, still required one aid peg. Ron Fawcett finally eliminated this *"driven into a roof – upside down"* nemesis in 1977 at 6b.

∧ Ed Drummond and Dave Pearce hanging out on Wen Slab during the first ascent of **Dream** photo: Leo Dickinson

The first ascent of **Dream of White Horses** HVS 5a, with wild seas crashing into Wen Zawn photo: Leo Dickinson >

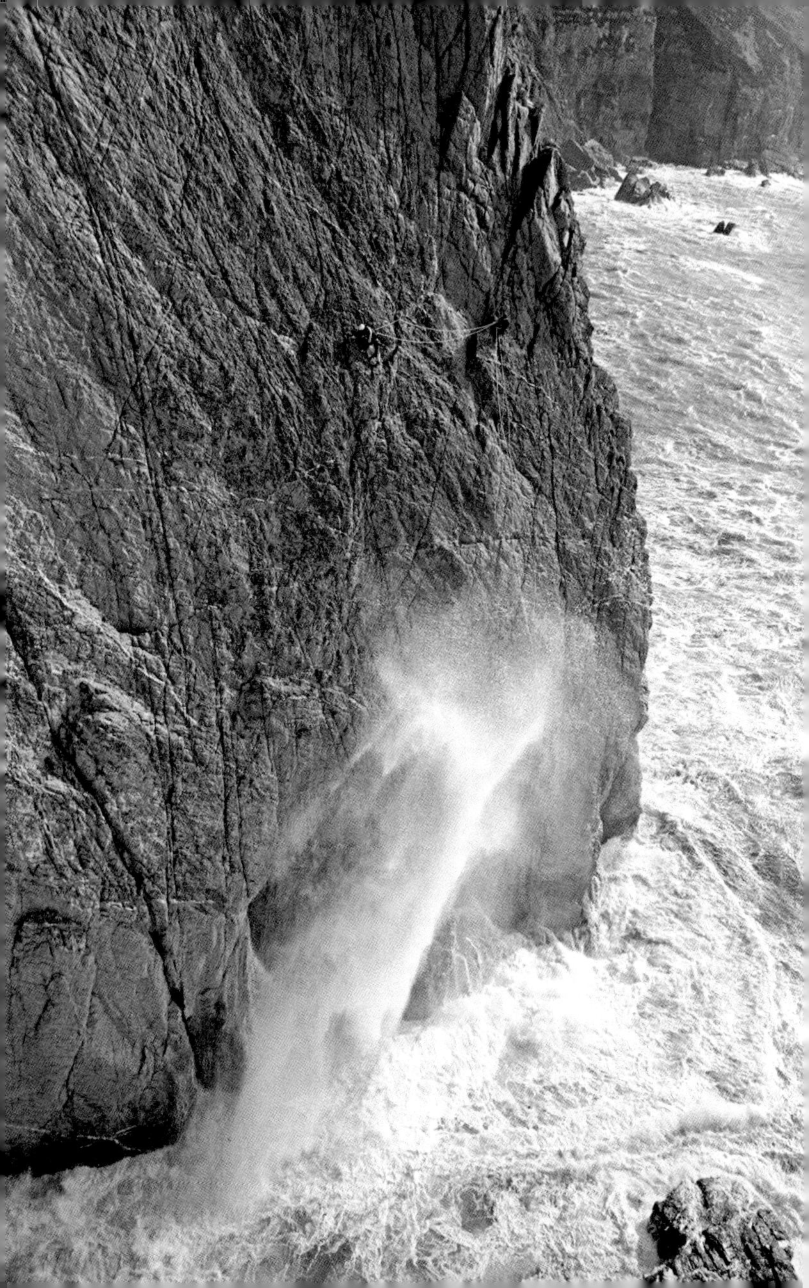

1969 saw Drummond ascend the bogus route **Gael's Wall** using four aid points and renaming it **Afreet Street** (XS). He then completed **The Horizon** with Ben Campbell Kelly, a marathon 300m girdle starting near **Syringe** at Main Cliff's left side and finishing up **Ormuzd** in Easter Island Gully, originally with six aid points. More obviously impressive was Laurie Holliwell's **Wonderwall** in Easter Island Gully about which second Dave Potts had this to say:

"It looked preposterous to me: it wasn't as though he was making for anything, just more overhanging rock. I was very impressed: he got right out to the lip before jacking it in. The point of this is that he was quite prepared to try anything. That doesn't sound much now, but it astonished me then."

Succumbing with two aid points, it went free at E3 6a on the fifth ascent in 1974 to Alec Sharp and Hank Pasquil, but was also later the scene for Alan Rouse to comment:

"I slumped back onto the peg and realised I had become a mountaineer."

In 1986, climbing with Craig Smith, Martin Crook climbed the direct finish, ***I Wonder Why*** (E5 6a), later described by Paul Williams as somewhat *"pumpsome youth."*

Now with over 130 routes Crew's *Anglesey–Gogarth Climbers's Guide* had morphed from the interim into a respectable, though still relatively slim, volume which hit the press in the summer of 1969. In the same year Dave Durkan wrote and published the Mona guide, which provided information on the Rhoscolyn and Holyhead Mountain routes. The latter outcrop style crag had been developed during the sixties by members of the RAF Valley mountain rescue team and a group of keen locals.

In September John Gosling with friends from the Black and Tans club added **Falls Road** (XS, 6 points) between **Gogarth** and **The Rat Race** whose final crack developed a considerable reputation after falls during repeat attempts by Alan Rouse and Bill Lounds. Ray Evans with Chris Rogers made a second ascent eliminating all but one aid point, before Pete Livesey finally repeated the route completely free in 1974.

∧ Front covers of Pete Crew's 1969 Anglesey-Gogarth guide and Dave Durkan's Mona guide
Positron first ascencionist Al Rouse repeating **Wonder Wall** E3 6a, Easter Island >
Gully in 1974 photo: Leo Dickinson

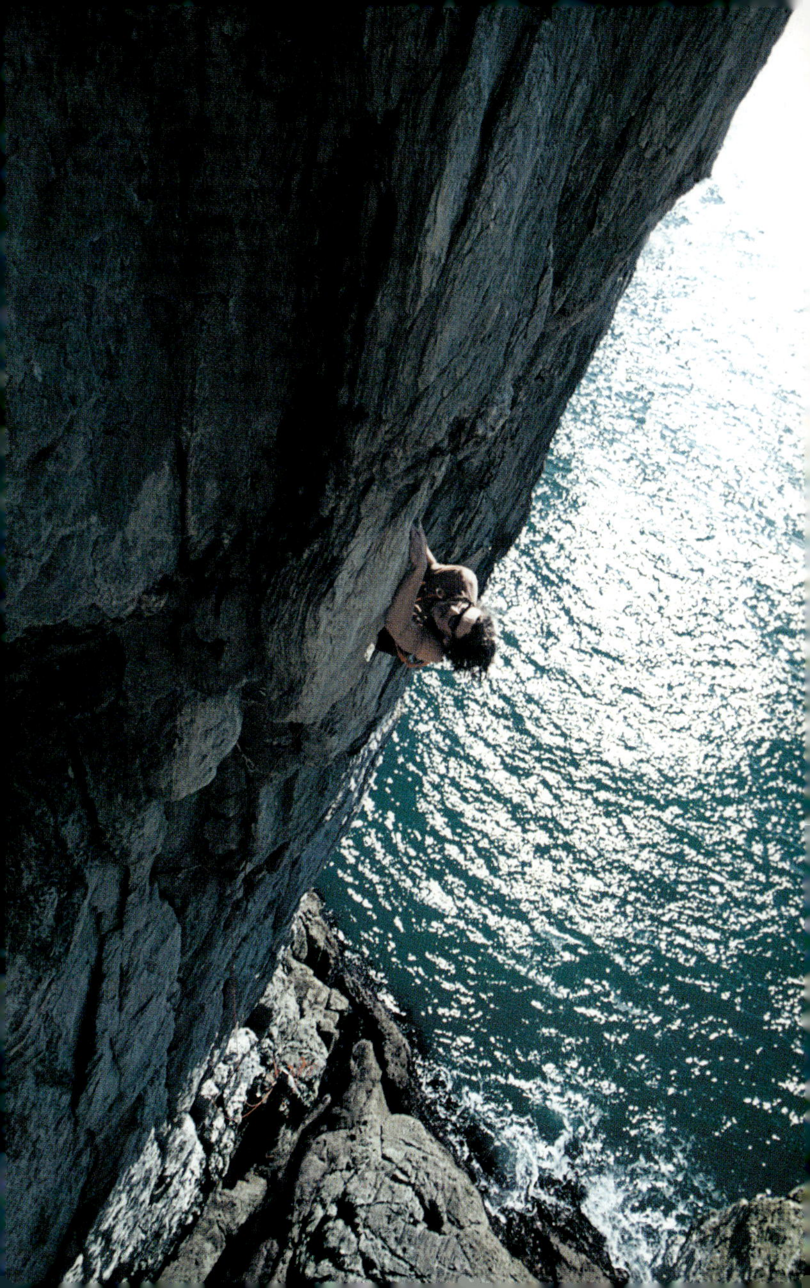

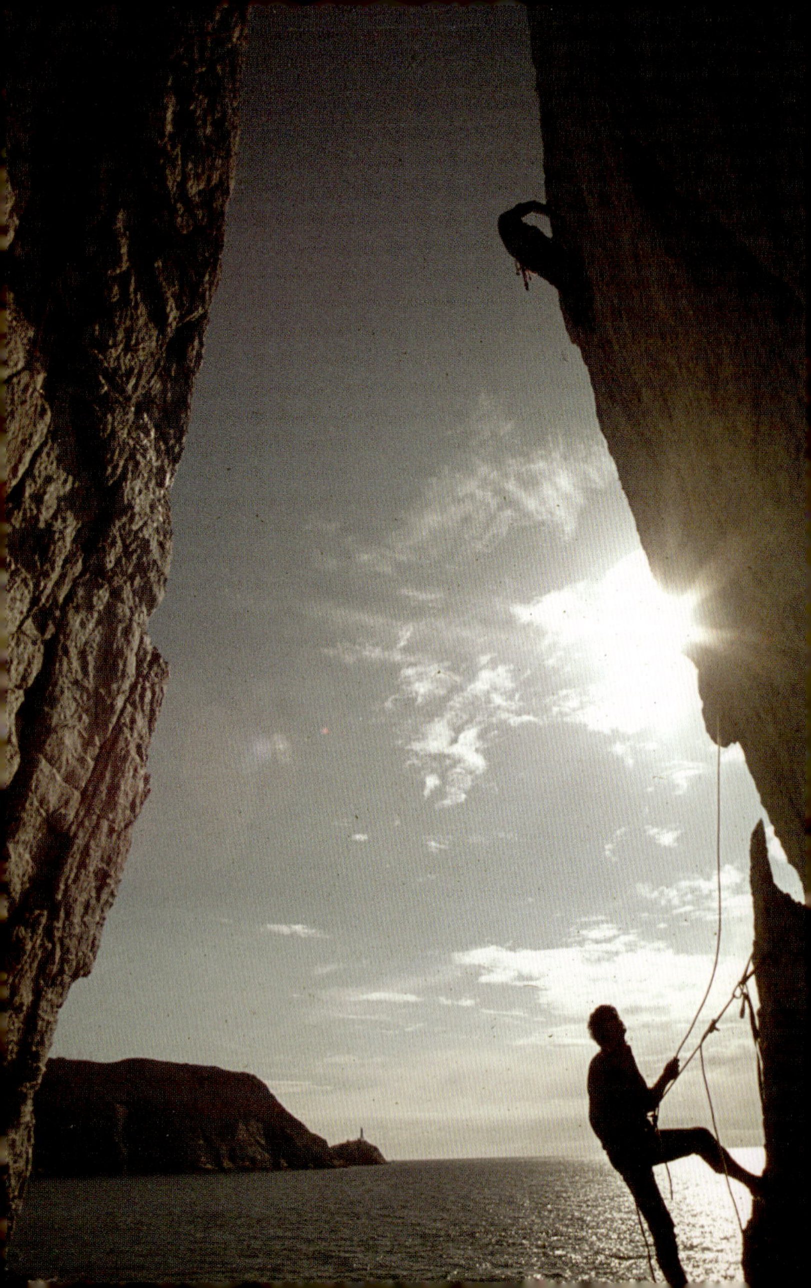

In 1971 Alan Rouse added **Positron** to Main Cliff, a climb that would gain legendary status within a relatively short time owing to difficulty and audacious position, extreme even by Gogarth standards. Pete Minks seconding had simply prussiked up listening to a radio strapped to his waist whilst Malcolm Howells and Dave Pearce, both well experienced Gogarth activists, were surprised to find when attempting an early repeat that:

"The second pitch is okay until you have to move down left and into a groove. These moves are appalling – they stick in the mind as a horror. Now it is Dave's turn to work. He is in good spirits, looking forward to the battle. The rope goes out – a pause – then comes rapidly back. Dave reappears, looking amazed and slightly rattled that the crag could do this to him."

Rouse, probably the finest rock climber of his generation, spent two days completing **Positron** and its ascent upped the Gogarth anti even with five aid points. At least one of these was only taken in-extremis, after Rouse, having climbed as far as possible into the crux with a 'Moac' nut between his teeth, managed a precarious placement then dropped onto it with arms blown. Although he had previously reached the same position, he had been unable to release either hand to reach for a runner and eventually took air after his fingers uncurled. In November 1975 Alec Sharp climbed **Positron's** main pitch free as part of his own impressive **Ordinary Route**, a sensational Main Cliff girdle, now E5, before Ron Fawcett followed minutes later by Pete Livesey made complete free ascents in 1976.

Back in 1971 at the Upper Tier Martin Boysen, with Dave Alcock, tackled a line made obvious by its intermittent large pockets on a steep sea grassed wall left of **Winking Crack**. **Fifteen Men on a Dead Man's Chest, Yo Ho Ho and a Bottle of Rum, Drink and the Devil Have Done For the Rest, Yo Ho Ho** (at XS) was so named in an attempt to make a route name larger than its description; an attempt that largely failed and along with its original three aid points, eliminated by South Walian, Andy Sharp in 1983, has generally been cut to **Fifteen Men etc**.

1971 also saw the first in a series of hard routes from Ray Evans, a quiet profit of purism, whose first contribution to Main Cliff was **Bubbly Situation Blues** based on strenuous grooves left of **Gogarth**. However the next few years saw only sporadic additions to the cliffs; most notably **The Needle** and **Puzzle Me Quick** from Evans. Around the same time Alec Sharp, a maths student at Bangor University, developed a special relationship with the cliff concentrating on eliminating or reducing aid points as well as finding quality routes:

"Having repeated Puzzle Me Quick and Citadel with two points of aid, it seemed time to search for new routes while there were still some left to be had."

Thus followed **The Camel**, an exacting crack between **Hypodermic** and **The Needle**; a place, according to the old saying, that such a beast could not pass through. Sharp, with John Zangwill, did so in 1974 before completing **Supercrack** in Easter Island Gully, a route first done by the Holliwells with some aid, but left unrecorded.

< Gogarth pioneer Alec Sharp leading **Supercrack** E3 5c, Easter Island Gully in 1974
photo: Leo Dickinson

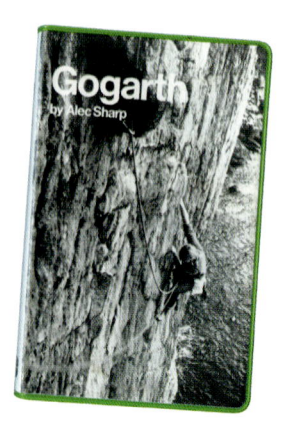

The next year saw his ascent of the aptly named **Eternal Optimist**, the last bogus route the 1967/8 Gogarth hoax affair to be done on Upper Tier. Moving once again to Easter Island, Sharp used a rare aid point on **Annihilator**, another impressive extreme near **Ormuzd**. **Horse Above Water**, essentially a knee deep chimney with a puzzling 5c entrance, near **Phaedra** on Main Cliff, and then the previously mentioned **Ordinary Route** compounded Sharp's domination at the time. Undoubtedly a true devotee, he was to produce a new Gogarth guide for the Climbers' Club which came out in 1977. Before this he made his final contribution to Main Cliff; **Graduation Ceremony**, another steep addition with harsh crack climbing on pitch two.

The introduction of the new guide marked the end of the Sharp era, yet as he left for the States he could not have known that it would act as a precursor to a new Gogarth blitz. In 1978 the cliffs received intense scrutiny and action from a number of protagonists, keen on further aid elimination and searching out new lines. This situation was helped with the introduction of added security provided by 'Friends', the American camming device. Spearheading this new Gogarth thrust was Jim Moran; a tough gritstone-trained, super-enthusiast now living in Wales.

In 1978 he was virtually camped out at Gogarth, often in the company of Geoff Milburn and Al Evans. Initially it was Ben and Marion Wintringham's ascent of **Bitter Days**, a steep arete near Shag Rock on the Upper Tier that kicked off the new season in March. Joe Brown, climbing with Smiler Cuthbertson and Jim Jewel found **Flytrap**, the top quality E2 in the caves between North Stack and Wen Zawn. Moran's initial foray into Easter Island Gully gave the steep and problematic **Pequod** at E3, whilst the very strong team of Pete Whillance and Dave Armstrong, from the Lakes, began with **Energy Crisis** on Upper Tier; a steep and exacting line with a baffling crux, which latterly became something of a test piece at E5 6a. However, it was Moran's **Barbarossa** ascent that proved pivotal. At first Moran doubted it could be climbed and was cajoled into an attempt by Al Evans who had abbed and cleaned it. While a pre-placed peg, some distance up the first section, gave something to go for, Moran could not continue without its aid. After two days of effort the Moran – Evans team had produced a magnificent hard route, which opened up an apparently blank section of wall between existing routes and thus pointed to further possibilities in this vein like a clarion call. With this route came a change in style, one previously ushered in by Livesey and the emergence of indoor climbing walls, which although rudimentary at that time allowed climbers to train during the winter months. Ed Drummond had been derided by leading Welsh activists in the late 60s for climbing training, as if it were a form of cheating, yet now it was becoming generally acceptable throughout the British climbing scene, though many still preferred training in the pub.

∧ Front cover of the 1977 CC guide showing Alec Sharp's shot of Chris Dale on the main **Positron** pitch on Main Cliff

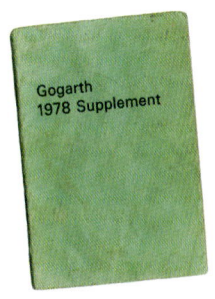

Tactics such as yo-yoing a route to a high point in order to boulder it out before returning to make a complete ascent were, although debated as much as the initial overtures concerning the use of chalk, becoming acceptable to complete climbs, **Barbarossa** being a good example. Preparation might now include abseil inspections and pre-cleaning. This applied also on Main Cliff when Moran, Milburn and Evans added **The Assassin** after abseil inspection, a route tried previously by Ray Evans, then Ben Wintringham, on sight.

By 1978 Pat Littlejohn was already a Gogarth veteran, yet it was rumoured that he too had began training a la' Livesey to enhance performance. Whatever the case Littlejohn simply turned up below Main Cliff in June with Chris King and climbed the impending wall between **Citadel** and **Mammoth** ground up and on sight to give **Hunger**; powerful and impressive at E5. In July the Moran team went for the wall left of **Fifteen Men** etc. to give **Horroshow**, originally E4 6a with one aid point, it was another high standard technical route with hard fingery climbing and a big feel. With Al Evans taking the lead they then dispatched the wall right of **Emulator** to give **Aardvark**, an instant classic, well protected but thin and good value at E2. Whilst Evans and Milburn may not have been the most gifted climbers operating at this time they were a driving force in exploring new possibilities; a point well illustrated when in July with Moran and Simon Horrox they opened up North Stack Wall with **Nice and Sleazy**.

Previously Cliff Phillips had climbed **Wall of Horrors** with some aid and Doug Scott had done **The Whip**, both at the right hand, loosest point of the cliff early in the 70s. However the best quality climbing was further left; a fact now apparent to Evans et al. Thus followed **Talking Heads** (E2 5b) and **South Sea Bubble** (E3 5c).

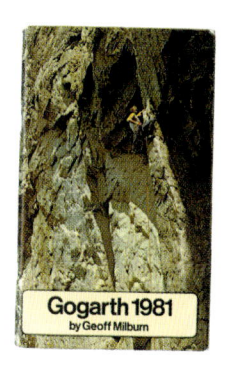

Although both lead by Moran on the same day, it was Evans' cleaning of what would later become **The Cad**, which eventually raised the bar, albeit controversially. Firstly Evans and Moran top roped it with no intention of a lead, then Evans and Milburn decided somewhat mischievously to begin a rumour that their top roped line was in fact the best unclimbed wall in Wales. As Milburn later noted, it probably was. Two months later Ron Fawcett turned up with Chris Gibb, placed two bolts and a peg and did it. Pete Whillance narrowly beaten to this major first ascent by little more than half an hour, settled for a repeat dispensing with the first bolt. John Redhead eliminated the peg during a third ascent, though it was not until 1987 that Nick Dixon finally by-passed the remaining protection bolt, although the de-flowered stud remains in position to this day, just about clippable with a hooked wire loop.

The 1978 and 1981 CC Gogarth supplements, the latter showing Paul Williams' shot of Ron Fawcett on **The Big Sleep** E6 6b on Main Cliff

While **The Cad**, in 1978, was a highly coveted route placing the wall firmly on the climber's map, the next few years saw less activity. Some awe inspiring excursions both at Main Cliff and out at North Stack were, however, climbed. These included **The Tet Offensive** (E5 6b) and **Sebastopol** (E5 6a) from Moran, now teamed with Paul Williams, and **The Long Run** (E5 6a); another North Stack frightener from Pete Whillance.

As the 70s morphed into the 80s super fit Ron Fawcett, climbing with Moran and Williams, did **The Big Sleep** (E6 6b) and **Wall of Fossils** (E6 6b); not the strongest lines on the crag, but very difficult undertakings. Not that big Ron was much put out; as Williams put it *"Ron never got a pump on youth"*. At this point Littlejohn climbed the stunning and fierce **Alien**, which by way of a contrast was one of the most striking lines on Main Cliff, and subsequently acquired a prodigious reputation, spitting off would be leaders time and time again.

Soon the limelight fell back on North Stack Wall. Here John Redhead made his big move, climbing **The Bells! The Bells!** At E7 (the first in Britain), which essentially started up **The Cad** before traversing out right, continuing boldly up difficult territory, passing a poor black peg which offered scant protection, to a welcome finish. Climbing with Chris Shorter (their respective partners relaxing into a picnic hamper above), Redhead recalls being *"Surreally gripped"* before closing his eyes, head against rock, in tentative balance, then climbing through with a fall unthinkable, into easier climbing.

A general lull in activity occurred during the next few years until in April 1984 Redhead returned for another big North Stack lead, **The Clown** (E7 6b), with Dave Towse and John Silvestor. The previous year saw Boreal 'Fire' rock shoes, with their revolutionary 'sticky rubber' soles introduced from Spain. Everybody wanted a pair since Jerry Moffatt had lead a version of Cloggy's **Master's Wall**, utilizing them during summer 1983. With slate 'happening' at the time and the true line of **Master's** still not resolved, almost all subsequent new routes, not only at Gogarth, but throughout Wales, were done in 'stickys'. The old familiar blue and white EBs were rapidly discarded all over the country.

In May Andy Pollitt freed **Mammoth** of its remaining two aid points then returned to do battle with **Skinhead Moonstomp** (E6 6b) a powerful, ultra strenuous Main Cliff adventure that took two days. Initially Pollitt with Steve Andrews had started on-sight carrying pegs. Pitch two proved so *"strenny"* that the team abbed off, returning next day for a successful complete ascent. Next he accompanied Redhead on a North Stack sojourn where he followed **Birth Trauma**, then lead **Art Groupie**; both serious E6 undertakings right of the main wall. The day after Pollitt went back to Main Cliff and did the elegant **Mammoth Direct** (E5/6 6b); a quiet cruised lead of one of the few remaining big lines.

Meanwhile Redhead continued his North Stack campaign with Dave Towse. On **The Demons of Bosch** Redhead placed, as the name suggests, a bolt, which mysteriously *"unclipped itself"* during the lead. (This was, in any case ,erased by Andy Pollitt a few years later in 1988.) Finally, as if an afterthought, Moran reappeared with Paul Williams to give **The Cruise**; a superb Upper Tier crack climb previously aided in 1970 by Dave Durkan as **The Nod**. It proved to be a well-protected E5 of utmost quality.

Dave Towse, John Redhead and Martin Crook on the North Stack Wall in the early 1980s photo: Martin Crook

< John Redhead climbs with **The Clown** E7 6b, North Stack Wall photo: Andy Newton

^ Andy Pollitt blasting up **Skinhead Moonstomp** E6 6b, Main Cliff photo: Glenn Robbins

1985 saw a virtual drought in exploration, but served as a calm before 1986's storm when new faces began joining the Gogarth fold keen to make a mark in an upsurge of intensity. Redhead was again first off the mark completing a serious E7 girdle of North Stack Wall, **Stroke of the Fiend** with Dave Towse, then **Flower of Evil**, also E7. Over in Wen Zawn, opposite the slab, Johnny Dawes with Simon Donahue climbed the very impressive looking **Conan the Librarian**; a multi pitch E7 with 1 point of aid, later returning with Craig Smith to add what he considered the true line of **Janitor Finish**. Dawes recalls:

"**The Janitor**. Loose blocks with loose holds made out of talc! The first pitch (E6 6b) was half wet; it was raining, but the crux groove was dry, protected by the roofs."

Craig Smith, resident in Llanberis for the summer, then worked out the desperate **Psychocandy** (E6/7 6c) on Upper Tier's innocuous right hand side. Andy Pollitt succeeded on a coveted repeat when he did **The Bells! The Bells!**, and then made his own contribution to North Stack with **The Hollow Man**; at E7/8 arguably the hardest line on the wall.

^ Johnny Dawes on the first ascent of **Conan the Librarian** E7 6c, Wen Zawn in 1986
photo: Craig Smith

In 1987 Paul Pritchard revisited the **Conan** arch and climbed directly up the large groove at its left side giving **The Unrideable Donkey**; a loose, serious E7 with Nick Dixon, which has since suffered from serious rockfall on its second pitch. Whilst Dawes headed over to Easter Island Gully with Noel Craine for the steep wall left of **Ormuzd**, which turned out to be a quality E5 named **The Red Sofa**. Back beneath the **Conan's** arch nestles The Cryptic Rift, entered through a kind of caving trip. Here Crispin Waddy and Dave Holmes found **Evidently Chickentown**, a subterranean E5 unusual even for Gogarth and a significant find that puzzled would be repeaters for some time.

Meanwhile, as the new year of 1988 arrived, a steep and very compact quarried wall in the Breakwater Country Park caught the eye of the Llanberis lads. Devoid of conventional runner placements it seemed an ideal candidate for a pair of bolt protected sport climbs. Paul Pritchard took the honours on the right hand line to give **The Crimson Crimp** (F7b), whilst George Smith spent several sessions working out and redpointing the left hand line to give **The Terrible Thing** (F7c+).

Back on the cliff proper George Smith began probing caves opposite North Stack Wall finding **Arachnid**, a steep jug-equipped chimney groove at E4. This made a companion route to the previous year's offering in the same area, **20,000 Leagues Under the Sea**, which had been climbed by Martin Crook with 'Diver' Dave Kendall (who had been submerged by a massive wave during initial exploration whilst belaying).

Stevie Haston appeared to 'turbo glide' across Mordor Zawn onto a hanging undercut fin, before climbing it to give **Seal's Song** (E5 6b) with Celia Bull. Then came an astounding ground up E7 in Wen Zawn. Climbers now had sticky boots, Friends and RPs, which had superseded Chouinard Stoppers in the early 80s, together with Rocks. Despite these technological improvements it was still the leader's skill and nerve that counted most and on-sight ascents were valued above all others. Thus Johnny Dawes did the wall right of **T-Rex** with Bob Drury in the best possible style to give **Hardback Thesaurus**, a still rarely repeated E7 6b route. Dawes's ascent was spread over several days, each attempt gaining more height while unlocking the secrets of this intimidating line, until finally he found himself fully committed, with hard moves guarding access to the jugs on **T-Rex,** and the prospect of a big fall snapping at his heels. The final successful summit push, as well as a few eye-popping falls, were captured on film by Al Hughes and featured in his Gogarth film. Andy Pollitt revisited North Stack for a **Wreath of Deadly Nightshade**, a bold arete left of Blue Peter, followed later in the year by Dave Towse who lead John Redhead up **The Angle Man**, another fine E7, to this now crowded cliff. As Pollitt put it: *"lovely place to climb – lonely place to climb"*.

Further important additions were added to Upper Tier and Main Cliff respectively. These were Paul Pritchard's **Hang Ten in the Green Room**; a crimpy arete left of **Campion** at E6/7 6c, then **Eraserhead** (originally given E6, but now considered to be top end E5) squeezed in between **Positron** and **Skinhead Moonstomp** by Grant Farquhar and Crispin Waddy. Having tossed a coin for the second pitch on the latter route, Waddy won the lead but soon found himself racing upwards to avoid an advancing rainstorm with an inadequate rack. Waddy also added a direct version of **Hunger's** second pitch: **Ramadan**, a lean E5 outing.

As the '80s drew towards their twilight a new guide was imminent, the production of which neatly summed up the moods of the times with the bold routes of the '80s, and inspired the next decade of development, which proved once again that Gogarth was far from worked out. By summer 1991 it was known that one big Main Cliff challenge not yet done centred on the wall right of **Hunger**. It would undoubtedly be very hard and eventually succumbed to Steve Mayers, who having tried it ground up, decided to abseil inspect and place a peg. The outcome was, even with the psychological support of the in situ protection, not easily gained. The resulting route was named **Extinction**, a sure fire E8 contender and still one of Gogarth's coveted big leads. In 1993 it was repeated in a very impressive ground up style by the powerful young Scottish climber, Stuart Cameron. Paul Pritchard stepped in to ground up the remaining continuation groove of **Graduation Ceremony's** first pitch to give **Food**, which he described as "*a nice runout E6*".

Elsewhere action centred around prolific development of the **Spider's Web** area when George Smith, after a three day event succeeded on **Barfly**, an E7 roof crack, before freeing **Spider's Web** with Tim Bonner at the disturbingly modest grade of E5 6a. Commenting later Smith recalled:

"*Had we done the right thing or perhaps pursued too narrow a discipline?*"

Smith returned with 'Diver' Dave Kendall to add another excellent E5, **The Boston Struggler**. Crispin Waddy re-entered the fray, beginning development off the small island under **Spider's Web** with attempts on the ludicrous three pitch crackline which eventually became **The Heinous Flytrap** (E7 6b) with Smith. This formidable piece of climbing took a few years to complete and was responsible for some madcap 'rubber inner-tube' inventions in an attempt to tame the numerous knee bars required for success. With the approach to the island mapped out, transforming the right hand crack line into **Billy Bud** (E6 6b) was a formality for Smith, producing another steep and safe piece of climbing on perfect quartzite. This was an area and a style that Smith came to dominate over the next few years as he scoured various coves and zawns for interesting 'upside down' features. In September/October of the same year Pat Littlejohn weighed in two additions to a relatively neglected area on the cusp between Main Cliff and Upper Tier: **Achilles** (E3 5c), a crack left of **Diogenes**, then **Coming on Strong**, the orange face left again at E6. It was also around this time that Paul Pritchard and Leigh McGinley, climbing on sight, accepted responsibility for perhaps Wen Zawn's most striking, but loosest line, the conglomerate stuffed fissure which **Concrete Chimney** studiously avoids to give **Rubble**, a three pitch E7 with technical grades no harder than 6a hinting at its seriousness and an outing best summed up in one word by McGinley: "Twitch!"

Steve Mayers on his Main Cliff test piece **Extinction** E8 6c photo: Ray Wood
Front cover of the 1990 CC guide showing Bernard Newman's shot of Andy Pollitt on **The Bells, The Bells** E7 6b on North Stack
Gogarth roof crack specialist, George Smith photo: Glenn Robbins
George Smith in the upside down world of **Barfly** E6/7 6b in wen Zawn photo: Ray Wood

Next year saw Adam Wainwright adding **Drink** (E5 6b), a logical second pitch to **Food** on Main Cliff with Waddy, who had first noticed the line. (Wainwright returned in 2006 with Tom Briggs and made a continuous ascent of the combination: **Food and Drink** E6). Steve Mayers, whilst not surpassing his previous year's effort on **Extinction**, nevertheless provided another testing E7 excursion with a direct start to **Conan the Librarian**, before doing that route's original second pitch free at E6.

The next few years were relatively lean in exploratory terms, yet good lines continued to emerge. **Sex and Religion** (E7 6c), Grant Farquhar's left hand finish to **Blackleg** on Upper Tier for example, was said to be, *"more serious than Panorama"*. Whilst Farquhar's other offering hereabouts, **Dead and Bloated** (E6 6c), a direct finish to Strike with four protection pegs, was slightly less so. Adam Wainwright and George Smith began seriously probing Wen Zawn's back wall in typically adventurous Gogarth ground up style, getting into and then out of trouble on the tremendous **Mister Softy** (E6 6b) late in 1994; about which Wainwright had this to say:

"In the 1990s Wen Zawn's back wall was still one of the greatest prizes left in North Wales, as it had been for a long time having seen off attempts from various suitors. It was in 1994 when I finally convinced myself of a viable line through the wall, initially persuading a reluctant Noel Craine to give me a belay, in return for me holding his ropes on Ludwig. Noel had been involved in the line before, belaying a hungover Paul Pritchard in his dalliance with the wall and was steadfast in his opinion of the wall's unclimbability. Ten metres up I was faced with a pull round a small roof on admittedly poor rock which gave access to a far better view of the problems above, when a small voice came from below, 'That's as far as the Pritchard got', implying that my time was up." It was to be the first of many encounters."

The following year Irish star Eddie Cooper, climbing with Pat Littlejohn succeeded on a direct finish to **Mammoth**, whilst Smith went back for one of his many sessions on a line first tried by Stevie Haston in the early 80's above the **Seal's Song** fin. Eventually solving this desperate roof problem already known as **Roof Rack** at E7 6c, Smith recalls:

"The name was Stevie Haston's – he had heard an angry individual during a fracas on Deiniolen High Street chanting 'roof rack, roof rack, around your head' whilst brandishing said item in a threatening manner towards his opponent!"

∧ Wen Zawn activist Adam Wainwright photo: Ray Wood

George Smith going for it on **The Mad Brown** E7 6b, Wen Zawn photo: Chris Plant ↗

Unconcerned by such trivia as a street brawl, Haston's thoughts were of a different rack, with the great roof poised around his head and above the sea.

The second half of the '90s saw the main action centred around Wen Zawn's Cryptic Rift and Back Wall where routes as adventurous in style and undertaking as anything that had gone before continued to be done. Smith and Wainwright revisited the Back Wall for a four pitch E7; **The Mad Brown** was an excursion which pushed these experienced protagonists far beyond any comfort zone and forced Smith, after three days of ground up effort, to abseil inspect a severely loose area above their high point. Even after this they did not reach the **Conan** traverse until nightfall. Thus a further day was required for the top pitch, which Wainwright recalls was done:

"...in the company of the paparazzi, with photographer Ray Wood spinning in space like a spider. With G leading, Ray tried to direct his model into an aesthetic position producing the memorable response from George, 'fuck the camera Ray, this time it's for real - what's that next hold like?"

The same year also saw Smith produce **Instant Van Goch** at E5 6b on a "beautiful painted" wall underneath Wen Zawn arch with James Harrison. He then took development in the Cryptic Rift into a new area by climbing into the very centre of the main arch to an abseil point to produce **The Wild Underdog** (E7 6b), whilst Wainwright now entered **The 4th Dimension**; yet another very physical E7 on the severely overhanging wall beneath **Spider's Web**.

A few years later, in 1997, Nick Dixon and Noel Craine climbed **It's a Broad Church** (E6/7 6b) taking the very overhanging groove between **Mister Softy** and **Games Climbers Play**, utilising the now popular 'ground up' tactics. This route saw a remarkable on sight second ascent from Johnny Dawes, who managed a full 360 degree spin inside the groove, and together with Nick's alternative left hand start to the route, **The Collection Plate** (E7 6b) brought development on this wall to a period of respite.

Climbers now began to require a new guide which, by the first year of the new century, might provide an emerging generation with further information and old hands with food for thought. Be that as it may, armed with the same description used by many would be ascencionists, Will Perrin and Pete Robins finally solved a long standing Gogarth puzzle in free climbing **Tsunami** in Tsunami Zawn beyond North Stack at E5 5b. It had been tried at least since the late '70s by the likes of Jim Moran and co. since it originally used four or five aid points, yet no one could determine the correct line. It is now described as *"very loose and very serious"* - terms which all Gogarth visitors past, present and future might, as a general rule, greet with affection and be pleasantly surprised on routes where this is not so. As if to stamp his authority on the roof cracks of Gogarth, George Smith turned his attention to Flytrap Zawn, producing a string of upside down creations such as **The Shadowy World of the Nemotode** (E5 6b) with Tom Briggs, **The Porcelain Arena** (E6 6b) with Simon Melia and perhaps most significantly **The Ultraviolet Exterminator** (E7 6b), bringing this zawn firmly up to date in time for the new guide.

More recently, and on a sad note to end this account of development on one of the worlds finest and most ethical of traditional climbing venues, a bolt ladder (one hundred or so in total) appeared in Parliament House Cave. If not for the length of time and economic outlay, it may have been a practical joke. Whatever the reasons for their placement they were destined to come out again. Local climbers Mark Reeves and Andy Newton stepped up and cleaned up the matter.

As a general theme Gogarth is synonymous with adventure climbing. Despite anomalies in style over the years, for the most part devotees have created an ethical code which relies on a no-bolting policy and favours new routes first attempted on-sight, with ground up ascents being the next best thing once a fall has taken place. As may be gleaned from this historical section Gogarth by its very nature is a serious sea cliff venue in the trad climbing ethos. Whoever writes it's future history through their routes, will hopefully share these values and be the better for it since even a poor man may be rich in stone...

Martin Crook March 2008

Adam Wainwright fully engaged with the super steep **The 4th Dimension** E7 6c on the underside of the Wen Zawn arch photo: Ray Wood

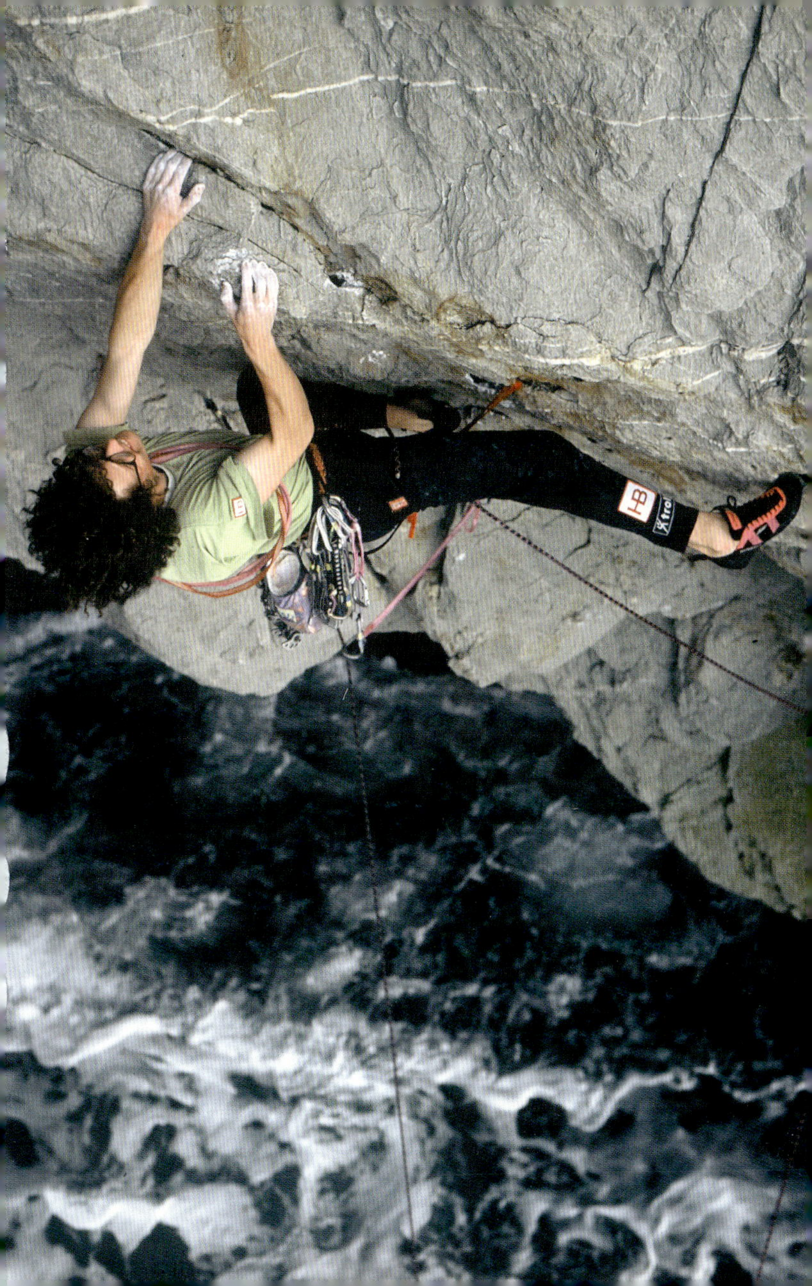

322 Route Index

▶ (It's a) Broad Church 189
(Will Mawr gets the)
Vulcan Lip Lock 202
?? Dee 263
20,000 Leagues Under the Sea 218
42 Moves 285
▶ Aardvark 103
Achilles 101
Acid 62
Afreet Street 86
Agrophobia 194
Ahriman 174
Albany Lodge 55
Albin & Co. 285
Alien 118
Aliens Ate My Bewick 255
Amphitheatre Wall 81
Andover 50
Annie's Arch 204
Annihilator 172
Another Groove 237
An Unimportant Wave 174
Apostrophe 51
Arachnid 216
Archway 201
Art Groupie 226
Away With the Fairies 252
A Dream of White Horses 183
A Groove 237
A Limpet Trip 256
A Pocketful of Pockets 277
A Quiet American 277
A Seagull Ate My Crisps 45
A Seagull called My Name 42
A Sea Change 258
A Slow Brew 49
A Wreath of Deadly Nightshade 227
▶ Babes in Consumer Land 258
Back in Black 288
Bank Holiday Bypass 234
Barbarossa 65
Bar Fly 201
Belial 171
Belial Direct 171
Belvedere 174
Bezel 87
Big Gut 169
Big Jim 47
Big Wednesday 255
Billy Bud 199
Birthday Passage 42
Birth Trauma 224

Bitter Days 75
Blackfoot 52
Blackleg 64
Black and Tan 51
Black Owen 54
Black Rod 223
Black Spot 75
Blind Pew 72
Bloody Chimney 65
Bloody Fingers 45
Blowout 202
Blue Oyster Cult 72
Blue Peter 226
Boil All Irishmen 169
Boogie Woogie 193
Boreal Boot Tester 252
Boulderdash 252
Boys From the Black Stuff 279
Bran Flake 46
Breakaway 37
Breaking the Barrier 51
Britomartis 198
Broadway 80
Broken Mirror 193
Brown Split 262
Bruvers 51
Bubbly Situation Blues 114
Bullitt 211
Bull Rush 260
Bunty 283
Bury My Knee 214
Bye Bye Sunday Blues 255
▶ C'est la Vie 43
Camel Crack 258
Campion 70
Candlestick 34
Candystore Rock 272
Canned Laughter 68
Captain Mark Phillips 257
Carlsberg Crack 272
Carol 205
Carousel Ambra 274
Cartwheel 86
Catalogue Man's Big Adventure 169
Caught by the Skerries 251
Ceilidh 82
Central Park 78
Central Reservation 268
Charlie Don't Surf 238
Chimney Climb 240
Christmas Cracker 269
Citadel 124

Colditz 212
Comfortably Numb 55
Coming on Strong 101
Conan the Librarian 192
Contestant 52
Contraflow 269
Cordon Bleu 102
Corkscrew 34
Costa Del Benllech 270
Crack 44
Cracked Slab 240
Cracked Up 241
Crackers 240
Cracking Sport 277
Crackpot Crack 270
Crane Fly 283
Crazy Horse 256
Croissant 47
Crossover 169
Crowbar 73
Cruise on Through 71
Cursing 40
Curtains 40
▶ D'Elephant 55
Dai Lemming! 218
Dangerous Rhythm 68
Dazed and Confused 273
Dde 183
Dead and Bloated 64
Delicate 57
Dementia 245
Derek and Clive 258
Devil's Marbles 108
Devotee 109
Diagonal 174
Diagonal Dash 252
Diatom 175
Dinosaur 120
Diogenes 100
Diogenes Direct Start 101
Direct start to Alien 120
Dirtigo 62
Dislocation Dance 194
Doomsville 80
Down to the Waterline 279
Drag 171
Dreaming of Home 52
Dream Seller 147
Driller Killer 263
Drink 127
Dropout 62
Drum Solo 275
Drying Out 49
Duffel 43

Route Index 323

Dwlban Arete 269
▶ Echo Beach 184
Elephant Talk 263
Emulator 104
Enchanter's Nightshade 262
End Game 234
Energy Crisis 85
Eraserhead 116
Escape Route 269
ET 117
Evidently Chickentown 194
Exit Chimney 171
Exit Groove 165
Extinction 123
▶ Fail Safe 86
Faller at the First 259
Falls Road 111
Fatty on Sight 258
Fifteen Men on a Dead Man's Chest 72
Fifth Avenue 76
Final Solution 48
Flooze 206
Flower of Evil 227
Fluke 168
Flytrap 214
Flytrap Roof 214
Food 127
Food and Drink 127
Force 8 69
Forgery 202
For Madmen Only 172
For those about to Rock... 288
Fossil Zone 271
Frazer's direct 284
Free Bourn 258
Friday's Extendable Arms 196
▶ Gael's Wall 86
Games Climbers Play 189
Games Climbers Play, Original Start 187
Gazebo 174
Gelli 57
Genuflex 202
Gerontion 244
Get The Stroll 68
Gladiator 81
Gobbler's Arête 198
God's Bone 241
Gogarth 109
Gone Fishing 271
Graduation Ceremony 126
Greaseball 269
Green Gilbert 226

Grendel 40
Gringo 156
Guitar Solo 275
Gumshoe 258
▶ Hamamatsu Flies Again 263
Hammer 57
Hang Ten (in the Green Room) 70
Hardback Thesaurus 188
Hardcore Prawn 252
Hard Shoulder 268
Hash 211
Hat 57
Hazy Memories 250
Headbutt 226
Heinous Flytrap 200
Heroin 148
Heulwen 277
High Noon 156
High Pressure 185
Hip to be Square 283
Hit me like a Hammer 279
Holyhead Revisited 216
Hombre 169
Horse Above Water 148
Horse Play 259
Hud 152
Huncho 206
Hunger 123
Hurricane 84
Hyde Park 79
Hydrophobia 183
Hyena 143
Hypodermic 140
▶ Ibby Dibby 251
Idris Mad Dog 252
If 184
Igdrazil 193
Imitator 104
Instant Van Goch 195
Interpolator 98
Interrogator 98
In the Next Room 214
Ipso Facto 204
Ipso Fatso 202
I Wonder Why 166
▶ Jaborandi 136
Jam Yesterday, Jam Tomorrow, but Never Jam Today 261
Jones' Crack 46
Jug Patrol 218
▶ King Bee Crack 47
Kira His 81

Kit Kat 44
Kraken 204
▶ L'Affreuse 224
Lardvark 104
Les Vacances 286
Le Bon Sauveur 233
Le Cadeau de Vacances 260
Little Women 41
Live at the Witch Trials 232
Lord Snooty 246
Lost Hope 54
Lost In Space 170
▶ M...M...Mother 34
Mammoth 122
Mammoth Direct 123
Mammoth Direct Finish 122
Manor Park 78
Maverick 206
Mayfair 79
Mental Block 42
Merchant Man 168
Mestizo 153
Metal Guru 188
Microdot 175
Micron 175
Mike's Glory 284
Mill Street Junction 81
Minime 44
Minnesota Fats 160
Minute Man 196
Mirrored in the Cleft 47
Mistaken Identity 100, 212
Mister Softy 191
Miura 206
Mobil 262
Molesting Mollusc 251
Momser 54
Monday Club Blues 183
Mondo Hard 82
Monsoon 92
Mordor 212
Mordor Newydd 212
Morphine 138
Mother Ship 273
Mr. Seal 205
Mrs Murdock 42
Mr Hulo 287
Mulatto 152
Mustang 205
M Wall 34
▶ Nagging Doubt 259
Nameless Arete 84
Nautical Mile 260
Neigh Bother 259

324 Route Index

Neutrino 171
New Boots and Panties 42
Nice 'n' Sleazy 232
Nightride 147
Noddy 71
Nomad 61
North by North West 251
North Face Route 262
Not Fade Away 232
Nuts 40
▶ Oh Man, I Gotta Have a Wildebeast 42
Oijee Wall 219
Old Boots and Cut-Offs 42
Old Wedge Route 262
Ordinary Route 115
Ormuzd 172
Overlapped Groove 240
▶ P.C.H. 37
Pantin 66
Paper Moves 274
Park Lane 79
Passions of Fools 263
Patience 49
Pawn 234
Pebbledash 252
Peepshow 135
Pencil Crack 274
Penelope Underclung 232
Penny 48
Pentathol 134
Pequod 171
Perpendicular 174
Phaedra 150
Phagocyte 168
Pigeon Hole Crack 36
Piglet's Left Boot 152
Pigs in Space 223
Pisa 44
Pleasant Surprise 42
Plimsole 40
Point Blank 219
Point Taken 51
Poison Ivy 268
Positron 116
Praetor 170
Primrose Hill 36
Primrose Hill Gutter 37
Progeria 245
Prom 211
Psychocandy 62
Puffin 69
Puffin Direct Start 69
Puffin Shuffle 35

Pulling For Two 232
Puppy Power 279
Puzzle Me Quick 134
▶ Quirky Hip Gyrations 263
▶ Ramadan 124
Ramble On 273
Red Wharf Groove 262
Reflections 274
Registration Blues 273
Relief 51
Remus 35
Reptile 238
Resolution 106
Resolution Direct 108
Return to Garth Gog 110
Revelation 102
Rhiannon 42
Rickety Fence Route 234
River of Steel 285
Rockferry 289
Rock and Ice 55
Rock Island Line 169
Rock Monster 289
Rolla Costa 87
Romulus 35
Roof Rack 212
Rotten Gut 168
Route 66 54, 219
Rubble 186
Run Fast, Run Free 68
▶ Sai Dancing 48
Sarah Green 226
Scavenger 144
Scavenger Direct 146
Scissorhands 54
Scream to a Sigh 287
Seal's Song 211
Sebastopol 127
Seeyerlater 103
See Emily Play 50
Sexy Garcon 283
Sex and Religion 64
Sex Lobster 171
Shagger's Start 165
Shagorado 75
Shag Rock 75
Shell Shock 238
Shreddies 46
Simulator 105
Sincerely El Cohen 233
Sirplum 287
Sir Lobalot 287
Sisters Crack 51
Six Blade Knife 279

Six White Boomers 212
Skerries Wall 250
Skinhead Moonstomp 118
Skinned Up 41
Skippy 219
Slab Direct 54
Slippers 54
Slow Dancer 87
Small Gut 168
Snakebite Wall 48
Sneaky Seal 250
Snowfall 55
South Sea Bubble 231
Spider's Web 200
Spider Wall 199
Sportingly Pocketed 277
Sporting Crack 277
Spreadeagle Crack 38
Sprung 196
Stairs 38
Stairs Direct 38
Stanley's Arch 205
Star of the Sea 196
Statement of Roof 287
Staying Alive 82
Step on the Wild Side 41
Stimulator 105
Street Survivor 78
Strike 64
Strike Direct 64
Stroke of the Fiend 231
Sue P. 239
Sulcus 87
Sump Direct 44
Sunstroke 100
Supercake 165
Supercrack 165
Surprise 57
Suspender 89
Swastika 170
Syringe 138
S W Arête 262
▶ T. Rex 188
Talking Heads 232
Tape Worm 168
Teaser 41
Teenage Kicks 38
Tempest 52
Tension 51
Tequila Sunrise 76
The 4th Dimension 199
The Abbey 43
The Amphibian 238
The Ancient Mariner 172

Route Index

The Angle Man 227
The Archie Gemmell Variant 204
The Arrow 50
The Assassin 143
The Bells! The Bells! 228
The Big Groove 131
The Big Groove Direct 132
The Big Overhang 224
The Big Sleep 121
The Bluebottle 199
The Boston Struggler 202
The Cad 228
The Cad Direct Start 231
The Camel 139
The Chimney 241
The Clown 228
The Concrete Chimney 185
The Crack 241
The Cracks 81
The Crimson Crimp 246
The Crossing 257
The Cruise 71
The Dark Side of Growth 258
The Demons of Bosch 231
The Dope 211
The Echoes 51
The Electric Lady Charlotte 49
The Electric Spanking of War Babies 49
The Elephant's Arse 44
The Emotionary 72
The Escapegoat 194
The Eternal Optimist 86
The Fast Buck 160
The Finisher 160
The Gauntlet 84
The Girdle Traverse 157
The Golden Bough Finish 188, 192
The Grim Reaper 73
The Grip 38
The Groove 241
The Hitcher 218
The Hollow Man 227
The Horizon 158
The Horrorshow 73
The Hustler 154
The Janitor Finish 192
The Jigs Up 234
The Long Run 231
The Long Run Direct 231
The Lost Pillar of Scheiser 261
The Mad Brown 191
The Mad Hatter 246
The Man Who Would be String 283
The Missing Link 289
The Mustapha Twins 246
The Needle 142
The Needle Alternative Finish 143
The Nemotode Strikes Out 214
The Night Prowler 146
The Original Finish 185
The Paranoid Duck 250
The Porcelain Arena 216
The Quartz Icicle 185
The Ragged Runnel 166
The Ramp 85
The Rat Race 114
The Raver 45
The Real Keel 172
The Red Sofa 172
The Rift 62
The Right Hand Finish 57
The Sad Cow 198
The Seventh Wave 279
The Shadowy World of the Nemotodes 216
The Song Remains the Same 273
The Strand 79
The Sump 43
The Tail 206
The Terrible Thing 246
The Tet Offensive 128
The Third Man 154
The Three Amigos 38
The Three Musketeers 153
The Tide is Turning 270
The Trap 196
The Trots 259
The Twilight Zone 246
The Ultraviolet Exterminator 216
The Unblue Crack 50
The Underground 89
The Undertaker 192
The Unrideable Donkey 192
The Walls of Jericho 219
The Wandering Primrose 36
The Wasp Factory 284
The Wastelands 130
The Whip 226
The Whispers 273
The Wild Underdog 195
The Wrath of Deadly Lampshade 233
This Year's Model 170
Thor 193
Thread 45
Three Day Event 257
Thumbscrew 34
Tidal Wave 241
Times Square 76
Time to Reflect 52
Tinseltown Rebellion 54
Toiler on the Sea 198
Tom's Shredded Slippers 226
Too Cold for Comfort 239
Touching Cloth 219
Trampled Underfoot 272
Transatlantic Crossing 80
Trhern Arête 48
Tricky Fruitbat 283
Trigonometry 270
Trogg's Way 61
Trouser Snake 48
Trunk Line 158
Tsunami 238
Tumbling Dice 174
Twilight Zone 49
▷ U.F.O. 66
Uhuru 46, 193
Unclimbed 287
▷ Vegetable Garden 34
Vend-T 198
Vicious Fish 171
Vi Et Armis 275
Volcano 166
▷ Waking the Witch 279
Wally's Folly 36
Wall of Fossils 122
Wall of Horrors 224
Wandering Wall 166
Watership Down 165
Wen 184
We Salute You! 288
Who Was EB? 71
Wind 46
Wind of Change 275
Winking Crack 71
Wonderwall 166
Wrangler 156
▷ Yellow Scar 84
Zed 150
Zeus 184
Ziggurat 84

Acknowledgements

Heartfelt thanks go to the core group of contributors and researchers whose extensive knowledge, enthusiasm and hard work have underpinned the production of this book. First and foremost in that long list is Adam Wainwright. His clear judgment and vital guiding presence throughout the whole project has provided a solid platform without which this book may not have happened at all. Next, Simon Marsh for his astonishing one man research mission on Main Cliff where he climbed, shunted and abseil-inspected every single route (barring one notable exception) on the crag. Graham Desroy for the Easter Island Gully, Craig Badrig and Porthllechog scripts, plus his unwavering enthusiasm and ever-striking attire. Al Leary for his Upper Tier script and trainspotter's eye for detail. George Smith for his humorous presence and knowledge of all things upside down. James McHaffie for his North Stack expertise, and Pete Robins for enthusiastic and knowledgeable input, Ian Lloyd Jones, Phil Targett and Tristan Peers for their bolting work at Fedw Fawr and Benllech, Chris Parkin for re-equipping White Beach Crag and for his commendable work in setting up and maintaining the North Wales Bolt Fund (Donations can be sent to: NWBF, Llysfaen, Lon Brynteg, Glyn Garth, Menai Brridge, LL59 5NU). Jon Ratcliffe for his help with the Benllech and Fedw Fawr scripts, Andy Newton for his work on the Holyhead Mountain script and Porthllechog script and supportive presence throughout. Kelvin Neal for his original Holyhead Mountain script. Andy Walker for the sea level traversing section. Martin Crook for his superb History section. Rob Wilson for helping to make Ground Up happen in the first place. Andy Godber for the Access and Conservation section and general advice on local access situations on Anglesey. Mike Hammill for geology advice and help with the Fedw Fawr script. Gareth Williams (www.goseafishing.biz) for the original boat trip around Gogarth. Martin Kocsis and Mark Hundleby for eagle eye proof reading. Mark Reeves and Grant Farquahar for making the Gogarth wiki happen. Nick Bullock for his help with the Porthllechog and North Stack script. Dave Durkan for help with the Holyhead Mountain script and his early guidebook work. Steve Laddiman and Andy Goater for services to Anglesey bouldering. Mark Goodwin for his Dream poem and Ed Belthorpe for his prize winning Gogarth story.

A great debt of thanks is also owed to the talented photographers who provided a range of stunning images: Ray Wood, Jethro Kiernan (www.onsight.com), John Cleare, Leo Dickinson, Dave Kendall, Glenn Robbins, Al Leary, Graham Desroy, Nick Bullock, Craig Smith, Gill Lovick, Andy Newton, Chris Plant, Adam Wainwright, Martin Crook and Rob Lamey.

And for various reasons, the following people deserve thanks: Mick Tolley, Joe Brown, Twid Turner, Clive Davis, Simon Jones, Pete Griffiths, Mark Richards, Lee Roberts, Dave Simpson, Dave Towse, Glenda Huxter, Rachael Barlow, Mike Raine, Guy Keating (BMC), Kevin Stephens, Mark Hounslea, Martin Dale, Neil Dickson, Steve Long, Dan Warren, Mark Lynden, Andy Scott, Crispin Waddy, Craig Smith, Neil Foster, Dai Lampard, Steve Mayers, Drew Withey, Jack Geldard, Johnny Dawes, Noel Craine, Rob Greenwood, Howard Jones, Gill Lovick, Keith Robertson, Bob Moulton, Ritchie Patterson, Chris Rowlands, Stuart Cathcart, Anita Gray, Gareth Aston, Dick Turnbull, Dave Cheetham Graham Hoey, Nick Dixon, Leigh McGinley, Rick Newcombe, Carole Becker, Helen John, Grant Mitchell, Andy Short, Pete Johnson, Davey Howard Jones, Dave Holmes, Andy Boorman, Alex Williams, Bryn Williams, Cath Wilson, Katherine Bromfield, Mike Lewis, Ben and Marion Wintringham, Mike Bailey, John Darling, Stan Lowe, Jamie Holding and the rest of the Ogwen Cottage staff, Leanne Callaghan, Paul James, Jack Street, Chris Watkins, Ruth Berry, James Margot, Mike Pyecroft, Ian Hey, Andy Bunage, Keith Robertson, Anne Vowles, Catrin Thomas, Sam Leary, Dave Torrington, Gary Smith, Chris Wright, Perry Hawkins, Judy Yates, Al Evans, Dan McManus and John Peake.

Bibliography • Advertising Directory • Acknowledgements

Although this guide has been extensively researched out on the crags, it very much builds upon the foundation of previous Gogarth guidebooks which were initially produced independently, and then by the Climbers' Club. A debt of gratitude is owed to the writers and editors, in particular Pete Crew, Dave Durkan, Alec Sharp, Geoff Milburn, Al Evans, Andy Newton Andy Pollitt, Steve Haston, Paul Williams and Mike Gresham, but also the many local and visiting climbers who have helped to the keep the definitive record going.

A very big thank you is also due to Al Williams, Ground Up's resident designer, who continues to produce the very highest standards in guidebook design.

And lastly a huge thank you to my wife Clare, and my kids, Cadi and Charlie for putting up with me and putting a smile on my face.

Simon Panton Nov 2008

Bibliography

Craig Gogarth - 1st Edition (Peter Crew, 1966)
Craig Gogarth - 1st Edition Revised (Peter Crew, 1967)
Holyhead Mountain - Dave Durkan, 1967
Anglesey - Gogarth (Peter Crew, West Col, 1969)
Mona - Dave Durkan, 1969
Gogarth - 1st Edition (Alec Sharp, Climbers' Club, 1977)
Gogarth - 1978 Supplement (Geoff Milburn and Al Evans, Climbers' Club, 1978)
Gogarth - 1981 Supplement (Geoff Milburn, Climbers' Club, 1981)
Gogarth - 2nd Edition (Andy Newton, Andy Pollitt, Steve Haston, Paul Williams and Mike Gresham, Climbers' Club, 1990)

Advertising Directory

Ground Up would like to thank the advertisers who helped to support this guidebook:

Andy Newton – page 5
01286 872 317
www.andynewtonmic.org

Anglesey Adventures – Page 26
01407 761777
www.angleseyadventures.co.uk

Anita's B&B – page 26
Llanberis
01286 870087 / 0776 9851681

The Beacon – page 26
01286 650045
www.beaconclimbing.com

Bendcrete – page 10
0800 146778
www.bendcrete.com

BMC – page 18
0870 010 4878
www.thebmc.co.uk

DMM – page 207
www.dmmwales.com

Highsports – page 5
01743 231649
www.highsports.co.uk

Outdoor Alternative – page 26
01407 860469
www.outdooralternative.org

Plas y Brenin – page 10
01690 720214
www.pyb.co.uk

Snowdonia Active – page 14
www.snowdonia-active.com

The Indy Climbing Wall - page 25
01248 716058

V12 Outdoor – page 3
01286 871534
www.v12outdoor.com

Wild Country – page 17
www.wildcountry.co.uk

Paul Pritchard on **The 4th Dimension**
E7 6c, Wen Zawn photo: Dave Kendall

V12 OUTDOOR
rock climbing specialists

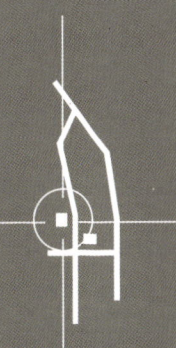

North Wales' premier climbing shop

Old Baptist Chapel, High Street,
Llanberis, Gwynedd, LL55 4EN

Tel: 01286 871534

www.v12outdoor.com

The glorious sea cliffs of Gogarth, situated on the western tip of Anglesey, provide an impressive range of exciting traditional routes. Nowhere else in the UK will you find such a concentration of classic and adventurous climbs.

Gogarth North covers Holyhead Mountain, Upper Tier, Main Cliff, Easter Island Gully, Wen Zawn, Flytrap Area, North Stack, Tsunami Zawn, Breakwater Quarry and the north coast crags of Craig Badrig, Porthllechog, Benllech and Fedw Fawr.

- Over 600 action packed routes
- Full colour topos
- Extensive area maps and individual crag approach maps
- In depth history section
- Atmospheric and inspiring action shots from the best climbing photographers including: Ray Wood, Jethro Kiernan, Glenn Robbins and Dave Kendall

The **Ground Up** team responsible for this guide are: Simon Panton (editor), Simon Marsh, Graham Desroy, Al Leary, Adam Wainwright, Martin Crook, George Smith, Pete Robins and James McHaffie.

A sister volume, **Gogarth South** (covering all the crags from South Stack to Trearddur Bay) is due to be published in 2009.

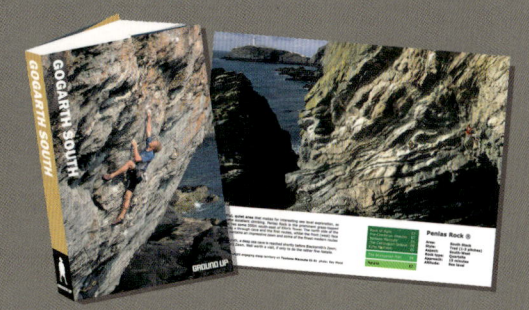

www.groundupclimbing.com

Ground Up *v.* a climbing style that is both authentic and aspirational, but also one that all climbers, no matter what their relative standard, can relate to.

Book Price £18.95
ISBN-13 978-0-9554417-1-4

GROUND UP
#2